DATE DUE

Marital and Family
Processes in Depression

Marital and Family Processes in *Depression:*

A Scientific Foundation for Clinical Practice

EDITED BY STEVEN R. H. BEACH

American Psychological Association
Washington, DC

Published by
American Psychological Association
750 First Street, NE
Washington, DC 20002

Copies may be ordered from
APA Order Department
P.O. Box 92984
Washington, DC 20090-2984

In the U.K., Europe, Africa, and the Middle East, copies may be ordered from
American Psychological Association
3 Henrietta Street
Covent Garden, London
WC2E 8LU England

Typeset in Times Roman by GGS Information Services, York, PA

Printer: Edwards Brothers, Inc., Ann Arbor, MI
Cover Designer: Kathy Keler Graphics, Washington, DC
Technical/Production Editor: Eleanor Inskip

The opinions and statements published are the responsibility of the authors, and such opinions and statements do not necessarily represent the policies of the APA.

Library of Congress Cataloging-in-Publication Data
   Marital and family processes in depression : a scientific foundation for clinical practice/
   edited by Steven R.H. Beach.
          p. cm.
      Includes bibliographical references and index.
      ISBN: 1-55798-695-9
      1. Depression, Mental—Treatment. 2. Marital psychotherapy. 3. Family psychotherapy
   4. Married people—Mental health.   I. Beach, Steven R.H.
   RC537.M358 2000
   616.85'270651—dc21

                                                                              00-029321

British Library Cataloguing-in-Publication Data
A CIP record is available from the British Library

Printed in the United States
First Edition

CONTENTS

CONTRIBUTORS

Steven R. H. Beach, PhD, University of Georgia

Nili R. Benazon, PhD, Wayne State University

Thomas N. Bradbury, PhD, University of California, Los Angeles

Amy Brooks, PhD, Emory University, Atlanta, Georgia

Annmarie Cano, PhD, Wayne State University, Detroit, Michigan

James V. Cordova, PhD, University of Illinois at Urbana-Champaign

James C. Coyne, PhD, University of Pennsylvania Health System

E. Mark Cummings, PhD, University of Notre Dame

Joanne Davila, PhD, State University of New York at Buffalo

Gina DeArth-Pendley, MA, University of Notre Dame

Frank D. Fincham, PhD, State University of New York at Buffalo

Christina B. Gee, MA, University of Illinois at Urbana-Champaign

Thomas E. Joiner, Jr., PhD, Florida State University

Benjamin R. Karney, PhD, University of Florida

Nadine J. Kaslow, PhD, Emory University, Atlanta, Geogia

Jennifer Katz, PhD, Washington State University

K. Daniel O'Leary, PhD, State University of New York at Stony Brook

Bettie Reynolds, MS, Emory University, Atlanta, Georgia

Tina Du Rocher Schudlich, MA, University of Notre Dame

David A. Smith, PhD, University of Notre Dame

Martie Thompson, PhD, Centers for Disease Control and Prevention

Heather Twomey, PhD, Emory University, Atlanta, Georgia

Mark A. Whisman, PhD, University of Colorado at Boulder

Preface

Marital and Family Processes in Depression: A Scientific Foundation for Clinical Practice

This collection of original chapters is meant to highlight the melding of basic and clinical science that has occurred over the last decade in the area of marital and family processes in depression. This emerging area has little tradition to constrain its development. As a result, this book brings together several perspectives and provides a set of new ideas about the way that marital and family difficulties come to be related to one another. This book should be of value whether one's primary interest in the topic derives from a clinical, developmental, or preventive perspective.

As will be clear throughout, the contributors to this book share the belief that the juxtaposition of basic science and clinically rich phenomena will produce exciting new insights for both clinicians and researchers. On the clinical side, there is the potential for new ideas about the process of intervention and ways to intervene with families and marital partners of individuals with depression. On the research side, there is the potential to examine basic behavioral processes in light of the complexity of clinical phenomena and develop insights about clinically relevant outcomes. By encouraging the juxtaposition of basic science and clinical phenomena, this book is meant to stimulate innovation in marital and family interventions for depression. I hope that reading this book also will stimulate, intrigue, and provide enjoyment to those interested in the connection between the intimate environments of marriage or family on the one hand and dysphoria and depression on the other. In addition, the chapter authors provide an excellent summary of the literature relevant to marital and family processes in depression.

The history of this book began several years ago. At the time, I was working simultaneously in a research setting, an inpatient setting, and an outpatient treatment setting. Having already conducted outcomes research on the use of marital therapy in treatment of depression, I was interested in the potential of applying this approach in various clinical settings. Information about the ways in which marital and family processes might be related to depression was still scarce, but there was an obvious and pressing need for work with the spouses and families of individuals with depression. As I quickly discovered, however, because of time limits, patient needs and characteristics, and unusual circumstances, it was not a simple matter to implement the treatment protocols as others and I had outlined them for the purposes of outcomes research. As a result, my own clinical work with the spouses and families of depressed individuals often became a crazy quilt of bits and pieces of therapy from different sources, with the central theme or focus of therapy hard to discern. At the same time, little was appearing in the literature that seemed directly relevant to working with close relationships under these difficult circumstances. Happily, however, during the past decade, the strains on marital and family relationships that occur in the context of depression have been the subject of new empirical scrutiny, with much of the work aimed at developing more powerful theoretical frameworks rooted in basic science.

However, along with the blessing of an increasingly diverse, sophisticated, and voluminous literature on marital and family processes related to depression, there remains the problem of finding clinically useful and coherent patterns in the basic data. In addition, because the literature is spread out over several areas and sub-disciplines, there is the potential for fragmentation, with common themes potentially being overlooked. One goal of this book was to bring together under one cover several threads of this fast-developing area and then to draw out their common clinical implications. I hope that this book will help stimulate and guide clinical work for those occasions when clinical approaches have to be modified and innovations are required by patient characteristics. My own experience suggests that such occasions are numerous.

An issue in designing a book such as this one is to determine how broadly or narrowly to configure the contributions. I wanted to focus on marital relationships, but I also wanted to have this focus occur in the context of developmental psychopathology research and in a broad social and cultural context. To adequately deal with these issues and to draw out potential implications for treatment required bringing together a unique group of scholars who were comfortable with crossing areas of inquiry and ignoring traditional boundaries. As a result, all of the contributors share the characteristic of cutting across traditional disciplinary boundaries. To further facilitate the process of interchange and cross-fertilization of ideas I decided to bring the group together for a period of discussion before the chapters were finalized. Fortunately, the University of Georgia was interested in supporting innovative conferences. As a result, I was able to host a "State of the Art" conference at the Center for Continuing Education at the University of Georgia in August 1998.

The office of the vice president for academic affairs provided financial support. In addition, the Institute for Behavioral Research provided logistical and financial support. Without this help, the exchange of ideas that is apparent in this book would have been much more difficult. The resulting conference allowed the authors to discuss emerging issues and to examine implications of various basic findings for the use of marital therapy for depression. The interchange of ideas continued throughout the process of revising and updating the chapters. As a result, each chapter has benefited from the input of all the other authors. This influence can be seen throughout the book, but it is perhaps most easily seen in the therapy chapters that complete it.

As with any effort of this sort, there are many individuals to thank and many without whose support and work the conference and this book could not have become reality. I particularly want to thank Rex Forehand; in his capacity as director of the Institute for Behavioral Research at the University of Georgia, his support of the project included encouragement and conference attendance; the conference could not have occurred without his help. I also thank Sharron Thompson, Diana Shelnutt, Beverly Bradshaw, and Sandy Gary for their invaluable assistance with numerous aspects of the conference and the production of the book. Robert Weiss and Karen Prager provided comments on an earlier draft of the book, and their help was much appreciated. I also thank each of the contributors. They kept the book on schedule and made the process of creating it fun and informative for me. I hope that some of this fun will be apparent to the reader as well.

On a more personal note, I also thank my family for their support and tolerance. They were quick to forgive and slow to criticize the disruptions and inconveniences occasioned by my involvement in bringing this book to fruition. Special thanks go also to Gene Brody, Abraham Tesser, and Paul Roman for their insights and advice on putting the conference together and for their mentorship over the years.

Introduction: Overview and Synthesis

Steven R. H. Beach and Frank D. Fincham

This book brings together a diverse group of authors. However, all are united in their desire to better understand depression and the nature of its connection to marital and family environments. Each chapter author brings to the book a unique perspective, perspectives born in part from the differing intellectual traditions that each represents. The authors share, however, the characteristics of easily crossing traditional disciplinary boundaries and being open to alternative perspectives. These characteristics create an open, but theoretically grounded, series of chapters designed to push the frontiers of theory and practice. This book also collects into a single volume developments in several different areas and so provides an index of the collective gains researchers have made, the areas of overlap between various approaches, and possible cautionary notes for the field as a whole. It is hoped that, as a result, this book will stimulate new thinking about the process of therapy, suggest new possible points of therapeutic intervention, and guide new efforts to prevent marital discord and depression.

Coyne and Benazon (chapter 2) suggest that the most enthusiastic therapists may sometimes promise more than they can deliver. As their chapter illustrates, one of the benefits of a book such as this one is bringing some discipline to claims regarding the therapeutic possibilities of marital therapy. On the other hand, by expanding the underpinnings of marital therapy for depression to include developmental psychopathology, personal relationships research, and research on the broader social context of close relationships, this book also holds out the promise of new ways to use marital relationships to promote the mental health of spouses. This book documents the existence of a large population of depressed individuals who may need help with marital and family relationship difficulties (Whisman, chapter 1; O'Leary and Cano, chapter 9); and the potential of marital therapy to be of benefit for depressed individuals (O'Leary and Cano, chapter 9; Cordova and Gee, chapter 10). In addition, there are many suggestions about ways to use marital therapy in helping alleviate depression (Coyne and Benazon, chapter 2; Cordova and Gee, chapter 10; Beach, chapter 11).

As is evident throughout the book, the authors are familiar with each other's work and refer to other chapters in the book. This familiarity was by design and is meant to increase the coherence between chapters. It also reflects a central theme of the book, that is that there is continuity of knowledge across applied and basic areas of inquiry and that advances in clinical application are intimately connected to advances in theory and basic research (see also Beach & Fincham, 2000; Beach, chapter 11). The clinical implications presented in the various chapters nicely illustrate the point that advances in intervention often are connected to advances in theory and basic research. In this book, the interplay of theory, basic research, and clinical innovation is obvious and intense.

In less than 15 years, the field of marital and family processes in depression has grown from infancy to adolescence, with this book marking another milestone in its development. Given that the first proposals regarding the use of marital interventions in the treatment of depression were made in the mid-1980s, it is remarkable that the field has progressed so rapidly and with such strength. Perhaps as a result, the topic has proven attractive to many new researchers. Reflecting this trend, included among the chapters are those by a new generation of authors who bring fresh perspectives to the subject. At the same time, the book's title, *Marital and Family Processes in Depression: A Scientific Foundation for Clinical Practice,* marks an explicit recognition that the field has broadened to recognize points of continuity with broader family issues, with romantic relationship precursors, and with the scientific literature outside the clinical area.

Despite the field's relative youth, the clinical and basic research roots of marital therapy for depression are deep and extensive. On the clinical side, influences include substantial contributions to and influence from behavioral (e.g., Lewinsohn, Weinstein, & Shaw, 1969; McClean, Ogston, & Grauer, 1973), interpersonal (e.g., Klerman, Weissman, Rounsaville, & Chevron, 1984), systems (e.g., Coyne, 1976), and cognitive (e.g., Beck, Rush, Shaw, & Emery, 1979) perspectives. Likewise, there is a basic science foundation for this approach with contributions from experimental social psychologists (e.g. Swann, 1983; Thibaut & Kelley, 1959), developmental psychopathologists (e.g., Hammen, 1991), depression researchers (e.g., Gotlib, Lewinsohn, & Seeley, 1998), epidemiologists (e.g., Weissman, 1987), and sociologists (e.g., Brown & Harris, 1978), among others. In addition, the history of each of these lines may be extended further, highlighting contributions from psychoanalytic and object relations theorists, early behaviorists, and humanistic psychologists (see Joiner, Coyne, & Blalock, 1999, for a more extensive discussion). Projecting into the future, the scientific underpinnings of this area are likely to be influenced by the ongoing development of the field of personal relationships. The study of personal relationships is also relatively new, but like the study of marital and family processes in depression, it has shown remarkable vitality and growth; this book highlights the connection of the field of marital and family processes in depression to basic developments in the area of personal relationships research.

How to Approach This Book

Reading this book from cover to cover and reading each chapter in the order it appears is one approach to this book that is likely to be rewarding. The chapters are presented in a logical progression, with issues relating to the description of the basic phenomena and cautionary notes presented in part 1, issues related to theory development presented in part 2, important contextual issues discussed in part 3, applications presented in part 4, and an integrative commentary by Thomas Bradbury completing the book. However, not all readers will be equally interested in all sections of the book, and some may wish to read chapters in a different order. To prepare the reader for the contributions that follow, a brief discussion of the constituencies toward whom the book is directed and how it may be helpful to each constituency is provided. Also presented is an overview of the book and the contents of each chapter. Finally, some predictions about future developmental tasks and challenges confronting the field are offered.

Who Should Read This Book?

Because the contributors all share an openness to ideas, it is likely that this book will be of greatest interest to individuals who enjoy pushing intellectual limits and see value in expanding the range of marital therapy for depression. Such individuals may find much that is of interest to them in parts 1 and 2, but they also will find stimulation in parts 3, 4, and the integrative commentary. Such individuals may also realize that, regardless of their particular constituency, this book is not meant to merely inform them. Instead, it is also meant to invite them into active participation in the growth and development of this approach to the treatment of depression.

Marital Therapists

Marital therapists may find much to enjoy in this book. They may find themselves identifying with the conclusion that marital therapy is sometimes a useful intervention for depressed individuals. Additionally, they may appreciate the discussions of marital therapy and the implications for intervention and prevention and the help provided in justifying to various third parties the use of marital therapy for depression. Because part 4 and the commentary address applied issues, they may be of particular interest. But marital therapists may also enjoy and benefit from the discussion of cautionary notes regarding marital therapy and depression, the attention to limitations of marital therapy as it is currently conducted, the careful discussion of processes linking dyadic transactions with depression, and the discussion of important contextual variables. This may draw their attention back to parts 1, 2, and 3. The book also may serve as a useful introduction to the literature on self-esteem, self-verification, and other self-processes as they relate to depression and potentially mediate various marital and family effects on depression. These processes may be particularly useful in guiding the application of marital therapy and in enhancing an emerging understanding of the reciprocal effects of depressive symptoms and relationship context.

Marital therapists also may appreciate the fact that the book is designed to increase their options in conducting marital therapy with depressed patients rather than claiming that there is one right way to conduct marital therapy. Three models of marital therapy are presented (Coyne and Benazon, chapter 2; Cordova and Gee, chapter 10; and Beach, chapter 11), and marital therapists may appreciate the flexibility offered within each of the models. At the same time, however, the contributors recognize this as a time of growth and expansion for marital approaches to depression. Accordingly, marital therapists may appreciate the sense of excitement about new possibilities that pervade the book.

Clinical Psychologists

Clinical psychologists interested in depression are well aware that there has been a significant increase in interest in the interpersonal aspects of depression (see, e.g., Joiner et al, 1999). For such readers, this book may provide an opportunity to delve more deeply into the role of marital, romantic, and family-of-origin relationships in the development and persistence of depression. Curiosity about the empirical foundation of this new theoretical direction may draw readers to the chapters in part 1. Marital relationships and the broader family systems within which they are embedded seem to play a role in the course of depression and to become interwoven in a self-maintaining pattern of suffering and despair. As a result, clinical psychologists dealing with depressed individuals may be interested in better understanding the potential influence of depression on these close relationships. Likewise, because family members are often involved in treatment, understanding the ways in which depressed individuals may evoke or maintain negative reactions from family members may be quite useful. Such interests are likely to attract clinical psychologists to part 2. An interest in the role of violence or ethnicity may draw the reader's attention to part 3. Finally, clinical psychologists may find themselves interested in the potential of this new approach. Because many of their clients are married, marital therapy may be an option that is currently underused as either a primary mode of intervention or as an adjunct to other forms of treatment. This may lead them to focus on part 4, in which specific suggestions regarding intervention are offered.

Personal Relationships Researchers

Understanding the connection between the self and its relational context is of central concern for all personal relationships researchers, regardless of the focus of their research. Depression in relational context provides an ideal set of phenomena for examining the rich interconnections between self- and dyadic processes, as well as providing intriguing methodological and developmental issues. Such interests will draw attention to parts 1 and 2, in which theory, data, and hints of grander theories yet to come are presented. It is likely that the issues of measurement and continuity, the relationship of self-view to the responses of others, and the impact of enduring personal vulnerabilities on the unfolding of personal relationships over time will seem familiar to many personal relationships researchers, and their discussion in this context will prove interesting and stimulating. Likewise, the stimulating review of contextual processes in part 3 will be of interest to many personal relationship researchers. Accordingly, even for the pure researcher who may be uninterested in the applied issues of therapy, there is much in this book that is likely to be stimulating and engaging. The commentary by Bradbury will likely be of particular interest.

Prevention Researchers

To the extent that potentially controllable aspects of the interpersonal environment are implicated in the development of depression, marital therapy is necessarily of interest to prevention researchers. Likewise, to the extent that depression leads to deterioration in marital and family relations in predictable ways, this also may be of interest to prevention researchers. The research reviewed in part 2 suggests the possibility that depression and interpersonal problems could be uncoupled and that serious sequelae of depression could be prevented if attention were given to marital functioning and if marital functioning could be successfully enhanced among individuals with chronic or recurrent depression. In particular, prevention researchers may be interested in the implications of Davila's developmental model (chapter 4), Cummings, DeArth-Pendley, Schudlich, and Smith's family transmission model (chapter 5), and Joiner's proposed integrative model (chapter 7) because of strong implications for potential secondary intervention strategies.

Graduate Students

Perhaps it goes without saying, but one intended audience for this book is graduate students looking for exciting directions for their dissertation research. In each of the chapters there is discussion of the areas that remain un- or underexplored. Likewise, the chapters are rich in citations to related areas and to the empirical literature. For graduate students looking for potential dissertation topics, the chapter by Joiner (chapter 7) may prove particularly exciting. Although the broad sweep of this chapter outstrips current evidence, this also makes it a gold mine of testable research hypotheses. Graduate students also may wish to pay particular attention to the end of each chapter, where the authors discuss particular types of future research and present possible testable hypotheses.

Overview of the Book

It also may be useful to have some hints about the specific contents of each of the chapters. Although each is excellent and deals in detail with a specific, important aspect of the relationship between marital or family processes and depression, they diverge considerably in their focus. The chapter by Whisman (chapter 1) lays some important groundwork for the subsequent chapters. Whisman reviews the evidence for an association between depression, whether construed as variations in symptoms or the presence of a diagnosable disorder, and problems in close romantic relationships. Because covariation is a logical requirement for the inference of a causal connection, careful examination of the data on covariation provides an empirical foundation for the remainder of the book. Although marital discord is not ubiquitous among people with depression, hints of such problems are present even when depressed individuals report that their current romantic relationships are satisfactory (e.g., Schmaling & Jacobson, 1990). Whisman's review of the literature suggests that, regardless of whether one asks about depressive symptoms within the normal range or about diagnostic state, it is not difficult to observe concurrent associations between depression and marital problems. Equally important, however, is his observation (along with that by Coyne and Benazon in chapter 2) that covariation per se does not indicate a particular direction of causality between depression and marital satisfaction. Likewise, that relationship problems seem equally strongly associated with symptoms of depression as with diagnostic status need not imply that the nature of that relationship is exactly the same. Accordingly, Whisman's chapter not only provides a foundation for the remaining chapters but also raises the question of how the observed relationships between symptoms of depression and disturbance in close relationships are best understood.

Is it possible that marital discord is the "Agent Blue" that causes depression? This question, raised tongue-in-cheek by Coyne and Benazon (chapter 2), is the conceptual twin of the question raised by Whisman in chapter 1. However, for Coyne and Benazon it serves as a prompt to consider various characteristics of depression and the futility of positing that marital discord alone is a sufficient condition for the onset of a depressive episode. Echoing this view, Davila (chapter 4) discusses the role of enduring individual characteristics as they may affect the depression-marital discord relationship. This view is similarly reflected in Joiner's (chapter 7) interest in combining within a single model cognitive characteristics, personal dispositions, and interpersonal processes. The question of how to best understand the relationship of depression and marital processes over time also provides a foundation for Katz's (chapter 6) investigation of self-processes in depression. Katz reports evidence that self-processes may moderate the effects of depression on interpersonal rejection and the effects of partner behavior on level of depressive symptoms. Methodological questions about how to best address the longitudinal relationship between depression and marital processes are the focus of Karney's chapter (chapter 3). Accordingly, many of the book's chapters may be seen as responding to the challenge of better specifying the nature of the link between depression and marital discord. At the same time, however, there is general recognition that standard longitudinal designs may have limited ability to tease apart the complex relationships of interest in this area.

Coyne and Benazon (chapter 2) also raise the issue of the decreasing age of onset of major depression throughout the industrialized world (Klerman, 1988). Decreasing age of onset suggests the importance of broadening marital models to include earlier family precursors and adopting a developmental framework that may better capture the heterotypic continuity of factors resulting in vulnerability to depression (see Cummings et al., chapter 5). This chapter discusses the link between parental depression and subsequent child vulnerability to depression and so highlights intergenerational transmission of depressive vulnerability. Davila (chapter 4) also presents a developmental framework, elaborating Hammen's (1991) stress generation model. Davila makes salient the importance of a developmental perspective on interconnected histories of depression and relationship stress. As she points out, to understand this connection one cannot be satisfied with "snapshots" of their interrelationship. Rather, one must be alert for longer-term patterning, related individual vulnerability factors, interpersonal stress generation processes, and the effects of interpersonal stress on subsequent depression. Interestingly, this is a point that is underscored by Coyne and Benazon (chapter 2) in their observation that depressed individuals often spend a significant portion of their adult life in a depressive episode and may often make lifestyle changes that reflect this rather dismal reality. As a result, for someone who has been recurrently depressed, it may be unreasonable to assume that social adjustment is immune to the number and intensity of previous episodes.

Following up this thread of the discussion with a methodological illustration, Karney (chapter 3) notes that assessing the connection between two time-varying constructs, as in the case of depression and marital dissatisfaction, poses formidable analytic problems for longitudinal research. Karney's chapter highlights the complexity of attempting to observe the longitudinal connection between depression and marital satisfaction. Still, as suggested by Karney's illustration, given sufficiently large sample sizes and strategically selected populations and time frames it may be possible to rule out some patterns of interconnection and provide support for other patterns of causality. Adopting such research strategies and recognizing the limits of any inferences made are likely to be important in attempting to better address the issue of the precise nature of the causal relationship between depression and relationship difficulties. Broadening the discussion still further, Davila (chapter 4); Cummings et al. (chapter 5); and Kalsow, Twomey, Brooks, Thompson, and Reynolds (chapter 8) suggest that theoretical progress might follow from disregarding boundaries between marriage, premarital relationships, and family-of-origin relationships. In this view, an exclusive focus on marriage is limiting not only because it excludes relevant theoretical developments in related areas, but also because it limits the ability to adequately model change over time. Developmental models provide the best chance to capture the continuity that may exist as individuals move from their family of origin to the formation of new relationships to marriage and, in some cases, to marital dissolution and remarriage.

As is clear from the integrative models put forward by Katz (chapter 6) and Joiner (chapter 7) as well as in the work reviewed by Davila (chapter 4) on stress generation processes, the literature on self-processes can inform understanding the link between depressive symptoms and close relationships. Likewise, as is clear in Kaslow et al's (chapter 8) careful attempt to contextualize interpersonal processes related to suicide, it is important to examine relationships other than marriage to investigate the impact of romantic relationships among important but too often overlooked populations. In addition, in examining populations with special stresses (see, e.g., Kaslow et al., chapter 8, and O'Leary and Cano, chapter 9), there are opportunities for variables such as family violence to emerge as powerful predictors of depression or else to be predicted by depression. It is important that any new framework allow for such effects and not be limited in scope to events occurring "within the head" of the depressed individual (cf. Coyne and Benazon, chapter 2).

Although both Whisman (chapter 1) and Coyne and Benazon (chapter 2) sound cautionary notes, the call for integrative theory is strong and consistent throughout the book. What evidence is there that the time may be right for theoretical convergence? Perhaps Joiner (chapter 7) best captures this mood in his discussion of "points of consilience." As Joiner notes, several interpersonal theories of depression have proceeded along relatively independent lines for many years. Yet, as his analysis suggests, there may be room for mutually informative exchange. Joiner focuses on theories positing (a) negative effects of depression on interpersonal relationships, (b) negative effects of cognitive processes on depression, (c) operation of self-processes in depression, (d) stress induction and stress reactivity in depression, and (e) stable dispositional and personality factors in depression. Although broad and inclusive, Joiner's chapter also may be viewed as merely an initial invitation to consider the still broader integrative potential that exists in this area. At the same time, several chapters, including those by Cordova and Gee (chapter 10) and Beach (chapter 11), and the commentary by Bradbury discuss the potential for new and more effective interventions for depression that may be based on the improved (or improving) understanding of the connection between depressive symptoms and interpersonal relationships.

Interest in sex differences and depression has been robust, and this interest is reflected in the chapters as well. A number of the book's chapters discuss ways in which gender roles or sex differences may contribute to the processes linking marriage and depression. For example, Whisman (chapter 1) reviews evidence for and against sex differences in the link between marital discord and depression, and Karney (chapter 3) helps to highlight the point that marital relationships provide an interesting opportunity to examine differences attributable to gender. Cummings et al. (chapter 5) carefully discuss possible gender effects in family transmission of depression, and Davila (chapter 4) notes that much of the available developmental psychopathology research is best viewed as research on depressed women, leading her to call for greater attention to gender effects in future developmental research on depression. Alternatively, as suggested by Joiner's broadly integrative model (chapter 7) or Katz's self-verification perspective (chapter 6), it may be that the intersection of several intra- and interpersonal factors need to be considered to adequately understand the emergence of gender differences in levels of depression. As these examples suggest, each chapter provides some attention to the likely importance of gender and sex differences in depression. At the same time, this is clearly an area in need of further development as the field continues to expand.

How Will Marital Therapy for Depression Continue to Develop?

Greater Attention to Effectiveness

As Coyne and Benazon (chapter 2) note, there is good reason to believe that many discordant couples in which one partner is depressed will not avail themselves of currently available forms of marital therapy. This suggests a problem with the effectiveness (i.e., usefulness and consumability) of current forms of marital therapy even if these approaches show good efficacy (i.e., good response among those accepting treatment). If so, considerable progress can be made by decreasing barriers to the consumption of marital therapy for depression. Indeed, many of the concrete suggestions offered by Coyne and Benazon for modifying current marital approaches may be seen as ways to make therapeutic intervention more palatable and therefore more widely used and effective. Likewise, the suggestion by Cordova and Gee (chapter 10) to extend marital therapy to depressed individuals who are not reporting marital problems may be seen as a way to dramatically increase the applicability and effectiveness of marital therapy. The chapters by Kaslow et al. (chapter 8) and O'Leary and Cano (chapter 9) also may be viewed as implicitly extending the range of marital intervention to populations that have previously been viewed as beyond the bounds of marital therapy (i.e., those in violent relationships and those who are not in marital relationships). In contrast, the chapter by Beach (chapter 11) emphasizes potential limitations of marital therapy for depression and subpopulations for whom traditional behavioral marital therapy might be less useful (e.g., those in nondiscordant marital relationships).

Better Theoretical Grounding for Marital Therapy for Depression

Each of the authors expresses the hope that we can put marital or "personal relationship" therapy for depression on a more solid theoretical footing. Motivating this hope is the exceptation that attention to basic literature will provide guidance for clinical research and practice. In particular, grounding marital interventions in empirically supported theory should lead to the identifaction of new points of intervention, better guidance for therapeutic activity, and more useful process research.

Although the basic research cited varies across authors, the areas of basic research highlighted include three fast growing areas: personal relationship research (Davila, chapter 4), research on developmental psychopathology (Cummings et al., chapter 5), and research on self-processes (Katz, chapter 6; Joiner, chapter 7). To the extent that research activity in these areas can be used to identify new points of therapeutic intervention it would be a powerful force for progress and continued development in the area. As is illustrated by Beach (chapter 11), attention to the emerging basic research literature is a good way to generate intervention strategies that may increase the efficacy of marital therapy for depression. In addition, linking intervention with theory provides a foundation for clinical judgement and the appropriate substitution of techniques when warranted. Thus, an empirically grounded theoretical framework can guide the process of tailoring clinical intervention to the needs of particular client couples.

Attention to basic research also provides opportunities to investigate more effectively the process of change in therapy. Because empirically grounded theories of change often provide good measurement technologies, they are ideal for generating testable hypotheses about mechanisms of change in therapy. Alternatively, if we have not identifed the basic processes that inform the techniques being proposed, we are in a poor position to capture these processes and estimate their relative importance (see Beach & Fincham, 2000; Borkovec & Castonguay, 1998; Whisman & Synder, 1997). In addition, empirically grounded theories are well positioned to support sustained progress and collaborative efforts in the area. Indeed, the history of behavioral marital therapy illustrates the importance of an empirically grounded theoretical framework for enabling cross-laboratory collaboration and cumulative progress (see Beach & Fincham, 2000).

Combining Marital Therapy With Pharmacotherapy for Depression

There is little empirical guidance regarding the use of marital and family interventions with concurrent antidepressant medication. Because of the likely importance of combination treatments for many depressed individuals (see Coyne and Benazon, chapter 2), better documentation is badly needed. Several of the models presented in this book suggest the strong potential for synergistic effects (e.g., Coyne and Benazon, chapter 2; Beach, chapter 11). However, the argument for synergistic effects has not yet been directly tested. Given the importance of this question, direct investigation of the additive benefit of marital therapy for suitable depressed individuals seems particularly timely.

Conclusion

At the same time that the contributions to this book are inspiring in terms of the breadth of their coverage, they also are humbling in light of three key issues. First, the diversity of the contributions to this book is a reminder that there is a long way to go before a well-specified and satisfactory theory of the link between marital and family relationship difficulties on the one hand and depression on the other can be claimed. Second, as several of the contributions make clear, there remain important measurement, statistical, and conceptual issues that must be resolved before research can provide a consistent picture of the link between depression and changes in intrapersonal and interpersonal processes. And, third, as is suggested explicitly by several of the authors, it is time for efforts directed at synthesizing disparate sets of data into a more coherent whole. At the same time, as noted by O'Leary and Cano (chapter 9) and Cordova and Gee (chapter 10), there is an increasingly solid empirical foundation for the expectation that marital therapy will be beneficial in the treatment of depression. In addition to the behavioral marital therapy format discussed by Beach (chapter 11), there are potentially useful approaches to the treatment of depression that are based on integrative couples therapy (Cordova and Gee, chapter 10), emotion-focused therapy, cognitive marital therapy, and others (see Coyne and Benazon, chapter 2). However, the strongest message in this book is that the field of marital therapy may now be ready to develop new marital interventions that are more specifically tailored to address depressogenic aspects of marital relationships. As the field continues to progress, those working in it will do well to maintain the current solid connection to basic research.

References

Beach, S. R. H., & Fincham, F. D. (2000). Marital therapy and social psychology: Will we choose explicit partnership or cryptomnesia? In G. Fletcher & M. Clark (Eds.), *Blackwell handbook of social psychology: Volume 2, interpersonal processes.* Oxford, NC: Blackwell.

Beck, A. T., Rush, A. J., Shaw, B. F., & Emery, G. (1979). *Cognitive therapy of depression.* New York: Guilford Press.

Borkovec, T. D., & Castonguay, L. G. (1998). What is the scientific meaning of empirically supported therapy? *Journal of Consulting and Clinical Psychology, 66,* 136–142.

Brown, G. W., & Harris, T. (1978). *Social origins of depression: A study of psychiatric disorders in women.* New York: Free Press.

Coyne, J. C. (1976). Toward an interactional description of depression. *Psychiatry, 39,* 28–40.

Gotlib, I. H., Lewinsohn, P. M., & Seeley, J. R. (1998). Consequences of depression during adolescence: Marital status and marital functioning in early adulthood. *Journal of Abnormal Psychology, 107,* 686–690.

Hammen, C. L. (1991). The generation of stress in the course of unipolar depression. *Journal of Abnormal Psychology, 100,* 555–561.

Joiner, T., Coyne, J. C., & Blalock, J. (1999). On the interpersonal nature of depression: Overview and synthesis. In T. Joiner & J. C. Coyne (Eds.), *The interactional nature of depression: Advances in interpersonal approaches.* Washington, DC: American Psychological Association.

Klerman, G. L. (1988). The treatment of depressive conditions. *In Perspectives on depressive disorders: A review of recent research.* Rockville, MD: National Institute of Mental Health.

Klerman, G. L., Weissman, M. M., Rounsaville, B. J., & Chevron, E. S. (1984). *Interpersonal therapy for depression.* New York: Basic Books.

Lewinsohn, P. M., Weinstein, M. S., & Shaw, D. A. (1969). Depression: A clinical research approach. In R. D. Rubin & C. M. Franks (Eds.), *Advances in behavior therapy* (pp. 229–248). New York: Academic Press.

McClean, P. D., Ogston, K., Grauer, L. (1973). A behavioral approach to the treatment of depression. *Journal of Behavior Therapy and Experimental Psychiatry, 4,* 323–330.

Schmaling, K. B., & Jacobson, N. S. (1990). Marital interaction and depression. *Journal of Abnormal Psychology, 99,* 229–236.

Swann, W. B. (1983). Self-verification: Bringing social reality into harmony with the self. In J. Suls & A. G. Greenwald (Eds.), *Social psychology perspectives* (Vol. 2, pp. 33–66). Hillsdale, NJ: Erlbaum.

Thibaut, J., & Kelley, H. H. (1959). *The social psychology of groups.* New York: Wiley.

Weissman, M. M. (1987). Advances in psychiatric epidemiology: Rates and risks for major depression. *American Journal of Public Health, 77,* 445–451.

Whisman, M. A., & Snyder, D. K. (1997). Evaluating and improving the efficacy of conjoint marital therapy. In W. K. Halford & H. J. Markman (Eds.), *Clinical handbook of marriage and couples intervention.* (pp. 679–693). New York: Wiley.

PART I

MARITAL DISSATISFACTION AND DEPRESSION: UNDERSTANDING THE LINK

1
The Association Between Depression
and Marital Dissatisfaction

Mark A. Whisman

[Marriage is] a condition of life appointed by God himself in Paradise, an honourable and
happy estate, and as great a felicity as can befall a man in this world, if the parties can agree....
But if they be unequally matched, or at discord, a greater misery cannot be expected.

Robert Burton
Anatomy of Melancholia (1671)

There has been a long-standing recognition that depression and relationship problems (e.g.,
marital dissatisfaction) are likely to co-occur. Early research by Weissman and Paykel
(1974), in which it was shown that depressed women reported problems in their marriages,
and Brown and Harris (1978), in which it was shown that lack of a confiding intimate
relationship was a risk factor for depression in women, spurred empirical research into the
association between depression and intimate relationships. In recent years, there has been a
growing body of empirical research in the role of marital functioning in the onset, remission,
and treatment of depression. For example, Weissman (1987) identified being in an
"unhappy marriage" as one of the "firm risk factors for major depression" (p. 445).
Although the literature contains several reviews of the association between depression and
marital functioning (e.g., Beach, Sandeen, & O'Leary, 1990), this chapter expands on
previous reviews by providing a comprehensive, systematic, and quantitative review of the
literature on the association between depression and marital dissatisfaction.

The focus of this chapter is on the nature and magnitude of the association between
depression and marital dissatisfaction (i.e., partners' subjective evaluations of their relationship). The cross-sectional and longitudinal research on the association between depression
(assessed in terms of both symptomatology and diagnostic disorder) and marital dissatisfaction is first reviewed, followed by a presentation of the theoretical perspectives on this
association. The chapter concludes with a discussion of the need for a second generation of
research on depression and marital dissatisfaction that focuses on the moderators and
mediators of this association.

It should be noted that in limiting this review to the literature on depression and marital
dissatisfaction, the true relation between depression and marital functioning may be
underestimated if "important depressogenic marital processes are not fully reflected in self-
reported marital adjustment" (Beach & O'Leary, 1993b, p. 416). However, as marital
satisfaction assumes such a central role in research on marital relationships, an exclusive
focus on marital dissatisfaction appears to be a defensible starting point in evaluating the
importance of marital functioning in depression. Establishing the magnitude of the
association between depression and marital dissatisfaction is also important for providing a
solid foundation for recommending marital treatments for depression (see Cordova and Gee,
chapter 10; Beach, chapter 11). In general, research on depression has examined one of two
aspects of depression: (a) symptoms of depression, obtained most often in community
samples, and (b) diagnostic depression, obtained most frequently in clinical samples of

*Preparation of this chapter was supported by Grant MH54732 from the National Institute of
Mental Health. I thank the investigators who provided me with their raw data to include in the
meta-analyses.*

individuals seeking treatment or epidemiological surveys of community households. Because it has been argued that symptoms of depression and diagnostic depression have different characteristics, causes, and courses (cf. Coyne, 1994), studies of depressive symptoms and diagnostic depression are addressed separately in this chapter.

Cross-Sectional Association Between Depression and Marital Dissatisfaction

Depressive Symptoms

Several studies have included data on the association between depressive symptoms and marital dissatisfaction. One goal of this chapter was to produce summary statistics (i.e., meta-analysis) of the magnitude of this association across studies. Studies were identified through computer literature and citation searches and were included in the review if they used standardized measures of depressive symptoms and marital dissatisfaction. Studies were not included in the review if participants were drawn from populations with physical conditions (e.g., pregnancy) or physical or mental illness other than depression, which is discussed later. This exclusionary criterion was included to (a) exclude studies in which there may have been a third variable that contributed to depressive symptoms or marital dissatisfaction and (b) maximize the generalizability of the association between depression and marital dissatisfaction to married individuals. Also, if it was clear that multiple studies were drawn from the same data set, the results were included in the meta-analysis only once. Furthermore, because multiple findings from a single study may be nonindependent, only one estimate of effect size was included from each study. Therefore, if more than one measure of depression or marital dissatisfaction was used in a study, or if data were collected over more than one period, a weighted effect size was used as a single estimate of effect size. The studies that met the criteria for the meta-analysis are summarized in Table 1.1. For each study, data were analyzed separately for women and men, which allowed for evaluating sex differences in the association between depressive symptoms and marital dissatisfaction. As can be seen in Table 1.1, depressive symptoms were inversely related to marital quality; that is, greater depression severity was associated with greater marital dissatisfaction. As described by Hedges and Olkin (1985), a common correlation coefficient was estimated across these studies by first transforming each correlation into a Fisher z score, then calculating the weighted mean of the standard scores. This weighted mean Fisher z score was then transformed back into a correlation coefficient equivalent. Using this method, the weighted mean effect size (i.e., correlation) between depressive symptoms and marital satisfaction across the 26 studies in Table 1.1 was -42 for women and $-.37$ for men. Both of these mean effect sizes are significantly different from 0 ($ps < .001$), indicating that depressive symptoms have a statistically significant association with marital dissatisfaction for both women and men. The magnitude of these correlations implies that 18% of the variance in wives' and 14% of the variance in husbands' depressive symptoms is attributable to their level of marital dissatisfaction. In interpreting the magnitude of these effect sizes, it may be helpful to keep in mind Cohen's (1988) discussion of small ($r = .10$), medium ($r = .30$), and large ($r = .50$) effect sizes. Thus, the association between depressive symptoms and marital dissatisfaction falls in Cohen's medium-to-large effect size range. Furthermore, because these correlations were obtained from a large number of participants (3,745 women and 2,700 men) with varied demographic characteristics, and because findings were obtained using several different measures of depressive symptoms and marital dissatisfaction, it can be assumed that these values are reliable estimates of the association between depressive symptoms and marital dissatisfaction. The difference in the magnitude of the correlations between depressive symptoms and marital dissatisfaction for women and men was significant, $z = -1.98$, $p < .05$, indicating that the association between depressive symptoms and marital dissatisfaction was greater for women than for men.

Diagnostic Depression

Two types of studies are conducted to evaluate the cross-sectional association between diagnostic depression and marital dissatisfaction. In the first type, clinical samples of depressed individuals (most often seeking treatment) and nondepressed control individuals are compared as to their level of marital dissatisfaction. As with depressive symptoms, one goal of this chapter was to produce summary statistics (i.e., meta-analysis) of the magnitude of this association across studies. Studies were identified through computer literature and citation searches and were included in the review if they included an assessment of diagnostic depression and one or more standardized measures of marital dissatisfaction. Studies that defined depression in terms of cutoff scores on symptom severity measures were not included because previous studies have shown that not all individuals falling above such cutoff scores meet the criteria for diagnostic depression (cf. Fechner-Bates, Coyne, & Schwenk, 1994). It should be noted, however, that such studies have consistently found that individuals with dysphoria report greater marital dissatisfaction than individuals without (e.g., Blumenthal & Dielman, 1975; O'Leary, Christian, & Mendell, 1994; Ruscher & Gotlib, 1988; Smolen, Spiegel, Khan, & Schwartz, 1988; Thompson, Whiffen, & Blain, 1995). Similarly, studies in which participants had to be both depressed and maritally dissatisfied were excluded because depression and marital dissatisfaction are intractably confounded in such studies. Furthermore, studies that collapsed marital quality data for depressed individuals and their spouses were not included unless the original data were available for reanalysis because collapsing marital quality data did not allow for testing the unique relation between depression and marital dissatisfaction among depressed individuals. Finally, as described above for depressive symptoms, studies that identified participants from populations with physical conditions (e.g., pregnancy) or physical or mental illness other than depression were excluded because of potential third variable problems and limited generalizability. Findings from the identified studies are summarized in Table 1.2.

As can be seen in Table 1.2, the presence of diagnostic depression was associated with greater marital dissatisfaction. The weighted mean effect size (d) across the studies in Table 1.2 was 1.75, indicating that depressed individuals differed from nondepressed individuals by an average of approximately 1 3/4 standard deviations. In interpreting the magnitude of this mean effect size, it may be helpful to keep in mind Cohen's (1988) discussion of small ($d = .20$), medium ($d = .50$), and large ($d = .80$) effect sizes. Thus, the mean effect size for the association between diagnostic depression and marital dissatisfaction clearly falls in the large effect size range, indicating the presence of a strong association. Because some prefer to think of effect sizes for mean differences in terms of correlations, this mean effect size was converted to a correlation coefficient. The obtained effect size converted to a correlation coefficient of .66, indicating that an average of 44% of the variance in diagnostic depression could be accounted for by degree of marital dissatisfaction.

Finally, because control couples often are recruited using nonrandom methods, it might be argued that samples of control couples may not be representative of the population of nondepressed individuals. Because nearly all of the studies in Table 1.2 used the same measure of marital quality—the Dyadic Adjustment Scale (DAS; Spanier, 1976)—it was possible to compute the weighted mean and standard deviation across these studies and compare this mean with normative information. Before doing so, however, DAS scores from

Table 1.1—*Association between depression symptoms and marital dissatisfaction*

Investigation	Description of Sample	Measure		Depres-sion	Marr-iage		
		Women	Men				
Assh & Byers (1996)	Married women	CES-D	DAS	124	-.30	-	-
Beach, Arias, & O'Leary (1986)	Married couples	BDI-SF	MAT	136	-.16	131	-.33
Beach & O'Leary (1993b)	Newlywed couples	BDI	MAT	241	-.44	241	-.41
Cohan & Bradbury (1997)	Newlywed couples	BDI	QMI	60	-.22	60	-.22
Culp & Beach (1998)	Married couples	BDI	QMI	134	-.54	126	-.50
Davies et al. (1999)[a]	Mothers of adolescents	CES-D	KMSS	506	-.34	-	-
Dehle & Weiss (1998)	Recently married couples	BDI	DAS	45	-.53	45	-.60
Dimitrovsky et al. (1994)	Newlywed couples	SDS	DAS	60	-.65	-	-
Fincham & Bradbury (1993)	Married couples	BDI	MAT	94	-.39	96	-.38
Fincham et al. (1989)	Married women	BDI	MAT	40	-.37	-	-
Fincham et al. (1997)	Newlywed couples	BDI	MAT	116	-.51	116	-.38
Goldberg (1990)	Parents of preschool-aged children	CES-D	DAS	96	-.20	96	-.19
Gotlib et al. (1998)[b]	Married couples	CES-D	DAS	258	-.49	158	-.46
Horneffer & Fincham (1995)	Married couples	BDI	MAT	150	-.44	150	-.40
Karney et al. (1994)	Married couples	BDI	MAT, QMI, KMSS	78	-.39	78	-.35

Study	Sample	Depression measure	Marital measure	N	r	N	r
Katz, Beach, & Anderson (1996)	Married women	BDI	QMI	138	-.54	-	-
O'Leary et al. (1994)	Married couples	BDI	MAT	300	-.49	299	-.42
Olin & Fenell (1989)	Married couples	SDS	DAS	89	-.46	89	-.24
Purnine & Carey (1997)	Married couples	DAS		76	-.35	76	-.48
Sandberg & Harper (1999)	Preretirement- and retirement-aged couples	CES-D	MSI	252	-.43	252	-.19
Senchak & Leonard (1993)	Newlywed couples	CES-D	MAT	312	-.45	312	-.27
Smolen, Spiegel, & Martin (1986)	Married couples	SDS	DAS	75	-.37	75	-.35
Stoneman, Brody, & Burke (1989)	Parents of two same-sex children	BDI	DAS	47	-.28	47	-.28
Thompson (1995)	Married (68%) and cohabiting couples	BDI	DAS	106	-.40	41	-.52
Whiffen et al. (in press)	Married couples	BDI	DAS	108	-.40	108	-.51
Weiss & Aved (1978)	Married couples	SDS	MAT	104	-.40	104	-.49

Note. BDI = Beck Depression Inventory, BDI-SF = Beck Depression Inventory - Short Form, CES-D = Center for Epidemiologic Studies Depression Scale, DAS = Dyadic Adjustment Scale, KMSS = Kansas Marital Satisfaction Scale, MAT = Marital Adjustment Test, MSI = Marital Satisfaction Inventory (Global Distress Scale), QMI = Quality of Marriage Index, SDS = Zung Self-Rating Depression Scale.
[a] P. Davies, personal communication, July 1999.
[b] J. Seeley, personal communication, December 1998.
— Some studies do not include men in the analyses

Table 1.2—*Association between diagnostic depression and marital dissatisfaction*

Investigation	Description of Depressed Sample	Sex	Depression Criteria	Marital Measure	Sample Sized	Clinic	Control
Basco et al. (1992)[a]	Patients, students	Mixed	DSM-III-R (SCID), HRSD > 13	DAS	16	36	.65
Bauserman et al. (1995)	Inpatients	Mixed	DSM-III-R	DAS	27	30	.83
Biglan et al. (1985)[b]	Outpatients	Women	RDC (SADS), BDI > 17	DAS	27	25	3.60
Cicchetti et al. (1998)[c]	Mothers of toddlers	Women	DSM-III-R (DIS)	DAS	99	51	1.25
Dobson (1987)	Inpatients	Women	DSM-III (SADS)	DAS	12	12	2.38
Frankel & Harmon (1996)[d]	Community	Women	RDC	DAS	20	32	1.18
Sacco et al. (1993)	Community	Women	DSM-III-R (SCID)	MAT	22	23	1.68
Stravynski et al. (1995)	Inpatients	Mixed	DSM-III, BDI > 19, HRSD > 16	DAS	20	20	1.61
Vega et al. (1996)	Outpatients	Women	DSM-III-R, HRSD > 13	DAS	61	60	2.61
Whiffen & Gotlib (1993)	Community	Women	RDC	DAS	32	18	1.56

Note. BDI = Beck Depression Inventory, DAS = Dyadic Adjustment Scale, DIS = Diagnostic Interview Schedule III-R, DSM = *Diagnostic and Statistical Manual of Mental Disorders*, HRSD = Hamilton Rating Scale for Depression, MAT = Marital Adjustment Test, RDC = Research Diagnostic Criteria, SADS = Schedule of Affective Disorders and Schizophrenia, SCID = Structured Clinical Interview for *DSM-III-R*.

[a]M. Basco, personal communication, April 1999.
[b]Nondistressed and distressed depressed samples were pooled prior to comparison with control samples.
[c]D. Cicchetti, personal communication, April 1999.
[d]Only those depressed individuals in a current episode were included in the depressed group.

four studies that did not include a nonpsychiatric control group (thereby precluding their inclusion in the meta-analysis) were included in the computation of the grand mean and standard deviation. The four studies were by Hickie, Parker, Wilhelm, and Tennant (1991), which included a mixed sample of outpatients with nonendogenous depression; Hooley and Teasdale (1989); J. Hooley, personal communication, April 1999), which included a mixed sample of depressed inpatients; Patton and Waring (1991), which included a sample of depressed outpatient women; and Staebler, Pollard, and Merkel (1993), which included a mixed sample of depressed inpatients. Because the Marital Adjustment Test (MAT) was used in the studies by Patton and Waring and Staebler et al., the mean score for depressed individuals in these studies was converted to an equivalent DAS score using the formula provided by Crane, Allgood, Larson, and Griffin (1990). The mean MAT score obtained by Sacco, Dumont, and Dow (1993), which was included in the meta-analysis, was also converted into an equivalent DAS score. The grand mean and standard deviation on the DAS for the pooled clinical samples were 93.71 and 25.17, respectively. These figures were based on 493 depressed individuals, pooled across 14 studies. According to the DAS manual (Spanier, 1989), a mean of 94 translates into a t score of 38, which indicates that the average score for clinically depressed individuals was approximately 2 standard deviations below the normative mean. This mean is also below the cutoff of 97 that is commonly used for identifying marital dissatisfaction (Jacobson et al., 1984), indicating that the mean DAS score for depressed individuals falls in the dissatisfied range.

Although suggestive that clinically depressed individuals differ from nondepressed control individuals, there are limitations with existing studies in terms of generalization of findings based on the kinds of samples being studied. For example, for depressed samples, many of the studies in Table 1.2 included only individuals seeking treatment. Previous studies, however, have indicated that only a small percentage of individuals with psychiatric disorders seek treatment. For example, epidemiological studies have indicated that only approximately 20% of individuals with a recent or active (i.e., 6- or 12-month) disorder obtained professional help for their disorder (Kessler et al., 1994; Shapiro et al., 1984). Therefore, it is not yet known how much the results obtained from depressed individuals seeking treatment generalize to all depressed individuals. That is, it is unclear to what extent findings are artifacts of treatment seeking versus the presence of depression per se. For example, if higher proportions of individuals with depression and marital problems seek therapy than individuals with depression and no marital problems (perhaps because of insufficient support to cope with their problems; cf. Halford & Bouma, 1997), then the association between depression and marital dissatisfaction would in part be an artifact of the sample studied.

Because of these limitations, epidemiological studies evaluating the association between marital dissatisfaction and diagnostic depression in representative samples are needed to supplement the studies comparing depressed and nondepressed individuals. To date, three studies have evaluated this association in population-based community samples. Weissman (1987) analyzed data from the New Haven Epidemiologic Catchment Area (ECA) program and reported that married women and men who were not getting along with their spouses were 25 times more likely to have major depression than married individuals who were getting along with their spouses. Goering, Lin, Campbell, Boyle, and Offord (1996) analyzed data from the Mental Health Supplement to the Ontario Health Survey and reported that being in a ''troubled'' spousal relationship increased the odds of having an affective disorder by approximately fourfold. The discrepancy between these two studies may be partly due to differences in the samples used in the two studies. Specifically, the group reported on by Goering et al. were respondents with affective disorders, which included major depression, mania, and dysthymia. In addition, respondents were included in this group if they met criteria only for affective disorders (i.e., if they did not meet criteria for co-occurring anxiety disorders or substance abuse). In comparison, Weissman's study was based on the association between not getting along with one's spouse and the prevalence of major depression (and not other affective disorders), and co-occurring disorders were not considered. Finally, whereas these two studies evaluated marital dissatisfaction as a categorical variable, Whisman (1999) analyzed the association between major depression and marital dissatisfaction on a continuum using data from the National Comorbidity Survey (NCS). He found an effect size (i.e., difference in dissatisfaction between individuals with and without major depression expressed in standard deviation units) of .70 for women and .36 for men.

These results, therefore, indicate that diagnostic depression is associated with marital dissatisfaction in both treatment-seeking and population-based samples. However, these findings do not address whether this association is specific to depression. That is, epidemiological studies have indicated that approximately 44% of individuals with a lifetime psychiatric disorder have only one disorder, approximately 27% have two disorders, and approximately 29% have three or more disorders (Kessler et al., 1994). Because most existing studies have not controlled for the presence of other disorders (for an exception, see Goering et al., 1996), it is not known whether the observed associations are due to depression, a secondary disorder, or a combination of disorders (i.e., comorbidity). This is an important methodological consideration, because previous studies have found that marital dissatisfaction is associated with psychiatric disorders other than depression (e.g., McLeod, 1994). Thus, Whisman (1999) reanalyzed the association between marital dissatisfaction and major depressive disorder in the NCS, controlling for the presence of other Axis I disorders. Marital dissatisfaction was significantly associated with major depressive disorder for women but not for men in this sample (although there was a significant difference in dissatisfaction for married men with and without dysthymia), thereby supporting the specificity of the association between depression and marital dissatisfaction in women. Similarly, Crowther (1985) found that patients with major depression reported significantly greater marital dissatisfaction than a sample of patients with mixed psychiatric diagnoses, and Staebler et al. (1993) found that patients with major depression reported significantly greater marital dissatisfaction than patients with either obsessive–compulsive disorder or panic disorder. Thus, the results from these studies provide support for the specificity of the association between diagnostic depression and marital dissatisfaction.

Summary and Critique

There is a sizeable body of literature supporting an association between depressive symptoms and marital dissatisfaction. The meta-analysis reported in this chapter indicated that across 26 studies involving more than 3,700 women and 2,700 men marital dissatisfaction was shown to account for approximately 18% of the variance in wives' and 14% of the variance in husbands' depressive symptoms. These correlations are significantly different from 0 and suggest that the association between depressive symptoms and marital dissatisfaction is in the medium-to-large effect size range. Furthermore, the correlation between depressive symptoms and marital dissatisfaction was significantly greater for women than for men. As many existing studies have not tested for sex differences in this association, future empirical studies and theoretical developments should consider this important variable.

Each of the studies reviewed evaluated the association between marital dissatisfaction and total scores on measures of depressive symptoms. Factor analytic studies, however, have indicated that these self-report measures are composed of several factors. For example, factor analyses of the Beck Depression Inventory (Beck, Rush, Shaw, & Emery, 1979) have shown that its factor structure represents one underlying general syndrome of depression, which can be subdivided into three highly interrelated factors reflecting Negative Attitudes Toward Self, Performance Impairment, and Somatic Disturbance (as reviewed by Beck, Steer, & Garbin, 1988). Research is needed to evaluate whether marital dissatisfaction exhibits a similar association with different symptom factors (particularly somatic symptoms).

There have been comparatively fewer studies evaluating the association between diagnostic depression and marital dissatisfaction. Specifically, 10 studies involving a total of 336 participants were identified. The results from these studies indicated that depressed individuals differ from nondepressed individuals in marital dissatisfaction (weighted mean d = 1.75) such that level of marital dissatisfaction accounts for approximately 44% of the variation between depressed and nondepressed individuals. However, the sample sizes in most of these studies were relatively small, and additional research is needed to evaluate the marital dissatisfaction of depressed individuals in larger clinical samples. In particular, such research is needed in studies not explicitly recruiting participants for research on marital functioning, as only a subset of depressed individuals may participate in such studies, thereby potentially confounding the assessment of marital dissatisfaction with the type of research study. However, that two population-based epidemiological studies also found differences in marital dissatisfaction for individuals with and without major depressive disorder and another epidemiological study found differences in spousal relationships between individuals with and without an affective disorder increases the likelihood that this association is significant.

Most existing studies evaluating the association between depression and marital dissatisfaction, particularly those based on depressive symptoms, have relied heavily on self-report measures of both constructs. It could be argued, therefore, that the observed association between the two constructs could, at least in part, be an artifact of the use of self-report measures. For example, it could be argued that some of the association between these two constructs could be due to shared method variance. In addition, these self-report measures could be influenced by response styles, and the reports of marital dissatisfaction could be the result of depressed mood. Several lines of evidence, however, have argued against the association between depressive symptoms and marital dissatisfaction being an artifact of self-report measures. First, spouses of depressed individuals also have reported lower levels of marital quality (e.g., Bauserman, Arias, & Craighead, 1995; Gotlib & Whiffen, 1989; Sacco et al., 1993), and wives' level of depressive symptoms have been shown to correlate with husbands' marital dissatisfaction (Olin & Fenell, 1989). Second, therapists' ratings of spouses' depression and the couple's marital conflict have been shown to be correlated (e.g., Coleman & Miller, 1975; Crowther, 1985). Third, observational studies have indicated that the marital interactions of couples with a depressed spouse are more negative than those of a couple without a depressed spouse (e.g., Biglan et al., 1985; Nelson & Beach, 1990; Schmaling & Jacobson, 1990), indicating that observers can detect differences in the communication patterns of couples with a depressed spouse. However, future research on the association between depression and marital dissatisfaction would benefit from multimethod assessment of both constructs. That is, there are interview measures of both depression (e.g., Hamilton, 1960) and marital dissatisfaction (e.g., Quinton, Rutter, & Rowlands, 1976). The inclusion of multitrait, multimethod assessment in future research using measures with established psychometric properties would help increase confidence in the observed association between depression and marital dissatisfaction.

Longitudinal Association Between Depression and Marital Dissatisfaction

Depressive Symptoms

In evaluating the temporal association between depressive symptoms and marital dissatisfaction, investigators have most often conducted short-term longitudinal studies in which both depressive symptoms and marital dissatisfaction are assessed on two occasions. The results from these studies have yielded mixed findings. Ulrich-Jakubowski, Russell, and O'Hara (1988) reported that depressive symptoms predicted subsequent level of marital dissatisfaction using structural equation modeling (SEM) in a sample of community men who were participating in a 15-month longitudinal study on the effects of retirement. Beach and O'Leary (1993b) used regression analyses and reported that marital dissatisfaction predicted subsequent depressive symptoms in a sample of newlywed couples who participated in an 18-month longitudinal study. Fincham and Bradbury (1993) used regression analyses and found that marital dissatisfaction predicted subsequent depressive symptoms for men (but not for women) in a sample of married couples who participated in a 12-month longitudinal study. In comparison, Fincham, Beach, Harold, and Osborne (1997) used SEM in a sample of newlywed couples who were followed for 18 months and reported that marital dissatisfaction predicted subsequent depressive symptoms for women, whereas depressive symptoms predicted subsequent marital dissatisfaction for men. Similarly, Dehle and Weiss (1998) used regression analysis in a sample of recently married couples and found that marital dissatisfaction was a better predictor for 3-month longitudinal change in depressive symptoms for women than for men. They also found that greater depressive symptoms predicted longitudinal declines in marital dissatisfaction for both women and men. Whereas each of these studies found primacy of either depressive symptoms or marital dissatisfaction in predicting longitudinal change in the other construct, Kurdek (1998) used hierarchical linear modeling and found evidence for concomitant change in both variables (i.e., increases in depressive symptoms were accompanied by decreases in marital quality). On the basis of these findings, Kurdek advocated the need for a ''doubly developmental perspective'' that examines the trajectory of change in ''risk factors'' for marital dissatisfaction (e.g., depressive symptoms), the trajectory of change in marital dissatisfaction, and the link between the two trajectories (p. 494).

Diagnostic Depression

Early studies on the temporal association between diagnostic depression and marital dissatisfaction relied primarily on retrospective methods. For example, Paykel et al. (1969) surveyed depressed individuals about the kinds of life stressors preceding the onset of their depression. Increase in arguments with their spouse was the most frequently reported life event. Other studies using retrospective methods have found that depressed individuals commonly experience problems and events in the area of partner relationships (e.g., Matussek & Wiegand, 1985) and report having a poor marriage or marital problems that predate the occurrence of their depression (e.g., Kendler, Karkowski, & Prescott, 1999; Roy, 1987; Stravynski, Tremblay, & Verreault, 1995).

Other investigators have specifically attempted to determine whether marital dissatisfaction preceded the onset of depression by directly asking depressed individuals about the temporal association between the two. For example, Birtchnell and Kennard (1983) reported that depressed individuals believed their marital dissatisfaction preceded their symptoms more often than the reverse. Similarly, O'Leary, Riso, and Beach (1990) asked a group of depressed, maritally dissatisfied women seeking treatment to make precedence judgments (i.e., whether depression or marital dissatisfaction preceded the other problem) and attributions about the primary cause of their depression (i.e., whether marital dissatisfaction or some other factor caused their depression). Results indicated that these women "had a general tendency to believe that their marital problems preceded their depression . . . [and] a tendency to view their marital problems as causing their depression" (p. 417).

Although there have been several retrospective studies on the temporal association between diagnostic depression and marital dissatisfaction, there have been few prospective studies. Burns, Sayers, and Moras (1994) evaluated the temporal association between marital dissatisfaction and change in depression for individuals undergoing treatment for depression; however, the results of this study were limited in that the intervention itself might have disrupted the natural history of and association between depression and marital dissatisfaction. To date there has been only one prospective study evaluating the impact of marital dissatisfaction and onset of diagnostic depression in a representative, community sample. Whisman and Bruce (1999) used a prospective cohort design to evaluate the association between marital dissatisfaction at baseline and 12-month incidence of major depressive episode (MDE) in a community sample of married individuals from the New Haven ECA program. None of the respondents met the criteria for MDE at baseline. Results indicated that risk for incidence of MDE at follow-up varied as a function of the level of marital dissatisfaction at baseline. Specifically, marital dissatisfaction was associated with a significant risk ratio of 2.7 and an attributable risk of 29.5%. Thus, dissatisfied spouses were nearly 3 times more likely than nondissatisfied spouses to develop MDE during the year, and nearly 30% of the new occurrences of MDE were associated with marital dissatisfaction. The association between marital dissatisfaction and risk of MDE remained significant when demographic characteristics and history of MDE were controlled. Furthermore, this association was not moderated by either sex or history of MDE, indicating that this association is invariant with respect to these two factors that have been associated with increased risk of incidence of depression in previous research.

Whereas most prospective studies evaluating the longitudinal association between depression and marital dissatisfaction have been based on relatively short periods (e.g., 1 year or less), Gotlib, Lewinsohn, and Seeley (1998) evaluated the consequences of major depressive disorder (and nonaffective psychiatric disorder) during adolescence on marital status and marital functioning in early adulthood. What is applicable to this review is that the results indicated that history of major depressive disorder during adolescence was associated with lower level of marital quality (i.e., greater marital dissatisfaction) during early adulthood. It remains possible, of course, that third variables such as family relationships during adolescence or deficits in interpersonal skills account for this apparent longitudinal association (see Davila, chapter 4). However, that these investigators found that this association appeared to be specific to history of major depression (i.e., history of nonaffective disorder was not associated with lower marital quality during adulthood) supports the perspective that depression history may be causally related to subsequent interpersonal difficulties. Findings such as these also underscore the importance of recognizing developmental precursors of both depression and marital difficulties (see Cummings, DeArth-Pendley, Schudlich, and Smith, chapter 5).

In addition to conducting prospective evaluations of the association between diagnostic depression and marital dissatisfaction, investigators have begun to evaluate the association between marital dissatisfaction and the course of depression. For example, Hooley and Teasdale (1989) evaluated the association between marital dissatisfaction (assessed shortly after hospitalization) and 9-month relapse rates in a sample of formerly hospitalized depressed inpatients. Marital dissatisfaction was predictive of greater likelihood of relapse. Similar findings were reported by Hickie and Parker (1992), who found that level of marital dissatisfaction at baseline was associated with outcome (i.e., percentage improvement) in an 18-month longitudinal study of individuals with nonmelancholic depression. Although Hickie and Parker were particularly interested in the role of partner care on outcome, they also assessed marital dissatisfaction and found that greater marital quality (i.e., less dissatisfaction) was associated with better outcome, particularly among those individuals who remained with their partner. Interestingly, they also reported that those individuals who separated from a relationship that had been classified as dysfunctional (i.e., those with low partner care) at baseline evidenced long-term recovery that approximated the recovery of those who remained in relationships classified as functional at baseline. Finally, Goering, Lancee, and Freeman (1992) reported that recovery from depression in an inpatient sample of depressed women was predicted by spouses' (but not patients') ratings of the marriage at baseline and patients' (but not spouses') ratings of the marriage at follow-up.

Summary and Critique

The findings regarding the longitudinal association between depressive symptoms and marital dissatisfaction have been mixed and inconclusive. Difference among studies may be due to differences in methodology, including differences in participant characteristics (e.g., newlyweds, married couples, retirees), length of follow-up (which has ranged from 3 to 18 months), and type of analyses (e.g., regression vs. SEM). Furthermore, there is some evidence that marital dissatisfaction may be a better predictor of longitudinal changes in depressive symptoms for women than for men. Given this potential sex difference, future studies should evaluate these associations separately for women and men. In addition, Kurdek's (1998) proposal to evaluate the independent trajectories of depressive symptoms and marital dissatisfaction, and the link between these trajectories, seems to be an important consideration for future research.

A clearer association has been obtained between diagnostic depression and marital dissatisfaction. It would seem from existing studies that marital dissatisfaction precedes diagnostic depression and therefore is potentially causally related to depression. As previously noted, however, most existing studies have relied on retrospective accounts of this association. Although indicative that marital dissatisfaction may be causally related to depression, the use of retrospective reports has some methodological limitations, including that such reports may be influenced by depressed mood and response biases. In addition, if social environmental stress is a commonly held explanation for the cause of depression (e.g., Jorm et al., 1997), then depressed individuals may be more likely to say that marital problems preceded their depression because such an explanation fits with the depressed individual's causal model of depression. Furthermore, each of the retrospective studies included only depressed individuals seeking treatment. As previously discussed, because only a fraction of depressed individuals seek treatment, further empirical research is needed to determine the generalizability of these findings to non-treatment-seeking depressed individuals. However, the findings that marital dissatisfaction predicted increased risk of incidence of diagnostic depression (Whisman & Bruce, 1999) and that marital dissatisfaction is associated with the course of formerly depressed individuals (Goering et al., 1992; Hickie & Parker, 1992; Hooley & Teasdale, 1989) offers additional support for the position that marital dissatisfaction is associated with the onset and course of depression.

One important methodological issue that has not been addressed in most longitudinal studies on diagnostic depression and marital dissatisfaction concerns single versus recurrent MDE. The strongest support for a causal association between marital dissatisfaction and onset of diagnostic depression would be to show that marital dissatisfaction preceded depression among individuals without a history of depression. If individuals with recurrent MDE are included in the sample, it is possible that individuals who have more severe depression, as evidenced by more frequent recurrences, including early episodes of depression (cf. Gotlib et al., 1998) may have poorer marriages over the course of a longitudinal study. In this case, marital dissatisfaction, although possibly predating the onset of a particular episode, may be a consequence of prior episodes and not a cause of that particular episode. To rule out this possibility, future investigations could evaluate the association between marital dissatisfaction and only new episodes (i.e., first incidence) of diagnostic depression.

Most existing studies have tested the longitudinal association between depression and marital dissatisfaction by assessing each at baseline and using each construct to predict residual change over time in the other. However, as discussed by Kurdek (1998) and Davila (chapter 4), this design does not fully take into account the potential recursive nature of the association between these variables. Thus, as discussed in greater detail below, it is likely that depression and marital dissatisfaction influence, and are influenced by, one another. Furthermore, collecting data at two points in time may not adequately address the longitudinal association between depression and marital dissatisfaction. As discussed in greater detail by Karney (chapter 3), collecting data on these variables across multiple assessment periods and subsequently using analytic procedures appropriate for multiwave data may provide a stronger test of the longitudinal association between depression and marital dissatisfaction.

Theoretical Perspectives on the Association Between Depression and Marital Dissatisfaction

There have been several theoretical perspectives proposed to account for the association between depression and marital dissatisfaction. In general, these perspectives can be divided into (a) those that suggest that marital dissatisfaction leads to depression, (b) those that suggest that depression leads to marital dissatisfaction, and (c) those that suggest that a third variable contributes to both depression and marital dissatisfaction. It should be noted, however, that most of the following perspectives allow for bidirectional associations between depression and marital dissatisfaction (and, when relevant, third variables) and only suggest that one factor is most often likely to predate the other.

Beach et al. (1990) have most extensively discussed the perspective that marital dissatisfaction is most often likely to predate depression. According to Beach et al., marital dissatisfaction is likely to contribute to increased risk of depression by reducing available support (i.e., through reducing couple cohesion, acceptance of emotional expression, actual and perceived coping assistance, self-esteem support, spousal dependability, and intimacy) and increasing levels of stress and overt hostility (i.e., though increasing verbal and physical aggression; threats of separation and divorce; severe spousal denigration, criticism, or blame; severe disruption of scripted routines; and major idiosyncratic marital stressors). Similarly, Klerman, Weissman, Rounsaville, and Chevron (1984) proposed that interpersonal conflict, including marital conflict, can act as a precipitating factor for the onset of depression.

Coyne (1976) has most extensively discussed the perspective that depression is most often likely to predate marital dissatisfaction. According to this perspective, the behavior of depressed individuals is aversive to others, including significant others. However, the behavior of depressed individuals is also guilt inducing and inhibiting. Therefore, members of the social networks of depressed individuals (including marital and romantic partners) are likely to try to inhibit their negative responses to depressed individuals, but because this strategy is typically ineffective, their negative responses are likely to slip through and be perceived by depressed individuals. Thus, according to this theory, the responses of others serve to reinforce depression. A related perspective that depression predates marital dissatisfaction has been advanced by Hammen (1991; see also Davila, chapter 4), who proposed that depressed individuals ''by their symptoms, behaviors, characteristics, and social context generate stressful conditions, primarily interpersonal, that have the potential for contributing to the cycle of symptoms and stress that create chronic or intermittent depression'' (p. 555).

There are several perspectives that propose that a third variable may contribute to increased risk for both depression and marital dissatisfaction. For example, Birtchnell (e.g., Birtchnell, 1988; Birtchnell & Kennard, 1983) has proposed that certain personality characteristics (e.g., dependence, interpersonal sensitivity) may predispose an individual to both depression and interpersonal problems. It should be noted, however, that social functioning has been shown to influence the course of depression, even when potential confounding factors such as personality characteristics have been statistically controlled. For example, Miller et al. (1992) found that family functioning was associated with the course of major depression, even after controlling for the influence of neuroticism. Because such studies have not been conducted with marital functioning, however, investigations are needed to evaluate the association between marital dissatisfaction and risk for depression that is independent of the shared association with personality functioning.

An alternative model has been proposed by Koerner, Prince, and Jacobson (1994), who suggested that cultural factors, including power differences between men and women and socialization of gender roles, are key to understanding why women are at increased risk for depression. A woman who thinks that her needs, especially her needs for intimacy, are not being met in a relationship may request or demand changes in the relationship. If her husband avoids her or withdraws and denies her the opportunity for need fulfillment, she has few options. She may continue to demand, thereby escalating the polarization and perhaps increasing marital conflict, or she may silence her demands in an effort to maintain harmony in the relationship. In either case, her needs, including her desire for intimacy, are not met. In addition to marital dissatisfaction, depression is a likely outcome, given the importance of the marital relationship as a primary source of reinforcement, support, and sense of self. In a related vein, Halloran (1998) proposed that inequality in marital power might be a third variable that explains how depression and marital dissatisfaction are related.

Summary and Critique

Several theoretical perspectives have been advanced to account for the association between depression and marital dissatisfaction. Although each stresses primacy of a particular causal factor (or factors), it is most likely that the associations between depression, marital dissatisfaction, and third variables are bidirectional. That is, it may be most likely that depression, marital dissatisfaction, and other factors both influence and are influenced by each other. In addition, although there have been recent efforts to test some of these theoretical perspectives, many aspects of these theories await empirical evaluation.

Although these theoretical positions represent important contributions, they also possess certain limitations. One limitation with most of the existing accounts of the association between depression and marital dissatisfaction is that these perspectives often have not accounted for other findings known about depression. As proposed by Lewinsohn, Hoberman, Teri, and Hautzinger (1985), an adequate theory of depression needs to be able to explain several significant research findings.

First, one of the most consistent findings in the demographics of depression is that the prevalence of depression among women is approximately twice that among men (Nolen-Hoeksema, 1987). Furthermore, results from the meta-analysis of depressive symptoms discussed in this chapter indicated that the association between depressive symptoms and marital dissatisfaction was significantly greater for women than for men, and the results from longitudinal studies indicated that marital dissatisfaction may be a better predictor of longitudinal change in depressive symptoms for women. However, although the theories proposed by Koerner et al. (1994) and Halloran (1998) provided an explanation for this demographic finding, the other theories have not addressed sex differences in depression or in the association between depression and marital dissatisfaction.

Second, an adequate theory of depression should consider age of onset. In the New Haven ECA study, the mean age of onset for major depression was 26.5 years (Weissman, Bruce, Leaf, Florio, & Holzer, 1991). In comparison, the median age at marriage is 26.7 years for women and 28.7 years for men (Centers for Disease Control and Prevention, 1990). Consequently, "most episodes of depression observed in a randomly selected married population will be recurrences rather than 'new' cases" (Beach & O'Leary, 1993b, p. 418). Therefore, theoretical perspectives of the association between depression and marital dissatisfaction need to account for these differences in demographics and address the issue of first onset versus recurrence of depression.

Third, a related aspect of depression that needs to be addressed in an adequate theory of depression concerns the recurrent nature of depression. As reviewed by Belsher and Costello (1988), "relapse rates of around 20% at 2 months postrecovery increase to around 30% at 6 months postrecovery, level off at about 40% by 12 months postrecovery, and stabilize around 50% by 2 years after recovery" (p. 89). Future research is needed to address the issue of marital dissatisfaction and depression relapse, particularly in light of the relative stability of marital quality. Theoretical advances proposed by Post (1992) might prove to be useful toward this end. In brief, Post's theory suggests that repeated environmental stimuli (i.e., psychosocial stress) lead to progressively greater neural responses, which in turn affect brain excitability and behavioral responsiveness in a long-lasting fashion. Thus, stress is believed to set in motion intracellular changes at the level of gene transcription, producing long-lasting alteration in neuropeptides and synaptic and neural structures. Consequently, such stress may leave residual vulnerability to further occurrences of depression. Therefore, an individual with a previous episode of depression may be more vulnerable to subsequent episodes resulting from ever-decreasing levels of psychosocial stress. Applied to marital functioning, this model suggests that vulnerable individuals may become susceptible to responding with depression in reaction to increasingly minor variations in their level of marital dissatisfaction. Theoretical and empirical work is needed to more fully understand the association between marital dissatisfaction and the recurrence of depression.

Toward a Second Generation of Research on Depression and Marital Dissatisfaction

The existing research has indicated a strong association between marital dissatisfaction and depression, treated both as a continuous variable and as a discrete disorder. Given the magnitude of this association, a fruitful area of future research may be to evaluate the moderators and mediators of this association.

A moderating variable is a qualitative or quantitative variable that affects "the direction and/or strength of the relation between an independent or predictor variable and a dependent or criterion variable" (Baron & Kenny, 1986, p. 1174). Thus, moderators are variables that address the question of who is at risk for depression in the face of marital dissatisfaction (and vice versa). That is, because not all maritally dissatisfied individuals are depressed (and not all depressed individuals are maritally dissatisfied), research is needed to identify variables that affect the strength of the cross-sectional and longitudinal association between depression and marital dissatisfaction.

Investigators have only recently begun to address the issue of moderators of the association between depression and marital dissatisfaction. For example, Culp and Beach (1998) reported that self-esteem moderated the association between marital dissatisfaction and depressive symptoms for men but not for women. Regarding the longitudinal association between marital dissatisfaction and depressive symptoms, Beach and O'Leary (1993a) reported that newlyweds with chronic dysphoria were more vulnerable to changes in marital quality (and associated interpersonal stress) in their 18-month prospective study. Because so few studies have been conducted in this area, continued investigation into the moderators of the association between depression and marital dissatisfaction is clearly needed. Future studies are needed to identify the biological, psychological, and social factors that moderate these associations. Furthermore, insofar as existing studies of the cross-sectional and longitudinal association between depression and marital dissatisfaction have focused primarily on White samples, future research is needed to determine if demographic characteristics such as race or ethnicity moderate these associations (see Kaslow, Twomey, Brooks, Thompson, and Reynolds, chapter 8).

In comparison to a moderator, a mediator is a variable that "accounts for the relation between the predictor and the criterion . . . [and] speaks to how or why such effects occur" (Baron & Kenny, 1986, p. 1176). To date, there has been relatively little empirical research on the mediators of the association between depression and marital dissatisfaction. In one of the few studies conducted evaluating mediation, Culp and Beach (1998) reported that the cross-sectional association between these two variables was mediated by self-esteem for women but not for men. Given the paucity of research in this area, future research is needed to identify the variables that intervene and account for the cross-sectional and longitudinal association between depression and marital dissatisfaction.

Although there has been relatively little empirical research in this area, there have been several theoretical perspectives proposed to account for the association between depression and marital dissatisfaction. Some of these perspectives have been reviewed previously. For example, Beach et al. (1990) suggested that marital dissatisfaction contributes to depression through reducing support and increasing stress and overt hostility. In identifying mechanisms of this association, future research is needed to account for the heterogeneity of symptoms of depression. In particular, future research is needed to identify the mechanisms of the association between marital dissatisfaction and the somatic symptoms of depression (e.g., sleep, appetite, and libido disturbance). For example, Ehlers, Frank, and Kupfer (1988) suggested that social disruptions lead to depression through the creation of instability of biological circadian rhythms (e.g., sleep patterns). Finally, it should be noted that marital dissatisfaction could itself be a mediator between other correlates of depression and the manifestation of depression (see Katz, chapter 6).

Conclusion

A review of the existing literature indicates that marital dissatisfaction is strongly associated with both depressive symptoms and diagnostic depression and that the association between marital dissatisfaction and depressive symptoms is greater for women than for men. The temporal association between these variables, however, is inconclusive. It appears that marital dissatisfaction may predate depressive symptoms, although there is some indication that, similar to the cross-sectional association, this effect may be greater for women than for men. It also appears that marital dissatisfaction is associated with the onset and course of diagnostic depression, although these conclusions should be tempered by the fact that there are relatively few existing studies. Although theoretical accounts of this association have been proposed, there are comparatively few empirical studies evaluating most of these perspectives. Future gains in understanding the magnitude and nature of the association between depression and marital dissatisfaction are most likely to be made from (a) longitudinal studies evaluating the association between marital dissatisfaction and the onset and course of diagnostic depression, (b) theoretical developments in accounting for this association that also take into account other known factors regarding both depression and marital dissatisfaction, and (c) studies evaluating the moderators and mediators of this association. Such studies not only should increase understanding of the onset and course of depression and marital dissatisfaction, but also may have important implications regarding prevention and treatment.

References

Assh, S. D., & Byers, E. S. (1996). Understanding the co-occurrence of marital distress and depression in women. *Journal of Social and Personal Relationships, 13,* 537–552.

Baron, R. M., & Kenny, D. A. (1986). The moderator-mediator variable distinction in social psychological research: Conceptual, strategic, and statistical considerations. *Journal of Personality and Social Psychology, 51,* 1173–1182.

Basco, M. R., Prager, K. J., Pita, J. M., Tamir, L. M., & Stephens, J. J. (1992). Communication and intimacy in the marriages of depressed patients. *Journal of Family Psychology, 6,* 184–194.

Bauserman, S. A. K., Arias, I., & Craighead, W. E. (1995). Marital attributions in spouses of depressed patients. *Journal of Psychopathology and Behavioral Assessment, 17,* 231–249.

Beach, S. R., Arias, I., & O'Leary, K. D. (1986). The relationship of marital satisfaction and social support to depressive symptomatology. *Journal of Psychopathology and Behavioral Assessment, 8,* 305–316.

Beach, S. R., & O'Leary, K. D. (1993a). Dysphoria and marital discord: Are dysphoric individuals at risk for marital maladjustment? *Journal of Marital and Family Therapy, 19,* 355–368.

Beach, S. R., & O'Leary, K. D. (1993b). Marital discord and dysphoria: For whom does the marital relationship predict depressive symptomatology? *Journal of Social and Personal Relationships, 10,* 405–420.

Beach, S. R. H., Sandeen, E. E., & O'Leary, K. D. (1990). *Depression in marriage: A model for etiology and treatment.* New York: Guilford Press.

Beck, A. T., Rush, A. J., Shaw, B. F., & Emery, G. (1979). *Cognitive therapy of depression.* New York: Guilford Press.

Beck, A. T., Steer, R. A., & Garbin, M. G. (1988). Psychometric properties of the Beck Depression Inventory: Twenty-five years of evaluation. *Clinical Psychology Review, 8,* 77–100.

Belsher, G., & Costello, C. G. (1988). Relapse after recovery from unipolar depression: A critical review. *Psychological Bulletin, 104,* 84–96.

Biglan, A., Hops, H., Sherman, L., Friedman, L. S., Arthur, J., & Osteen, V. (1985). Problem-solving interactions of depressed women and their husbands. *Behavior Therapy, 16,* 431–451.

Birtchnell, J. (1988). Depression and family relationships: A study of young, married women on a London housing estate. *British Journal of Psychiatry, 153,* 758–769.

Birtchnell, J., & Kennard, J. (1983). Does marital maladjustment lead to mental illness? *Social Psychiatry, 18,* 79–88.

Blumenthal, M. D., & Dielman, T. E. (1975). Depressive symptomatology and role function in a general population. *Archives of General Psychiatry, 32,* 985–991.

Brown, G. W., & Harris, T. (1978). *Social origins of depression: A study of psychiatric disorder in women.* London: Tavistock,

Burns, D., Sayers, S., & Moras, K. (1994). Intimate relationships and depression: Is there a causal connection? *Journal of Consulting and Clinical Psychology, 62,* 1033–1043.

Centers for Disease Control and Prevention. (1990). *Monthly Vital Statistics Report, 43.*

Cicchetti, D., Rogosch, F. A., & Toth, S. L. (1998). Maternal depressive disorder and contextual risk: Contributions to the development of attachment insecurity and behavior problems in toddlerhood. *Development and Psychopathology, 10,* 283–300.

Cohan, C. L., & Bradbury, T. N. (1997). Negative life events, marital interaction, and the longitudinal course of newlywed marriage. *Journal of Personality and Social Psychology, 73,* 114–128.

Cohen, J. (1988). *Statistical power analysis for the behavioral sciences* (2nd ed.). Hillsdale, NJ: Erlbaum.

Coleman, R. E., & Miller, A. G. (1975). The relationship between depression and marital maladjustment in a clinic population: A multi-trait-multimethod study. *Journal of Consulting and Clinical Psychology, 43,* 647–651.

Coyne, J. C. (1976). Toward an interactional description of depression. *Psychiatry, 39,* 28–40.

Coyne, J. C. (1994). Self-reported distress: Analog or ersatz depression? *Psychological Bulletin, 116,* 29–45.

Crane, D. R., Allgood, S. M., Larson, J. H., & Griffin, W. (1990). Assessing marital quality with distressed and nondistressed couples: A comparison and equivalency table for three frequently used measures. *Journal of Marriage and the Family, 52,* 87–93.

Crowther, J. H. (1985). The relationship between depression and marital maladjustment: A descriptive study. *Journal of Nervous and Mental Disease, 173,* 227–231.

Culp, L. N., & Beach, S. R. H. (1998). Marriage and depressive symptoms: The role and bases of self-esteem differ by gender. *Psychology of Women Quarterly, 22,* 647–663.

Davies, P. T., Dumenci, L., & Windle, M. (1999). The interplay between maternal depressive symptoms and marital distress in prediction of adolescent adjustment. *Journal of Marriage and the Family, 61,* 238–254.

Dehle, C., & Weiss, R. (1998). Sex differences in prospective associations between marital quality and depressed mood. *Journal of Marriage and the Family, 60,* 1002–1011.

Dimitrovsky, L., Schapira-Beck, E., & Itskowitz, R. (1994). Locus of control of Israeli women during the transition to marriage. *Journal of Psychology, 128,* 537–545.

Dobson, K. S. (1987). Marital and social adjustment in depressed and remitted married women. *Journal of Clinical Psychology, 43,* 261–265.

Ehlers, C. L., Frank, E., & Kupfer, D. J. (1988). Social zeitgebers and biological rhythms: A unified approach to understanding the etiology of depression. *Archives of General Psychiatry, 45,* 948–952.

Fechner-Bates, S., Coyne, J. C., & Schwenk, T. L. (1994). The relationship of self-reported distress to depression and other psychopathology. *Journal of Consulting and Clinical Psychology, 62,* 549–558.

Fincham, F. D., Beach, S. R., & Bradbury, T. N. (1989). Marital distress, depression, and attributions: Is the marital distress-attribution association an artifact of depression? *Journal of Consulting and Clinical Psychology, 57,* 768–771.

Fincham, F. D., Beach, S. R. H., Harold, G. T., & Osborne, L. N. (1997). Marital satisfaction and depression: Different causal relationships for men and women? *Psychological Science, 8,* 351–357.

Fincham, F. D., & Bradbury, T. N. (1993). Marital satisfaction, depression, and attributions: A longitudinal analysis. *Journal of Personality and Social Psychology, 64,* 442–452.

Frankel, K. A., & Harmon, R. J. (1996). Depressed mothers: They don't always look as bad as they feel. *Journal of the American Academy of Child and Adolescent Psychiatry, 35,* 289–298.

Goering, P., Lin, E., Campbell, D., Boyle, M. H., & Offord, D. R. (1996). Psychiatric disability in Ontario. *Canadian Journal of Psychiatry, 41,* 564–571.

Goering, P. N., Lancee, W. J., & Freeman, J. J. (1992). Marital support and recovery from depression. *British Journal of Psychiatry, 160,* 76–82.

Goldberg, W. A. (1990). Marital quality, parental personality, and spouse agreement about perceptions and expectations for children. *Merrill-Palmer Quarterly, 36,* 531–556.

Gotlib, I. H., Lewinsohn, P. M., & Seeley, J. R. (1998). Consequences of depression during adolescence: Marital status and marital functioning in early adulthood. *Journal of Abnormal Psychology, 107,* 686–690.

Gotlib, I. H., & Whiffen, V. E. (1989). Depression and marital functioning: An examination of specificity and gender differences. *Journal of Abnormal Psychology, 98,* 23–30.

Halford, W. K., & Bouma, R. (1997). Individual psychopathology and marital distress. In W. K. Halford & H. J. Markman (Eds.), *Clinical handbook of marriage and couples intervention* (pp. 291–321). New York: Wiley.

Halloran, E. C. (1998). The role of marital power in depression and marital distress. *American Journal of Family Therapy, 26,* 3–14.

Hamilton, M. (1960). A rating scale for depression. *Journal of Neurology, Neurosurgery and Psychiatry, 12,* 56–62.

Hammen, C. L. (1991). The generation of stress in the course of unipolar depression. *Journal of Abnormal Psychology, 100,* 555–561.

Hedges, L. V., & Olkin, I. (1985). *Statistical methods for meta-analysis.* Orlando, FL: Academic Press.

Hickie, I., & Parker, G. (1992). The impact of an uncaring partner on improvement in non-melancholic depression. *Journal of Affective Disorders, 25,* 147–160.

Hickie, I., Parker, G., Wilhelm, K., & Tennant, C. (1991). Perceived interpersonal risk factors of non-endogenous depression. *Psychological Medicine, 21,* 399–412.

Hooley, J. M., & Teasdale, J. D. (1989). Predictors of relapse in unipolar depressives: Expressed emotion, marital distress, and perceived criticism. *Journal of Abnormal Psychology, 98,* 229–235.

Horneffer, K. J., & Fincham, F. D. (1995). Construct of attributional style in depression and marital distress. *Journal of Family Psychology, 9,* 186–195.

Jacobson, N. S., Follette, W. C., Revenstorf, D., Baucom, D. H., Hahlweg, K., & Margolin, G. (1984). Variability in outcome and clinical significance of behavioral marital therapy: A reanalysis of outcome data. *Journal of Consulting and Clinical Psychology, 52,* 497–504.

Jorm, A. F., Korten, A. E., Jacomb, P. A., Christensen, H., Rodgers, B., & Pollitt, P. (1997). Public beliefs about causes and risk factors for depression and schizophrenia. *Social Psychiatry and Psychiatric Epidemiology, 32,* 143–148.

Karney, B. R., Bradbury, T. N., Fincham, F. D., & Sullivan, K. T. (1994). The role of negative affectivity in the association between attributions and marital satisfaction. *Journal of Personality and Social Psychology, 66,* 413–424.

Katz, J., Beach, S. R. H., & Anderson, P. (1996). Self-enhancement versus self-verification: Does spousal support always help? *Cognitive Therapy and Research, 20,* 345–360.

Kendler, K. S., Karkowski, L. M., & Prescott, C. A. (1999). Causal relationship between stressful life events and the onset of major depression. *American Journal of Psychiatry, 156,* 837–841.

Kessler, R. C., McGonagle, K. A., Zhao, S., Nelson, C. B., Hughes, M., Eshleman, S., Wittchen, H.-U., & Kendler, K. S. (1994). Lifetime and 12–month prevalence of DSM-III-R psychiatric disorders in the United States: Results from the National Comorbidity Survey. *Archives of General Psychiatry, 51,* 8–19.

Klerman, G. L., Weissman, M. M., Rounsaville, B. J., & Chevron, E. (1984). *Interpersonal psychotherapy of depression.* New York: Basic Books.

Koerner, K., Prince, S., & Jacobson, N. S. (1994). Enhancing the treatment and prevention of depression in women: The role of integrative behavioral couple therapy. *Behavior Therapy, 25,* 373–390.

Kurdek, L. A. (1998). The nature and predictors of the trajectory of change in marital quality over the first 4 years of marriage for first-married husbands and wives. *Journal of Family Psychology, 12,* 494–510.

Lewinsohn, P. M., Hoberman, H., Teri, L., & Hautzinger, M. (1985). An integrative theory of depression. In S. Reiss & R. Bootzin (Eds.), *Theoretical issues in behavior therapy* (pp. 331–359). New York: Academic Press.

Matussek, P., & Wiegand, M. (1985). Partnership problems as causes of endogenous and neurotic depressions. *Acta Psychiatrica Scandinavica, 71,* 95–104.

McLeod, J. D. (1994). Anxiety disorders and marital quality. *Journal of Abnormal Psychology, 103,* 767–776.

Miller, I. W., Keitner, G. I., Whisman, M. A., Ryan, C. E., Epstein, N. B., & Bishop, D. S. (1992). Depressed patients with dysfunctional families: Description and course of illness. *Journal of Abnormal Psychology, 101,* 637–646.

Nelson, G. M., & Beach, S. R. (1990). Sequential interaction in depression: Effects of depressive behavior on spousal aggression. *Behavior Therapy, 21,* 167–182.

Nolen-Hoeksema, S. (1987). Sex differences in unipolar depression: Evidence and theory. *Psychological Bulletin, 101,* 259–282.

O'Leary, D. A., Christian, J. L., & Mendell, N. R. (1994). A closer look at the link between marital discord and depressive symptomatology. *Journal of Social and Clinical Psychology, 13,* 33–41.

O'Leary, K. D., Riso, L. P., & Beach, S. R. (1990). Attributions about the marital discord/depression link and therapy outcome. *Behavior Therapy, 21,* 413–422.

Olin, G. V., & Fenell, D. L. (1989). The relationship between depression and marital adjustment in a general population. *Family Therapy, 16,* 11–20.

Patton, D., & Waring, E. M. (1991). Criterion validity of two methods of evaluating marital relationships. *Journal of Sex and Marital Therapy, 17,* 22–26.

Paykel, E. S., Myers, J. K., Dienelt, M. N., Klerman, G. L., Lindenthal, J. J., & Pepper, M. P. (1969). Life events and depression: A controlled study. *Archives of General Psychiatry, 21,* 753–760.

Post, R. M. (1992). Transduction of psychosocial stress into the neurobiology of recurrent affective disorder. *American Journal of Psychiatry, 149,* 999–1010.

Purnine, D. M., & Carey, M. P. (1997). Interpersonal communication and sexual adjustment: The roles of understanding and agreement. *Journal of Consulting and Clinical Psychology, 65,* 1017–1025.

Quinton, D., Rutter, M., & Rowlands, O. (1976). An evaluation of an interview assessment of marriage. *Psychological Medicine, 6,* 577–586.

Roy, A. (1987). Five risk factors for depression. *British Journal of Psychiatry, 150,* 536–541.

Ruscher, S. M., & Gotlib, I. H. (1988). Marital interaction patterns of couples with and without a depressed partner. *Behavior Therapy, 19,* 455–470.

Sacco, W. P., Dumont, C. P., & Dow, M. G. (1993). Attributional, perceptual, and affective responses to depressed and nondepressed marital partners. *Journal of Consulting and Clinical Psychology, 61,* 1076–1082.

Sandberg, J. G., & Harper, J. M. (1999). Depression in mature marriages: Impact and implications for marital therapy. *Journal of Marital and Family Therapy, 25,* 393–406.

Schmaling, K. B., & Jacobson, N. S. (1990). Marital interaction and depression. *Journal of Abnormal Psychology, 99,* 229–236.

Senchak, M., & Leonard, K. E. (1993). The role of spouses' depression and anger in the attribution-marital satisfaction relation. *Cognitive Therapy and Research, 17,* 397–409.

Shapiro, S., Skinner, E. A., Kessler, L. G., Korff, M. V., German, P. S., Tischler, G. L., Leaf, P. J., Benham, L., Cottler, L., & Regier, D. A. (1984). Utilization of health and mental health services: Three Epidemiologic Catchment Area sites. *Archives of General Psychiatry, 41,* 971–978.

Smolen, R. C., Spiegel, D. A., Khan, S. A., & Schwartz, J. F. (1988). Examination of marital adjustment and marital assertion in depressed and nondepressed women. *Journal of Social and Clinical Psychology, 7,* 284–289.

Smolen, R. C., Spiegel, D. A., & Martin, C. J. (1986). Patterns of marital interaction associated with marital dissatisfaction and depression. *Journal of Behaviour Therapy and Experimental Psychiatry, 17,* 261–266.

Spanier, G. B. (1976). Measuring dyadic adjustment: New scales for assessing the quality of marriage and similar dyads. *Journal of Marriage and the Family, 38,* 15–28.

Spanier, G. B. (1989). *Dyadic Adjustment Scale manual.* North Tonawanda, NY: Multi-Health Systems.

Staebler, C. R., Pollard, C. A., & Merkel, W. T. (1993). Sexual history and quality of current relationships in patients with obsessive-compulsive disorder: A comparison with two other psychiatric samples. *Journal of Sex and Marital Therapy, 19,* 147–153.

Stoneman, Z., Brody, G. H., & Burke, M. (1989). Marital quality, depression, and inconsistent parenting: Relationship with observed mother-child conflict. *American Journal of Orthopsychiatry, 59,* 105–117.

Stravynski, A., Tremblay, M., & Verreault, R. (1995). Marital adjustment and depression. *Psychopathology, 28,* 112–117.

Thompson, J. M. (1995). Silencing the self: Depressive symptomatology and close relationships. *Psychology of Women Quarterly, 19,* 337–353.

Thompson, J. M., Whiffen, V. M., & Blain, M. D. (1995). Depressive symptoms, sex and perceptions of intimate relationships. *Journal of Social and Personal Relationships, 12,* 49–66.

Ulrich-Jakubowski, D., Russell, D. W., & O'Hara, M. W. (1988). Marital adjustment difficulties: Cause or consequence of depressive symptomatology? *Journal of Social and Clinical Psychology, 7,* 312–318.

Vega, B. R., Cañas, F., Bayón, C., Franco, B., Salvador, M., Graell, M., & Santo-Domingo, J. (1996). Interpersonal factors in female depression. *European Journal of Psychiatry, 10,* 16–24.

Weiss, R. L., & Aved, B. M. (1978). Marital satisfaction and depression as predictors of physical health status. *Journal of Consulting and Clinical Psychology, 46,* 1379–1384.

Weissman, M. M. (1987). Advances in psychiatric epidemiology: Rates and risks for major depression. *American Journal of Public Health, 77,* 445–451.

Weissman, M. M., Bruce, M., Leaf, P., Florio, L., & Holzer, C. (1991). Affective disorders. In L. Robins & E. Regier (Eds.), *Psychiatric disorders in America* (pp. 53–80). New York: Free Press.

Weissman, M. M., & Paykel, E. S. (1974). *The depressed woman: A study of social relationships.* Chicago: University of Chicago Press.

Whiffen, V. E., Aubé, J. A., Thompson, J. M., & Campbell, T. L. (in press). Attachment beliefs and interpersonal context associated with dependency and self-criticism. *Journal of Social and Clinical Psychology.*

Whiffen, V. E., & Gotlib, I. H. (1993). Comparison of postpartum and nonpostpartum depression: Clinical presentation, psychiatric history, and psychosocial functioning. *Journal of Consulting and Clinical Psychology, 61,* 485–494.

Whisman, M. A. (1999). Marital distress and psychiatric disorders in a community sample: Results from the National Comorbidity Survey. *Journal of Abnormal Psychology, 108,* 701–706.

Whisman, M. A., & Bruce, M. L. (1999). Marital distress and incidence of major depressive episode in a community sample. *Journal of Abnormal Psychology, 108,* 674–678.

2
Not Agent Blue: Effects of Marital Functioning on Depression and Implications for Treatment

James C. Coyne
Nili R. Benazon

Being married has been associated with greater psychological well-being (Wood, Rhodes, & Whelan, 1989), physical health (Joung et al., 1997), and longevity (Hu & Goldman, 1990). A 17-nation study consistently found that married individuals were happier than unmarried individuals (Stack & Eshleman, 1998). However, the advantages of being married may be limited to those who are happily married, and positive involvement in other relationships may not compensate for a distressed marriage (Coyne & DeLongis, 1986). The strong association between marital conflict and psychological distress (Beach, Sandeen, & O'Leary, 1990; Fincham, Beach, Harold, & Osborne, 1997) has led to the widespread conviction that marital problems play a causal role in clinical depression. It has repeatedly been suggested that findings of gender differences in depression can be explained by the greater impact of marital distress on women than men (Dehle & Weiss, 1998). Weissman's (1979) statement that the prototypic depressed patient is a woman experiencing marital problems remains widely cited, even if clinical and epidemiological evidence has suggested that the never and formerly married are overrepresented among depressed community-residing individuals and patients and that the married actually have the lowest rates of depression among women (Betrus, Elmore, Woods, & Hamilton, 1995; Schwenk, Coyne, & Fechner-Bates, 1996; Weissman, Bruce, Leaf, Florio, & Holzer, 1991). The notion that marital problems play a major role in depression has taken a firm hold in modern culture, as can be seen in the following advertisement soliciting clients for psychotherapy proclaiming seeming scientific authority:

> Depressed? Recent research has shown marital distress and criticism to be one of the leading causes of depression. If this is true for you or your partner, call us. We can help. (Advertisement, *Philadelphia Weekly,* 1998, p. 52)

Programs of research focused on phenómena such as mood contagion, self-verification, and reassurance seeking stake much of their claims to clinical significance on their presumed relevance to interpersonal processes in the marriages of depressed individuals, even if the bulk of such studies have focused on unmarried, distressed college students. This high-lighting of the role of marriage in depression would seem to indicate an area of vigorous empirical activity. However, despite strong claims and numerous articles on the subject of depression and marital distress, there has been relatively little in the way of new empirical work in the past decade examining the role of marriage and marital functioning in major depression. Most recent writings consist of integrative reviews and consolidations of existing data, and there is a relative paucity of new data being published. Indeed, Whisman (chapter 1) points out that to date there are still only a handful of published studies that included both a standardized measure of marital adjustment and a standardized diagnosis of depression and that otherwise met minimal methodological standards.

In contrast, the past few decades have been marked by considerable growth in researchers' understanding of the nature, natural history, and clinical epidemiology of depression. This chapter notes how this work has yet to have the impact in the psychological literature concerning depression and marriage that it is due. If data from community and clinical samples were taken into account, there would be fundamental shifts in the way questions about depression and marriage are framed, research is conducted, and therapeutic interventions in the marriages of depressed individuals are attempted. The relevance of much of the data cited in support of particular relations between depression and marriage would be thrown into doubt, and the confidence with which many statements made about the role of marital problems in depression would need to be tempered. Additionally, the need to consider alternatives to conventional marital therapy for depression as it is currently practiced would be more obvious.

With so much of the existing literature thus being open to intense criticism and skeptical reevaluation, the fine detail and firmness of conclusions that can be drawn are limited. However, a broad metastrategy for studying the relations between depression and marriage can be proposed. Namely, rather than simply importing more theory from social and cognitive clinical psychology, there is a pressing need for theory-informed, but phenomena-driven, research. It is important that the various theoretical schematics that are imposed on the complex phenomena of depression not miss some important nuances or fail to specify key features of this disorder and its context. Lacking an adequate grounding in the phenomena of depression, many of current psychological writings on the topic have a hypothetical, even fictional, quality. At the center of the standard—and, we believe, dubious—plot of this fiction is a heroine who would never have become depressed had she not encountered marital problems. Moreover, we argue that the recurrent, episodic nature of depression dictates a longitudinal, adult developmental perspective that is sorely lacking in current psychological theory and research. The bulk of recent theoretical work has abstracted a small number of variables and then generalized from observations made over an arbitrary brief length of time to long-term processes stretching across the life of a marriage, if not all of adulthood. Without actually studying clinically depressed individuals and doing so in a way that allows thinking to be shaped by their experiences and circumstances, what is left is theoretical elegance that may be irrelevant to the phenomena it is intended to explain.

This chapter begins by examining the nature of clinical depression as it is coming to be understood in psychiatric epidemiological studies. Next, how the theoretical perspectives on the relation between depression and marital distress must take into consideration the nature of clinical depression in formulating research questions and in interpreting existing data is considered. We argue that there has been an unfortunate reductionism and a fundamental misspecification of the relation between depression and marital distress in the bulk of previous work. Finally, the chapter concludes with a discussion of some of the important clinical implications of the depiction of the nature of depression and its association with marital distress. In particular, we argue that the appeal and use of couples therapy for depression could be substantially increased if therapists engaged spouses of depressed patients collaboratively rather than uniformly implying a causal role for them in either their relationship problems or their partners' depression.

Understanding the Nature of Depression: An Emergent Perspective

The limited database on which the psychological literature concerning depression and marriage depends consists largely of a few cross-sectional and short-term longitudinal studies of marital functioning during an acute episode of depression; a larger number of cross-sectional and short-term longitudinal studies of the relations of marital functioning and psychological distress; and a few studies of the association of marital variables and subsequent relapse, notably the expressed emotion literature. Throughout this literature, there are some unquestioned assumptions about the nature of depression that have proved to be erroneous. Namely, it has been assumed that depression is largely characterized by single episodes that are preceded and followed by relatively positive well periods. Vulnerability to clinical depression has been assumed to be broadly distributed in the population and on a continuum with everyday fluctuations in distress. Thus, retracing a reductionistic path that is well trodden by cognitive theorists, interpersonal theories have come to assume that a progression from mild distress to severe depression can be reduced to a matter of a limited number of psychological processes, but interpersonal or social–cognitive in nature, rather than cognitive. As a result, correlational studies of largely minor and short-term fluctuations in marital functioning and distress have been accepted as suitable models of the relations between marriage and the development of clinical disorder.

What has been ignored is a fundamental shift in the conceptualization of clinical depression that has occurred among psychiatrists and epidemiologists as a result of increasingly sophisticated clinical and community studies (Judd, 1998). Namely, depression is now seen as less of an acute, single-episode phenomenon, like appendicitis, and more of a chronic, episodic condition, like asthma (Klinkman, Schwenk, & Coyne, 1997). As with asthma, most current episodes of depression are going to be recurrences, and the best predictor of a future episode is having a past episode (Coyne, Pepper, & Flynn, 1999). Other data clearly show that depression neither appears ''out of the blue'' nor resolves completely for long periods. Instead, more than previously realized, depression is characterized by intermittent symptoms as well as full-blown relapses and recurrences (Judd et al., 1998). What has been abandoned is any notion of depression as a disorder occurring in single, discrete episodes and any sense that conditions under which everyone, or even most people, could be expected to become clinically depressed can be specified (Coyne & Racioppo, 1999).

Secular Trends

There also is evidence that over the past few decades there have been secular trends in the lifetime prevalence of depression and the timing of first episodes. Data from a number of countries, including the United States, Canada, Germany, and New Zealand, suggest that since 1935 there have been both a sharp increase in the rates and a drop in the age of onset of depression (Cross-National Collaborative Group, 1992). In the United States, the rates for women appeared to have stabilized since 1945, but they have continued to increase for men (Wickramaratne, Weissman, Leaf, & Holford, 1989). Data from the Epidemiologic Catchment Area (ECA) study revealed that only 1% of Americans born before 1905 had suffered a major depression by age 75, but among individuals born after 1955, 6% had their first depressive episode by age 24 (Burke, Burke, Rae, & Regier, 1991). Currently, women are most likely to be affected by age 27, and men by age 29 (Weissman et al., 1991). Moreover, results from the National Institute of Mental Health Collaborative Depression Study indicated that 33.5% of depressed patients had experienced episode onset before the age of

21 (Judd et al., 1998). Whereas clinical depression was once a disorder of middle age (Burke et al., 1991; Klerman, 1988), it now occurs early enough to influence the key transitions of early adulthood and the subsequent life-course trajectory (Sorenson, Rutter, & Aneshensel, 1991).

Depression As a Recurrent Condition

Accumulated natural history data have demonstrated that depression is a chronic, recurring condition (e.g., Keller, Lavori, Lewis, & Klerman, 1983; Keller, Lavori, Rice, Coryell, & Hirschfeld, 1986; Keller, Shapiro, Lavori, & Wolfe, 1982), and long-term follow-up of depressed psychiatric patients has suggested that few, if any, depressed patients experience only a single episode of depression (Keller et al., 1983). Similarly, in community and primary medical care samples, the best predictor that an individual will become depressed in the near future is by far a personal history of depression. Indeed, reanalyses of the ECA data revealed that individuals who become depressed in the course of a year are 40 times more likely to have been depressed in the past than individuals who do not become depressed in that year (Kessler & Magee, 1994). However, the criteria for diagnosing current depression in the ECA study may have contributed to an inflated estimate of the relationship of past to current depression. Respondents were considered to be currently suffering from major depression if they had ever met the criteria for major depression and they had experienced at least one symptom in the past month (see Dohrenwend, 1989, for a discussion). Thus, respondents who had experienced a single symptom of depression in the past month (e.g., sleep disturbance) would have been diagnosed as depressed if they had experienced a previous depressive episode. In a study of primary medical care patients, Coyne et al. (1999) used the *Diagnostic and Statistical Manual of Mental Disorders,* third edition, revised (*DSM-III-R;* American Psychiatric Association, 1987) and the Structured Clinical Interview for *DSM-III-R* (SCID; Spitzer, Williams, Gibbon, & First 1989), and obtained a more modest, but nonetheless impressive, relative risk of 8.0 for past depression predicting current depression. This figure dwarfs the typical risk of depression found to be associated with psychosocial variables.

Symptomatic Course of Depression

Angst (1986) estimated that once depressed individuals enter outpatient treatment, they are likely to spend 20% of their lives depressed. A 12-year prospective study of over 400 patients seeking treatment in psychiatric settings found that they spent 15% of this time meeting full criteria for major depression (Judd et al., 1998). However, the lives of these patients were also characterized by intermittent symptoms as well as by changes in symptom levels. Judd et al. (1998) distinguished four levels of symptoms: (a) no symptoms; (b) mild symptoms, but less than required for a diagnosis of minor depression; (c) moderate symptoms sufficient for a diagnosis of minor depression; and (d) full-syndrome major depression. Over the follow-up period, these patients, on average, had some symptoms 59% of the time; 9 out of 10 experienced 3 of the 4 symptom levels; and the average patient experienced 1.8 changes in symptom level per year.

The data reported by Judd et al. (1998) are richer than any that have previously been available. They are inconsistent with any conception of depression as a trait. For most of their adult lives, individuals who at some point become clinically depressed are not in a depressive episode. In explaining the depressive episodes that take up 15%–20% of the adult lives of depressed individuals, it is important to remain cognizant that 80%–85% of these individuals' adult lives are spent out of episode. In attempting to explain the occurrence of depression, researchers must be cautious not to develop theoretical explanations of depression that are unable to account for the long periods in which individuals vulnerable to depression are not in a depressive episode. Over time, individuals who become clinically depressed often have symptom levels in the range experienced by individuals who never in their lives become clinically depressed. For most individuals in the general population, mild symptoms do not progress to a full episode of depression, as only from 9% to 21% of women and 4% to 13% of men become clinically depressed in their lifetimes (Kessler et al., 1994; Weissman et al., 1991). Thus, there is a heterogeneity among individuals with mild depressive symptoms that needs to be accommodated in theory and research. For most individuals—the bulk of individuals studied in a community or student sample—mild symptoms represent variations in mood not tied to lifetime risk of depression (Coyne et al., 1999). For a minority of individuals, however, a longitudinal perspective reveals that mild symptoms are an expression of their adult life vulnerability to clinical depression, a disorder that is more variable in its manifestations over time than once thought. In the absence of a biological marker, researchers and practitioners are left with past history to serve as an indicator of some unspecified risk factor, not as the definition of the risk factor (Tien & Gallo, 1997), and yet it is a powerful and dependable indicator of risk.

Taking the Recurrent Nature of Depression Into Account

By the time they are identified for study, most depressed individuals have a history of numerous previous episodes of depression. Coyne et al. (1999) found that 85% of currently depressed primary care and 78% of currently depressed psychiatric outpatients were experiencing recurrences. These groups of patients, who had a mean age in their late 30s, had an average of over eight past episodes, with no differences between the two groups. In the Judd et al. (1998) study noted above, 71% of the patients had experienced an episode of depression before the one in which they enrolled in the study. Obtaining sufficient numbers of individuals experiencing first episodes of depression in a prospective study is a highly inefficient process. Hirschfeld et al. (1989) limited their study to 400 individuals with family histories, but no personal history, of depression and were able to obtain only 29 first episodes in 6 years. Eaton et al. (1997) obtained 12- and 15-year follow-up assessments of participants in the Baltimore site of the ECA study and found a rate of first episodes per year of 3 per 1,000 individuals. Put differently, 23,698 person-years of study yielded only 71 new cases of major depression. It should be clear that except under the most exceptional of circumstances, researchers are studying recurrences, not first episodes of depression, whether they use cross-sectional or longitudinal designs. Theories that assume that researchers whose focus is someone who has never previously been depressed are at best impractical in their requirements for testing and, more basically, simply inaccurate when applied to the typical depressed individual. Researchers need to consider the likelihood that the depressed individuals being studied have had previous episodes of depression.

Kessler and his colleagues (Kessler, Davis, & Kendler, 1997; Kessler, Gillis-Light, Magee, Kendler, & Eaves, 1997; Kessler & Magee, 1993, 1994) have begun to explore some of the profound implications of previous episodes of depression for the interpretation of research findings. The strength of history of depression as a predictor of subsequent risk is such that many psychosocial predictors of depression lose their significance once previous episodes of depression are taken into account. Kessler and Magee (1994) found this to be the case for 13 of the 14 risk factors they examined. Additional analyses of these and other data were interpreted as demonstrating that childhood adversity affected early onset of depression but had less effect on later onset and no effect on persistence of depression. On these bases, Kessler, Gillis-Light, et al. (1997) suggested that "many of the factors that mediate the effects childhood adversities on adult psychopathology are either in place prior to the first onset of disorder or are mediated by the effects of early onset on persistence" (p. 46).

The work of Kessler and his colleagues suggests that studies of depression in adulthood need to take into account previous depression not only as a control variable, but also as a potential mediator or moderator of other risk factors. Earlier depression appears to directly affect the risk of later depression, but it also may mediate the effects of background factors on later depression and moderate the risk posed by subsequent adversity. Earlier depression may also affect later adult circumstances by having shaped the trajectory of early adulthood transitions and the resolution of developmental tasks. One possibility suggested by this work is that psychosocial factors may affect the timing of first episodes of depression without affecting the overall lifetime risk: Childhood adversity hastens a first episode of depression, which ultimately would have occurred even in the absence of such adversity. If background factors such as childhood adversity are more of an influence on earlier episodes than on later ones, one implication is that studies of young depressed individuals may not generalize to studies of older depressed individuals because the role of background factors such as childhood adversity will be less in magnitude and more indirect for older depressed individuals.

Depression As a Source of Impairment

There is very little in the psychological literature acknowledging that depression is the source of impairment that it is. Instead, there is a tendency to consider the difficulties of depressed individuals in terms of preexisting deficiencies, such as a lack of social skills. And yet, the growing body of personal accounts of the experiences of depression is replete with references to this impairment:

> For in virtually any other serious sickness, a patient who felt similar devastation would be lying flat in bed, possibly sedated and hooked up to the tubes and wires of life-support systems, but at the very least in a posture of repose and in an isolated setting. His invalidism would be necessary, unquestioned and honorably attained. However, the sufferer from depression has no such option and therefore finds himself, like a walking casualty of war, thrust into the most intolerable social and family situations. (Styron, 1990, pp. 62–63)

Coyne et al. (1987) found that individuals living with a depressed individual were burdened by the depressed individual's symptoms and dysfunction, and this burden explained the heightened distress of these friends and family members (for a replication and extension of these findings with spouses of depressed individuals, see Benazon & Coyne, 1998). Unpublished data from the Coyne et al. study (1987) also suggested that individuals living with depressed individuals are ambivalent about the causes of this impairment. They attributed the depressed individuals difficulties to biology, but nonetheless blamed them for these problems. Thus, consistent with the quote from William Styron above, there apparently were doubts that the patients' impairment was necessary and honorably obtained.

However, during an episode of depression, the depressed individual experiences more personal and social impairment than that associated with many chronic medical conditions (Wells et al., 1989). Data from the World Health Organization indicated that, worldwide, depression was the leading cause of years lived with disability across developed and developing areas in 1990 and, in particular, the leading cause of an alternative measure of disability-adjusted life years for individuals aged 15 to 44 (Murray & Lopez 1996). Depression may precipitate vocational and marital problems (Dew & Bromet, 1991), including divorce (Briscoe & Smith, 1973; Bruce, 1998). Some depressed individuals' problems may persist after recovery (Coryell et al., 1993; Weissman & Paykel, 1974). More specifically, even after successful treatment (as judged by symptomatic recovery), former depressed outpatients continue to have occupational (Mintz, Mintz, Arruda, & Hwang, 1992) and sexual (Nofzinger et al., 1993) difficulties.

Vulnerability to depression may shape individuals' circumstances and how they negotiate their life course and handle interpersonal difficulties. The debilitation accompanying depression, repeated confrontations with evidence of impairment and incompetence, as well as negative responses from family members and others undoubtedly represent profound personal experiences (Coyne & Calarco, 1995). Moreover, in light of the possibility of recurrence, depressed individuals may organize their lives so as to avoid being in the position of being unable to meet demands of work, school, and close relationships, even if this entails forgoing the satisfactions that these involvements would bring (Coyne & Calarco, 1995). This could represent not only a continued cost of having experienced depression, but also a diminution of the resources useful in avoiding depression in the future (Calarco, 1992; Coyne & Calarco, 1995; Coyne, Gallo, Klinkman, & Calarco, 1998).

Implications for the Study of Depression and Marriage

Historical Relativity and Anachronism

In studying depression and marriage at the turn of the 21st century, current researchers may be dealing with different phenomena than what researchers observed in the studies of the 1970s or 1980s, when much of the existing data now being discussed in the literature were accumulated. Comparisons of the mean age of first onset of depression (Sorenson et al., 1991) and the mean age of marriage suggest that individuals have an increasing likelihood of first experiencing depression before getting married. In contrast to the declining age of first onset of depression, the mean age of first marriage for women increased from 22 in 1980 to 24 in 1991 (Ahlburg & DeVita, 1992). Most people who become depressed will have had their first experience with the disorder in their early 20s, either just before or while they were in the process of selecting a mate, getting married, and forming a family. Linking theories should be expected to accommodate such contextual details.

We caution against becoming too focused on these developmental details as necessary for the explanation of the relationship between depression and marriage. It was not long ago that depression was a disorder of middle age, manifesting itself in individuals in their 40s and in the context of established marital relationships, when raising small children was no longer a preoccupation. Furthermore, in the earlier literature on depression, too much was made of what later were found to be spurious relations between particular developmental stages and the onset of depression. For example, the earlier prominence in clinical writings of a supposed ''empty-nest syndrome'' probably reflected the coincidence of the age of first onset of depression and the approximate age at which children left the family home. Empirical data consistently have suggested that there generally is an improvement in parental well-being when children leave home (White & Edwards, 1990). Similarly, the supposed postmenopausal depression reflected a coincidence of a peak in women's risk for depression and the age of menopause (Winokur, 1973). The peak in women's risk for depression is now considerably younger (Klerman, 1988), whereas the mean age of menopause has moved from the middle 40s to the early 50s (Kato et al., 1998). With the earlier onset of depression and its correspondence to having school-age children in the home, it is tempting to revive the earlier feminist notion that "the presence of children in the home is the single most important factor contributing to depression in women" (Rothblum, 1982, p. 7). However, it should serve as a caution that maternal depression was once spuriously associated with the empty nest. Even when such pitfalls of interpreting secular trends are avoided, fine-grained, contextual theories adequate to explain data concerning depression and marriage in the 1970s and 1980s may of necessity be anachronistic when applied to data collected at the turn of the 21st century. The historical relativity of these theories and of any detailed explanations of the association between depression and marriage more generally must be kept in mind.

Accommodating the Nature of Depression in Marital Research

Formally speaking, models of depression and marriage need to accommodate the direct, mediating, and moderating effects of a recurrent, episodic disorder on current circumstances, including marital problems. This disorder is likely to have preceded the current marriage and may have contributed to a previous divorce. The magnitude of the risk of subsequent depression associated with a previous episode is so large that it is unlikely to be reducible to psychosocial factors, although current circumstances may both mediate and moderate the effects of history of depression. Put less technically, the depressed woman seeking therapy or enrolling in a study is likely to have been depressed previously, and directly and indirectly this depression may have contributed to her current marital problems. It can be assumed that theories have taken leave of the available data if they suggest (a) that marital problems are some sort of Agent Blue (Klerman, 1988) capable in themselves of explaining lifetime risk of depression, (b) that the typical depressed individual has never previously been depressed, or (c) that development of clinical depression is adequately explained by the same processes as the fluctuations in depressed mood found in the general population.

What, then, is left for theorists and researchers addressing the role of marriage and marital problems in depression? Certainly, our argument calls for less reductionistic theorizing concerning marriage and marital problems and an acknowledgment of individual differences in vulnerability to depression that may not be a result of marital or other psychosocial variables. Our argument also suggests that substantially less importance should be given to short-term longitudinal studies of marital problems and distress or depression if the intention is to address basic causal issues. Yet, although the causal or even the simply temporal priority of marital problems is thrown into doubt, important questions remain about the role of marital factors in the course of depression. Marital problems may affect the timing and resolution of depression among vulnerable individuals to a degree that is clinically significant. However, as soon as the focus is shifted from simple clinical predictions to the construction and testing of theoretical models, considerable complications are encountered. The apparent predictive value of marital variables may disappear when previous course of depression is taken into consideration (Mundt, Kronmueller, Backenstrass, Reck, & Fiedler, 1998).

Expressed Emotion

There has been a consistent failure in the literature concerning depression and marriage to accommodate the effects of depression on the lives of individuals vulnerable to the disorder, including their close relationships. There also has been a consistent bias in interpreting ambiguous data in terms of the interpersonal processes affecting depression, rather than vice versa. The literature examining the role of expressed emotion in predicting relapse of depressed patients is an example of this. One of the most often and confidently cited findings in the depression and marriage literature is that a component of expressed emotion, hostile criticism from the spouse, predicts relapse. A reader readily gets the sense that a robust finding is being reported, but only five studies report an association between expressed emotion during an acute episode and subsequent relapse. Of these, only two found a clear positive association. Claims concerning the role of expressed emotion in depression have been protected from critical scrutiny by a persistent lack of basic theory and a strong tradition in the literature of post hoc finessing of measurement and of overinterpretation of isolated bivariate associations between criticism and relapse.

However, recent data have suggested that negative spousal attitudes may not be antecedents so much as they are concomitants of depressive episodes. Specifically, Hayhurst and colleagues (Hayhurst, Cooper, Paykel, Vearnals, & Ramana, 1997) examined the stability of expressed emotion over time in the partners of depressed patients. The results of their study did not confirm previous findings that elevated levels of criticism predicted subsequent relapse among recovered depressed patients. Their results suggested, however, that over time, levels of criticism varied in ways that could be linked with the course of patients' depression. More specifically, levels of criticism declined as patients remitted, which appears to have been largely accounted for by the reduction in depression. Thus, although severity of depression and criticism were associated, it was the ongoing residual symptoms that appeared to be most crucial, thereby suggesting that expressed emotion is not an antecedent of depression, but a concomitant. This does not bar an important role for expressed emotion in the course of depression, but it does redefine the likely nature of this role.

Protective Advantage of a Positive Relationship With a Spouse

A number of authors have concluded that an individual's positive relationship with his or her spouse largely eliminates the effects of early adversity on risk for depression in adulthood (Birtchnell, 1980; Parker & Hadzi-Pavlovic, 1984; Quinton, Rutter, & Liddle, 1984). The model proposed by these authors is that childhood adversity causes depression, but this effect is moderated by the quality of the individual's relationship with his or her spouse (see Coyne, Burchill, & Stiles, 1991, and Coyne & Fechner-Bates, 1992, for enthusiastic endorsement of this view). Thus, Parker and Hadzi-Pavlovic (1984) concluded ''that an affectionate husband largely corrected any diathesis to greater depression exerted by uncaring parenting, while the protective effects of caring parenting on adult depressive experience were largely undone by marriage to an unaffectionate husband'' (p. 125). Birtchnell (1980) reported that among women whose mothers had died in childhood and who had a poor relationship with subsequent maternal figures, those who had a good relationship with their spouse and still became depressed did so almost a decade later than those with a bad relationship with their spouse. This is a plausible model of vulnerability to depression, but it becomes less convincing and more in need of qualification if the following possibilities are considered: (a) Childhood adversity moderates an underlying risk for depression, but it is not itself the key risk factor, and (b) mate selection is constrained by both childhood adversity and past depression. As Kessler, Gillis-Light, et al. (1997) implied, the quality of an individual's relationship with his or her spouse may be more of a marker for the accumulative effects of vulnerability to depression rather than a resiliency factor.

Divorce

Despite early recognition that depression may lead to divorce (Briscoe & Smith, 1973), until recently little systematic attention was paid to the extent to which divorce is a negative social consequence of depression or to how it can serve as a mediator of the effects of previous depression on the subsequent life course. Data from follow-up assessments in the ECA study and the National Comorbidity Survey (NCS; Bruce, 1998; Kessler, Walters, & Forthofer, 1998) have allowed some exploration of the relations between depression and divorce, but these same data also highlight some of the difficulties in attempting to explicate this seemingly simple bivariate relation. According to the original ECA data, individuals who had been divorced once were significantly more likely to be depressed in a year than the married or never married, and the risk of depression increased with a second divorce (Weissman et al., 1991). Using data from the NCS, Kessler et al. (1998) showed that a history of depression increased the likelihood of divorce and the number of years in adulthood out of marriage. Bruce (1998) reported results of analyses using follow-up data from the ECA study. Individuals with a history of major depression were 70% more likely than those without major depression to experience marital separation or divorce in the upcoming year. Additional analyses showed that among married individuals who both had a history of depression at baseline and subsequently experienced marital separation or divorce, 46% reported their first episode as occurring more than 10 years before the divorce. However, another 18% reported their first onset as occurring within 2 years of the baseline interview, thus allowing the possibility that marital problems contributing to divorce also contributed to depression. Despite a large community sample, the overall pattern of findings is ambiguous. Bruce noted:

> Although it is clear that a number of psychiatric disorders are associated with subsequent marital disruption, one cannot tell whether (1) the psychiatric disorders contributed to the problems in the marriage that resulted in divorce; (2) given problems in the marriage, a history of disorder increased a person's vulnerability to divorce; (3) the reported psychiatric episode was a reaction to marital problems that also resulted in divorce, or (4) the psychiatric reaction to marital problems increased the likelihood that those problems would prompt divorce. Hence, psychiatric problems may "cause" divorce, but they also may be a side effect of the divorce process or factor exacerbating the process. (p. 224)

Of course, these are not mutually exclusive possibilities.

Challenges and Pitfalls in Interpreting the Role of Previous History of Depression

In summary, we have been arguing that theory and research concerning marriage, marital problems, and depression need to acknowledge the powerful effects of depression on life course and the current circumstances of those who are vulnerable to the disorder. This argument leads to considerable skepticism about the conventional interpretations of existing research and the adequacy of standard methodologies. One conclusion is that the notion that marital problems cause depression needs to accommodate not only what is undoubtedly a set of bidirectional influences, but also the strong accumulative effects of vulnerability to depression on subsequent interpersonal problems. The interpretative task that has been termed an "unraveling of Gordian knot" (p. 303) of sorting the causal influences of depression or marital problems and vice versa, (Snyder & Heim, 1992), is even more complex than previously imagined. Clearly, efforts to clarify the nature of the association of depression and marital problems are at high risk for inaccurate conclusions if they rely on a balanced 2 x 2 design crossing depression and marital problems (e.g., Nelson & Beach, 1990; Schmaling & Jacobson, 1990). Although they have the appeal of tidiness, such designs deny the influences of past depression as seen in current marital problems and of past marital problems as seen in current depression.

Both theoretical statements and research designs need to accommodate history of depression as a direct influence and as a mediator and moderator of other factors. Yet, the challenge of reliably and validly assessing history of depression remains (Bromet, Dunn, Connell, Dew, & Schulberg, 1986; Kramer, von Korff, & Kessler, 1980; Rogler, Malgady, & Tyron, 1992). Comparisons of estimates of the incidence of depression based on recollection of short periods of time versus that obtained for longer periods of recall suggest that there is considerable reduction in respondents' recollection of episodes of depression (Eaton et al., 1997). The number of current and past symptoms, number and recency of previous episodes, and current and past treatment all bias reports of past history of depression (Kendler, Neale, Kesslcr, & Hcath, 1993). Furthermore, episodes of depression are not evenly distributed across the adulthood of vulnerable individuals. Those who have recently recovered from depression are considerably more vulnerable to new episodes than are individuals who have had long periods of wellness (Coyne & Whiffen, 1995). This finding is worthy of theoretical and empirical explication and can be exploited in research designs focused on the particularly high-risk group of recently recovered depressed individuals.

Exploration of the importance of a history of depression needs to be guided by a well-specified model. For most purposes, it does little good simply to include history as a control variable in a multivariate analysis, and a recent article highlighted the pitfalls of misspecifying the role of past depression. Gotlib, Lewinsohn, and Seeley (1998; Table 1) reported regression analyses in which a full range of variables, including current scores on the Center for Epidemiologic Studies-Depression Scale (CES-D; Radloff, 1977) and history of depression, were used to predict marital satisfaction, marital conflict, and the perception of spousal criticism. It appeared that when CES-D scores and history of depression were considered simultaneously, CES-D scores had substantial effects on these measures of marital functioning, whereas history of depression had a much more modest effect. However, missing from their analysis and interpretation of their data was any consideration of how past depression might be reflected in current depression and, therefore, in elevated CES-D scores. Current CES-D scores are plausibly an effect of the risk for depression, and so the CES-D should not be treated as a control variable in understanding the role of risk for depression in current marital problems. Such a strategy would be appropriate only if the researcher were interested in using additional analyses to examine the extent to which current symptoms mediated the effect of previous history on marital functioning. However, the Gotlib et al. (1998) analyses appear to pit two causal explanations against each other. This would be analogous to controlling for current alcohol consumption to examine the relationship of alcoholism to marital problems. It would seem odd, at best, to conclude that problem drinking had no substantial effect on relationship quality once the amount consumed in last night's binge was controlled for.

Implications for Treatment

Nothing we have said thus far contradicts the consistent empirical finding that depression and marital problems are associated or the reasonable inference that involving the spouse and addressing marital issues may be efficacious ways of resolving a depressive episode and perhaps reducing the likelihood of a future episode. However, the same misspecification of the nature of this association that we have critiqued in current theory and research carries over to treatment. Namely, the notion that marital turmoil is an Agent Blue, sufficient to explain the occurrence of depression, has become an ideology limiting the acceptability of marital therapy to couples with a depressed partner, as well as the development of alternative ways of addressing depression in a marital context. Blanket claims that marital problems are the root cause of depression are gross exaggerations, if not simply incorrect.

Numerous controlled clinical trials have demonstrated that depressed women in couples who are willing to accept randomization to marital therapy benefit from this treatment (O'Leary and Cano, chapter 9; Cordova and Gee, chapter 10). However, anyone who has tried to recruit for such trials or who has tried to make referrals of depressed individuals to marital therapy from psychiatric or primary medical care settings is well aware of the limited appeal of this approach. Many patients refuse such a referral immediately, whereas others accept it, only to fail to enlist their partner or to fail to come for subsequent sessions as a couple. A number of studies have demonstrated the efficacy of marital therapy for depression (for a review, see Beach, Smith, & Fincham, 1994). However, a rare effort to demonstrate that a behavioral marital therapy that had previously been shown to be efficacious in a clinical trial (McLean & Hakstian, 1979) would be effective in a primary care setting ended in failure when the physicians and depressed women could not enlist sufficient numbers of the women's husbands in therapy (McLean & Miles, 1975). There has been virtually no attention to the limited acceptability of marital therapy for depression and how this might be reconciled with the supposition that this therapeutic approach addresses the root cause of depression, marital turmoil.

Some difficulties in recruiting and retaining couples with a depressed individual in therapy may reflect the deteriorated state of their marriage when they present for treatment. Other problems may be inherent in attempting to enlist couples to collaborate in conjoint treatment when they are locked in conflict. However, we also believe that unnecessary problems are created by the implicit demand that couples accept as fact an ideology concerning the role of their marriage and their own behavior in the depression of one member of the couple. Namely, couples are asked to accept that their conflict has caused the depression and that the occurrence or recurrence of depression represents a failure of their coping skills and, by implication, evidence of their inadequacy. Such an ideology is vulnerable to embarrassment by a full range of clinical evidence and counter to the experience of many couples seeking therapy. To obtain treatment, they must accept as a basic premise what amounts to the invalidation of this experience.

Despite the correlation between depression and marital turmoil, many, perhaps almost half, of all couples with a depressed spouse do not experience substantial marital conflict. (For a psychologist's poignant account of her efforts to struggle with severe depression in the context of a supportive marital relationship, see Manning, 1994.) Therapy may nonetheless be useful in providing the couple with an understanding of the nature of depression and the role it has assumed in their relationship, and in assisting them in renegotiating their relationship to deal more effectively with the problems posed by depression. However, an emphasis on marital conflict and a couple's presumed lack of skills in dealing with it is likely to prove alienating and a distraction from these tasks. This may explain the notable lack of success of conventional behavioral marital therapy with couples who are not maritally distressed, but in which one individual is depressed (Jacobson, Dobson, Fruzzetti, Schmaling, & Salusky, 1991).

Even when marital conflict and depression co-occur, this observation should be the starting point for developing an understanding of a particular case, not the conclusion. Some couples clearly see that their marital conflict is precipitated by their efforts to deal with the return of depression that has occurred previously in their marriage and, very likely, previous to their marriage. Alternatively, there may be a clear temporal precedence of the current marital distress to the current episode of depression. However, regardless of which came first, depression may be impairing one partner's ability to participate in a renegotiation of the relationship and it may inhibit the nondepressed partner from articulating his or her own complaints or unmet needs in a timely, constructive fashion (Biglan, Rothlind, Hops, & Sherman, 1989; Kahn, Coyne, & Margolin, 1985). Depression may come to dominate the marital interactions of some couples so that it becomes an overwhelming barrier to affecting change in general communication and problem-solving skills. As long as anhedonia goes unacknowledged, for example, it is going to be difficult to implement strategies for change that depend on the reward experienced by the depressed individual for their maintenance. Moreover, a spouse who does not understand this is likely to aggravate the situation by blaming the patient.

However, some of the most embarrassing data for a reductionist marital turmoil perspective on depression lies in the overwhelming evidence that many couples, though far from perfect, are doing a remarkable job of coping with the challenges of depression in one partner. Their achievement is all the more remarkable given that they fail to have an adequate grasp of the nature of the problem with which they contend. Moreover, they may be coping well despite the oppressive evangelism of their therapist who communicates that if only they did the right thing, depression would be banished from their lives. By implication, the persistence of depression is a testimony to their shortcomings.

We are confident that sensitive, competent marital therapists come to appreciate what can be the powerful influence of depression on the lives of their patients and their patients' spouses. We also assume that therapists get glimpses of just how difficult depression can make problem solving and living in harmony. They may also come to appreciate the ability of many couples to maintain good relations despite the intrusion of depression in their lives. Yet, the dominant reductionist marital turmoil perspective on depression can get in the way of therapists obtaining the full benefit of such observations and it can keep this wisdom from being articulated in a way that is useful and validating for struggling couples. Furthermore, it is our sense that when many therapists find their assumptions challenged by the intractability of a patient's depression, they go into theoretical disarray, declaring that this particular case of depression, unlike most others they treat, is biological in nature and in need of a reductionist biological perspective to understand and treat it. Such therapists' ability to assist such a depressed individual and his or her spouse is thereby diminished.

Realistic Expectations and the Limited Sick Role

A better appreciation of the recurrent, episodic nature of depression and the complexity of its relation to marital problems can lead to a more realistic and humane set of expectations for what the therapist, the depressed individual, and the spouse must accomplish. As Cronkite

(1994) advised, ''For some, expectations of 'conquering' depression are unrealistic. Instead of fighting the truth, make space for it in your life, not by caving in, but by finding ways to adapt'' (p. 318). Similarly, a sociologist who experiences depression stated, ''For me, depression has a chronicity that makes it like a kind of mental arthritis; something that you just have to live with. My aim is to live with depression as well as I can'' (Karp, 1996, p. 10). Therapy could be premised on the notion that its goal is to see if depressive symptoms and perhaps the likelihood of recurrence can be reduced, but, for some couples, its greatest benefit would be to assist them to cope better with the intrusion of depression into their lives.

We believe that providing the depressed individual with a limited sick role, as is routinely done in interpersonal therapy for depression (Klerman Weissman, Rounsaville, & Chevron, 1984), can be of particular benefit in work with couples. This involves pointing out that some of the difficulties of depressed individuals reflect genuine impairment, and although there is a burden on them to manage these difficulties, it also must be accepted that they are not at their best and they need to lower expectations and renegotiate responsibilities correspondingly. This can then serve as a basis for assisting the couple in renegotiating their roles with respect to each other, including the degree of help, concern, and sympathy the depressed individual seeks and that the spouse is prepared to give. One possible outcome of such negotiation is that it will be decided that the interests of both parties will be served best by allowing the depressed individual to be left alone in assuming responsibility for managing his or her difficulties and by the spouse assuming more self-responsibility, rather than responsibility for the depressed individual's mood and other symptoms.

Attention to the Spouse

Legitimizing the sense of impairment of a depressed individual can facilitate legitimizing the spouse's sense of burden. This can serve as a basis for renegotiating their spouse's responsibilities for managing symptoms and for reestablishing their right to look after their own needs. If therapists drop the assumption that the occurrence of depression is a sign of the poor coping skills of depressed individuals and their spouses, then they can be more prepared to recognize both the well-meant but inappropriate coping efforts of spouses, as well as the genuine sacrifices and accomplishments represented in the couples' predicament not being worse. Rather than focusing on the presumed deficiencies of spouses, attention could profitably be focused on the special skills demanded by the partner's depression and notably the crucial virtues of patience and tolerance.

We have noted the ambiguity in the interpretation of the relation of expressed emotion to relapse for depression. Nonetheless, it appears that spouses who are high in expressed emotion—that is, high in criticism and living with a partner who is at greater likelihood of relapse—are also more likely to perceive symptoms of depression as controllable and themselves as active copers and good problem solvers (Hooley, 1998). Such attitudes increase with duration of disorder. Although these attitudes may reflect the erosion of support, it could also be that adopting a more resigned and accepting attitude could be beneficial for depressed individuals and their spouses. Rather than giving up on depressed partners, spouses could give up the illusion that they are responsible for their partners' symptoms and focus on their own contributions to improving the marital relationship and their own well-being.

Alternative Framing and Formats for Marital Therapy

Marital therapy remains an effective intervention for couples who accept its rationale and format. However, if too few couples with a depressed member seek and benefit from conjoint marital therapy, then perhaps the inflexibility in its format as it is typically offered should be reconsidered. Marital therapy does not require the premise that marital problems are the root of depression, but can proceed from a more agnostic position that a couple is obviously facing both marital problems and depression in one spouse. Furthermore, couples may be willing to work on their relationship as a way of assisting the recovery of the depressed individual but be thwarted by some combination of the intensity of their conflict, the impairment of the depressed individual, and the frustration and impatience of the spouse. In such cases, it might be useful to consider various ways of proceeding without relying primarily on conjoint sessions. Suitable formats include separate meetings with patients and spouses, with some effort at diplomacy (Coyne, 1984). Alternatively, psychoeducational and support groups might provide spouses with a chance to receive validation and information about the nature of depression and the special coping skills required to live effectively and humanely with a depressed individual (Anderson et al., 1986). Finally, individual therapy for the spouses of depressed individuals should be evaluated as a way for them to take responsibility for their own role in their difficulties as a couple (Watzlawick & Coyne, 1980) and for improving their well-being in the face of the stress of living with a depressed individual.

References

Advertisement. (1998, July 15). *Philadelphia Weekly,* p. 52.

Ahlburg, D. A., & DeVita, C. J. (1992). New realities of the American family. *Population Bulletin, 47,* 11–14.

American Psychiatric Association. (1987). *Diagnostic and statistical manual of mental disorders* (3rd ed, rev.). Washington, DC: Author.

Anderson, C. M., Griffin, S., Rossi, A., Pagonis, I., Holder, D. P., & Treiber, R. (1986). A comparative study of the impact of education vs. process groups for families of patients with affective disorders. *Family Process, 25,* 185–205.

Angst, J. (1986). The course of affective disorders. *Psychopathology, 19,* 47–52.

Beach, S. R. H., Sandeen, E. E., & O'Leary, K. D. (1990). *Depression in marriage: A model for etiology and treatment.* New York: Guilford Press.

Beach, S. R. H., Smith, D. A., & Fincham, F. D. (1994). Marital interventions for depression: Empirical foundation and future prospects. *Applied and Preventive Psychology, 3,* 233–250.

Benazon, N. R., & Coyne, J. C. (1998). *Living with a depressed spouse.* Manuscript submitted for publication.

Betrus, P. A., Elmore, S. K., Woods, N. F., & Hamilton, P. A. (1995). Women and depression. *Health Care for Women International, 16,* 243–252.

Biglan, A., Rothlind, J., Hops, H., & Sherman, L. (1989). Impact of distressed and aggressive behavior. *Journal of Abnormal Psychology, 98,* 218–228.

Birtchnell, J. (1980). Women whose mothers died in childhood: An outcome study. *Psychological Medicine, 10,* 699–713.

Briscoe, C. W., & Smith, J. B. (1973). Depression and marital turmoil. *Archives of General Psychiatry, 29,* 811–817.

Bromet, E. J., Dunn, L. O., Connell, M. M., Dew, M. A., & Schulberg, H. C. (1986). Long-term reliability of diagnosing lifetime major depression in a community sample. *Archives of General Psychiatry, 43,* 435–440.

Bruce, M. L. (1998). Divorce and psychopathology. In B. P. Dohrenwend (Ed.), *Adversity, stress, and psychopathology* (pp. 219–234). New York: Oxford University Press.

Burke, K. C., Burke, J. D., Rae, D.S., & Regier, D. A. (1991). Comparing age at onset of major depression and other psychiatric disorders by birth cohorts in five U.S. community populations. *Archives of General Psychiatry, 48,* 789–795.

Calarco, M. M. (1992). *Psychological and biological differences among first episode and recurrently depressed women during depression and recovery.* Unpublished doctoral dissertation, University of Michigan, Ann Arbor.

Coryell, W., Scheftner, W., Keller, M., Endicott, J., Maser, J., & Klerman, G. L. (1993). The enduring psychosocial consequences of mania and depression. *American Journal of Psychiatry, 150,* 720–727.

Coyne, J. C., (1984). Integrating structural interventions into strategic therapy: A–cautionary note. *Journal of Systemic and Strategic Therapies, 3,* 23–27.

Coyne, J. C., Burchill, S. A. L., & Stiles, W. B. (1991). An interactional perspective on depression. In C. R. Snyder & D. O. Forsyth (Eds.), *Handbook of social and clinical psychology: The health perspective* (pp. 327–349). New York: Pergamon.

Coyne, J. C., & Calarco, M. M. (1995). Effects of the experience of depression: Application of focus group and survey methodologies. *Psychiatry, 58,* 149–163.

Coyne, J. C., & DeLongis, A. M. (1986). Going beyond social support: The role of social relationships in adaptation. *Journal of Consulting and Clinical Psychology, 54,* 454–460.

Coyne, J. C., & Fechner-Bates, S. (1992). Depression, the family, and family therapy. *Australia and New Zealand Journal of Family Therapy, 13,* 203–208.

Coyne, J. C., Gallo, S. M., Klinkman, M. S., & Calarco, M. M. (1998). Effects of recent and past major depression and distress on self-concept and coping. *Journal of Abnormal Psychology, 107,* 86–96.

Coyne, J. C., Kessler, R. C., Tal, M., Turnbull, J., Wortman, C., & Greden, J. (1987). Living with a depressed person. *Journal of Consulting and Clinical Psychology, 55,* 347–352.

Coyne, J. C., Pepper, C. M., & Flynn, H. (1999). Significance of prior episodes of depression in two populations. *Journal of Consulting and Clinical Psychology, 67,* 76–81.

Coyne, J. C., & Racioppo, M. W. (1999). *But wouldn't anyone be depressed?* Unpublished manuscript.

Coyne, J. C., & Whiffen, V. E. (1995). Issues in personality as diathesis for depression: The case of sociotropy/dependency and autonomy/self-criticism. *Psychological Bulletin, 118,* 358–378.

Cronkite, K. (1994). *On the edge of darkness: Conversations about conquering depression.* New York: Doubleday.

Cross-National Collaborative Group. (1992). The changing rate of major depression. Cross-national comparisons. *Journal of the American Medical Association, 268,* 3098–3105.

Dehle, C., & Weiss, R. L. (1998). Sex differences in prospective associations between marital quality and depressed mood. *Journal of Marriage and the Family, 60,* 1002–1011.

Dew, M. A., & Bromet, E. J. (1991). Effects of depression on support in a community sample of women. In J. Eckenrode (Ed.), *The social context of coping* (pp. 189–210). New York: Plenum.

Dohrenwend, B. P. (1989). The problem of validity in field studies of psychological disorder revisited. In L. N. Robins & J. E. Barrett (Eds.), *The validity of psychiatric diagnosis* (pp. 35–56). New York: Raven Press.

Eaton, W. W., Anthony, J. C., Gallo, J., Cai, G. J., Tien, A., Romanoski, A., Lyketsos, C., & Chen, L. S. (1997). Natural history of Diagnostic Interview Schedule/DSM-IV major depression: The

Baltimore Epidemiologic Catchment Area follow-up. *Archives of General Psychiatry, 54,* 993–999.

Fincham, F. D., Beach, S. R. H., Harold, G. T., & Osborne, L. N. (1997). Marital satisfaction and depression: Different causal relationships for men and women? *Psychological Science, 8,* 351–357.

Gotlib, I. H., Lewinsohn, P. M., & Seeley, J. R. (1998). Consequences of depression during adolescence: Marital status and marital functioning in early adulthood. *Journal of Abnormal Psychology, 107,* 686–690.

Hayhurst, H., Cooper, Z., Paykel, E. S., Vearnals, S., & Ramana, R. (1997). Depressed emotion and depression. *British Journal of Psychiatry, 171,* 439–443.

Hirschfeld, R. M. A., Klerman, G. L., Lavori, P., Keller, M. B., Griffith, P., & Coryell, W. (1989). Premorbid personality assessments of major depression. *Archives of General Psychiatry, 46,* 345–350.

Hooley, J. (1998). Expressed emotion and psychiatric illness: From empirical data to clinical practice. *Behavior Therapy, 29,* 631–646.

Hu, Y.R., & Goldman, N. (1990). Mortality differentials by marital-status: An international comparison. *Demography, 27,* 233–250.

Jacobson, N. S., Dobson, K., Fruzzetti, A. E., Schmaling, K. B., & Salusky, S. (1991). Marital therapy as a treatment for depression. *Journal of Consulting and Clinical Psychology, 59,* 547–557.

Joung I.M.A., Stronks, K, vandeMheen, H., vanPoppel, F.W.A., vanderMeer, J.B.W., & Mackenbach, J. (1997). The contribution of intermediary factors to marital status differences in self-reported health. *Journal of Marriage and the Family, 59,* 476–490.

Judd, L. L. (1998). The clinical course of unipolar major depressive disorders. *Archives of General Psychiatry, 54,* 989–991.

Judd, L. L., Akiskal, H. S., Maser, J. D., Zeller, P. J., Endicott, J., Coryell, W., Paulus, M. P., Kunovac, J. L., Leon, A. C., Mueller, T. I., Rice, J. A., & Keller, M. B. (1998). A prospective 12–year study of subsyndromal and syndromal depressive symptoms in unipolar major depressive disorders. *Archives of General Psychiatry, 55,* 694–700.

Kahn, J., Coyne, J. C., & Margolin, G. (1985). Depression and marital disagreement: The social construction of despair. *Journal of Social and Personal Relationships, 2,* 447–462.

Karp, D. A. (1996). *Speaking of sadness: Depression, disconnection, and the meanings of illness.* New York: Oxford University Press.

Kato, I., Toniolo, P., Akhmedkhanov, A., Koenig, K. L., Shore, R., & Seleniuch-Jacquotte, A. (1998). Prospective study of factors influencing the onset of natural menopause. *Journal of Clinical Epidemiology, 51,* 1271–1276.

Keller, M. B., Lavori, P. W., Lewis, C. E., & Klerman, G. (1983). Predictors of relapse in major depressive disorder. *Journal of the American Medical Association, 250,* 3299–3304.

Keller, M. B., Lavori, P. W., Rice, J., Coryell, W., & Hirschfeld, R. M. (1986). The persistent risk of chronicity in recurrent episodes of nonbipolar major depressive disorder: A prospective follow-up. *American Journal of Psychiatry, 143,* 24–28.

Keller, M. B., Shapiro, R. W., Lavori, P. W., & Wolfe, N. (1982). Recovery in major depressive disorder: Analysis with the life table and regression models. *Archives of General Psychiatry, 39,* 905–910.

Kendler, K. S., Neale, M. C., Kessler, R. C., & Heath, A. C. (1993). The lifetime history of major depression in women: Reliability of diagnosis and heritability. *Archives of General Psychiatry, 50,* 863–870.

Kessler, R. C., Davis, C. G., & Kendler, K. S. (1997). Childhood adversity and adult psychiatric disorders in the U.S. National Comorbidity Survey. *Psychological Medicine, 27,* 1109–1119.

Kessler, R. C., Gillis-Light, J., Magee, W. J., Kendler, K. S., & Eaves, L. J. (1997). Childhood adversity and adult psychopathology. In I. H. Gotlib & B. Wheaton (Eds.), *Stress and adversity over the life course: Trajectories and turning points* (pp. 29–49). New York: Cambridge University Press.

Kessler, R. C., & Magee, W. J. (1993). Childhood adversities and adult depression: Basic patterns of association in a US national survey. *Psychological Medicine, 23,* 679–690.

Kessler, R. C., & Magee, W. J. (1994). The disaggregation of vulnerability to depression as a function of the determinants of onset and recurrence. In W. R. Avison & I. H. Gotlib (Eds.), *Stress and mental health: Contemporary issues and prospects for the future* (pp. 239–258). New York: Plenum Press.

Kessler, R.C., McGonagle, K.A., Zhao, S., Nelson, C.B., Hughes, M., Eshleman, S., Wittchen, H.U., Kendler, K.S. (1994). Lifetime and 12–month prevalence of DSM-II-R psychatric disorders in the United States. *Archives of General Psychiatry, 51,* 8–19.

Kessler, R. C., Walters, E. E., & Forthofer, M. S. (1998). The social consequences of psychiatric disorders, III: Probability of marital stability. *American Journal of Psychiatry, 155,* 1092–1096.

Klerman, G. L. (1988). The current age of youthful melancholia: Evidence for increase among adolescents and young adults. *British Journal of Psychiatry, 152,* 4–14.

Klerman, G. L., Weissman, M. M., Rounsaville, B.J., & Chevron, E. S. (1984). *Interpersonal psychotherapy of depression.* New York: Basic Books.

Klinkman, M. S., Schwenk, T. L., & Coyne, J. C. (1997). Depression in primary care—More like asthma than appendicitis: The Michigan Depression Project. *Canadian Journal of Psychiatry, 42,* 966–973.

Kramer, M., von Korff, M., & Kessler, L. (1980). The lifetime prevalence of mental disorders: Estimation, uses and limitations. *Psychological Medicine, 10,* 429–435.

Manning, M. (1994). *Undercurrents: A therapist's reckoning with her own depression.* New York: HarperCollins.

McLean, P. D., & Hakstian, A. R. (1979). Clinical depression: Comparative efficacy of outpatient treatments. *Journal of Consulting and Clinical Psychology, 47,* 818–836.

McLean, P. D., & Miles, J. E. (1975). Training family physicians in psychosocial care: An analysis of a program failure. *Journal of Medical Education, 50,* 900–902.

Mintz, J., Mintz, L. I., Arruda, M. J., & Hwang, S. S. (1992). Treatments of depression and the functional capacity to work. *Archives of General Psychiatry, 49,* 761–768.

Mundt, C., Kronmueller, K. T., Backenstrass, M., Reck, C., & Fiedler, P. (1998). The influence of psychopathology, personality, and marital interaction on the short-term course of major depression. *Psychopathology, 31,* 29–36.

Murray, C. L., & Lopez, A. D. (1996). Global and regional descriptive epidemiology of disability: Incidence, prevalence, health expectancies and years lived with disability. In C. L. Murray & A. D. Lopez (Eds.), *The global burden of disease* (pp. 201–246). Cambridge, MA: Harvard University Press.

Nelson, G. M., & Beach, S. R. (1990). Sequential interaction in depression: Effects of depressive behavior on spousal aggression. *Behavior Therapy, 21,* 167–182.

Nofzinger, E. A., Thase, M. E., Reynolds, C. F., Frank, E., Jennings, J. R., Garamoni, J. L., Fasiczka, A. L., & Kuper, D. J., (1993). Sexual function in depressed men: Assessment by self-report, behavioral, and nocturnal penile tumescence measures before and after treatment with cognitive behavior therapy. *Archives of General Psychiatry, 150,* 24–30.

Parker, G., & Hadzi-Pavlovic, D. (1984). Modification of levels of depression in mother-bereaved women by prenatal and marital relationships. *Psychological Medicine, 14,* 125–135.

Quinton, D., Rutter, M., & Liddle, C. (1984). Institutional rearing, parenting difficulties and marital support. *Psychological Medicine, 14,* 107–124.

Radloff, L. S. (1977). The CES-D scale: A self-report depression scale for research in the general population. *Applied Psychological Measurement, 1,* 385–401.

Rogler, L. H., Malgady, R. G., & Tyron, W. W. (1992). Evaluation of mental health: Issues of memory in the Diagnostic Interview Schedule. *Journal of Nervous and Mental Disease, 180,* 215–222.

Rothblum, E. D. (1982). Women's socialization and the prevalence of depression: The feminine mistake. *Women and Therapy, 1,* 5–13.

Schmaling, K. B., & Jacobson, N. S. (1990). Marital interaction and depression. *Journal of Abnormal Psychology, 99,* 229–236.

Schwenk, T. L., Coyne, J. C., & Fechner-Bates, S. (1996). Differences between detected and undetected depressed patients in primary care and depressed psychiatric patients. *General Hospital Psychiatry, 18,* 407–415.

Snyder, D. K., & Heim, S. C. (1992). Marriage, depression, and cognition: Unraveling the Gordian knot—Reply to Ettinger et al. *Journal of Marital and Family Therapy, 18,* 303–307.

Sorenson, S. B., Rutter, C. M., & Aneshensel, C. S. (1991). Depression in the community: An investigation into age of onset. *Journal of Consulting and Clinical Psychology, 59,* 541–546.

Spitzer, R. L., Williams, J. B., Gibbon, M. B., & First, M. B. (1989). *Structured Clinical Interview for DSM-III-R.* New York: New York State Psychiatric Institute, Biometrics Research Department.

Stack, S., & Eshleman, J. (1998). Marital status and happiness: A 17-nation study. *Journal of Marriage and the Family, 60,* 527–536.

Styron, W. (1990). *Darkness visible: A memoir of madness.* New York: Random House.

Tien, A. Y., & Gallo, J. J. (1997). Clinical diagnosis: A marker for disease? *Journal of Nervous and Mental Disease, 185,* 739–747.

Watzlawick, P. W., & Coyne, J. C. (1980). Depression following stroke: Brief problem-focused family treatment. *Family Process, 19,* 13–18.

Weissman, M. M. (1979). The psychological treatment of depression. *Archives of General Psychiatry, 36,* 1261–1269.

Weissman, M. M., Bruce, M. L., Leaf, P. J., Florio, L. P., & Holzer, C. III. (1991). Affective disorders. In L. N. Robins & D. A. Regier (Eds.), *Psychiatric disorders in America.* New York: Free Press.

Weissman, M. M., & Paykel, E. S. (1974). *The depressed woman: A study of social relationships.* Chicago: University of Chicago Press.

Wells, K. B., Stewart, A., Hays, R. D., Burnam, M. A., Rogers, W., Daniels, M., Berry, S., Greenfield, S., & Ware, J. (1989). The functioning and well-being of depressed patients: Results from the Medical Outcomes Study. *Journal of the American Medical Association, 262,* 914–919.

White, L., & Edwards, J. N. (1990). Emptying the nest and parental well-being: An analysis of national panel data. *American Sociological Review, 55,* 235–242.

Wickramaratne, P. J., Weissman, M. M., Leaf, P. J., & Holford, T. R. (1989). Age, period, and cohort effects on the risk of major depression: Results from five United States communities. *Journal of Clinical Epidemiology, 42,* 333–343.

Winokur, G. (1973). Depression in the menopause. *American Journal of Psychiatry, 130,* 92–93.

Wood, W., Rhodes, N., & Whelan, M. (1989). Sex differences in positive well-being: a consideration of emotional style and marital status. *Psychological Bulletin, 106,* 249–264.

3

Depressive Symptoms and Marital Satisfaction in the Early Years of Marriage: Narrowing the Gap Between Theory and Research

Benjamin R. Karney

The association between depression and marital quality is significant and has been demonstrated in clinical and nonclinical samples (Beach, Sandeen, & O'Leary, 1990; Burns, Sayers, & Moras, 1994), in married and cohabiting couples (Thompson, 1995), and with respect to depressive symptoms and diagnostic depression (Whisman, chapter 1). Across contexts, individuals who are clinically depressed or who report higher levels of depressive symptoms also report lower levels of satisfaction with their marriages.

The association between levels of depressive symptoms and marital satisfaction is so reliable that many researchers have proposed associations between changes in marital satisfaction and changes in depressive symptoms. For example, recent suggestions that marital counseling be recommended as a treatment for depression (e.g., Jacobson, Dobson, Fruzzetti, Schmaling, & Salusky, 1991) rest on the assumption that changes in marital satisfaction will lead to changes in an individual's level of depression. Similarly, recent models of stress generation among depressed individuals (e.g., Davila, chapter 4; Joiner, chapter 7) have hypothesized that increases in depressive symptoms should be associated with declines in the quality of an individual's intimate relationship.

These models of depression and marriage emphasize the dynamic relationships between depressive symptoms and marital satisfaction within individuals over time. The research supporting these models, however, has yet to address such relationships directly. Most of the research linking depressive symptoms and marriage has been cross-sectional, and even longitudinal studies of these two variables have relied exclusively on between-subjects analyses.

Thus, there appears to be a gap between theory and research. The purpose of this chapter is to offer a strategy of data analysis designed to bridge this gap and directly test assumptions about the dynamic relationship between depressive symptoms and marital satisfaction within individuals over time. To this end, the chapter is organized into four sections. First, the methods used in previous longitudinal research in this area are reviewed and the limitations of current approaches to analyzing relationships between variables that change over time are highlighted. Second, a relatively recent development in the analysis of change—growth curve analysis (GCA)—is described as a possible alternative approach to examining longitudinal within-subject effects. Third, the advantages of this approach are demonstrated with data from a 4-year study of depressive symptoms and marital satisfaction in newlyweds. Finally, the concluding section highlights some implications of this approach and offers several recommendations for future research on the causal relationships between depression and marital satisfaction.

Methods Used in Previous Research on Depression and Marital Satisfaction

In chapter 1, Whisman reviews a selection of longitudinal research on depression and marital quality and concludes that the findings of this research have been somewhat mixed. In chapter 4, Davila reviews evidence suggestive of bidirectional causation: Some research has supported depressive symptoms as precursors of marital distress, whereas other research has supported marital distress as a precursor of depressive symptoms. Why the confusion? It is possible that limitations in the methods used to examine the relationships between depressive symptoms and marital satisfaction over time have prevented earlier studies from making definitive statements about longitudinal effects between these two variables. In this section, the strategies used to examine longitudinal data in this area are described and their potential drawbacks are discussed.

Limitations of Two-Wave Longitudinal Designs

Most previous longitudinal studies of depressive symptoms and marital satisfaction share a common approach. In general, these studies assessed satisfaction and depressive symptoms using self-reports then assessed one or both of these variables again at a later time, typically after 1 to 3 years (e.g., Fincham, Beach, Harold, & Osborne, 1997; Schaefer & Burnett, 1987). In most cases, multiple regression or cross-lagged correlations were used to estimate the association between initial levels of one of these variables and regressed change in the other.

This approach to longitudinal research may have only a limited ability to reveal dynamic relationships between depressive symptoms and marital satisfaction, for several reasons. First, although researchers often are interested in drawing inferences about within-subject relationships, current approaches focus exclusively on between-subjects analyses. For example, as noted earlier, the recommendation that marital therapy be considered as a treatment for depression implies that changes in marital distress should lead to changes in an individual's depressive symptoms. Longitudinal research on these variables has yet to examine directly the association between changes in these two variables. Instead, two-wave longitudinal designs addressing whether individuals who differ in their initial levels of one variable experience different amounts of change in the other variable have been used. The significant associations revealed by these analyses suggest that changes in the two variables are also associated within individuals, but a direct test of this hypothesis may produce stronger effects.

Second, regression and correlational techniques emphasize prediction at the expense of description. For example, a multiple regression analysis estimates the association between initial levels of marital satisfaction and regressed changes in depressive symptoms without ever describing how depressive symptoms change over time, the average rate of change over time, or the presence or absence of individual differences in change over time. Without descriptive statistics on how these variables change or remain stable, attempts to account for individual differences in change may be difficult to interpret. Furthermore, as a result of reliance on these techniques, the accumulated longitudinal research on depressive symptoms in marriage has yet to provide a clear picture of how depressive symptoms develop in the context of long-term relationships.

Third, in the absence of an explicit description of how depressive symptoms and marital satisfaction change, current approaches assume that both of these variables change in the same way. A multiple regression analysis, for example, applies the same underlying model to estimate regressed change in both depressive symptoms and marital satisfaction.

However, this assumption is not supported by existing data on the behavior of depressive symptoms and marital satisfaction over time. Life span longitudinal studies suggest that marital satisfaction may change linearly and continuously (Johnson, Amoloza, & Booth, 1992; Vaillant & Vaillant, 1993), whereas depressive symptoms are thought to be recurrent and to wax and wane in cycles (Coyne and Benazon, chapter 2). Ideally, analyses of how these variables affect each other would incorporate distinct and appropriate models of change for each variable. Unfortunately, current approaches tend not to articulate explicit models of change for either variable.

Finally, using two waves of longitudinal data may be unreliable as a source of information on how two variables affect each other over time. As Rogosa (1980) has argued in some detail, the cross-lagged correlational design "is not a sound basis for causal inference" (p. 257). In particular, when the variables being examined are significantly correlated over time, measures of change derived from only two waves of data tend to be unreliable (Rogosa, Brant, & Zimowski, 1982). Despite these warnings, and despite the fact that depressive symptoms and marital satisfaction are significantly correlated over 1- to 3-year intervals, cross-lagged correlational analyses of two waves of data continue to be the basis for data analyses in this area (e.g., Fincham et al., 1997). When the reliability of the assessment of change is low, then the size of the observed effects on change will necessarily be low as well. This may account for the fact that, although the obtained cross-sectional associations between depressive symptoms and marital satisfaction have been substantial, the obtained longitudinal associations between depressive symptoms and marital satisfaction have been relatively modest (Whisman, chapter 1).

In sum, the techniques used to analyze data in previous longitudinal research on marital satisfaction and depressive symptoms may not be the ones most appropriate to addressing the questions of greatest theoretical interest to researchers. Continued reliance on these techniques may serve to obscure rather than illuminate the within-subject associations between changes in depressive symptoms and marital satisfaction over time.

The Problem of Multiwave Data

Understanding the association between individual change in depressive symptoms and marital satisfaction may require more than two assessments of each variable. To date, few studies of depressive symptoms and marital satisfaction have collected multiwave data (e.g., Beach & O'Leary, 1993a; 1993b; Gotlib, Lewinsohn, & Seeley, 1998). One reason for this may be the lack of available methods of analyzing more than two waves of data at a time. For example, even those researchers who have collected multiwave data have tended to analyze those data as a series of two-wave designs. In this light, the considerable expense of gathering more than two waves of data may not be worthwhile.

However, there may be important aspects of the relationship between depressive symptoms and marital satisfaction that cannot be addressed without multiwave data. To illustrate this point, Figure 3.1 presents eight waves of depressive symptom and marital satisfaction scores from two spouses. Depressive symptoms were measured using the Beck Depression Inventory (BDI; Beck, Steer, & Garbin, 1988), and marital satisfaction was assessed with the Marital Adjustment Test (MAT; Locke & Wallace, 1959). Both instruments were administered approximately every 6 months during the first 4 years of marriage. To facilitate comparisons between the timelines, scores for depressive symptoms were transformed so that their range more closely resembled the range of the marital satisfaction scores.

BENJAMIN R. KARNEY

BDI and MAT scores for Spouse A

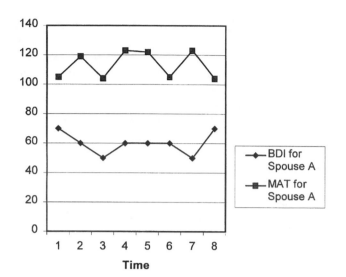

BDI and MAT scores for Spouse B

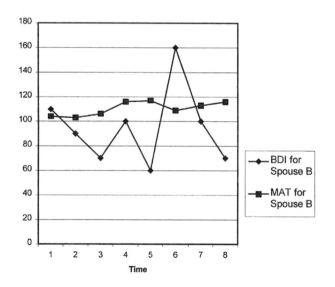

Figure 3.1. Eight Waves of Data on Depressive Symptoms and Marital Satisfaction for Two Spouses

The resulting timelines draw attention to the within-subject correlation between depressive symptoms and marital satisfaction over time. For Spouse A, this correlation was relatively high. Between assessments, when marital satisfaction increased, depressive symptoms tended to decrease, and when marital satisfaction held steady, depressive symptoms did also. In contrast, for Spouse B, this correlation was relatively low. The slight changes in marital satisfaction from assessment to assessment do not appear related to fluctuations in Spouse B's level of depressive symptoms. Across a sample of individuals followed over time, between-subjects variability in the within-subject correlation may be of considerable theoretical interest. For example, marital therapy presumably would be recommended as a treatment for depression only for those individuals for whom the within-subject correlation between depressive symptoms and marital satisfaction was high. For individuals for whom changes in these two variables were uncorrelated, marital therapy would not be the recommended treatment for depression.

Thus, examining even two cases of within-subject data points out the potential value in addressing directly the association between changes in depressive symptoms and changes in marital satisfaction. However, a thorough treatment of these issues requires not only multiple assessments of each variable but also methods of data analysis that allow researchers to conduct within-subject analyses and between-subjects analyses simultaneously. Until recently, such techniques were unavailable.

Analyzing Multiwave Longitudinal Data With Growth Curve Analysis

Recent developments in analyzing multiwave longitudinal data overcome the limitations of earlier methods and offer a new approach to answering questions about how changes in depressive symptoms and changes in marital satisfaction may be associated over time. This section provides a brief overview of GCA and then outlines a strategy using GCA to address the dynamics of two variables that are changing simultaneously.

Examining Individual Trajectories

In contrast to regression-based methods of analyzing longitudinal data, the dependent variable in GCA is not a participant's Time 2 status on a variable controlling for Time 1 status on that variable. Instead, GCA addresses the full trajectory of the variable across time. The analysis generally proceeds in two stages. In the first stage, multiple assessments of each participant are used to estimate a trajectory, or growth curve, that summarizes how each individual is changing over the course of the study. One simple function that can be used to summarize individual change is a straight line, described with the function $Y = mx + b$, where Y represents the value of a variable at any given time, x is some measure of elapsed time, m represents the rate of change in variable Y over time, and b represents the initial value of Y when x is 0. This function reduces a potentially large number of assessments to a limited number of parameters, in this case an *intercept,* capturing the initial level of the variable, and a *slope,* capturing the rate of change in the variable over time. More complex functions can be estimated as theoretically appropriate.

In the second stage of a GCA, the parameters summarizing the change of each individual are treated as new dependent variables in a multivariate between-subjects analysis. Thus, this approach accounts for between-subjects variability in change only after a model of change has been specified and the parameters of that model estimated for each individual in the sample (Rogosa et al., 1982). This second stage is similar to a multivariate regression in which between-subjects factors are used to account for variance in the within-subject parameters of change (see Karney & Bradbury, 1995a).

Determining the Advantages of Growth Curve Analysis

The growth curve approach to analyzing longitudinal data has a number of advantages over the methods used in previous research on depression and marital satisfaction. First, GCA emphasizes the importance of describing how variables change before attempting to account for individual differences in change. The descriptive step is crucial to planning subsequent analyses. For example, previous research has shown both depressive symptoms and marital satisfaction to be fairly stable over time. Explaining individual differences in change is appropriate only if (a) the variables in question are in fact changing over time and (b) individual differences in change exist. Previous approaches to longitudinal data have not addressed these preliminary questions, but GCA addresses them directly by requiring researchers to specify and evaluate a model of individual change before attempting to account for differences between participants.

Second, by requiring that researchers articulate a model of change for each dynamic variable, GCA offers researchers the flexibility to specify distinct models for different variables as appropriate. Whereas the conventional regression approach assumes an identical statistical model for each dependent variable, GCA can incorporate linear, curvilinear, and exponential models for different variables with equal ease. Thus, in an analysis of depressive symptoms and marital satisfaction, there is no need to specify the same model of change for both variables.

Third, defining individual trajectories in terms of specific parameters allows researchers to make more precise statements about effects on change over time. As Willett (1988) noted, "Once a suitable mathematical model has been selected to represent the individual growth, *vague* questions about interindividual differences in change can be replaced by *specific* questions about differences in the individual growth parameters" (p. 393). For example, rather than ask how initial levels of satisfaction affect change in depressive symptoms, estimating individual trajectories enables researchers to ask how satisfaction is associated with specific parameters of the individual change function.

Finally, because the first stage of the analysis estimates an individual trajectory from whatever data are available for each participant, GCA can address participants that may or may not have completed the study. In marital research that uses two-wave designs, data from couples who dissolve before the second wave must be discarded, forcing researchers to waste valuable data and to ignore the couples who may be the most interesting. In GCA, trajectories can be estimated from whatever data the couple provided before withdrawing. Thus, the changes experienced by couples who dissolve and couples who remain intact can be compared.

Examining Two Variables That Change Together Over Time

In most research using GCA, trajectories are estimated for variables that change over time and then variance in those trajectories is accounted for with variables that are presumed not to change. For example, Tate and Hokanson (1993) assessed depression three times over a period of 2 to 3 months in a sample of college students. To account for changes in symptoms over that period, Tate and Hokanson examined personality traits that they assumed would be relatively stable over the same period.

When both variables to be examined change over time, as depressive symptoms and marital satisfaction appear to do, the analysis becomes more complex. For example, given that marital satisfaction is also changing, it would not be appropriate to enter a single value of marital satisfaction in the second stage of the analysis to account for changes in depressive symptoms over time. One strategy to account for changes in both variables at once is to enter each variable as a time-varying covariate in the within-subject function specified for the other variable in the first stage of the analysis (Bryk & Raudenbush, 1992; Karney & Bradbury, 2000). In this strategy, the within-subject analysis, rather than treating the dependent variable strictly as a function of the time at each assessment, treats the dependent variable as a function of the time at each assessment and the value of the second variable at each assessment. The second variable is thus a time-varying covariate in the function that describes the trajectory of the first variable.

To examine dynamic relationships between depressive symptoms and marital satisfaction, a GCA would proceed in the following way. First, multiple assessments of depressive symptoms and multiple assessments of marital satisfaction would be examined separately to determine the appropriate functions that describe change in each variable over time. Once an adequate function was determined to describe change in each variable, the other variable would then be added to that function as a time-varying covariate. For example, to address the effects of changes in depressive symptoms on the trajectory of marital satisfaction, depressive symptoms would be entered as a time-varying covariate in the within-subject function that describes the trajectory of marital satisfaction. The coefficient of the time-varying covariate estimates the extent to which changes in depressive symptoms between assessments affect marital satisfaction at each assessment, controlling for the overall trajectory of marital satisfaction across time. The significance of this coefficient addresses the following question: Do changes in depressive symptoms between assessments predict deviations from an individual's overall trajectory of marital satisfaction? A second analysis then reverses the positions of the two variables. Depressive symptoms would now be treated as the dependent variable, with marital satisfaction as the within-subject time-varying covariate. The question in this case would be the reverse of the previous: Do changes in marital satisfaction between assessments predict deviations from an individual's baseline trajectory of depressive symptoms over time?

It is important to note that the two analyses are not identical. The first analysis asks whether changes in depressive symptoms are associated with variations in concurrent levels of marital satisfaction, controlling for the individual's overall trajectory of marital satisfaction. The second analysis asks whether changes in marital satisfaction are associated with variations in concurrent levels of depressive symptoms, controlling for the individual's overall trajectory of depressive symptoms. Thus, each analysis estimates the within-subject association between the two variables, controlling for a different trajectory.

A unique advantage of this approach is that the coefficient of the time-varying covariate in each analysis can be examined as a between-subjects variable in the second stage of the analysis. In other words, not only does this approach estimate the associations between changes in depressive symptoms and changes in marital satisfaction within each individual, it also allows the use of other variables to account for between-subjects variability in the magnitude of these associations.

A Study of Change in Depressive Symptoms and Marital Satisfaction Over the First 4 Years of Marriage

This section explores the implications of a growth curve approach to analyzing depressive symptoms in marriage using data drawn from a 4-year study of depressive symptoms and marital satisfaction in newlyweds (Karney & Bradbury, 1997, 2000). The analyses summarized in this chapter had three goals. The first was simply to describe how depressive symptoms and marital satisfaction change on average across the first 4 years of marriage. The second was to estimate associations between changes in satisfaction and changes in depressive symptoms within spouses. The third was to account for individual differences in the size of these associations with other variables, specifically neuroticism and marital dissolution.

Data Set

Data to address these issues came from 60 newlywed couples solicited from the Los Angeles, California, area through newspaper advertisements. At Time 1, the couples had been married an average of 12.0 (*SD* = 6.2) weeks. Husbands averaged 25.4 (*SD* = 3.4) years of age, and wives averaged 24.0 (*SD* = 2.9) years of age. Seventy percent of the sample had cohabited premaritally, and 75% of husbands and wives were White.

At their initial assessment, the couples were invited to research rooms on campus, where they completed self-report instruments and participated in recorded marital interaction tasks. At 6-month intervals following the initial assessment, spouses were mailed packets to complete at home and return through the mail. At each phase of measurement, spouses were instructed to complete their forms independently of one another and were paid for their participation.

Four years later, the couples had been assessed eight times. By Time 8, marital status was known for 56 (93%) of the original 60 couples. Eighteen of those couples (32%) had reported a divorce or permanent separation. Of the 18 dissolved marriages, 16 had provided multiple waves of data before dissolving. Thus, the analyses requiring multiple waves of data had data for 54 couples (for more details on this data set, see Karney & Bradbury, 1997).

Measurement

Marital Satisfaction

Although the most frequently administered measures of marital satisfaction are omnibus measures that ask spouses to evaluate multiple aspects of the marriage, some researchers have argued for conceptually clearer measures that assess global sentiments toward the marriage exclusively (Fincham & Bradbury, 1987; Huston, McHale, & Crouter, 1986; Norton, 1983). In this study, both kinds of measures were administered at each phase of data collection.

The one omnibus measure was the MAT (Locke & Wallace, 1959), a widely used scale that assesses spouses' global evaluations of the marriage; the amount of disagreement across different areas of possible conflict; and aspects of conflict resolution, cohesion, and communication. Yielding scores ranging from 2 to 158, the MAT demonstrates adequate cross-sectional reliability (split-half = .90) and discriminates between nondistressed spouses and spouses with documented marital problems.

In addition, couples completed three measures that assessed their global evaluations of the marriage exclusively. The first global measure was the Quality Marriage Index (QMI; Norton, 1983), a 6-item scale asking spouses to rate the extent to which they agree with general statements about their marriage (e.g., ''We have a good marriage'' and ''I really feel like part of a team with my partner''). The QMI yields scores from 6 to 45. The second global measure was the Kansas Marital Satisfaction Scale (KMSS; Schumm et al., 1986), a 3-item instrument that asks spouses to rate their satisfaction with their marriage, their spouse, and their relationship with their spouse on 7-point scales. The KMSS yields scores from 3 to 21. The third global measure was a version of the Semantic Differential (SMD; Osgood, Suci, & Tannenbaum, 1957), a method of quantifying evaluations of concepts by asking participants to rate their perception of that concept on 7-point scales between two opposite adjectives. In this study, spouses rated how they felt about their marriage on 15 adjective pairs (e.g., ''bad-good,'' ''dissatisfied-satisfied,'' and ''unpleasant-pleasant''), yielding scores from 15 to 105. The internal consistency of all three global measures was quite high (across measures and waves of measurement, coefficient alpha averaged above .9 for each spouse). Throughout the analyses that follow, significant results are given more weight to the extent that they replicate across specific measures of marital satisfaction.

Depressive Symptoms

At each phase of data collection, both spouses completed the BDI (Beck & Beamesderfer, 1974), an instrument used widely for assessing this construct (see Whisman, chapter 1). For nonpsychiatric samples, coefficient alpha on the BDI consistently exceeds .80, and test–retest correlations consistently exceed .7 over 2- to 3-week intervals (see Beck et al., 1988). Scores on this 21-item measure can range from 0 to 63.

Neuroticism

At Times 1 and 2, neuroticism, a key indicator of negative affectivity (Watson & Clark, 1984), was assessed with the Neuroticism scale of the Eysenck Personality Questionnaire (EPQN; Eysenck & Eysenck, 1978), a 23-item measure asking spouses to answer yes or no questions about their negative affectivity (e.g., "Are you a worrier?" and "Does your mood go up and down often?"). Yielding scores ranging from 0 to 23, the EPQN has demonstrated high internal consistency (.84; Eysenck & Eysenck, 1978). In this study, 6-month test–retest reliability was .74 for husbands and .75 for wives.

Marital dissolution was also assessed at each phase of measurement. A marriage was defined as dissolved if either spouse reported, either on a questionnaire or over the telephone, that the marriage had ended in divorce or permanent separation since the previous assessment period. In all analyses, dissolution was dummy coded as a dichotomous variable such that 0 = intact and 1 = divorced or permanently separated. At each wave of assessment, marital satisfaction data were entered only for intact couples.

Data Analyses

Growth curve analyses were conducted using hierarchical linear modeling (HLM; Bryk & Raudenbush, 1992) and the HLM/2L computer program (Bryk, Raudenbush, & Congdon, 1994), for several reasons. First, unlike other approaches to analyzing trajectories (e.g., structural equation modeling), HLM does not assume that all data are collected simultaneously from all participants at equally spaced intervals. Instead, HLM uses all available data from each participant to estimate a trajectory for that participant, controlling for the timing of that individual's measurements. Second, HLM provides maximally efficient estimates of trajectories by weighting individual parameter estimates by their precision, according to empirical Bayes theory. When an individual's trajectory can be estimated precisely, the final estimate relies heavily on the individual data. When an individual's trajectory cannot be estimated precisely, the final estimate relies more heavily on the mean of the sample. Because the most precise estimates therefore contribute more to the final estimated variance of the sample, variances estimated in this way tend to be smaller and more conservative than those obtained through traditional Optimal Least Squares (OLS) method. Third, HLM computes effects on each parameter through simultaneous equations; therefore, effects on one parameter of change are estimated controlling for effects on other parameters of change. In all of these analyses, husbands' and wives' trajectories were estimated simultaneously in a couple-level model according to procedures outlined by Raudenbush, Brennan, and Barnett (1995).

Specific Questions and Hypotheses

How Do Depressive Symptoms and Marital Satisfaction Change Over the First Years of Marriage?

Previous longitudinal research regarding marital satisfaction has consistently demonstrated that satisfaction declines linearly over time (e.g., Johnson et al., 1992; Vaillant & Vaillant, 1993). Accordingly, we expected that a declining linear model would adequately describe couples' scores on all measures of marital satisfaction over the first 4 years of marriage. Previous research regarding depressive symptoms has offered no reason to expect that symptoms change continuously over time. On the contrary, for many individuals, depressive symptoms wax and wane spontaneously over the course of their lives (see Coyne and Benazon, chapter 2). Accordingly, we expected that a simpler model of variability around a mean value would describe spouses' scores on the BDI across assessments.

How Are Changes in Depressive Symptoms and Changes in Marital Satisfaction Associated Within Individuals?

Given the well-established cross-sectional association between levels of depressive symptoms and levels of marital satisfaction, we expected that changes in depressive symptoms and changes in marital satisfaction would also be associated within individuals. That is, increases in marital satisfaction should be associated with decreases in depressive symptoms, and vice versa. However, the GCA strategy allows some refinement of this initial prediction. By treating each variable as a time-varying covariate in the function predicting the other variable, the analyses in this study could compare the extent that changes in marital satisfaction were associated with deviations from the overall trajectory of depressive symptoms to the extent that changes in depressive symptoms were associated with deviations from the overall trajectory of marital satisfaction. Should there be a difference in the magnitude of the association depending on which overall trajectory is being controlled? In the absence of previous research using this approach, we could offer no formal hypotheses. However, we speculated that changes in depressive symptoms would be more strongly linked to deviations from the trajectory of marital satisfaction than changes in marital satisfaction would be linked to deviations from the trajectory of depressive symptoms, mostly because we expected that marital satisfaction scores would have a more clearly defined trajectory from which to deviate.

How Does Neuroticism Predict the Within-Subject Associations Between Depressive Symptoms and Marital Satisfaction?

Individuals for whom the associations between changes in depressive symptoms and marital satisfaction are strong appear to be at great risk for negative life outcomes. Relative to individuals for whom these associations are low, these individuals are at greater risk for depression (if their marital satisfaction should decline) and at greater risk for marital distress (if they experience elevated depressive symptoms). In a series of longitudinal analyses, Beach and O'Leary (1993a, 1993b) addressed the hypothesis that chronic negative affectivity accounted for the heightened vulnerability of these individuals. They found that the longitudinal associations between depressive symptoms and marital satisfaction were stronger for chronically negatively affective spouses. However, these analyses were unable to examine the effects of negative affectivity on the associations between changes in the two variables. Using GCA, this study was able to reexamine and elaborate on the earlier findings. Consistent with the implications of the Beach and O'Leary studies (1993a, 1993b), we predicted that changes in depressive symptoms and changes in marital satisfaction would be more strongly associated for spouses who scored higher on neuroticism.

How Do the Within-Subject Associations Between Depressive Symptoms and Marital Satisfaction Predict Marital Dissolution?

For the reasons described earlier, previous longitudinal research on depressive symptoms and marital satisfaction has been unable to address the effects of the association between these variables on whether or not a marriage eventually dissolves. The approach used in this study allowed us to address this question by comparing the size of the association in couples who experienced each of these outcomes. We predicted that changes in depressive symptoms and changes in marital satisfaction would be more strongly associated in couples who dissolved their marriages within the first 4 years than in couples who remained intact.

Descriptive Statistics and Preliminary Analyses

Table 3.1 presents spouses' mean scores for each measure at each phase of assessment for the 38 couples who provided data at every assessment. Recalculating the means from all of the couples providing data at each assessment did not change the patterns described below in any way.

With respect to marital satisfaction, average marital satisfaction declined over the first 4 years of marriage for both spouses on all four measures administered. Mean scores for husbands and wives did not differ significantly at any time point, and spouses' marital satisfaction scores were significantly correlated with each other at each time point (range: $-.38$ to .76). With respect to depressive symptoms, average BDI scores did not change systematically over time, regardless of whether the full sample or the intact sample was examined. Scores for wives were higher than scores for husbands at most time points, but this difference was statistically significant only at Time 7. Unlike their marital satisfaction scores, husbands' and wives' BDI scores were not significantly correlated with each other at seven out of the eight assessments.

Replicating previous cross-sectional research, the correlation between BDI scores and marital satisfaction scores was significant at most waves for both spouses. For example, for husbands, the average correlation between BDI scores and MAT scores was $-.29$ (range: .04 to $-.49$), and the average correlation between BDI scores and SMD scores was $-.38$ (range: $-.12$ to $-.64$). For wives, the average correlation between BDI scores and MAT scores was $-.34$ (range: $-.17$ to $-.66$), and the average correlation between BDI scores and SMD scores was $-.47$ (range: $-.31$ to $-.78$). The magnitude of the correlation did not appear to change systematically over the eight waves of measurement.

With respect to neuroticism, scores on the EPQN were significantly correlated with BDI scores for both husbands and wives (at Time 1, for husbands, $r = .64$, for wives, $r = .66$; at Time 2, for husbands, $r = .74$, for wives, $r = .70$). However, consistent with the view that neuroticism is a relatively stable aspect of personality, EPQN scores were more stable over 6 months (for husbands, $r = .74$; for wives, $r = .75$) than BDI scores over the same period (for husbands, $r = .67$; for wives, $r = .46$). Neither neuroticism (for husbands, $r = .09$; for wives, $r = .07$) nor depressive symptoms (for husbands, $r = -.01$; for wives, $r = .14$) at Time 1 were associated with whether or not a couple dissolved their marriage during the course of the study.

Table 3.1—*Means and Standard Deviations of Depressive Symptoms and Marital Satisfaction Across Eight Waves of Measurement*

Instrument Spouse	Time 1	Time 2	Time 3	Time 4	Time 5	Time 6	Time 7	Time 8
Marital Adjustment Test								
Husbands								
M	117.2	118.3	111.8	113.7	108.1	107.6	108.0	108.7
SD	21.0	17.1	20.9	20.4	22.3	26.8	28.7	24.2
Wives								
M	118.3	118.4	110.6	114.7	110.1	105.7	110.4	113.2
SD	18.1	22.4	24.4	21.4	25.0	30.0	25.2	23.8
Quality Marriage Index								
Husbands								
M	39.2	39.4	37.1	38.7	36.4	36.3	36.2	36.3
SD	6.1	5.1	7.3	6.4	8.2	7.9	8.9	8.4
Wives								
M	39.0	38.0	36.2	37.2	36.4	33.7	36.0	35.3
SD	6.3	6.8	8.8	7.6	7.8	9.4	8.5	8.5
Kansas Marital Satisfaction Survey								
Husbands								
M	18.5	18.6	17.4	18.1	17.4	17.0	17.2	17.0
SD	2.9	2.4	3.2	3.0	3.4	3.5	3.8	3.2
Wives								
M	18.4	17.9	16.6	16.9	16.4	15.5	16.4	16.3
SD	2.7	2.7	3.7	3.8	4.0	4.4	3.7	3.9
Semantic Differential								
Husbands								
M	91.6	93.1	87.0	89.5	86.7	86.2	86.4	85.8
SD	13.3	9.9	16.0	14.8	16.8	17.0	19.3	16.7
Wives								
M	90.2	89.4	85.6	89.4	85.4	81.2	85.9	83.84
SD	12.6	15.4	17.7	16.4	17.3	20.7	18.2	17.7
Beck Depression Inventory								
Husbands								
M	5.5	5.2	5.0	5.5	5.8	5.2	5.7	6.2
SD	5.7	6.1	6.8	7.6	7.4	5.9	5.7	6.6
Wives								
M	6.5	6.9	6.2	7.3	7.0	6.7	7.6	6.0
SD	6.2	5.9	5.4	7.9	6.7	4.9	6.8	4.4

All of the variables assessed for these analyses appeared to perform as expected. The established negative associations between depressive symptoms and marital dissatisfaction were replicated through significant cross-sectional correlations at each time point. The associations among the between-subjects variables suggested that it was reasonable to examine each variable for its independent effects on the association between depressive symptoms and marital satisfaction. Finally, examining the mean scores for depressive symptoms and marital satisfaction offered preliminary support for one of our hypotheses about how depressive symptoms and marital satisfaction may change over time. Whereas the average marital satisfaction of this sample declined over time, the average level of depressive symptoms varied across assessments but did not appear to change systematically. To evaluate whether different models described individual changes in the two variables, we examined these data using GCA.

Within-Subject Analyses: Modeling Individual Change

Conventional analyses of multiwave data focus solely on patterns of mean change over time, potentially obscuring individual differences in change. By specifying a model of individual change and estimating that function for each spouse, GCA allows individual differences in change to be described more precisely.

Specifying a Model of Marital Satisfaction Over Time

With respect to marital satisfaction, the pattern of decline in the mean scores suggested that individual change could be described adequately with a linear function. The linear model can be understood as a within-subject regression of an individual's marital satisfaction scores onto the time of each assessment. To evaluate this model, the following function was specified to describe the data from each individual:

$$(1) \qquad Y_{ij} = \beta_{0j} + \beta_{1j}(\text{Time}) + r_{ij}.$$

where Y_{ij} is the marital satisfaction of individual j at Time i; β_{0j} is the marital satisfaction of individual j at Time 0 (i.e., the initial satisfaction of individual j); β_{1j} is the rate of the linear change in marital satisfaction for individual j; and r_{ij} is the residual variance in repeated measurements for individual j, assumed to be independent and normally distributed across participants.

For all four measures of satisfaction, the resulting model produced reliable estimates of all parameters. Thus, the trajectory of each individual's marital satisfaction was described with an intercept, capturing the initial level of the trajectory, and a slope, capturing the subsequent rate of change in the trajectory across time. These analyses are reported in greater detail in Karney and Bradbury (1997).

Specifying a Model of Depressive Symptoms Over Time

In contrast to the mean marital satisfaction scores, mean BDI scores revealed no obvious trends to guide the choice of a model to describe individual change. Thus, two different models were specified and compared as possible descriptions of these data. The first was a mean and variance model, suggesting that depressive symptoms do not develop systematically over time, but rather vary at each assessment around an individual's mean level. To evaluate this model, the following function was specified to describe the data from each individual:

$$(2) \qquad Y_{ij} = \beta_{0j} + r_{ij}.$$

where Y_{ij} is the level of depressive symptoms of individual j at time i; β_{0j} is the mean level of depressive symptoms of individual j across assessments; and r_{ij} is the deviation from the mean level at each assessment.

This model provided reliable estimates of husbands' and wives' mean levels of depressive symptoms (reliabilities of .83 and .91, respectively).

The alternative model examined in this study was a linear model analogous to the one described for marital satisfaction in Equation 1. This model allows for the possibility that depressive symptoms do not vary randomly but rather change systematically over time. Using this model produced reliable estimates of the intercepts (.71 and .76 for wives and husbands, respectively) but far less reliable estimates of the slopes (.41 and .22 for wives and husbands, respectively), indicating some difficulties in estimating linear change in depressive symptoms over time. Furthermore, the mean estimated slope for wives did not differ significantly from zero ($t = .71, p = .48$), although there was significant interindividual variability among wives. In contrast, slopes for husbands were significantly different from zero and positive (slope $= .06, t = 1.9, p = .06$, two-tailed). However, this value did not vary significantly across husbands.

To compare the appropriateness of the two models, we conducted a chi-square test of their goodness-of-fit statistics. The difference between the models was not significant, ($\chi^2 = 10.08, df = 7, p > .05$), suggesting that both models described the data equally well. In light of this test and the difficulties estimating slopes in the second model, we elected to examine the more parsimonious mean and variance model in the remainder of the analyses.

Describing Individual Change

Specifying an appropriate model for the change in each variable allowed a more precise description of the development of depressive symptoms and marital satisfaction than was possible from examining the mean scores alone. The means and variances of each parameter for both functions are presented in Table 3.2. Generally, these statistics confirm the patterns suggested by the mean scores. Marital satisfaction began relatively high, then declined linearly over time, regardless of the instrument examined. For expressive symptoms assessed with the BDI, wives' average level of depressive symptoms across the first 4 years of marriage was 7.2 ($SD = 3.7$), and husbands' average was 5.9 ($SD = 5.4$). These means were not significantly different from each other, and spouses' means were significantly correlated ($r = .25, df = 54, p < .05$).

The GCA then expanded on this description in several ways. First, t tests of the marital satisfaction slope parameter indicated that overall declines in marital satisfaction over time were significantly different from zero (Column 3 of Table 3.2). Second, chi-square tests of the variance among the parameter estimates indicated that significant interindividual differences existed in the marital satisfaction intercept, the marital satisfaction slope, and the BDI means, justifying further analyses to account for between-subjects variance in these parameters. Third, because GCA provides unbiased estimates of each parameter, the correlation between the marital satisfaction slope and intercept parameters is an accurate estimate of the relationship between initial levels of marital satisfaction and subsequent rates of change in marital satisfaction. In this study, for example, that correlation, aggregated across the four measures of marital satisfaction, was .41 ($p < .01$) for husbands and .17 (ns) for wives. Thus, for husbands, a higher initial level of marital satisfaction is associated with more positive slopes over time, whereas for wives these parameters are relatively independent.

Summary

The following were the first questions to be addressed in these analyses: How do depressive symptoms and marital satisfaction change over the first years of marriage? Does

Table 3.2—*Mean Trajectories of Depressive Symptoms and Marital Satisfaction Across 4 Years*
(N = 54 Couples)

Instrument Spouse	M	SE	t^a	χ^2
Satisfaction intercepts				
MAT				
Husbands	117.9	2.1	—	158.0***
Wives	117.9	2.4	—	205.8***
QMI				
Husbands	39.2	.66	—	109.3***
Wives	38.6	.80	—	169.8***
KMS				
Husbands	18.4	.31	—	134.0***
Wives	18.0	.33	—	163.1***
SMD				
Husbands	91.6	1.4	—	125.6***
Wives	90.2	1.8	—	198.6***
Satisfaction slopes				
MAT				
Husbands	-.91	.21	-4.3***	182.4***
Wives	-.78	.19	-4.0***	165.0***
QMI				
Husbands	-.28	.06	-4.6***	139.9***
Wives	-.31	.06	-5.1***	152.9***
KMSS				
Husbands	-.11	.02	-4.5***	133.2***
Wives	-.15	.03	-5.6***	145.7***
SMD				
Husbands	-.54	.14	-3.9***	148.1***
Wives	-.58	.14	-4.0***	166.3***
Depressive symptom means				
BDI				
Husbands	5.9	5.4	7.8***	739.0***
Wives	7.2	3.7	13.1***	375.0***

Note. For *t* chi-square tests, *df* = 53. N = 54 couples. MAT = Marital Adjustment Test (Locke & Wallace, 1959); QMI = Quality Marriage Index (Norton, 1983); KMSS = Kansas Marital Satisfaction Survey (Schumm et al., 1986); SMD = Semantic Differential (Osgood, Suci, & Tannenbaum, 1957); BDI = Beck Depression Inventory (Beck, Steer, & Garbin, 1988).

[a]The *t* test addresses the hypothesis that a given parameter differs significantly from 0. Because the lowest possible score on the marital satisfaction intercepts is greater than 0, these tests are not meaningful and hence are not reported.

***$p < .001$, one-tailed.

the same model adequately describe the trajectory of both variables? The results of the GCA supported our predictions. Specifically, whereas a linear model described how marital satisfaction scores declined significantly for both spouses, a simpler mean and variance model was adequate to describe how BDI scores varied over time without changing systematically. These results support the argument made earlier that it is unwarranted to examine these two variables longitudinally without accounting for the fact that they change differently over time.

Within-Subject Analyses: Changes in Depressive Symptoms
and Marital Satisfaction

Once models of change have been specified for each variable, these models can be adapted to examine how levels of one variable at each assessment are associated with individual trajectories of the other variable.

Do Changes in Depressive Symptoms Affect the Trajectory of Marital Satisfaction?

To address this question, each spouse's scores on the BDI at each assessment were centered on their own mean and then entered into Equation 1 as a time-varying covariate. The new within-subject function became as follows:

$$(3) \qquad Y_{ij} = \beta_{0j} + \beta_{1j}(\text{Time}) + \beta_{2j}(\text{BDI}) + r_{ij}.$$

The coefficient of the time-varying covariate, β_{2j}, estimates the extent to which changes in depressive symptoms are associated with changes in marital satisfaction, controlling for the overall trajectory of marital satisfaction.

Separate models were estimated for each of the satisfaction measures examined. Estimates of the time-varying coefficients in each model are presented in the left side of Table 3.3. The effect of changes in depressive symptoms on the trajectory of marital satisfaction was significant across spouses and measures. Elevations in reported depressive symptoms were associated with declines in marital satisfaction regardless of the instrument used to measure marital satisfaction. It is noteworthy that the overall size of this effect, summarized by the aggregate effect sizes in Table 3.3, is substantially higher than the effect sizes obtained in previous longitudinal research on this association, supporting the idea that the effects of depressive symptoms on marital satisfaction may be best observed through within-subject analyses (Whisman, chapter 1; see also Karney & Bradbury, 1995b).

Do Changes in Marital Satisfaction Affect the Trajectory of Depressive Symptoms?

The previous set of analyses treated marital satisfaction as a dependent variable and depressive symptoms as a time-varying covariate. The next set of analyses reversed the positions of the two variables. Spouses' scores on each measure of marital satisfaction were centered on their own mean and then added as a time-varying covariate to Equation 2. The new within-subject function to describe depressive symptoms over time became as follows

$$(4) \qquad Y_{j} = \beta_{0j} + \beta_{1j}(\text{satisfaction}) + r_{ij}.$$

The coefficient of the time-varying covariate, β_{1j}, estimates the extent to which changes in satisfaction are associated with elevated or lowered levels of symptoms, controlling for mean levels of symptoms.

Separate models were estimated for each of the satisfaction measures examined. Estimates of the time-varying coefficients are presented in the right side of Table 3.3. As the table indicates, the coefficients of this time-varying covariate were also significant across spouses and measures. For both spouses, elevations in marital satisfaction were

Table 3.3—*Within-Subject Associations Between Depressive Symptoms and Marital Satisfaction Over Time (N = 54 Couples)*

	BDI ->satisfaction			Satisfaction ->BDI		
Instrument	Coefficient	t	Effect size	Coefficient	t	Effect size
			Husbands			
MAT	-.98	-4.7***	-.54	-.06	-4.6***	-.53
QMI	-.34	-5.6***	-.61	-.21	-5.2***	-.57
KMSS	-.17	-5.7***	-.62	-.55	-5.6***	-.60
SMD	-.92	-7.1***	-.70	-.14	-6.8***	-.68
	Aggregate effect size =		-.62***	Aggregate effect size =		-.60***
			Wives			
MAT	-1.0	-6.8***	-.68	-.10	-7.8***	-.72
QMI	-.36	-7.4***	-.71	-.29	-8.1***	-.74
KMSS	-.16	-7.2***	-.70	-.58	-7.9***	-.73
SMD	-1.0	-9.7***	-.80	-.14	-9.3***	-.78
	Aggregate effect size =		-.73***	Aggregate effect size =		-.74***

Note. For the BDI ->satisfaction t tests, $df = 53$. For the satisfaction ->BDI t tests, $df = 55$. MAT = Marital Adjustment Test (Locke & Wallace, 1959); QMI = Quality Marriage Index (Norton, 1983); KMSS = Kansas Marital Satisfaction Survey (Schumm et al., 1986); SMD = Semantic Differential (Osgood, Suci, & Tannenbaum, 1957); BDI = Beck Depression Inventory (Beck, Steer, & Garbin, 1988).
***$p < .001$, one-tailed.

associated with lower levels of depressive symptoms, controlling for mean levels of symptoms. It is noteworthy that the size of the associations between changes in satisfaction and the trajectory of depression were very similar to the size of the associations between change in depression and the trajectory of satisfaction reported in the left side of the table. Contrary to our admittedly tentative speculations, there was no evidence from a within-subject analysis that the direction of causality between these two variables is stronger in one direction than in the other.

Summary

The second question addressed in these analyses was the following: Are changes in depressive symptoms and changes in marital satisfaction associated within individuals? The results of this set of analyses support the hypothesis that changes in these two variables are significantly associated. This finding offers direct support for the suggestion that therapies designed to alleviate marital distress may simultaneously relieve depressive symptoms as well. Contrary to our tentative speculations, there was no evidence that effects in one direction differed from effects in the other direction.

Between-Subjects Analyses: The Effect of Neuroticism

Having estimated the within-subject associations between depressive symptoms and marital satisfaction over time, the second stage of the GCA attempted to account for between-subjects variability in the size of these associations. One of the between-subjects analyses examined the effects of neuroticism. Specifically, this analysis allowed us to revisit a hypothesis put forth by Beach and O'Leary (1993b) and elaborated by Beach and Fincham (1994) suggesting that a stable tendency to experience negative affect, often measured as neuroticism (Watson & Clark, 1984), may give rise to both depressive symptoms and marital satisfaction (see also Davila, chapter 4). Therefore, changes in these two variables should be more strongly linked for spouses who are higher in neuroticism.

In these analyses, this possibility was addressed in two ways. First, to examine the extent to which neuroticism moderates the association between BDI scores and the trajectory of marital satisfaction, each spouse's neuroticism score was entered into the second stage of the GCA as a predictor of each parameter of the within-subject function described in Equation 3. In this way, the association between neuroticism and the time-varying coefficient of BDI scores was estimated controlling for the association between neuroticism and each of the other parameters of the marital satisfaction trajectory. These coefficients are reported for both spouses and for each marital satisfaction measure on the left side of Table 3.4.

As Table 3.4 indicates, the moderating effect of neuroticism, controlling for the other associations between neuroticism and the trajectory of marital satisfaction (see Karney & Bradbury, 1997) was significant for husbands (aggregate $r = .24, p < .05$) but negligible for wives (aggregate $r = .01, ns$). The effect for husbands was in the positive direction, indicating that, contrary to our hypotheses, changes in depressive symptoms were less strongly associated with deviations from the marital satisfaction trajectory for husbands who scored higher in neuroticism. In other words, for the more neurotic husbands in our sample, increases in depressive symptoms were not as likely to lead to decreases in marital satisfaction than for the less neurotic husbands.

A second way to address this issue is to examine the extent to which neuroticism moderates the association between changes in marital satisfaction and the trajectory of depressive symptoms. To address this possibility, each spouse's neuroticism score was entered into the second stage of the GCA as a predictor of each parameter of the within-subject function described in Equation 4. The associations between neuroticism scores and the time-varying coefficient of marital satisfaction are presented on the right side of Table 3.4. As the aggregate effect sizes reveal, the effect of neuroticism, controlling for the association between neuroticism and mean levels of depressive symptoms, was negligible for husbands (aggregate $r = -.06, ns$) and marginally significant for wives (aggregate $r = -.18, p < .10$). Here the effect for wives was negative, indicating that, consistent with predictions, declines in marital satisfaction were slightly more strongly associated with increases in depressive symptoms for wives who scored higher in neuroticism.

Across different measures, spouses' levels of neuroticism do appear to moderate the association between changes in marital satisfaction and changes in depressive symptoms over time. However, the nature of this moderation appears to vary according to gender and the direction of the effect being estimated. For husbands, neuroticism appears to moderate the effect of changes in depressive symptoms on the trajectory of marital satisfaction. This effect suggests that changes in depressive symptoms are less likely to influence the marital satisfaction trajectory for husbands who are more neurotic. For wives, neuroticism appears to moderate the effect of changes in satisfaction on the trajectory of depressive symptoms. In contrast to the effect for husbands, this effect suggests that changes in satisfaction are more likely to influence the trajectory of depressive symptoms for wives who are more neurotic.

Table 3.4—*Effects of Neuroticism Scores on the Association Between Depressive Symptoms and Marital Satisfaction*

	Effect on BDI ->satisfaction			Effect on satisfaction ->BDI		
Instrument	Coefficient	t	Effect size	Coefficient	t	Effect size
			Husbands			
MAT	.06	1.9**	.25	.00	.02	.00
QMI	.01	1.4	.19	.00	.30	.04
KMSS	.01	1.6	.22	.00	-.52	-.07
SMD	.04	2.2**	.29	.00	-.64	-.09
Aggregate effect size =			.24**			-.06
			Wives			
MAT	-.02	-.76	-.10	-.00	-2.3**	-.30
QMI	.01	.75	.10	.00	-.79	-.11
KMSS	.00	.46	.06	.01	-.53	-.07
SMD	-.01	-.26	-.04	-.00	-1.8**	-.24
Aggregate effect size =			.01			-.18*

Note. For the BDI ->satisfaction t tests, $df = 52$. For the satisfaction ->BDI t tests, $df = 54$. MAT = Marital Adjustment Test (Locke & Wallace, 1959); QMI = Quality Marriage Index (Norton, 1983); KMSS = Kansas Marital Satisfaction Survey (Schumm et al., 1986); SMD = Semantic Differential (Osgood, Suci, & Tannenbaum, 1957); BDI = Beck Depression Inventory (Beck, Steer, & Garbin, 1988).

$*p < .10$, one-tailed; $**p < .05$, one-tailed.

Between-Subjects Analyses: Effects on Dissolution

One advantage of the GCA approach is the ability to estimate within-subject associations for couples who may not have completed the study. As long as a couple provides multiple waves of data before dissolving or withdrawing, a trajectory can be computed. Thus it was possible in the analyses described here to compare the size of the associations between depressive symptoms and marital satisfaction in couples who dissolved their marriages in the first 4 years and in couples who remained intact. The central question was whether changes in depressive symptoms and marital satisfaction were more strongly linked in the couples who eventually dissolved.

Effects on marital dissolution were examined with respect to both types of within-subject functions (e.g., Equations 3 and 4). In each case, a categorical variable indicating whether or not the couple dissolved within the first 4 years of marriage was entered into the second stage of the GCA as a predictor of each parameter of the within-subject functions. This analysis was functionally equivalent to a *t* test of the difference between the time-varying coefficients in the two groups of couples, controlling for the association between dissolution and each of the other parameters in the within-subject models.

With respect to the effects of changes in depressive symptoms on deviations from the marital satisfaction trajectory, the coefficients for intact couples and dissolved couples are presented on the left side of Table 3.5. As the aggregate effect sizes indicate, across measures and spouses this association was marginally stronger among the couples who dissolved. In other words, consistent with predictions, increases in depressive symptoms were slightly more likely to lead to declines in marital satisfaction within marriages that dissolved than within marriages that remained intact.

With respect to the association between changes in marital satisfaction and deviations from the trajectory of depressive symptoms, the coefficients for intact and dissolved couples are presented on the right side of Table 3.5. These aggregate effect sizes illustrate a different result. For husbands, whether or not the marriage dissolved was not related to the size of the association between changes in depressive symptoms and changes in marital satisfaction (aggregate $r = .05$, ns). For wives, however, this effect was significant and in the opposite direction (aggregate $r = .23$, $p < .05$). For wives, declines in satisfaction were less strongly associated with increases in depressive symptoms in the marriages that dissolved than in the marriages that remained intact.

As with neuroticism, the results of the analyses of marital dissolution varied according to gender and the direction of the effect being estimated. To the extent that changes in depressive symptoms influence the marital satisfaction trajectory, the size of this effect was marginally larger for both spouses in marriages that dissolved. However, to the extent that changes in marital satisfaction influence levels of depressive symptoms, the size of this association was significantly smaller for wives in marriages that dissolved.

Conclusion: Implications of Growth Curve Analysis

The analyses reported in this chapter are not meant to be the definitive word on depressive symptoms and marital satisfaction over time. The size of the sample is smaller than ideal, and, as a result, some of the effects are of marginal significance. However, the pattern of results and the overall analytic strategy suggest several important aspects of the dynamics between these two variables that may have been overlooked in previous research. This concluding section describes three broader implications of GCA for the study of depression in the context of marriage.

Nature of the Dependent Variable

What most distinguishes GCA from conventional approaches to longitudinal data analysis is the nature of the dependent variable. In many current approaches, the nature of the dependent variable is left slightly vague. For example, in a multiple regression analysis the dependent variable is regressed change (i.e., the level of a variable at Time 2 controlling for the initial level of the variable at Time 1). Is this what researchers interested in depressive symptoms and marital satisfaction are trying to explain? That is not the impression one gets from reading the chapters in this book. Rather, current theories discuss the course of depressive symptoms, the trajectory of marital satisfaction, and the relationships between changes in these variables within an individual over time. The two-stage approach of GCA requires that researchers specify exactly these constructs of greatest interest and then address them directly as the dependent variables in longitudinal data analyses.

As this chapter describes, treating individual change as the dependent variable suggests questions and phenomena that have been overlooked in previous research. For example, the causes, consequences, and recommended treatment for depression in married individuals may vary depending on the size of the within-subject correlation between depressive symptoms and marital satisfaction across time. In research that has relied on two-wave designs, these dynamic relationships have been inaccessible. With GCA, indi-

Table 3.5—*Associations Between Depressive Symptoms and Marital Satisfaction in Couples Who Remained Intact and Couples Who Dissolved*

	BDI ->satisfaction				satisfaction ->BDI			
Instrument	Intact (n = 38)	Dissolved (n = 16)	t	Effect size	Intact (n = 38)	Dissolved (n = 16)	t	Effect size
				Husbands				
MAT	-.70	-1.56	-1.8*	-.24	-.06	-.06	-.18	-.02
QMI	-.28	-.48	-1.4+	-.19	-.21	-.22	-.08	-.01
KMSS	-.14	-.23	-1.3+	-.18	-.58	-.53	.26	.04
SMD	-.84	-1.08	-.82	-.11	-.17	-.11	1.5	.20
	Aggregate effect size =			-.18*				= .05
				Wives				
MAT	-.85	-1.43	-1.7**	-.23	-.11	-.08	1.4	.19
QMI	-.32	-.46	-1.2*	-.16	-.35	-.22	1.8**	.24
KMSS	-.14	-.20	-1.1	-.15	-.67	-.46	1.4	.19
SMD	-.92	-1.17	-1.0	-.14	-.17	-.10	2.3**	.30
	Aggregate effect size =			-.17*				= .23**

Note. For the BDI ->satisfaction t tests, df = 52. For the satisfaction ->BDI t-tests, df = 54. MAT = Marital Adjustment Test (Locke & Wallace, 1959); QMI = Quality Marriage Index (Norton, 1983); KMSS = Kansas Marital Satisfaction Survey (Schumm et al., 1986); SMD = Semantic Differential (Osgood, Suci, & Tannenbaum, 1957); BDI = Beck Depression Inventory (Beck, Steer, & Garbin, 1988).

*p < .10, one-tailed; **p < .05, one-tailed.

vidual change is the dependent variable, to be specified clearly, described precisely, and then explained (possibly) with other variables.

The specific analyses described in this chapter suggest that more research needs to be done to refine the dependent variable further. For example, although the models specified in this chapter provided adequate descriptions of how depressive symptoms and marital satisfaction changed over time, they were limited by the relatively small number of assessments of each variable. More frequent assessments may allow the specification of more sophisticated models. Furthermore, it may be possible that different models may describe the same variables for different subgroups of a population. Whereas a linear model was not necessary to describe changes in depressive symptoms in this sample, it may have been a better description of change for some individuals. Larger samples would allow researchers to explore hypotheses about the different models that may best describe change for different groups. Continued progress in understanding the etiology and treatment of depression in marriage is likely to depend on a clear focus on individual change as the dependent variable of central interest.

Direction in Cases of Bidirectional Causality

Previous research has described the causal relationships between depressive symptoms as bidirectional, based on the finding that initial levels of depressive symptoms have been shown to predict later levels of marital satisfaction and initial levels of marital satisfaction have been shown to predict later levels of depressive symptoms. Because these findings were all the products of between-subjects analyses, these descriptions have assumed that the two directions of causality have similar implications.

By estimating within-subject associations between these two variables with GCA, the analyses described in this chapter could examine whether each direction of the effect had different correlates and consequences. Although the discussion in this chapter generally resisted causal language, the analytic strategy described suggests within-subject causality in much the same way that cross-lagged correlations suggest between-subjects causality. To the extent that changes in BDI scores are associated with changes in marital satisfaction, controlling for the overall trajectory of marital satisfaction, this association may be thought to capture the degree to which fluctuating depressive symptoms lead to changes in marital satisfaction. To the extent that changes in marital satisfaction are associated with changes in depressive symptoms, controlling for individual mean levels of depressive symptoms, this association may be thought to capture the degree to which fluctuating marital satisfaction leads to changes in depressive symptoms.

Considered this way, it is noteworthy that the correlates and consequences of the within-subject associations differed depending on gender and on the direction of the effect. The pattern of results for neuroticism, for example, suggests that the direction of causal effects may be different for husbands and wives. Among those husbands at greater risk for elevated symptoms of depression (i.e., those higher in neuroticism), there is evidence that depressive symptoms have a significantly weaker effect on the development of marital satisfaction. At the same time, husbands' neuroticism does not appear to moderate the effect of marital satisfaction on changes in depressive symptoms. Conversely, for wives who are higher in neuroticism, there is evidence of an increased effect of marital satisfaction on changes in depressive symptoms. However, wives' neuroticism does not appear to moderate the effect of depressive symptoms on change in marital satisfaction.

The analyses in this chapter do little to explain such effects, but they do provide additional support for efforts to investigate the role of personality in the longitudinal association between marital satisfaction and depression (see Davila, chapter 4). In addition, these analyses suggest the value of examining gender differences in the areas of self that are most salient and vulnerable among those high in neuroticism and lend support to the proposal that depressive symptoms may follow more strongly from marital distress for neurotic women than for neurotic men.

The direction of causality proved equally important when the implications of these effects on marital dissolution were examined. Among couples who eventually dissolved, there was evidence that depressive symptoms were more likely to lead to declines in marital satisfaction. However, for the wives in these couples, marital satisfaction appeared to be significantly less likely to lead to increases in depressive symptoms. Again, the current analyses do not suggest an explanation for this pattern of results, but they do emphasize the value of examining marital quality and marital dissolution as independent outcomes in marital research. Furthermore, they support the idea that marital dissolution may result from the interaction between depressive symptoms and marital satisfaction more than from either variable independently.

Thus, the direction of the effect appears to matter in the case of bidirectional causality. The challenge for future research is to develop models of depression and marital satisfaction that account for the possibility of differential effects in each direction.

Old Data Sets, New Analyses

One way to advance an understanding of the marital context of depression is to collect new data. It is hoped that the growing availability of useful techniques for analyzing multiwave data will suggest that the added expense of collecting such data is worthwhile. However, researchers interested in applying these techniques need not wait for new data to be collected. Several existing data sets contain multiple assessments of depression and marital satisfaction. An emphasis on individual change over time highlights new questions that can be pursued using these data sets and offers a way to address those questions. One of the more exciting implications of this approach is that there may exist, overlooked within old data sets, important new findings waiting to be uncovered.

References

Beach, S. R. H., & Fincham, F. D. (1994). Toward an integrated model of negative affectivity in marriage. In S. M. Johnson & L. S. Greenberg (Eds.), *The heart of the matter: Perspectives on emotion in marital therapy* (pp. 227–255). New York: Brunner/Mazel.

Beach, S. R. H., & O'Leary, K. D. (1993a). Dysphoria and marital discord: Are dysphoric individuals at risk for marital maladjustment? *Journal of Marital and Family Therapy, 19,* 355–368.

Beach, S. R. H., & O'Leary, K. D. (1993b). Marital discord and dysphoria: For whom does the marital relationship predict depressive symptomatology? *Journal of Social and Personal Relationships, 10,* 405–420.

Beach, S. R. H., Sandeen, E. E., & O'Leary, K. D. (1990). *Depression in marriage.* New York: Guilford Press.

Beck, A. T., & Beamesderfer, A. (1974). Assessment of depression: The Depression Inventory. In P. Pinchot (Ed.), *Modern problems in pharmacopsychiatry* (pp. 151–169). Basel, Switzerland: Karger.

Beck, A. T., Steer, R. A., & Garbin, M. G. (1988). Psychometric properties of the Beck Depression Inventory: Twenty-five years of evaluation. *Clinical Psychology Review, 8,* 77–100.

Bryk, A. S., & Raudenbush, S. W. (1992). *Hierarchical linear models: Applications and data analysis methods.* Newbury Park, CA: Sage.

Bryk, A. S., Raudenbush, S. W., & Congdon, R. T. (1994). *HLM: Hierarchical linear modelling with the HLM/2L and HLM/3L programs.* Chicago: Scientific Software International.

Burns, D. D., Sayers, S. L., & Moras, K. (1994). Intimate relationships and depression: Is there a causal connection? *Journal of Consulting and Clinical Psychology, 62,* 1033–1043.

Eysenck, H. J., & Eysenck, S. B. G. (1978). *Manual for the Eysenck Personality Questionnaire.* Kent, England: Hodder & Stoughton.

Fincham, F. D., Beach, S. R. H., Harold, G. T., & Osborne, L. N. (1997). Marital satisfaction and depression: Different causal relationships for men and women? *Psychological Science, 8,* 351–357.

Fincham, F. D., & Bradbury, T. N. (1987). The assessment of marital quality: A reevaluation. *Journal of Marriage and the Family, 49,* 797–809.

Gotlib, I. H., Lewinsohn, P. M., & Seeley, J. R. (1998). Consequences of depression during adolescence: Marital status and marital functioning in early adulthood. *Journal of Abnormal Psychology, 107,* 686–690.

Huston, T. L., McHale, S. M., & Crouter, A. C. (1986). When the honeymoon's over: Changes in the marriage relationship over the first year. In R. Gilmore & S. Duck (Eds.), *The emerging field of personal relationships* (pp. 109–132). Hillsdale, NJ: Erlbaum.

Jacobson, N. S., Dobson, K., Fruzzetti, A. E., Schmaling, K. B., & Salusky, S. (1991). Marital therapy as a treatment for depression. *Journal of Consulting and Clinical Psychology, 59,* 547–557.

Johnson, D. R., Amoloza, T. O., & Booth, A. (1992). Stability and developmental change in marital quality: A three-wave panel analysis. *Journal of Marriage and the Family, 54,* 582–594.

Karney, B. R., & Bradbury, T. N. (1995a). Assessing longitudinal change in marriage: An introduction to the analysis of growth curves. *Journal of Marriage and the Family, 57,* 1091–1108.

Karney, B. R., & Bradbury, T. N. (1995b). The longitudinal course of marital quality and stability: A review of theory, method, and research. *Psychological Bulletin, 118,* 3–34.

Karney, B. R., & Bradbury, T. N. (1997). Neuroticism, marital interaction, and the trajectory of marital satisfaction. *Journal of Personality and Social Psychology, 72,* 1075–1092.

Karney, B. R., & Bradbury, T. N. (2000). Attributions in marriage: State or trait? A growth curve analysis. *Journal of Personality and Social Psychology, 78,* 295–309.

Locke, H. J., & Wallace, K. M. (1959). Short marital adjustment prediction tests: Their reliability and validity. *Marriage and Family Living, 21,* 251–255.

Norton, R. (1983). Measuring marital quality: A critical look at the dependent variable. *Journal of Marriage and the Family, 45,* 141–151.

Osgood, C. E., Suci, G. J., & Tannenbaum, P. H. (1957). *The measurement of meaning.* Urbana: University of Illinois Press.

Raudenbush, S. W., Brennan, R. T., & Barnett, R. C. (1995). A multivariate hierarchical model for studying psychological change within married couples. *Journal of Family Psychology, 9,* 161–174.

Rogosa, D. (1980). A critique of cross-lagged correlation. *Psychological Bulletin, 88,* 245–258.

Rogosa, D., Brant, D., & Zimowski, M. (1982). A growth curve approach to the measurement of change. *Psychological Bulletin, 92,* 726–748.

Schaefer, E. S., & Burnett, C. K. (1987). Stability and predictability of quality of women's marital relationships and demoralization. *Journal of Personality and Social Psychology, 53,* 1129–1136.

Schumm, W. R., Paff-Bergen, L. A., Hatch, R. C., Obiorah, F. C., Copeland, J. M., Meens, L. D., & Bugaighis, M. A. (1986). Concurrent and discriminant validity of the Kansas Marital Satisfaction Scale. *Journal of Marriage and the Family, 48,* 381–387.

Tate, R. L., & Hokanson, J. E. (1993). Analyzing individual status and change with hierarchical linear models: Illustration with depression in college students. *Journal of Personality, 61,* 181–206.

Thompson, J. M. (1995). Silencing the self: Depressive symptomatology and close relationships. *Psychology of Women Quarterly, 19,* 337–353.

Vaillant, C. O., & Vaillant, G. E. (1993). Is the U-curve of marital satisfaction an illusion? A 40–year study of marriage. *Journal of Marriage and the Family, 55,* 230–239.

Watson, D., & Clark, L. A. (1984). Negative affectivity: The disposition to experience aversive emotional states. *Psychological Bulletin, 96,* 465–490.

Willett, J. B. (1988). Questions and answers in the measurement of change. In E. Z. Rothkopf (Ed.), *Review of research in education* (Vol. 15, pp. 345–422). Washington, DC: American Educational Research Association.

PART II

EXPANDING MODELS FOR RESEARCH AND TREATMENT: THEORETICAL CONSIDERATIONS

4

Paths to Unhappiness: The Overlapping Courses of Depression and Romantic Dysfunction

Joanne Davila

Researchers have been examining associations between depression and romantic dysfunction, and specifically marital dysfunction, for more than two decades, resulting in a considerable body of literature. One goal of this book was to consider the contributions and limitations of this literature and to propose directions for future research in this area. Therefore, this chapter asks two questions: What have researchers learned over the years, and where should researchers go now?

What researchers have learned can be described broadly as follows: (a) Negative marital events such as conflicts, chronically stressful and unsupportive circumstances, and divorce can lead to dysphoria and depression; (b) dysphoria and depression can lead to negative marital events such as dissatisfaction and chronically stressful circumstances; and (c) dysphoric and depressed spouses and their partners behave in a negative fashion toward one another (for more detail see Whisman, chapter 1). Until relatively recently, however, these three broad categories of findings were studied and considered separately. The point of this chapter, and one answer to where researchers should go now, is that progress in our understanding of the associations between depression and marital functioning would benefit from considering these three findings together. That is, the associations between depression and marital functioning may be best understood if depression and marital functioning are conceived of as following relatively parallel courses and exerting reciprocal influences on one another through both intrapersonal experiences and interpersonal interactions. Moreover, these reciprocal influences will be best understood by focusing on the development of depression and early romantic dysfunction in addition to focusing on depression in the context of existing marriages. This chapter presents a brief discussion of each of the three broad categories of findings followed by an elaboration of the reciprocal and developmental perspectives.

Marital Dysfunction As a Precursor to Depression

Numerous studies have shown that marital dysfunction puts individuals at risk for depression. Brown and Harris (1978) were among the first to suggest that the lack of a confiding, intimate relationship made individuals vulnerable to depression. Subsequent research has indicated that low levels of marital satisfaction are associated with increasing levels of dysphoria (e.g., Beach & O'Leary, 1993b), that the absence of a supportive marital relationship increases vulnerability to depression (e.g., Jacobson, Fruzzetti, Dobson, Whisman, & Hops, 1993; Monroe, Bromet, Connell, & Steiner, 1986), and that severe marital events increase the chances that spouses who have never been depressed before will become so (Christian-Herman, O'Leary, & Avery-Leaf, in press). Even research examining the relative contributions of genetics and life stressors has indicated that serious marital problems and divorce each independently increase the risk of experiencing depression more than 10-fold, controlling for genetic factors (Kendler et al., 1995). It is clear that marital dysfunction is a precursor of depression (although not necessarily a precursor to first onset of depression; see Coyne and Benazon, chapter 2).

Depression As a Precursor to Marital Dysfunction

There has been much less research examining the effects of depression on marital dysfunction than there is research examining the effects of marital dysfunction on depression. However, that depression might affect marital dysfunction is not a new idea. It has its roots in the early work on depression and social functioning (e.g., Coyne, 1976; Lewinsohn, 1974). One of the most influential hypotheses was elaborated by Coyne (1976), who suggested that depressed individuals behave in ways that lead others to reject them. If this is the case, then it follows that for married depressed individuals, marital dysfunction might ensue. Indeed, longitudinal research has indicated that depressive symptoms lead to lower levels of marital satisfaction (e.g., Beach & O'Leary,1993a; Davila, Bradbury, Cohan, & Tochluk, 1997; Fincham, Beach, Harold, & Osborne, 1997). These studies, however, typically have been conducted on nonclinical samples. Cross-sectional studies of both clinical and nonclinical samples have consistently indicated that depression is associated with low levels of marital satisfaction (e.g., Billings, Cronkite, & Moos, 1983; O'Leary, Christian, & Mendell, 1994), and longitudinal studies of clinical samples have shown that depression is associated with high levels of subsequent interpersonal stress (e.g., Hammen, 1991b). Hence, although further research is needed, evidence to date has suggested that dysphoria and depression may be precursors to marital dysfunction.

Negative Marital Behavior Associated With Depression

Research has indicated that spouses who are dysphoric or depressed think negatively about and behave negatively toward their partners. For example, dysphoric spouses expect less support from their partners and show diminished capacity to provide support to and receive support from their partners (e.g., Cutrona & Suhr, 1994; Davila et al., 1997). Dysphoric and depressed spouses make negative marital attributions and exhibit high levels of conflict, tension, negativity, ambivalence, hostility, and criticism when attempting to resolve problems with their partners (e.g., Gotlib & Whiffen, 1989; see Gotlib & Beach, 1995, for a review). Depressed spouses also display depressive behaviors such as depressed affect, self-denigration, and physical and psychological complaints when interacting with their partners (e.g., Biglan et al., 1985).

Research also has indicated that partners of dysphoric or depressed spouses think negatively about and behave negatively toward their partners. For example, partners tend to disagree with their depressed spouses and evaluate them negatively (e.g., Hautzinger, Linden, & Hoffman, 1982). Partners also tend to feel sad, angry, and hostile after interacting with their depressed spouses (e.g., Kahn, Coyne, & Margolin, 1985). Overall, the interactions between depressed spouses and their partners are consistently characterized by negative communication, poor problem solving, and poor affect regulation (e.g., Gotlib & Whiffen, 1989; McCabe & Gotlib, 1993; see Gotlib & Beach, 1995, for a review).

Conceptualizing Depression and Marital Dysfunction As Reciprocal Processes

The brief review above should make it clear that depression and marital dysfunction are closely linked. It is now time to integrate the three broad categories of findings so that the complexities of their link can be understood. It is time to abandon the idea of determining whether marital dysfunction is a better predictor of depression or vice versa and to focus instead on the ongoing association of the two over time and on the mechanisms of this association (see also Coyne and Benazon, chapter 2; Karney, chapter 3).[1] A number of researchers have moved in this direction (e.g., Gotlib & Beach, 1995; Hops, Perry, & Davis, 1997), and it is a goal of this chapter to encourage more to follow.

Why Consider Depression and Marital Dysfunction As Reciprocal Processes? What Are the Benefits?

One straightforward reason is because such a perspective captures the ongoing circumstances of individuals' lives. No one would argue that depression does not affect the lives of the individuals experiencing it. So why, for example, should researchers be satisfied to know that marital dysfunction increases vulnerability to depression? Would it not be equally as important to understand the aftermath of depression? Furthermore, numerous perspectives have suggested that it is incomplete to think of the relation between depression and interpersonal dysfunction as unidirectional. For example, interpersonal perspectives on depression (e.g., Coyne, 1976; Gotlib & Hammen, 1992) have suggested that depression and interpersonal dysfunction reciprocally influence one another, as do transactional perspectives that espouse the idea that as individuals move through life they both construct their lives and respond to existing circumstances (e.g., Cicchetti, Rogosch, & Toth, 1994). Accordingly, such perspectives provide a natural point of connection between clinical and developmental theories of depression (see also Cummings, DeArth-Pendley, Schudlich, and Smith, chapter 5).

Another reason to examine the overlapping courses of depression and interpersonal dysfunction, particularly in the case of depression and marital dysfunction, is because they almost always involve the life of another individual (or other individuals). In the case of marriage, the partner of the depressed spouse affects and is affected by the course of the spouse's depression and can play an instrumental role in the treatment for both the depression and the associated marital dysfunction (see Gotlib & Beach, 1995). Therefore, a better understanding of the course of depression and marital dysfunction could further both prevention and treatment efforts.

How Should the Reciprocal Association Between Depression and Marital Dysfunction Be Characterized?

Although there are likely to be a number of ways to conceptualize reciprocal associations between depression and marital dysfunction, the conceptualization presented in this chapter is built around the model of stress generation in unipolar depression (Hammen, 1991b). Hammen described stress generation as the process by which depressed individuals contribute to the occurrence of stress in their lives and thereby contribute to their experience of depression. That is, depressed individuals, in part, cause their own stressful experiences, which then lead to further depression. Research has supported this proposition and further indicated that depressed individuals are especially likely to create interpersonal stress, such as interpersonal conflicts with others, which then leads to increases in depression (e.g.,

---

[1]It is important to note that gender differences in these processes may still need to be explored as the bulk of this work has examined depressed women.

Adrian & Hammen, 1993; Davila, Hammen, Burge, Paley, & Daley, 1995; Hammen, 1991b; Pothoff, Holahan, & Joiner, 1995).[2]

Applying this model to marriage, depressed spouses should contribute to stressful marital circumstances that should then maintain or lead to increases in the depressed spouses' depression. Thus, in this model, depression is both a cause and a consequence of marital dysfunction. Hence, this model integrates the three broad findings about depression and marital dysfunction in a straightforward manner: Depression, because it is characterized by negative marital behaviors and negative cognition, results in stressful marital circumstances, which then maintain or increase vulnerability to further depression.

An initial test of the marital stress generation model supported its hypotheses for dysphoric wives (Davila et al., 1997). My colleagues and I proposed that social support would be one mechanism of marital stress generation. That is, depressed spouses would have negative cognitions about marital social support and would lack the capacity to seek and provide marital social support, thereby resulting in increased levels of marital stress and increased levels of depressive symptoms. Why focus on social support? Because negative social support perceptions and behaviors are related to both negative marital outcomes (e.g., Pasch & Bradbury, 1998) and increased levels of depressive symptoms (e.g., Jacobson et al., 1993; Monroe et al., 1986). Social support may thus be one link between the overlapping courses of depression and marital dysfunction.

To test these hypotheses, we (Davila et al., 1997) followed 154 newlywed couples over the first year of marriage. The couples were recruited from marriage licenses filed in Los Angeles County, California. The couples participated in an initial laboratory session and a follow-up session 1 year later. At the initial session, their levels of depressive symptoms, their levels of ongoing marital stress (using an objectively coded interview), their social support behaviors when interacting with their partners (using an objectively coded marital interaction), and their expectations of support from their partners immediately preceding the support interaction were assessed. Depressive symptoms and marital stress were reassessed 1 year later.

The data were analyzed using structural equation modeling, and husbands' and wives' models were analyzed separately. Although a marital stress generation process was not evident for husbands, wives' data confirmed our predictions. Among wives, initial depressive symptoms were associated with expecting husbands to be negative and critical during the social support discussion and with behaving in a negative manner when being on both the receiving end and the providing end during the support discussion. That is, dysphoric wives expected their husbands to be negative and critical and subsequently were themselves negative and critical when attempting to both receive support from and provide support to their husbands.[3] Moreover, this behavior was associated with increases in marital stress over the 1-year period, and this stress was associated with increases in subsequent depressive

---

[2]Although the stress generation model originally was designed to explain a process characteristic of unipolar depression, it recently has been shown to occur in individuals with only mild or moderate levels of depressive symptoms (e.g., Davila, Hammen, Burge, Paley, & Daley, 1995; Pothoff, Holahan, & Joiner, 1995). Additionally, subclinical levels of depression have been shown to lead to impairment in functioning (e.g., Wells et al., 1989), particularly social role impairment (e.g., not getting along well with others, difficulty negotiating disagreements; Beach, Martin, Blum, & Roman, 1993). Hence, a stress generation process appears to occur at various levels of dysphoria and depression.

[3]To be more precise, according to the Social Support Interaction Coding System (Bradbury & Pasch, 1992), which was used in this study, negative social support behavior includes the following types of behavior: criticism, rejection, blaming, minimization, exaggeration, inattention, disengagement, demanding, accusing, whining, and complaining.

symptoms. Hence, for wives, depressive symptoms were manifested in negative thoughts and behaviors that increased the stress in their marriages and led to further depressive symptoms.

These results begin to help researchers understand, at least for wives, how depression and marital dysfunction follow overlapping courses. To the extent that depression impairs the ability to both give and receive support, the marriage will suffer, and to the extent that the marriage suffers, depression increases, thus resulting in a potentially serious vicious cycle. This vicious cycle is similar to that proposed by Gotlib and Beach (1995) in their marital and family discord model of depression and earlier by Beach, Sandeen, and O'Leary (1990) in their marital discord model of depression. These models suggest that marital and family discord, which are manifested in decreases in various types of adaptive behaviors and increases in negative behaviors, leads to subsequent depression, which is then manifested in further maladaptive types of interpersonal behaviors and, ultimately, further marital and family discord. These models provide important information about the ongoing link between depression and marital discord that alert researchers to the ways in which spouses might get trapped in a vicious cycle of depression and marital dysfunction.

Admittedly, however, this vicious cycle is unlikely to result in a linear progression toward increasing depressive symptoms over time. One clear indicator of this is that not all couples in which one spouse is depressed are discordant. There are likely to be some individuals for whom depression and marital dysfunction are more strongly linked than others (see also Beach & Fincham, 1994; Whisman, chapter 1; Katz, chapter 6). This leads to the next issue to be addressed: Who is most likely to fall into this vicious cycle of depression and marital dysfunction? What makes the courses of depression and marital dysfunction more or less overlapping? No doubt there are a number of factors involved. This chapter focuses on two factors—those related to the personality and interpersonal styles of the depressed individual and those related to the developmental history of the depressed individual.

The Role of Personality and Interpersonal Factors in the Association Between Depression and Relationship Dysfunction

Various types of chronic, maladaptive interpersonal styles are associated with depression. Personality disorders, which are defined largely in terms of interpersonal dysfunction, are highly comorbid with depression. Recent estimates indicate that 30% to 70% of individuals with depression have a comorbid personality disorder (see Farmer & Nelson-Gray, 1990). In addition to diagnosable personality disorders, various personality styles such as sociotropy and autonomy are related to depression and associated with interpersonal dysfunction (see Nietzel & Harris, 1990, for a review). Similarly, an insecure attachment style, that is characterized by maladaptive interpersonal relating, is related to depression (e.g., Carnelley, Pietromonaco, & Jaffe, 1994; Cole-Detke & Kobak, 1996; Rosenstein & Horowitz, 1996; Toth & Cicchetti, 1996). All of these associations provide an indication of the types of dysfunctional interpersonal patterns that depressed individuals may engage in. These patterns provide information about the factors that keep individuals vulnerable to depression in the context of interpersonal relationships.

A growing body of research has indicated that personality disorders, typically measured as Axis II symptoms, are associated with numerous risk factors and negative outcomes for depressed individuals. For example, personality disorders are associated with an earlier age at onset of depression (e.g., Fava et al., 1996); poorer social support and more severe stressors (e.g., Pfohl, Stangl, & Zimmerman, 1984); poorer social adjustment (e.g., Shea et al., 1990); poorer response to treatment, including pharmacotherapy; and a higher and faster relapse rate (e.g., Ilardi, Craighead, & Evans, 1997; Shea, Widiger, & Klein, 1992). To illustrate this last point, Ilardi et al. (1997) examined the extent to which Axis II symptoms predicted depression relapse, controlling for possible confounding variables, including dysfunctional attitudes, depressive attributional style, number of previous depressive episodes, presence of dysthymia, depression severity, and residual depressive symptoms. Axis II pathology was a significant predictor of relapse. Analyses indicated that patients without a personality disorder had an expected period of remission approximately 7.4 times longer than patients with comorbid personality disorder. The greatest risk for relapse occurred within the first 6 months postrecovery and was among patients with Cluster B (borderline, histrionic, narcissistic, and antisocial) and Cluster C (avoidant, dependent, and obsessive–compulsive) personality pathology. Thus, depressed individuals with comorbid personality pathology are at risk for worse outcomes than depressed individuals without comorbid personality pathology.

What is it about personality disorders that makes this the case? Although the mechanisms of the relation between personality pathology and depression have received little empirical attention, researchers have suggested that the chronic, rigid nature of the personality pathology furthers exposure to stressful life circumstances, which then increases risk for depression (e.g., Daley, Hammen, Davila, & Burge, 1998; Johnson, Hyler, Skodol, Bornstein, & Sherman, 1995; Klein, Wonderlich, & Shea, 1993). Hence, personality pathology may be associated with a stress generation process. Indeed, research has begun to support this hypothesis.

Daley et al. (1998) hypothesized that the relationship between personality pathology and onset of depression follows a stress generation process. They predicted that people with high levels of personality pathology would generate increased interpersonal stress in their lives and thereby experience increased depression. Daley et al. examined this hypothesis in a 2-year longitudinal study of late adolescent women during the transition to adulthood using interview measures of depression and life stress and a self-report measure of Axis II pathology (the Personality Diagnostic Questionnaire; Hyler & Rieder, 1987). Path analyses indicated that, controlling for initial levels of depressive symptoms and stress, Cluster A and Cluster B symptoms predicted subsequent interpersonal stress, which then predicted subsequent depressive symptoms.

This work clearly supports the hypothesis that personality pathology is associated with subsequent interpersonal stress and depression, but it does not specifically address romantic or marital stress. My colleagues and I have addressed this issue, in part, by examining whether personality pathology among young people is associated with a romantic stress generation process and by examining specific interpersonal patterns associated with early manifestations of romantic stress (Davila, Cobb, & Lindberg, 2000). We are currently following 94 young men and women as they make the transition to college. To examine how these young people developed relationships over time, the sample was selected to include a large proportion of participants who were not in a romantic relationship when they began the study at the beginning of freshman year. At the initial session, interview measures of depression, Axis II personality pathology, and overall quality of romantic experiences to date were collected. At the 6-month follow-up, interview measures of depression and romantic stress were collected. Path analyses indicated that, controlling for initial depression and prior romantic experience quality, Axis II pathology was associated with subsequent romantic stress, which was in turn associated with increased depressive symptoms. In particular, symptoms of dependent personality disorder and obsessive–compulsive personality disorder uniquely predicted romantic stress and depressive symptoms.

These findings suggest that there are two interpersonal styles that may be most related to romantic stress generation processes. One interpersonal style, indicative of dependent symptoms, reflects submissive, dependent behaviors; a reliance on the views of others for self-esteem; and fears of abandonment. The second, indicative of an obsessive–compulsive style, reflects perfectionism, rigidity, and distrust in the abilities of others. These findings are remarkably similar to other personality-based conceptions of depression that focus on sociotropy and autonomy (Beck, 1983) or dependent and self-critical interpersonal styles (Blatt, Quinlan, Chevron, McDonald, & Zuroff, 1982). The sociotropic/dependent styles are very consistent with dependent personality disorder, and the autonomous/self-critical styles are consistent with obsessive–compulsive personality disorder. These findings further support the notion that pervasive traits of the dependent and self-critical nature maintain individuals' risk for depression, and they do so, at least in part, because they increase romantic stress.

The above results clearly illustrate that (a) a romantic stress generation process is evident even relatively early in individuals' romantic "careers," and (b) personality pathology functions as a mechanism of this process. As an additional test of the mechanisms of romantic stress generation, and to further clarify the interpersonal patterns most associated with stress generation, my colleagues and I (Davila, Cobb, Lindberg, Polsky, & Baliotis, 1999) used a procedure that assesses interpersonal patterns over time— Bartholomew's Family and Peer Attachment Interview (FPAI; Bartholomew, 1998). The FPAI, which is similar in some ways to the Adult Attachment Interview (Main & Goldwyn, 1991) and the Couple Attachment Interview (Silver & Cohn, 1992), assesses individuals' representations of their relationship experiences (family, friends, and romantic), and interviewers rate individuals' adult attachment patterns based on these representations. However, relationship experiences are probed to elicit specific behavioral indicators of relationship events and circumstances so that ratings are based on both objective (relatively speaking) and subjective material. As such, the ratings should map onto specific behavioral patterns. Hence, we examined whether any of these behavioral patterns acted as mechanisms of stress generation.

The FPAI assesses four attachment patterns based on Bartholomew's four-category model of attachment (Bartholomew, 1990; Bartholomew & Horowitz, 1991). A secure pattern is characterized by the capacity to maintain a close relationship without losing autonomy, the valuing of intimate relationships, a positive sense of self, and coherence and insight about relationships. A dismissing pattern is characterized by the downplaying of close relationships, restricted emotionality, compulsive self-reliance, a positive (possibly excessively so) sense of self, and poor insight into and defensiveness about relationships. A preoccupied pattern is characterized by overinvolvement in close relationships, a strong desire for closeness, a dependence on other peoples' acceptance for a sense of self-worth, a tendency to idealize people, exaggerated emotionality, and low insight into relationships. Finally, a fearful pattern is characterized by avoidance of close relationships because of a fear of rejection, low self-worth, distrust of others, interpersonal sensitivity, and concealment of emotions.

We focused on the three insecure styles (dismissing, preoccupied, and fearful), as those would provide the most specific information about the maladaptive interpersonal styles operating in a stress generation process. Ratings on the preoccupied and fearful styles were correlated at the zero-order level with depressive symptoms, romantic stress, and Axis II symptoms, rendering them appropriate for further analyses. Dismissing attachment was not correlated with depressive symptoms or stress. Path analyses controlling for initial levels of depressive symptoms, romantic quality, and overall Axis II symptoms indicated a significant association between the preoccupied interpersonal pattern and subsequent romantic stress. Axis II symptoms were, as before, also a significant predictor. These results suggest that, in addition to interpersonal styles characteristic of dependent and obsessive–compulsive personality disorders, an interpersonal style characterized by a strong need for attention and relationships, high levels of emotional and interpersonal dependence, sensitivity to rejection, and fear of abandonment results in subsequent romantic stress and depression.

The findings regarding the preoccupied attachment pattern and dependent personality disorder symptoms are consistent with research indicating that excessive reassurance seeking is associated with a stress generation process among young people (e.g., Pothoff et al., 1995). Excessive reassurance seeking, that is, the tendency to desire and ask for continued reassurance about personal worth (e.g., Joiner, Alfano, & Metalsky, 1992), is a correlate of depression and leads to various types of interpersonal stress and rejection. Recent theory and research has suggested that excessive reassurance seeking may be a mechanism in the stress generation process (e.g., Pothoff et al., 1995; Joiner, chapter 7). That is, one reason that depressed individuals generate interpersonal stress is that they seek excessive reassurance from others. Because this behavior never results in felt reassurance by depressed individuals, their continued attempts cause interpersonal tension and conflict, resulting in interpersonal stress. The findings of this study support this hypothesis in that both dependent personality disorder symptoms and a preoccupied attachment pattern are characterized by behaviors consistent with excessive reassurance seeking (e.g., emotional dependence on others, reliance on others for a sense of self). We are currently exploring associations between reassurance seeking, personality disorders, and attachment patterns (Davila, 2000).

In summary, personality and interpersonal factors are clearly implicated in the association between depression and romantic dysfunction. Such factors likely work to keep individuals vulnerable to depression in the context of interpersonal relationships. In particular, a needy/dependent style characteristic of a preoccupied attachment style and symptoms of dependent personality disorder and a rigid, perfectionistic style characteristic of symptoms of obsessive–compulsive personality disorder may be most responsible for the generation of romantic stress and vulnerability to depression. Whether this is also the case in marriage remains to be studied.

Development of Depression and Romantic Dysfunction

The second set of factors relevant to the extent to which the courses of depression and romantic dysfunction, particularly marital dysfunction, overlap are factors related to the developmental history of the individual. In attempting to understand the relation between depression and marital dysfunction, researchers have done the obvious, appropriate thing. They have studied married couples. However, to more fully understand the complex links between depression and marital dysfunction, researchers need to understand not only what goes on in a marriage, but also what went on in the lives of depressed individuals before they got to the marriage. Specifically, the early course of their depression and the extent to which it was related to their early romantic history needs to be understood. The obvious hypothesis is that for some individuals the link between depression and romantic dysfunction begins early and continues throughout their lives. These are likely to be the individuals who are most at risk for both depression and marital dysfunction and who may have the most difficulty breaking the link between the two.

Associations Between Interpersonal Dysfunction and Depression
in Childhood and Adolescence

A large, diverse body of research has suggested that for many individuals depression starts early. Recent prevalence rates of childhood depression are approximately 2% (e.g., Anderson, Williams, McGee, & Silva, 1987; Costello et al., 1988). The rates of adolescent depression are on the rise and match those of adults (i.e., approximately 4% to 8%; e.g., Kashani et al., 1987; Lewinsohn, Hops, Roberts, Seeley, & Andrews, 1993). Given that previous episodes of depression greatly increase an individual's risk for later episodes (e.g., Belsher & Costello, 1988; Lewinsohn, Zeiss, & Duncan, 1989), individuals with childhood or adolescent depression are at great risk for a lifetime of depression. Even if depression reaches only subclinical levels, it will still exert a significant negative effect on psychosocial functioning (e.g., Wells et al., 1989).

Early-onset depression (i.e., depression in childhood and adolescence) has been consistently linked to interpersonal difficulties (e.g., Puig-Antich et al., 1985, 1993). Depression in childhood and adolescence is associated with both family and peer dysfunction. For example, depressed children and adolescents tend to come from families whose members have high levels of psychopathology (e.g., Mitchell, McCauley, Burke, Calderon, & Schloredt, 1989; Puig-Antich et al., 1989) and in which there are high levels of various types of family conflict and poor cohesion (e.g., Kashani, Allan, Dahlmeier, Rezvani, & Reid, 1995; McKeown et al., 1997; see Kaslow, Deering, & Ash, 1996, for a review). Depressed children and adolescents tend to exhibit insecure attachments to their parents (e.g., Armsden, McCauley, Greenberg, Burke, & Mitchell, 1990; Rosenstein & Horowitz, 1996; Shaw, Keenan, Vondra, Delliquadri, & Giovanelli, 1997) and view their families negatively (e.g., Rudolph, Hammen, & Burge, 1997; Stark, Humphrey, Crook, & Lewis, 1990). When depressed children and adolescents interact with their parents, their interactions are characterized by a host of potentially problematic behaviors. Their interactions tend to be typified by low levels of friendliness and involvement (e.g., Lasko et al., 1997). Parents' behaviors may be dominant and controlling (e.g., Amanat & Butler, 1984), reinforcing of depressive behavior (e.g., Sheeber, Hops, Andrews, Alpert, & Davis, 1998), or inappropriate with regard to levels of emotional involvement (e.g., Asarnow, Ben-Meir, & Goldstein, 1987). Research on children of depressed mothers (who are thus at risk for depression themselves) indicates that mother–child interactions are characterized by negativity, criticism, and poor problem solving. These dysfunctional interactions are influenced by the characteristics of both the child and the mother and have negative effects on the child's functioning (see Hammen, 1991a).

Research has shown similar deficits in the peer relations of depressed children and adolescents. Depressed children and adolescents show poor social problem-solving skills (e.g., Rudolph, Hammen, & Burge, 1994) and perceive themselves as being poor social problem solvers (Sacco & Graves, 1984). They are isolated (e.g., Larson, Raffaelli, Richards, Ham, & Jewell, 1990), spend a lot of time alone (e.g., Altmann & Gotlib, 1988), and feel insecure in their peer relationships (e.g., Armsden et al., 1990). Depressed children and adolescents experience negative interactions with peers (e.g., Altmann & Gotlib, 1988). For example, depressed children show poor affect regulation and poor conflict negotiation during conflict interactions with peers, their interactions are rated by observers as being less adaptive, and their interaction partners behave more negatively (e.g., Rudolph et al., 1994). Similarly, depressed adolescents view and are viewed negatively by their interaction partners (e.g., Baker, Milich, & Manolis, 1996). Not surprisingly, research has consistently indicated that depressed children and adolescents are disliked and rejected by peers (e.g., Baker et al., 1996; Rudolph et al., 1994).

Longitudinal studies show that childhood and adolescent depression are also associated with significant psychosocial impairment in adulthood. For example, Garber, Kriss, Koch, and Lindholm (1988) found that depressed adolescents evidenced high levels of social, family, and romantic dysfunction in adulthood. Moreover, two studies have shown that early-onset depression is associated with subsequent marital dysfunctioning. Forthofer, Kessler, Story, and Gotlib (1996) found that being depressed increased the likelihood of early marriage among women. Similarly, Gotlib, Lewinsohn, and Seeley (1998) found that, among young women, depression in adolescence was associated with early marriage and with high levels of marital dysfunction. Among men, depression in adolescence was associated with high levels of marital disagreements. These findings are particularly important for the present conceptualization of depression and romantic dysfunction because they support the basic premise that both depression and romantic dysfunction begin early and travel along overlapping courses.

Predictions From Developmental Psychopathology

Not surprisingly, child and adolescent depression researchers typically approach the problem of depression in young people from a developmental perspective, and more specifically from a developmental psychopathology perspective (e.g., Cicchetti et al., 1994). This perspective suggests that psychopathology is best understood using a life span development approach that takes into account how the successful negotiation and attainment of earlier developmental tasks affects individuals' capacities to successfully manage later tasks. Individuals may travel down one of many paths, and their success or failure at various junctures along the way determines the path they follow.

Although this model has gained a lot of attention by child and adolescent psychopathology researchers, it seems highly relevant for researchers of adult psychopathology, and particularly relevant for researchers studying the association between adult depression and interpersonal functioning. Some developmental psychopathologists (e.g., Cummings & Cicchetti, 1990) have conceptualized the earliest psychosocial precursors to depression as arising out of early parent–child relations (see also Cummings et al., chapter 5). Following predictions of attachment theory (Bowlby, 1969, 1973, 1980), these researchers have suggested that the early parent–child relationship results in internal representations of self, others, and relationships that guide interpersonal functioning and risk for psychopathology across the life span. This notion provides a useful theoretical framework for understanding the overlapping courses of depression and romantic dysfunction. Specifically, it suggests that earlier deficits in relational functioning may leave individuals unprepared to successfully negotiate later interpersonal situations. The framework does not imply, however, that individuals have no capacity for change. Although internal representations tend to be self-confirming and remain stable, they also can accommodate new information and experiences over time. This notion is consistent with the person–environment (transactional) perspective discussed earlier and with the developmental psychopathology perspective on multiple pathways. Still, the notion of continuity is an important one in that it suggests that some individuals, because of earlier difficulties (e.g., depression, interpersonal dysfunction), will come to their adult romantic relationships, including marriage, lacking adequate interpersonal skills. Recent long-term longitudinal research is now emerging to support this hypothesis. Poor parent–child relations and peer relations are associated with poor romantic relations in adulthood (e.g., Collins, 1998). In addition, recent work on the effect of parental depression and marital discord on children's outcomes (e.g., Cummings et al., chapter 5) has provided hypotheses about the developmental antecedents of the link between depression and romantic dysfunction by helping to identify how some young people both fail to develop adequate interpersonal skills and are at risk for depression.

To summarize, then, a large body of research has suggested that depression is associated with interpersonal dysfunction at all ages across the life span and that both depression and interpersonal dysfunction tend to follow chronic courses. This research strongly points to the idea that the association between depression and romantic dysfunction starts early and follows an overlapping course. Furthermore, a developmental psychopathology perspective on this process would suggest that as individuals move along the path of depression and interpersonal dysfunction they may ultimately end up in a marriage for which they do not possess the skills that would make their relationship successful. This perspective may help marital researchers and clinicians better conceptualize the association between depression and marital dysfunction by identifying a group of individuals (a) who will be most at risk for depression and marital dysfunction, (b) for whom depression and marital dysfunction will be most strongly linked and, (c) consequently, for whom depression and marital dysfunction may be most difficult to treat because of the long-standing nature of their association and of the interpersonal skill deficits.

Conclusion and Future Directions

The goal of this chapter was to elaborate two hypotheses about the association between depression and romantic dysfunction. First, the association between depression and romantic dysfunction, especially marital dysfunction, is best understood as a reciprocal one. Depression and romantic dysfunction follow overlapping paths along which they mutually affect one another. Second, some individuals may be more likely than others to evidence strong, ongoing associations between depression and romantic functioning. These are likely to be individuals for whom the overlapping paths of depression and romantic dysfunction began early in life. In this case, the paths have their history in the association between more general interpersonal dysfunction and depression in childhood and adolescence, and their link continues into adult romantic relationships, in part due to ongoing deficits in interpersonal skills. A second factor that is likely to maintain the ongoing association between depression and romantic dysfunction is the personality and interpersonal patterns that individuals exhibit. Rigidly enacted patterns characteristic of neediness, dependency, and perfectionism may be most likely to keep individuals stuck in a vicious cycle of depression and poor romantic functioning. This conceptualization offers researchers and clinicians a way to better understand who is most likely to be at risk for depression and romantic dysfunction, especially marital dysfunction, provides information about the factors that keep individuals vulnerable to depression in the context of interpersonal relationships, and has clinical implications.

For example, if chronic maladaptive interpersonal patterns keep individuals at risk for depression and marital dysfunction, then prevention programs might want to assess for their presence, help couples identify their existence and implications, and include techniques designed to disrupt such patterns (or at least refer individuals to treatments that can assist in this effort). Therefore, treatment programs for the depressed and maritally dissatisfied might want to include a focus on such chronic maladaptive patterns and on how couples can understand, tolerate, and work to change them.

Of course, these hypotheses about chronic maladaptive patterns and the association of depression and marital dysfunction raise a number of issues that must be addressed in future work. Research on the associations between personality and interpersonal patterns and actual behavior would provide important information about how such patterns translate into actual interpersonal transactions between members of the couple. In addition, because the association between depression and romantic dysfunction is inherently interpersonal it will be necessary to examine cross-partner associations among the variables to more fully understand the dyadic processes that contribute to the maintenance of the association. Another important issue regards gender differences in these processes. The hypotheses put forth in this chapter did not include gender differences. However, given that much of the research on depression and interpersonal dysfunction has examined women, the present hypotheses may be most applicable to women. Gender differences in these processes would thus be a critical avenue for exploration.

It is also important to consider the likelihood that the nature of the relation between depression and romantic dysfunction may be different at different developmental phases throughout the life span and, as stated throughout the chapter, that only a subset of depressed individuals may actually experience the processes outlined here. These processes are characteristic of a specific group of individuals who are hypothesized to experience an ongoing, repetitive course of depression and romantic dysfunction throughout their lives. Other courses certainly exist, and research directed at specifying relations between depression and interpersonal dysfunction at various ages and life stages is warranted (see also Coyne and Benazon, chapter 2). Finally, researchers should continue to investigate additional mechanisms of the association between depression and romantic dysfunction. For example, Beach and Fincham (1994) have proposed that emotion regulation strategies may play a role in the association between depression and marital discord. Pursuing such hypotheses will further refine researchers' understanding of why and for whom the courses of depression and romantic dysfunction overlap.

References

Adrian, C., & Hammen, C. (1993). Stress exposure and stress generation in children of depressed mothers. *Journal of Consulting and Clinical Psychology, 61,* 354–359.

Altman, E. O., & Gotlib, I. H. (1988). The social behavior of depressed children: An observational study. *Journal of Abnormal Child Psychology, 16,* 29–44.

Amanat, E., & Butler, C. (1984). Oppressive behaviors in the families of depressed children. *Family Therapy, 11,* 65–75.

Anderson, J. C., Williams, S., McGee, R., & Silva, P. A., (1987). DSM III disorders in preadolescent children: Prevalence in a large sample from the general population. *Archives of General Psychiatry, 44,* 69–76.

Armsden, G. C., McCauley, E., Greenberg, M. T., Burke, P. M., & Mitchell, J. R. (1990). Parent and peer attachment in early adolescent depression. *Journal of Abnormal Child Psychology, 18,* 683–697.

Asarnow, J. R., Ben-Meir, S. L., & Goldstein, M. J. (1987). Family factors in childhood depressive and schizophrenia spectrum disorders: A preliminary report. In K. Hahlweg & M. J. Goldstein (Eds.), *Understanding major mental disorder: The contribution of family interaction research* (pp. 123–138). New York: Family Process Press.

Baker, M., Milich, R., & Manolis, M. B. (1996). Peer interaction of dysphoric adolescents. *Journal of Abnormal Child Psychology, 24,* 241–255.

Bartholomew, K. (1990). Adult avoidance of intimacy: An attachment perspective. *Journal of Social and Personal Relationships, 7,* 147–178.

Bartholomew, K., & Horowitz, L. M. (1991). Attachment styles among young adults: A test of a four category model. *Journal of Personality and Social Psychology, 61,* 226–244.

Bartholomew, K. (1998). *The Family and Peer Attachment Interview.* Unpublished manuscript, Simon Fraser University, Burnaby, British Columbia, Canada.

Beach, S. R. H., & Fincham, F. D. (1994). Toward an integrated model of negative affectivity in marriage. In S. M. Johnson & L. S. Greenberg (Eds.), *The heart of the matter: Perspectives on emotion in marital therapy* (pp. 227–255). New York: Brunner/Mazel.

Beach, S. R. H., Martin, J. K., Blum, T. C., & Roman, P. M. (1993). Subclinical depression and role fulfillment in domestic settings: Spurious relationships, imagined problems, or real effects? *Journal of Psychopathology and Behavioral Assessment, 15,* 113–128.

Beach, S. R. H., & O'Leary, K. D. (1993a). Dysphoria and marital discord: Are dysphoric individuals at risk for marital maladjustment? *Journal of Marital and Family Therapy, 19,* 355–368.

Beach, S. R. H., & O'Leary, K. D. (1993b). Marital discord and dysphoria: For whom does the marital relationship predict depressive symptomatology? *Journal of Social and Personal Relationships, 10,* 405–420.

Beach, S. R. H., Sandeen, E. E., & O'Leary, K. D. (1990). *Depression in marriage: A model for etiology and treatment.* New York: Guilford Press.

Beck, A. T. (1983). Cognitive therapy of depression: New perspectives. In P. J. Clayton & J. E. Barrett (Eds.), *Treatment of depression: Old controversies and new approaches* (pp. 265–290). New York: Raven Press.

Belsher, G., & Costello, C. G. (1988). Relapse after recovery from unipolar depression: A critical review. *Psychological Bulletin, 104,* 84–96.

Biglan, A., Hops, H., Sherman, L., Friedman, L. S., Arthur, J., & Osteen, V. (1985). Problem solving interactions of depressed women and their husbands. *Behavior Therapy, 16,* 431–451.

Billings, A. G., Cronkite, R. C., & Moos, R. H. (1983). Social-environmental factors in unipolar depression: Comparisons of depressed patients and nondepressed controls. *Journal of Abnormal Psychology, 92,* 119–133.

Blatt, S. J., Quinlan, D. M., Chevron, E. S., McDonald, C., & Zuroff, D. (1982). Dependency and self-criticism: Psychological dimensions of depression. *Journal of Consulting and Clinical Psychology, 50,* 113–124.

Bowlby, J. (1969). *Attachment and loss: Vol. 1. Attachment.* New York: Basic Books.

Bowlby, J. (1973). *Attachment and loss: Vol. 2. Separation: Anxiety and anger.* New York: Basic Books.

Bowlby, J. (1980). *Attachment and loss: Vol. 3. Loss: Sadness and depression.* New York: Basic Books

Bradbury, T. N., & Pasch, L. A. (1992). *The Social Support Interaction Coding System.* Unpublished manuscript, University of California, Los Angeles.

Brown, G. W., & Harris, T. O. (1978). *Social origins of depression: A study of psychiatric disorders in women.* London: Free Press.

Carnelley, K. B., Pietromonaco, P. R., & Jaffe, K. (1994). Depression, working models of others, and relationship functioning. *Journal of Personality and Social Psychology, 66,* 127–140.

Christian-Herman, J., O'Leary, K. D., & Avery-Leaf, S. (in press) The impact of severe negative life events in marriage on depression. *Journal of Social and Clinical Psychology.*

Cicchetti, D., Rogosch, F. A., & Toth, S. L. (1994). A developmental psychopathology perspective on depression in children and adolescents. In W. M. Reynolds & H. F. Johnson (Eds.), *Handbook of depression in children and adolescents.* New York: Plenum.

Cole-Detke, H., & Kobak, R. (1996). Attachment processes in eating disorder and depression. *Journal of Consulting and Clinical Psychology, 64,* 282–290.

Collins, W. A. (1998, February). *Late adolescent competence in developmental perspective: Issues from a 19–year study.* Paper presented at the seventh biannual meeting of the Society for Research in Adolescence, San Diego, CA.

Costello, E. J., Costello, A., Edelbrock, C., Burns, B. J., Dulcan, M. K., Brent, D., & Janiszewski, S. (1988). Psychiatric disorders in pediatric primary care: Prevalence and risk factors. *Archives of General Psychiatry, 45,* 1107–1116.

Coyne, J. C. (1976). Toward an interactional description of depression. *Psychiatry, 39,* 28–40.

Cummings, E. M., & Cicchetti, D. (1990). Toward a transactional model of relations between attachment and depression. In M. T. Greenberg & E. M. Cummings (Eds.), *Attachment in the preschool years: Theory, research, and intervention* (pp. 339–372). Chicago: University of Chicago Press.

Cutrona, C. E., & Suhr, J. A. (1994). Social support communication in the context of marriage: An analysis of couples' supportive interaction. In B. R. Burleson, T. L. Albrecht, & I. G. Sarason (Eds.), *Communication of social support: Messages, interactions, relationships, and community* (pp. 113–135). Thousand Oaks, CA: Sage.

Daley, S. E., Hammen, C., Davila, J., & Burge, D. (1998). Axis II symptomatology, depression, and life stress during the transition from adolescence to adulthood. *Journal of Consulting and Clinical Psychology, 66,* 595–603.

Davila, J. (2000). *Refining the association between excessive reassurance seeking and depressive symptomatology: The role of related interpersonal constructs.* Manuscript submitted for publication.

Davila, J., Bradbury, T. N., Cohan, C. L., & Tochluk, S. (1997). Marital functioning and depressive symptoms: Evidence for a stress generation model. *Journal of Personality and Social Psychology, 73,* 849–861.

Davila, J., Cobb, R., & Lindberg, N. (2000). *Depressive symptoms, personality pathology, and early romantic dysfunction among young individuals: A test of a romantic stress generation model.* Manuscript submitted for publication.

Davila, J., Cobb, R., Lindberg, N., Polsky, R., & Baliotis, V. (1999). [Attachment and romantic functioning among young people]. Unpublished data, University of California, Los Angeles.

Davila, J., Hammen, C., Burge, D., Paley, B., & Daley, S. E. (1995). Poor interpersonal problem solving as a mechanism of stress generation in depression among adolescent women. *Journal of Abnormal Psychology, 104, 592–600.*

Farmer, R., & Nelson-Gray, R. O. (1990). Personality disorders and depression: Hypothetical relations, empirical findings, and methodological considerations. *Clinical Psychology Review, 10,* 453–476.

Fava, M., Alpert, J. E., Borus, J. S., Nierenberg, A. A., Pava, J. A., & Rosenbaum, J. F. (1996). Patterns of personality disorder comorbidity in early-onset versus late-onset major depression. *American Journal of Psychiatry, 153,* 1308–1312.

Fincham, F. D., Beach, S. R. H., Harold, G. T., & Osborne, L. N. (1997). Marital satisfaction and depression: Different causal relationships for men and women? *Psychological Science, 8,* 351–357.

Forthofer, M. S., Kessler, R. C., Story, A. L., & Gotlib, I. H. (1996). The effects of psychiatric disorders on the probability and timing of first marriage. *Journal of Health and Social Behavior, 37,* 121–132.

Garber, J., Kriss, M. R., Koch, M., & Lindholm, L. (1988). Recurrent depression in adolescents: A follow-up study. *Journal of the American Academy of Child and Adolescent Psychiatry, 27,* 49–54.

Gotlib, I. H., & Beach, S. R. H., (1995). A marital/family discord model of depression: Implications for therapeutic intervention. In N. S. Jacobson & A. S. Gurman (Eds.), *Clinical handbook of couple therapy* (pp. 411–436). New York: Guilford Press.

Gotlib, I. H., & Hammen, C. (1992). *Psychological aspects of depression: Toward a cognitive-interpersonal integration.* Chicester, England: Wiley.

Gotlib, I. H., Lewinsohn, P. M., & Seeley, J. R. (1998). Consequences of depression during adolescence: Marital status and marital functioning in early adulthood. *Journal of Abnormal Psychology, 107,* 686–690.

Gotlib, I. H., & Whiffen, V. E. (1989). Depression and marital functioning: An examination of specificity and gender differences. *Journal of Abnormal Psychology, 98,* 23–30.

Hammen, C. (1991a). *Depression runs in families: The social context of risk and resilience in children of depressed mothers.* New York: Springer-Verlag.

Hammen, C. L. (1991b). The generation of stress in the course of unipolar depression. *Journal of Abnormal Psychology, 100,* 555–561.

Hautzinger, M., Linden, M., & Hoffman, N. (1982). Distressed couples with and without a depressed partner: An analysis of their verbal interaction. *Journal of Behavior Therapy and Experimental Psychology, 13,* 307–314.

Hops, H., Perry, B. A., & Davis, B. (1997). Marital discord and depression. In W. K. Halford & H. J. Markman (Eds.), *Clinical handbook of marriage and couples interventions* (pp. 537–554). Chichester, England: Wiley.

Hyler, S., & Rieder, R. (1987). *PDQ-R: Personality Diagnostic Questionnaire-Revised.* New York: New York State Psychiatric Institute.

Ilardi, S. S., Craighead, W. E., & Evans, D. D. (1997). Modeling relapse in unipolar depression: The effects of dysfunctional cognitions and personality disorders. *Journal of Consulting and Clinical Psychology, 65,* 381–391.

Jacobson, N. S., Fruzzetti, A. E., Dobson, K., Whisman, M., & Hops, H. (1993). Couple therapy as a treatment for depression. II: The effects of relationship quality and therapy on depressive relapse. *Journal of Consulting and Clinical Psychology, 61,* 516–519.

Johnson, J. G., Hyler, S. E., Skodol, A. E., Bornstein, R. F., & Sherman, M. (1995). Personality disorder symptomatology associated with adolescent depression and substance abuse. *Journal of Personality Disorders, 9,* 318–329.

Joiner, T. E., Alfano, M. S., & Metalsky, G. I. (1992). When depression breeds contempt: Reassurance seeking, self-esteem, and rejection of depressed college students by their roommates. *Journal of Abnormal Psychology, 101,* 165–173.

Kahn, J., Coyne, J. C., & Margolin, G. (1985). Depression and marital disagreement: The social construction of despair. *Journal of Social and Personal Relationships, 2,* 447–461.

Kashani, J. H., Allan, W. D., Dahlmeier, J. M., Rezvani, M., & Reid, J. C. (1995). An examination of family functioning utilizing the circumplex model in psychiatrically hospitalized children with depression. *Journal of Affective Disorders, 35,* 65–73.

Kashani, J. H., Carlson, G. A., Beck, N. C., Hoeper, E. W., Corcoran, C. M., McAllister, J. A., Fallahi, C., Rosenberg, T. K., & Reid, J. C. (1987). Depression, depressive symptoms, and depressed mood among a community sample of adolescents. *American Journal of Psychiatry, 144,* 931–934.

Kaslow, N. J., Deering, C. G., & Ash, P. (1996). Relational diagnosis of child and adolescent depression. In F. W. Kaslow (Ed.), *Handbook of relational diagnosis and dysfunctional family patterns* (pp. 171–185). New York: Wiley.

Kendler, K. S., Kessler, R. C., Walters, E. E., MacLean, C., Neale, M. C., Heath, A. C., & Eaves, L. J. (1995). Stressful life events, genetic liability, and onset of episode of major depression in women. *American Journal of Psychiatry, 162,* 833–842.

Klein, M. H., Wonderlich, S., & Shea, M. T. (1993). Models of relationships between personality and depression: Toward a framework for theory and research. In M. H. Klein, D. J. Kupfer, & M. T. Shea (Eds.), *Personality and depression: A current view: Mental health and psychopathology,* (pp. 1–54). New York: Guilford.

Larson, R. W., Raffaelli, M., Richards, M. H., Ham, M., & Jewell, L. (1990). Ecology of depression in late childhood and early adolescence: A profile of daily states and activities. *Journal of Abnormal Psychology, 99,* 92–102.

Lasko, D., Field, T., Bendell, D., Yando, R., Scafidi, F., La Grecs, A., & Trapani, L. (1997). Adolescent psychiatric patients' interactions with their mothers. *Adolescence, 32,* 977–988.

Lewinsohn, P. M. (1974). A behavioral approach to depression. In R. J. Friedman & M. M. Katz (Eds.), *The psychology of depression: Contemporary theory and research* (pp.157–178). New York: Wiley.

Lewinsohn. P. M., Hops, H., Roberts, R. E., Seeley, J. R., & Andrews, J. A. (1993). Adolescent psychopathology: I. Prevalence and incidence of depression and other DSM-III-R disorders in high school students. *Journal of Abnormal Psychology, 102,* 133–144.

Lewinsohn, P. M., Zeiss, A. M., & Duncan, E. M. (1989). Probability of relapse after recovery from an episode of depression. *Journal of Abnormal Psychology, 98,* 107–116.

Main, M., & Goldwyn, R. (1991). *Adult Attachment Classification System.* Unpublished manuscript, University of California, Berkeley.

McCabe, S. B., & Gotlib, I. H. (1993). Interactions of couples with and without a depressed spouse: Self-report and observations of problem-solving situations. *Journal of Social and Personal Relationships, 10,* 589–599.

McKeown, R. E., Garrison, C. Z., Jackson, K. L., Cuffe, S. P., Addy, C. L., & Waller, J. L. (1997). Family structure and cohesion, and depressive symptoms in adolescents. *Journal of Research on Adolescence, 7,* 267–281.

Mitchell, J., McCauley, E., Burke, P., Calderon, R., & Schloredt, K. (1989). Psychopathology in parents of depressed children and adolescents. *Journal of the American Academy of Child and Adolescent Psychiatry, 28,* 352–357.

Monroe, S. M., Bromet, E. J., Connell, M. M., & Steiner, S. C. (1986). Social support, life events, and depressive symptoms: A 1–year prospective study. *Journal of Consulting and Clinical Psychology, 54,* 424–431.

Nietzel, M., & Harris, M. J. (1990). Relationship of dependency and achievement/autonomy to depression. *Clinical Psychology Review, 10,* 279–297.

O'Leary, K. D., Christian, J. L., & Mendell, N. R. (1994). A closer look at the link between marital discord and depressive symptomatology. *Journal of Social and Clinical Psychology, 13,* 33–41.

Pasch, L. A., & Bradbury, T. N. (1998). Social support, conflict, and the development of marital dysfunction. *Journal of Consulting & Clinical Psychology, 66,* 219–230.

Pfohl, B., Stangl, D., & Zimmerman, M. (1984). The implications of DSM III personality disorders for patients with major depression. *Journal of Affective Disorders, 7,* 309–318.

Pothoff, J. G., Holahan, C. J., & Joiner, T. E. (1995). Reassurance seeking, stress generation, and depressive symptoms: An integrative model. *Journal of Personality and Social Psychology, 68,* 664–670.

Puig-Antich, J., Goetz, D., Davies, M., Kaplan, T., Davies, S., Ostrow, L., Asnis, L., Twomey, J., Iyengar, S., & Ryan, N. D. (1989). A controlled family history study for prepubertal major depressive disorder. *Archives of General Psychiatry, 46,* 406–418.

Puig-Antich, J., Kaufman, J., Ryan, N. D., Williamson, D. E., Dahl, R. E., Lukens, E., Todak, G., Ambrosini, P., Rabinovich, H., & Nelson, B. (1993). The psychosocial functioning and family environment of depressed adolescents. *Journal of the American Academy of Child and Adolescent Psychiatry, 32,* 244–253.

Puig-Antich, J., Lukens. E., Davies, M., Goetz, D., Brennan-Quattrock, J., & Todak, G. (1985). Psychosocial functioning in prepubertal major depressive disorders: I. Interpersonal relationships during the depressive episode. *Archives of General Psychiatry, 42,* 500–507.

Rosenstein, D. S., & Horowitz, H. A. (1996). Adolescent attachment and psychopathology. *Journal of Consulting and Clinical Psychology, 64,* 244–253.

Rudolph, K. D., Hammen, C., & Burge, D. (1994). Interpersonal functioning and depressive symptoms in childhood: Addressing the issues of specificity and comorbidity. *Journal of Abnormal Child Psychology, 22,* 355–371.

Rudolph, K. D., Hammen, C., & Burge, D. (1997). A cognitive-interpersonal approach to depressive symptoms in preadolescent children. *Journal of Abnormal Child Psychology, 25,* 33–45.

Sacco, W. P., & Graves, D. J. (1984). Childhood depression, interpersonal problem solving, and self ratings of performance. *Journal of Clinical Child Psychology, 13,* 10–15.

Shaw, D. S., Keenan, K., Vondra, J. I., Delliquadri, E., & Giovanelli, J. (1997). Antecedents of preschool children's internalizing problems: A longitudinal study of low-income families. *Journal of the American Academy of Child and Adolescent Psychiatry, 36,* 1760–1767.

Shea, M. T., Pilkonis, P. A., Beckham, E., Collins, J. F., Elkin, I., Sotsky, S. M., & Docherty, J. P. (1990). Personality disorders and treatment outcome in the NIMH treatment of depression collaborative research program. *American Journal of Psychiatry, 147,* 711–718.

Shea, M. T., Widiger, T. A., & Klein, M. H. (1992). Comorbidity of personality disorders and depression: Implications for treatment. *Journal of Consulting and Clinical Psychology, 60,* 857–868.

Sheeber, L., Hops, H., Andrews, J., Alpert, T., & Davis, B. (1998). Interactional processes in families with depressed and non-depressed adolescents: Reinforcement of depressive behavior. *Behaviour Research and Therapy, 36,* 417–427.

Silver, D. H., & Cohn. D. A. (1992). *Couple Attachment Interview.* Unpublished manuscript, University of California, Berkeley.

Stark, K. D., Humphrey, L. L., Crook, K., & Lewis, K. (1990). Perceived family environments of depressed and anxious children: Child's and maternal figure's perspective. *Journal of Abnormal Child Psychology, 18,* 527–547.

Toth, S. L., & Cicchetti, D. (1996). Patterns of relatedness, depressive symptomatology, and perceived competence in maltreated children. *Journal of Consulting and Clinical Psychology, 64,* 32–41.

Wells, K. B., Stewart, A, Hays, R. D., Burnam, M. A., Rogers, W., Daniels, M., Berry, S., Greenfield, S., & Ware, J. (1989). The functioning and well-being of depressed patients: Results from the Medical Outcomes Study. *Journal of the American Medical Association, 262,* 914–919.

5

Parental Depression and Family Functioning: Toward a Process-Oriented Model of Children's Adjustment

E. Mark Cummings
Gina DeArth-Pendley
Tina Du Rocher Schudlich
David A. Smith

Children of depressed parents are 2–5 times more likely to develop behavior problems than children of nondepressed parents (Beardslee, Bemporad, Keller, & Klerman, 1983). They are at greater risk not only for depression and mood disorders, but also for a variety of other forms of psychological and medical dysfunction (Weissman, Warner, Wickramaratne, Moreau, & Olfson, 1997). On the other hand, many children of depressed parents do not develop psychopathology. Thus, the children who do not develop psychopathology study is of interest also for the knowledge that can be gained about how children may cope effectively despite adversity.

The matrix of factors that contribute to risk for psychopathology in children of depressed parents is complex. Intraorganismic factors have often been implicated. The monozygotic-to-dyzygotic rate is approximately 46:20 for unipolar mood disorder and approximately 72:14 for bipolar mood disorder (McGuffin, Katz, Watkins, & Rutherford, 1996). Neurophysiological investigations of mood disorders, including studies of children (Birmaher et al., 1997), have specifically implicated the neurotransmitters norepinephrine and serotonin and neuroendocrine dysfunction (Goodwin & Jamison, 1990).

However, it is also clear that biological influences can only partially explain the association between depression in parents and maladjustment in children (Rende, Plomin, Reiss, & Hetherington, 1993) and are most appropriately conceptualized as interacting with environmental factors in influencing an individual's development (Cicchetti & Toth, 1998). Identifying biological processes does not necessarily indicate biological causation. Environmental stress can cause a neurophysiological sensitization that then enhances subsequent stress reactivity (Gold, Goodwin, & Chrousos, 1988).

The most investigated area of environmental influences on children's adjustment is the effect of family functioning associated with parental depression. The evidence overwhelmingly supports the role of family processes linked to parental depression in children's risk for maladjustment (Coyne, Downey, & Boergers, 1992; Cummings & Davies, 1994b; Downey & Coyne, 1990). A positive side to the evidence for the importance of family factors is that they are, at least potentially, changeable, so that understanding their effects, especially the key processes by which such influences occur, offers real hope for more effective prevention and treatment for these children (Beardslee et al., 1997).

This chapter is concerned with further explicating the relations between parental depression, family functioning, and child adjustment. In terms of family models, the emphasis is often on parent–child relations as the basis for conceptual understanding and clinical intervention (Emery, Fincham, & Cummings, 1992). A key proposition is that the broader family climate must be considered, especially the role of interparental relations in both parental depression and the risk for disorder in the children of depressed parents.

With regard to the former, impressive evidence has accumulated to indicate that parental depression and marital conflict are linked (Beach, Smith, & Fincham, 1994). Recent work has supported causal relations between these variables, although the effects are bidirectional (Whisman, chapter 1; Davila, chapter 4). It would be redundant to review this evidence here in any detail, given the extensive coverage provided elsewhere in this book. However, the evidence that parental depression and marital conflict are closely linked provides an additional, important impetus for examining marital conflict in models of the effect of these family environments on children.

Accordingly, this chapter is organized to advance several themes toward better understanding the role played by family factors, and especially marital relations, in the development of children of depressed parents. First, a framework for the familial influences that affect children in families with parental depression is revisited, and a brief overview of findings is provided to illustrate the nature of the evidence. However, coverage of the evidence for multiple familial influences is necessarily brief, given the recency of extensive reviews (Cummings & Davies, 1994b, 1999).

Second, the overview of a family model for the effects of parental depression on children is followed by a more focused treatment of marital conflict. In particular, it is concluded that evidence from the child development literature indicating that marital conflict predicts children's adjustment is substantial (Davies & Cummings, 1994; Grych & Fincham, 1990), including adjustment in families with parental depression (Cummings & Davies, 1994a; Downey & Coyne, 1990), emphasizing that the quality of marital relations as well as parenting must be considered in conceptualizing the effects of parental depression on children. A discussion of recent findings is provided, and a variety of empirical gaps that impede understanding relations between parental depression, marital conflict, and child adjustment are identified.

The third section focuses on the need for a theoretical model to account for relations between parental depression and family functioning on the one hand and child outcomes on the other. One problem is a lack of articulation about how to conceptualize process and developmental questions in such a model. Accordingly, this section briefly outlines principles for a process-oriented approach from a developmental perspective, influenced by the developmental psychopathology tradition (Cicchetti & Cohen, 1995).

Finally, a specific theoretical model for relations between parental depression, family functioning, and child development is presented. An emotional security hypothesis (Cummings & Davies, 1996; Davies & Cummings, 1994) is outlined as a model for an important subset of the processes mediating relations between parental depression and child adjustment. Notably, the evidence suggests that emotional security generally accounts for important variance in the effects of both parent–child relations (Colin, 1996) and marital conflict and distress (Davies & Cummings, 1998) on children's adjustment, thus providing a promising model for the effects of parental depression on child adjustment as affected by family processes (Cummings, 1995). General propositions in support of this model are considered, as is evidence for the operation of three specific subprocesses of emotional regulation, children's representations of family relations and other cognitions, and children's efforts to regulate parental behavior.

A Framework for Familial Influences on Children in Families With Parental Depression

As noted, there is considerable evidence to indicate that family processes, including marital conflict and distress, affect the development of children in families with parental depression (Coyne, Schwoeri, & Downey, 1994; Downey & Coyne, 1990; Schwoeri & Sholevar, 1994). Figure 5.1 presents a framework illustrating familial factors related to the adjustment of children in families with parental depression. The following factors appear to be associated with children's adjustment in these families (Cummings & Davies, 1994b, 1999): (a) exposure to parental depressive symptoms, (b) exposure to marital distress and conflict, (c) parenting practices, (d) parent–child attachment, and (e) children's characteristics. As the framework illustrates, these influences are interrelated rather than independent. For example, marital conflict and parenting have been posited to affect each other (Erel & Burman, 1995). This model places special emphasis on parent–child relations and marital conflict as key pathways of influence on children, but it also recognizes the role of the child in reciprocal family relationships. Notably, when parental depression leads to family disruption (e.g.,

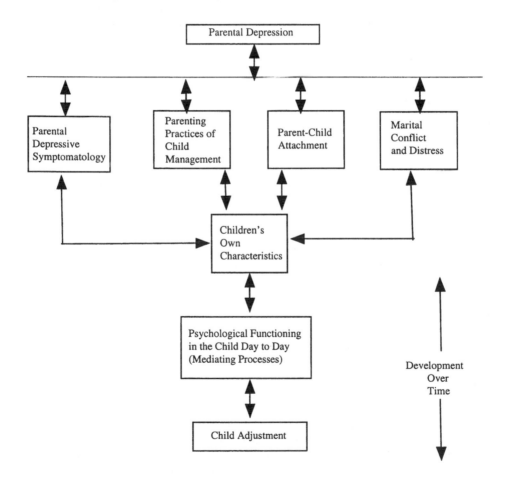

Figure 5.1. Framework for relations between parental depression, family functioning, and child adjustment.

divorce and breakup of the family, foster care), children are also at increased risk for psychopathology (Hetherington, Stanley-Hagen, & Anderson, 1989; Rutter & Quinton, 1984).

Parental Characteristics of Depressive Symptoms

The most direct and unambiguous pathway through which parental functioning may affect children is through children's exposure to parental characteristics of depression. Particularly intriguing are studies that have demonstrated the direct effect on children of the affective behavior associated with parental depressive symptoms. For example, in analog studies, exposure to face-to-face maternal displays of dysphoria and withdrawal has been shown to elicit responses of anger, reduced activity, dysphoria, and social withdrawal from infants (e.g., Cohn & Campbell, 1992). However, depressive symptoms are also characterized by high rates of irritability and aggression, which may also influence children's functioning through exposure to these expressions (Cummings, Zahn-Waxler, & Radke-Yarrow, 1981).

Children may also be affected by exposure to the cognitive, as well as the emotional, symptomatology of depression. Associations have been reported between maternal depression, negative cognitions about the children, and parenting impairments. For example, negative attributions for child behavior have been found to account for some of the relations between maternal depressed mood and child psychological problems by fueling harsh parenting practices (e.g., impulses to blame or respond negatively to the child; Geller & Johnston, 1995). Depressed parents may also communicate in ways that increase children's sense of responsibility and guilt for the adult depression. Thus, children of depressed parents are exposed to negative emotions, despair, and negative attributional strategies, that is, mixed expressions of personal responsibility and helplessness (see reviews in Cummings & Davies, 1994b, 1999).

Depression and Parenting Practices

On the one hand, in comparison to nondepressed parents, depressed parents are more inconsistent, lax, and ineffective in child management and discipline. On the other hand, when not yielding to the child's demands, depressed parents are more likely to engage in direct and forceful control strategies and less likely to end disagreements in compromise (Fendrich, Warner, & Weissman, 1990; see reviews in Cummings & Davies, 1994a, 1999). Support has been found for a model in which parental symptoms compromised child management practices, leading to children's deviance (Conger, Patterson, & Ge, 1995). Exemplifying the interrelations between family variables, McElwain and Volling (1997) reported that marital conflict mediated the relationship between depressed mood and parental intrusiveness.

Depression and Attachment

Parental depression has repeatedly been linked with insecure parent–child attachment (e.g., Radke-Yarrow, Cummings, Kuczynski, & Chapman, 1985; see reviews in Cummings & Davies, 1994a, 1999). Murray (1992) reported that diagnoses of maternal depression at 2 months postpartum increased children's risk for developing insecure attachments with the mother 16 months later. Another study found that maternal depression during infancy predicted insecure attachment 13 months later for infants and preschoolers (Teti, Gelfand, Messinger, & Isabella, 1995). Cicchetti, Rogosch, and Toth (1998) reported that more behavioral difficulties and insecure attachment were found among children with depressed parents than among children with nondepressed parents. Again exemplifying the interrelations between family influences, contextual factors, including marital satisfaction and family conflict, significantly added to the prediction of behavior problems in children of depressed parents. However, as with other studies of family processes, depression increases the probability of dysfunctional outcomes, but a wide range of outcomes has been found, including good adjustment.

Depression and Marital Conflict

Marital conflict has been reported to be a primary factor in the effects of parental depression on children's adjustment (see reviews in Cummings & Davies, 1994b, 1999). For example, Caplan et al. (1989) reported links between maternal depression and marital conflict in the early years of child rearing, with marital discord more closely related to behavior problems than parental depression. In another longitudinal study, Cox, Puckering, Pound, and Mills (1987) found that marital discord was more closely related to disturbances in mother–child relations than maternal depression. Thus, these studies and others provide impressive evidence to suggest that marital discord plays a key role in the effects of maternal depression on children and may even be a more proximate predictor of certain child outcomes than maternal depression (see discussion in Downey & Coyne, 1990). Unfortunately, little is known about relations between paternal depression, marital discord, and child adjustment. Nonetheless, these studies provide an important point of contact between the developmental and clinical literature on marital discord and depression (Whisman, chapter 1).

Children's Characteristics

Inherited dispositions may also play a role in increased risk for adjustment problems in children of depressed parents. However, aside from evidence implicating genetics and biological processes, little is known about these effects. There is modest evidence that children of depressed parents (a) have more difficult temperaments, at least as rated by their own mothers, and (b) are more unresponsive and lethargic in the first days of life (see reviews in Cummings & Davies, 1999). However, studies identifying specific processes at risk in children of depressed parents, especially regarding how child characteristics may affect family functioning, are scarce, and much more study of this issue is merited.

Improving Specifications of Relations: Parental Depression, Marital Conflict, and Child Adjustment

The evidence reviewed thus far provides a brief overview of family processes that may contribute to risk for adjustment problems in children of depressed parents. Given that the multiple family processes that may be affected by maternal depression are appropriately acknowledged, the next section focuses on the particular family process, that is, marital conflict, that is of particular interest in this book.

General Evidence for Relations Between Marital Conflict and Child Adjustment

The general evidence concerning effects of marital conflict on children's adjustment merits attention. Marital conflict induces powerful emotional, cognitive, and behavioral responses in children bystanders (Cummings & Davies, 1994a). Correlational studies have long indicated that children's stress and coping responses are related to their marital conflict history and their risk for adjustment problems (e.g., Cummings & Davies, 1994a; Laumakis, Margolin, & John, 1998; Margolin, Christensen, & John, 1996). Empirical support for mediational models, with children's emotional, cognitive, and behavioral reactions to marital conflict as mediators, has been reported (e.g., Davies & Cummings, 1998; Grych, 1998; Harold & Conger, 1997; Harold, Fincham, Osborne, & Conger, 1997). Marital conflict also negatively affects parenting and parent–child attachments (Davies & Cummings, 1994; Erel & Burman, 1995), but parenting does not fully account for these effects (Emery et al., 1992). Among the moderators of outcomes are children's age, children's gender (Cummings & Davies, 1994a), parental gender (Osborne & Fincham, 1996), and parental adjustment (Cummings & Davies, 1994b). Moreover, recent theory has provided a rich conceptual foundation for mediational and moderational models (e.g., Cummings & Davies, 1996; Emery, 1992; Grych & Fincham, 1990).

Studies of Links Among Parental Depression, Marital Conflict, and Child Outcomes

It is surprising that, after the impetus to study the effects of marital conflict in families with parental depression provided by the conclusions of earlier studies and reviews, few studies have examined this issue since the early 1990s. Davies and Windle (1997) recently reported that adolescent daughters of depressed mothers experienced more depressive symptoms, conduct problems, and academic difficulties than did adolescent sons of depressed mothers. Mediational tests showed that daughters' greater vulnerability to family discord mediated the effect of maternal depression on their social and emotional development. Evidence has also emerged to support distinguishing between mothers' and fathers' conflict behavior when there is parental depression. Miller, Cowan, Cowan, Hetherington, and Clingempeel (1993) reported that paternal depression was associated with increased marital conflict but that the link to children's externalizing problems was based on decreased child control. However, for depressed mothers, both increased marital conflict and decreased positive affect and warmth in parenting were associated with children's externalizing problems through separate pathways.

Diagnostic Procedures

Part of the reason for a slowing down of work in this area may be the need for a more sophisticated assessment both of parental depression and of children's responses to family patterns associated with parental depression, that is, a finer-grained and more informative assessment of these family environments and children's reactions to them. In particular, the criteria used for depression in research on depression in families and the distinction between depressive symptomatology and a clinically significant syndrome of depression warrant close consideration (cf. Whisman, chapter 1; Coyne and Benazon, chapter 2). Depression is assessed in two ways in the literature: depressive symptoms and diagnostic depression. Coyne and Downey (1991) have argued persuasively that it is important to distinguish between studies that assess depressive symptoms based on self-report instruments such as the Beck Depression Inventory (Beck, Rush, Shaw, & Emery, 1979) and those based on direct clinical interview instruments and formal diagnostic criteria. It is important that future research be increasingly mindful of this distinction as there is a need for more research toward understanding child outcomes in families with clinically significant disorders given the greater implications of such environments for the development of psychopathology in children. Ideally, because both sets of criteria tap significant elements of depressive phenomena in families, both sets of criteria should be used in research when possible. Another important issue is to begin to try to distinguish effects due to anxiety from those due to depression. Given the comorbidity of anxiety and depressive symptoms, the relative neglect of parental anxiety as an influence on child development is notable. Are effects altered when both anxiety and depression are present? Again, both questionnaire assessments and clinical interviews are likely to provide useful information about anxiety as a factor in family functioning.

Nature of Discord and Conflict

Some additional points have been suggested by recent work concerning characteristics of parental depression that may affect children (see Figure 5.1). For example, depressed individuals have characteristic speech patterns, including greater response latencies, hesitations, and silences; poor eye contact; and negative self-disclosures (Gotlib, 1982; Gotlib & Asarnow, 1979). In remarkably short times (3–5 min in some studies) these characteristic patterns can cause those with whom depressed individuals interact to feel anxious, dysphoric, and hostile and to behave in rejecting ways (Gotlib & Robinson, 1982; Strack & Coyne, 1983). Although considerable evidence has accumulated with regard to infants' reactions to face-to-face maternal displays of negativity and withdrawal (Cohn & Campbell, 1992), little is known about older children's reactions and the reactions of children to more general behavioral styles associated with depression, especially as shown by depressed parents in daily interactions.

Similarly, there is a need for new approaches to examining the effects on children of marital interaction patterns associated with parental depression (see Figure 5.1). Much of the work reported thus far has reflected relatively global assessments of marital conflict and distress based on questionnaire assessments. It is uncertain whether such assessments capture the most important dimensions of marital conflict associated with parental depression. What are these behaviors? Although the work of Hops and colleagues (Hops et al., 1987) has made important inroads in this area, it is important that the conflict styles of depressed individuals be examined, particularly in the context of everyday problem solving, and that both the relative incidence of constructive and destructive styles of marital conflict be charted. Recent work has called attention to the relative prevalence of constructive conflict styles (e.g., compromise, humor) in problem-solving situations in the home among nondepressed spouses (Cummings, Goeke-Morey, & Dukewich, 1998). What is the rate of constructive versus destructive conflict styles in depressed versus nondepressed marital dyads?

Children's Reactions to "Mere Exposure" to Marital Conflict by Depressed Parents

There is a similar need to develop new methodologies for examining children's reactions to marital conflict behaviors. Again, traditional questionnaire assessments may not be sensitive to the key dimensions of marital conflict behavior as enacted by depressed spouses. Children of depressed parents are likely to be exposed to emotional communications that are especially ambiguous, changeable, unreliable with regard to meaning, and negative, which may contribute to their sense of emotional insecurity (Cummings, 1995). Given that children have been shown to be sensitive to "mere exposure" (Cummings & Davies, 1994a, p. 61) to marital conflict, independent of effects on parenting, it is particularly important that children's reactions during exposure to marital conflict styles associated with parental depression be examined. Exposure to the attributional (e.g., hopelessness, self-blame) and interpersonal (e.g., reassurance seeking, confirmation of negative feedback) processes associated with depression in marital conflict may also affect children (Katz, chapter 6; Joiner, chapter 7), but there has been little investigation of the effect of these processes. Cultural and historical patterns associated with the ethnicities of families of origin or families of creation (e.g., African American families; see Kaslow, Twomey, Brooks, Thompson, and Reynolds, chapter 8) also may affect both the expression of family conflict and children's interpretations and responses but also have received scant study. Moreover, whereas some responses may be evident in children's overt behavioral responses (e.g., attempts to intervene in parental conflict), other responses may require interviewing children about their responses to marital conflict behaviors (e.g., feelings of anger, sadness; helplessness, self-blame, hopelessness). Thus, multiple methodologies are needed that can capture the various important dimensions of children's reactions to marital conflict.

It is important to recognize that although incidents of intense marital conflict may be relatively infrequent, even in high-conflict homes, the impact of these events on children's emotional, cognitive, and general functioning may outweigh the actual amount of time consumed by these events. That is, children's fundamental sense of emotional security regarding family functioning may derive from their exposure to interspousal relations, especially marital conflict and distress. Emotional security is a higher order construct that is intended to encompass multiple dimensions of children's emotional, cognitive, and behavioral functioning within an organizing rubric that reflects children's organizing goals regarding their emotional, cognitive, and behavioral responses to family events, including, but not limited to, marital conflict and distress.

Effects of Marital Conflict on Parenting Provided by Depressed Parents

Marital conflict also may have indirect effects on children's adjustment in families with parental depression by affecting parenting practices. It is important to recognize that marital conflict and distress can also affect emotional security indirectly by altering the security of parent–child attachments (see Figure 5.2). This result might follow because parent–child interactional styles are changed (e.g., parents become less responsive to children's signals because of the distracting influence of marital conflict), resulting in more insecure attachments between parent and child, or because children simply change their view of the relative safety and security offered by their parent as a result of observing the hostility of that parent toward his or her spouse. Marital conflict may also affect the quality and effectiveness of parents' discipline and other child management practices. Similarly, parenting practices (e.g., child management) and parent–child emotional relationships (e.g., attachment) may affect the quality of marital relations (see Figure 5.2). In fact, relations between marital conflict, parenting, and child adjustment are well established (Cummings & Davies, 1994a; Harold et al., 1997; see review provided by Erel & Burman, 1995). However, the patterns of these relations in families with parental depression are not well established and may differ in important respects from patterns observed in other families.

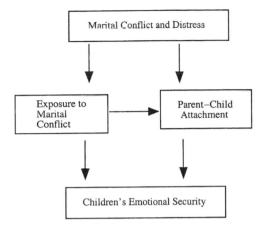

Figure 5.2. Direct and indirect effects of marital conflict on children's emotional security.

Gender of Parents and Children

The role of gender also has been relatively unexplored. Past research has suggested no consistent pattern of gender differences in vulnerability to family environments associated with parental depression (Cummings & Davies, 1994b). However, more recent research has provided some support for greater effects on girls than boys (cf. Whisman, chapter 1; Karney, chapter 3; Davila, chapter 4). Fergusson, Horwood, and Lynskey (1995) reported that maternal depressive symptoms were strongly correlated with subsequent depressive symptoms in adolescent daughters, but not in adolescent sons. Davies and Windle (1997) found that histories of maternal depressive symptoms were related to subsequent adolescent reports of depressive symptoms, conduct problems, and academic difficulties for girls but not for boys.

In addition, little is known about differences between children's exposure to maternal and paternal behavior as a function of marital conflict and the possibility of cross-gender effects. For example, relations between marital conflict and father–child relations provides information over and above that provided by including only the path from marital conflict to mother–child relations (Osborne & Fincham, 1996). As for cross-gender effects, Crockenberg and Forgays (1996) reported that girls judged fathers to be more angry than did boys despite the absence of differences in conflict behaviors between fathers of boys and girls according to independent observers. A particularly intriguing direction would be to examine maternal and paternal conflict behaviors in the context of families with parental depression and the direct effects of exposure to each parent's conflict behaviors on their children. Significant research issues include differentiating styles of marital conflict that are characteristic of depressed fathers versus depressed mothers. The prevalence and effect of nonverbal anger communication, anger mixed with dysphoria, unresolved conflict issues, and lack of explanation in families with depressed parents merit investigation (Cummings, 1995). Another interesting question is whether a lack of positive affect expression by parents exacerbates the effect of high rates of negative emotionality in these families (Campbell, Cohn, & Meyers, 1995).

Finally, it is important to distinguish between different types of outcomes in children of depressed parents, as multiple aspects of adjustment problems have been implicated, including depression, anxiety, and global adjustment as reflected by internalizing and externalizing problems. Moreover, children of depressed parents often are resilient, evidencing no clinical disorder. Thus, it is also important to assess social competence and other indices of positive functioning in these children.

Toward a Process-Oriented Approach

As Figure 5.3 illustrates, another key element for a process-oriented perspective is to conceptualize and account for development over time in children of depressed parents. Tests of causal relations require a longitudinal time frame. Important conceptual directions are to clarify what is meant by a process-oriented approach and the key elements of a developmental perspective on risk among children of depressed parents.

Themes for Process-Oriented Research

Research on children of depressed parents has made great strides over the past 2 decades. However, major gaps in understanding the processes that underlie risk remain. Typically, identifying a risk factor only increases, perhaps only marginally, the statistical probability that a negative outcome will occur. Moreover, many individuals experiencing a risk factor for a disorder will not develop the disorder and, furthermore, many individuals that do not experience the risk factor will develop the disorder. Thus, many children with depressed parents will not develop depression or other disorders, and some children without depressed parents will develop depression.

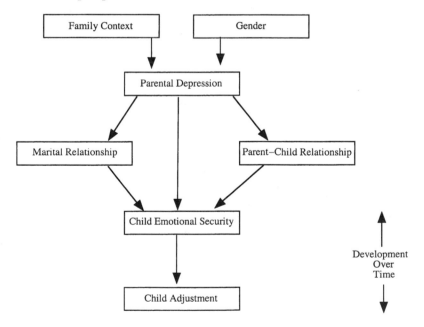

Figure 5.3. Mediators and moderators of relations between parental depression and children's adjustment.

It is clear that it is not enough to know that a risk factor may sometimes lead to a negative outcome. It also is important to know how and why (i.e., mediating processes), for whom (i.e., moderating processes), and the prognosis for the future (i.e., longitudinal time frame). More complex and sophisticated models for understanding how individuals develop in families with depression, that consider the operation of multiple factors or influences and their interaction over time, and that seek to identify the causal processes that underlie relations between exposure to risk and the development of psychopathology are needed.

Put another way, a first generation of research has successfully mapped many basic relations in children of depressed parents, including numerous factors associated with risk for the development of psychopathology (Fincham, 1994). However, this strategy has reached a point of diminishing returns. A second generation of research is needed to move the field beyond the documentation of correlations between risk factors (e.g., parental depression) and negative outcomes (e.g., children's behavior problems) to an increased understanding of the processes that underlie pathways of normal development and the development of psychopathology over time.

The aim of process-oriented research is to describe the specific responses and patterns, in the context of specific histories or developmental periods, that account, over time, for normal versus diagnostic outcomes. For example, as noted, having a depressed parent does not directly, immediately, or even necessarily result in depression in children (Cummings & Davies, 1994b). Risk for psychopathology in children of depressed parents is related to the development of specific patterns of responding (e.g., cognitive, emotional, physiological, neurological) to experiential contexts (e.g., stress, loss, challenge, relationship conflict, relationship insecurity) that, over time, lay a foundation for the development of depression. Understanding at this level of analysis can provide the understanding of the causal underpinnings of human development that is needed for advanced theoretical models and informed clinical prevention and intervention. At this point, the concepts of mediators and moderators are significant.

Mediators are the "generative mechanisms" through which an independent variable (e.g., parental depression) influences outcomes (e.g., child adjustment; Baron & Kenny, 1986, p. 1173). Thus, in the model illustrated in Figure 5.3, emotional security resulting from the quality of family relations is identified as a factor that mediates outcomes in children of depressed parents. Mediators, by definition, are conceptualized as explaining, at least in part, how and why risk factors (e.g., parental depression) lead to maladaptive outcomes (e.g., adjustment problems). Notably, emotional security is conceptualized as involving cognitive, emotional, and behavioral components; that is, it is a higher order construct for a class of response patterns hypothesized to mediate relations between family functioning and child outcomes.

Moderators specify the strength and direction of relations between an independent variable (e.g., parental depression) and an outcome (e.g., child adjustment: Baron & Kenny, 1986; Holmbeck, 1997). Moderators recognize that the nature and degree of risk are not necessarily uniform across different conditions and individuals. For example, in Figure 5.3, children's gender may serve as moderators of relations between family functioning associated with parental depression and child adjustment. In addition to specifying who is at risk, moderator models may also reflect when risk occurs. For example, risk for adjustment problems in children of depressed parents may be disproportionately greater when multiple family systems are dysfunctional (e.g., marital *and* parent–child relations) than when only one system is deviant. Additionally, the family context, including factors such as socioeconomic status and available social support, may also mediate child outcomes (Cicchetti & Toth, 1998).

Before the developmental psychopathology model is outlined, there are several gaps in research that merit comment. First, more attention needs to be paid to the contextual factors that characterize specific developmental periods and their possible significance to the role of childhood factors in adult adjustment. Second, extrafamilial influences such as peer groups also may affect children's risk and adjustment. Third, a particularly significant issue may be how parents validate children's emotional experiences, which may have implications for children's subsequent capacities for emotional regulation (Gottman, Katz, & Hooven, 1997).

Assumptions of a Developmental Model

Another critical issue for a process-oriented approach to understanding relations between parental depression, family functioning, and child outcomes is taking into account developmental factors. Clinical problems sometimes are implicitly treated as if they were adevelopmental. In fact, the way an individual responds to events is typically a function of past history or experience in addition to the current experiential stimuli. This means that study of ontogenesis or etiology is essential (Grych, 1998).

Another error is to assume that pathways between early and later development are relatively simple and straightforward (e.g., early depression predicts later depression; Harrington, Rutter, & Fombonne, 1996). In fact, apparently benign beginnings (e.g., taking care of a depressed parent) can have so-called "sleeper effects" (e.g., predict risk for later problems). For example, studies on discordant marital relationships have indicated greater adult psychopathology in female children who were preferred over spouses to be close confidantes to their parents (Jacobvitz & Bush, 1996). In addition, multiple pathways may lead to the same outcome (e.g., depression), or the same outcome may result from different patterns of influence (Harrington et al., 1996). Some additional principles that merit consideration when incorporating developmental processes into models of psychopathology in children of depressed parents are considered below (Cicchetti & Cohen, 1995; Cicchetti & Toth, 1998; Cummings, Davies, & Campbell, in press).

Maladaptive Trajectories of Development Are Governed by the Same General Principles That Govern Normal Development

As the discussion thus far has illustrated, no new processes are posited in families with parental depression than in families without parental depression. That is, the same classes of processes are invoked. It is assumed that more maladaptive forms of these classes of family functioning will be present, on average, but not that qualitatively different elements will occur. Thus, risk processes (e.g., insecure attachment) in children of depressed parents are expected to operate like those in other families rather than constitute a qualitatively distinct class of variables.

Disorder Reflects a Succession of Deviations Over Time

The development of disorder is assumed to occur as a result of repeated transactions between the individual and the environment over time, not as an immediate occurrence. Accordingly, when children of depressed parents develop disorders, this does not happen all of a sudden, but as the outcome of a long history of responses to the conditions of a dysfunctional family environment. This assumption puts a premium on the careful, microanalytic study of response processes in context, as they are assumed to underlie child outcomes, rather than a focus on diagnostic classification, as is typical in disease models.

More Than One Pathway May Lead to Similar Outcomes

Depression or other specific disorders in children do not necessarily result from a single causal chain of events, but may result from various, different pathways. For example, for some children psychopathology may be most influenced by genetic risk, whereas for others one or more traumatic historical experiences (e.g., marital conflict, divorce, severe parental depressive symptoms) may be most important. The notion that multiple pathways may lead to the same outcome is termed *equifinality,* and this premise supports the use of relatively complex—and individual—rather than variable-oriented—levels of analyses (Cummings, Davies, & Campbell, in press).

These notions reflect the opposite of a "one-size fits all" formula. For example, some psychiatric models are based on static, dichotomous frameworks that conceptualize individuals as either having a disease or being healthy, with the search for a single pathway reflecting the movement from risk status to actual disease. In contrast, pluralistic models emphasize that different outcomes and pathways are the byproduct of dynamic, bidirectional relations between contextual factors and the organism over time (Cummings, et al., in press).

The Same Pathway May Have Different Outcomes

The fact that two different individuals are following a similar pathway at a given point in time does not mean the later end result will be the same. Any one component during development (e.g., having a parent with depression) may function differently depending on the organizational system in which it operates, resulting in different outcomes later in development. Even if two individuals have the same characteristics or the same experiences at a point in time (e.g., similar family patterns associated with parental depression), the events that follow may result in different later outcomes. This notion is called *multifinality,* and it supports careful assessment of developmental pathways over time in children at risk (e.g., children of depressed parents).

Change Is Always Possible

Human development involves continual, dynamic transactions between an individual and his or her context. Accordingly, trajectories of development are never fixed. Instead, there is a constant process of adaptation, so that change from psychopathology to normality, or from normality to psychopathology, is always possible. Therefore, it is important not to infer that childhood problems (e.g., insecure attachment, school disorders) necessarily presage long-term psychopathology.

Change Is Constrained by Prior Adaptation

On the other hand, past adaptations influence future possibilities for development. Early structures become incorporated into later structures. In this way, the possibility of change is constrained by past functioning. Thus, signs of early problems in children from at-risk samples are a cause for concern.

Risk Is Probabilistic, Not Certain

An outcome of psychopathology in children, even in the presence of multiple significant risk factors, is never certain. Exposure to multiple risk factors (e.g., the multiple risk factors associated with parental depression; see Figure 5.1) does no more than probabilistically increase the likelihood of the development of psychopathology. On the other hand, some individuals confronted with apparently low-risk conditions develop serious adjustment problems. Thus, it is important not to equate risk for psychopathology with the necessary outcome of the development of psychopathology.

Summary

In summary, these concepts and notions specify a variety of parameters that merit consideration in moving models of risk for psychopathology in children of depressed parents beyond correlational models to second-generation models that conceptualize development in terms of dynamic processes of interaction between the individual and the environment over time.

Mediational Processes: An Emotional Security Hypothesis

As is evident in Figure 5.3, emotional security has been posited as a mediator of relations between parental depression and family functioning on the one hand and child adjustment on the other. Moreover, emotional security has been posited as an influence on an individual's development across his or her life span (Bowlby, 1969). Therefore, although the focus of this chapter is on emotional security as a mediator of children's development in families with parental depression, emotional security derived from childhood experiences may subsequently influence children's own later marital relations (Karney, chapter 3), thus ultimately contributing to relations between later depression and marital conflict patterns. That is, the patterns of emotional security that children develop in families have implications for later adult functioning, including risk for depression (Cummings & Cicchetti, 1990). Emotional security derived from marital relations influences risk for adjustment problems in adulthood (see review in Colin, 1996), suggesting additional implications of emotional security notions for an understanding of relations between adult depression and adjustment and marital conflict from a clinical perspective (Cordova and Gee, chapter 10). However, this chapter focuses on a more limited extension of emotional security theory to an understanding of the development of children in families with depressed parents.

General Propositions

The specific process model to be discussed extends the emotional security hypothesis (Cummings & Davies, 1996; Davies & Cummings, 1994) to an understanding of the development of children of depressed parents (Cummings & Davies, 1992, 1994b). According to this model, parental depression and child outcomes are linked through a complex interplay among child management impairments, child exposure to symptoms, marital discord, and child characteristics such as temperament and developmental level (Cummings & Davies, 1999). Among various direct and indirect connections, this diverse collection of phenomena and processes converge to threaten the child's emotional security, which then becomes an important locus for deleterious effects. Intermediary effects of threatened emotional security are evident in child responses to immediate family events and stresses. Ultimately, however, the cumulative effects of chronic threats to emotional security are likely to be seen in diagnosable childhood conditions.

The centrality (but not exclusivity) of emotional regulation to the emotional security approach is not unique. In fact, emotional regulation and emotional security are central constructs in other accounts of normal development and the development of psychopathology (Cole, Michel, & Teti, 1994). The idea that emotions serve regulatory functions is also not unique (Thompson, 1994; Thompson & Caulkins, 1996). It is the hypothesized network of relations in which emotional security is embedded that marks its unique contribution to the parental depression literature. We propose that emotional security is central to the regulation of action (see also Emery, 1992). In fact, it is a constructive and organizing process, not an epiphenomenal byproduct of experience that needs to be controlled and modulated owing to any presumed disorganizing nature. Emotional security is the goal-state of a homeostatic apparatus encompassing not only emotions but also behavior, thoughts, and physiological responses. Hence, it extends beyond conscious thoughts and feelings and subsumes both present and past situational influences. Although broad in scope and necessarily explicated in abstract terms for theoretical purposes, various propositions of the emotional security model can be readily tested with standard instruments and laboratory procedures (Cummings & Davies, 1996, 1999; Davies & Cummings, 1994, 1998).

In an important review and integration of data, Lee and Gotlib (1991) suggested that because many forms of family disturbance (e.g., marital discord, divorce, parental depression) were associated with similar child outcomes perhaps there is a common pathway through which such disturbances exert their effects (see also Cummings & Davies, 1994a; Davies & Cummings, 1994). Under rubrics such as ''parental availability'' (p. 172) and ''children's sense of security or confidence in his or her parents'' (p. 180), they argued that a family systems perspective was needed. Several other proposals are reminiscent of this model (Feldman & Downey, 1994; Thompson & Caulkins, 1996; Wierson & Forehand, 1992), as is the classic final common pathway model of depression itself (Akiskal & McKinney, 1975). Now that a fairly large database of findings has emerged, it seems reasonable to focus specifically on constructs related to the emotional security model.

Extension of Model to the Effect of Marital Conflict on Children

The idea that children's emotional security in parent–child relations is central to their functioning has a long history (Bowlby, 1969). One of the more consistent findings in the literature on children of depressed parents is that they are more likely to form insecure or even very insecure (Type A or C or Type D) attachments to their parents (Cummings & Cicchetti, 1990; Cummings & Davies, 1994b; Radke-Yarrow et al., 1985; Zahn-Waxler, Chapman, & Cummings, 1984). A key proposition of the emotional security hypothesis is that these notions can also be extended to understanding the effect of marital conflict in families on children. A proposition of this chapter is that emotional insecurity in children of depressed parents derives from insecurity caused by high marital conflict as well as more frequent insecure attachments to their parents.

There is presently consensus among researchers and theorists that (a) children react to the perceived meaning of conflicts for themselves and their families, not its occurrence or even its form; (b) the meaning is personal and emotional and evident in children's cognitive appraisals, emotional reactions, and coping behaviors; and (c) historical as well as current experience with marital conflict influences reactions (Crockenberg & Forgays, 1996; Davies & Cummings, 1994; Emery, 1992; Grych & Fincham, 1990). The emotional security model proposes that children assess a particular meaning, that is, the emotional security implications of marital conflict (Cummings & Davies, 1996), referencing a construct of long-demonstrated importance in developmental theory.

A critical assumption is that not all conflict styles are distressing to children. Thus, in addition to differentiating between negative conflict behaviors, it is necessary to distinguish between constructive and destructive conflict behaviors. It is assumed that not all marital conflict styles are distressing for children. Some marital conflict styles (e.g., physically aggressive, unresolved) may induce insecure emotions (e.g., anger, sadness, fear) and cognitions (e.g., negative attributions and representations about family, self-blame, threat), leading to behavioral dysregulation (aggressiveness) and motivating children to attempt to restore emotional security (e.g., by mediating in parental disputes). Repeated exposure results in children's sensitization to conflict (i.e., more negative emotional, behavioral, and cognitive responses), thereby increasing the probability of children's adjustment problems. Cummings and Davies (1996) hypothesized that children interpret these marital conflict styles, especially with repeated exposure, as a threat to their emotional security, with negative implications for their adjustment (see also Grych & Fincham, 1990). These conflict styles are assumed to underlie the negative effects of marital conflict on children.

However, other conflict styles (e.g., fully resolved verbal conflicts) only mildly or briefly induce distress and are not linked with adjustment problems. Cummings and Davies (1996) hypothesized that children exposed to such conflicts over time retain secure representations of their parents' marriage and family, with positive implications for social competence as a result of the predictability, stability, and positivity of models for marriage and family provided (see also Davies & Cummings, 1994). This distinction underscores the importance of separating different marital conflict styles in studying their effects on children. Given the prevalence of negative marital conflict behaviors in spouses with depression, another possible distinction between depressed and nondepressed spouses is the proportion of negative conflict styles enacted in front of children. Changes in parenting also influence adjustment, due to implications for children's emotional security, but also due to other processes; (e.g., modeling, attributional processes; Brody, Arias, & Fincham, 1996).

Specific Propositions of the Model

Emotional security is specifically proffered to be reflected in three interdependent processes: (a) emotional reactivity, (b) representations of family relations, and (c) regulation of exposure to family affect (Davies & Cummings, 1994). Assessing these component processes as distinct elements not only allows the emotional security model to be tested, but it also allows for tests of the significance of the subprocesses as mediators of adjustment without regard to assumptions of the higher order organization posited by the emotional security hypothesis.

However, in theory, emotional security is conceptualized as a control system within which interrelations between these three component processes and the latent goal of emotional security are inextricable and bidirectional. Thus, emotional security is a goal that governs or regulates the expression of the concrete component processes. For example, insecurity resulting from marital discord may increase children's incentive to regulate their exposure to the threatening parental event by escaping or intervening in the conflict. By the same token, emotional security is also a goal that is regulated by the component processes. Extending the previous example, the mediation in parental disputes that was originally motivated by felt insecurity subsequently serves as a means of restoring some sense of emotional security, at least in a temporary, superficial way. Thus, positing that emotional security is reflected in several specific, interdependent component processes advances the testability and specificity of the model.

Moreover, it is hypothesized that children's reactions to marital conflict (a) provide a valuable window into the meaning of marital conflict from their perspective as well as (b) reflect broader patterns of response process that mediate development (e.g., Davies & Cummings, 1998; Harold et al., 1997). Preliminary studies have supported distinguishing among emotional, cognitive, and coping responses as reflecting interrelated, but different, mediational pathways on relations between marital conflict and children's adjustment (e.g., Davies & Cummings, 1998). Thus, there is support for the notion that children's reactions reflect (a) their emotional security about marital conflict styles and (b) dynamic process-level mediators of their adjustment over time.

Emotional Regulation

Supporting the importance of affect regulation in relation to family depression and child outcomes are several findings on families with depressed members: (a) They are emotionally dysregulated and do not allow for repairing or resolving negative interactions; (b) they are dysfunctional in family communication, in problem solving, and in the capacity to express appropriate affect; (c) the parents interpret negative affect as overwhelming, intolerable, and frightening and do not teach their children, who are more likely to express negative affect, to regulate or express their negative or conflictual affect more maturely and appropriately; and (d) depressed mothers ineffectively socialize their children's emotions by oscillating between ignoring, explaining, denying, anxiously alluding to, and punishing them (Coyne et al., 1994; Greenberg, DeKlyen, Speltz, & Endriga, 1997; Schwoeri & Sholevar, 1994). A depressive environmental context and the ensuing stress increase children's risk for emotional insecurity; and when children are additionally affected by the dysfunctional and emotionally dysregulated interactions in their families, they are at an even greater risk for not being able to regulate themselves and thus are at even greater risk for emotional and behavioral problems.

Representation of Family Relationships

Not only do parents' views of themselves influence marital and family dynamics through self-verification (cf. Katz, chapter 6) and stress generation processes (cf. Davila, chapter 4), parental views, or working models, of relationships are also evident in the ways that they interpret and behave in marriage and family life (Cummings & Cicchetti, 1990). For example, Carnelley, Pietromonaco, and Jaffe (1994) examined depressive individuals' working models of others and the relative contribution of these models and depression to relationship functioning. Respondents reported on their childhood relationships, adult attachment style, and relationship functioning. Among college women, Carnelley et al. found that attachment style and depression status mediated relations between positive experiences with mother and better relationship functioning.

Efforts to Regulate Parental Emotions

Exposure to negative parental emotions and conflict has been shown in studies of children, both at home and in the laboratory, to increase children's caregiving toward parents (Cummings & Davies, 1994a; El-Sheikh & Cummings, 1995). Such caregiving appears to be motivated by children's desire to regulate, reduce, and terminate negative emotions or conflicts to maintain their own emotional security (Davies & Cummings, 1994). The insecure–disoriented–disorganized attachment pattern, which involves efforts to regulate parental emotions and take care of parents, has repeatedly been reported in children of depressed parents (Cummings & Davies, 1994b; Teti et al., 1995). However, although efforts to mediate, and thereby regulate, interparental conflict have repeatedly been found among children from high-conflict homes, investigation has not been extended to the study of children of depressed parents.

Conclusion

This chapter discussed the significance of family processes to the impact of parental depression on children. Research and theory supporting links between parental depression and marital conflict and parental depression, marital conflict, parenting dysfunction, and child adjustment, respectively, were considered. Next steps include movement toward (a) articulating the processes linking these factors, (b) adequate conceptualization of developmental pathways in children of depressed parents, and (c) over the longer term, extending the developmental framework along with the processes it highlights to the study of family relationships in adulthood and the way they become associated with depression (Karney, chapter 3). Arguments for a testable model of greater emotional insecurity due to greater parenting dysfunction and marital conflict as one class of important mediators of greater risk for adjustment problems in children of depressed parents were advanced. Finally, with regard to the themes of this book, this chapter proposed a point of contact between models in which parental marital discord leads to childhood depression and models derived from research on adults demonstrating that marital discord leads to adult depression and vice versa (Whisman, chapter 1). In a related vein, there may be intergenerational patterns of influence by which marital discord increases risk for depression both in the parents and in their children, with effects on children evident both in immediate functioning and in later developmental outcomes, including the likelihood of depression and discord in their own adult relationships. This and other chapters in this book provide intriguing empirical and theoretical bases for studying these processes from both a life span and a familywide perspective.

References

Akiskal, H., & McKinney, W. (1975). Overview of recent research in depression: Integration of ten conceptual models into a comprehensive clinical framework. *Archives of General Psychiatry, 32,* 285–305.

Baron, R. M., & Kenny, D. A. (1986). The moderator-mediator variable distinction in social psychological research: Conceptual, strategic, and statistical considerations. *Journal of Personality and Social Psychology, 51,* 1173–1182.

Beach, S. R. H., Smith, D. A., & Fincham, F. D. (1994). Marital interventions for depression: Empirical foundation and future prospects. *Applied and Preventive Psychology, 3,* 233–250.

Beardslee, W., Bemporad, J., Keller, M. B., & Klerman, G. L. (1983). Children of parents with a major affective disorder: A review. *American Journal of Psychiatry, 140,* 825–832.

Beardslee, W. R., Versage, E. M., Wright, E. J., Salt, P, Rothberg, P. C., Drezner, K., & Gladstone, T. R. G. (1997). Examination of preventive interventions for families with depression: Evidence of change. *Development and Psychopathology, 9,* 109–130.

Beck, A. T., Rush, A. J., Shaw, B. F., & Emery, G. (1979). *Cognitive therapy of depression.* New York: Guilford Press.

Birmaher, B., Kaufman, J., Brent, D., Dahl, R., Perel, J., Al-Shabbout, M., Nelson, B., Stahl, S., Rao, U., Waterman, G., Williamson, D., & Ryan, N. (1997). Neuroendocrine response to 5-hydroxy-l-trypotophan in prepubertal children at risk of major depressive disorder. *Archives of General Psychiatry, 54,* 1113–1119.

Bowlby, J. (1969). *Attachment.* New York: Basic Books.

Brody, G. H., Arias, I., & Fincham, F. D. (1996). Linking marital and child attributions to family processes and parent-child relationships. *Journal of Family Psychology, 10,* 408–421.

Campbell, S. B., Cohn, J. F., & Meyers, T. (1995). Depression in first-time mothers: Mother-infant interaction and depression chronicity. *Developmental Psychology, 31,* 349–357.

Caplan, H., Cogill, S., Alexandra, H., Robson, K., Katz, R., & Kumar, R. (1989). Maternal depression and the emotional development of the child. *British Journal of Psychiatry, 154,* 818–822.

Carnelly, K. B., Pietromonaco, P. R., & Jaffe, K. (1994). Depression, working models of others and relationship functioning. *Journal of Personality and Social Psychology, 66,* 127–141.

Cicchetti, D., & Cohen, D. (1995). Perspectives on developmental psychopathology. In D. Cicchetti & D. Cohen (Eds.), *Developmental psychopathology* (pp. 3–22). New York: Wiley.

Cicchetti, D., Rogosch, F., & Toth, S. L. (1998). Maternal depressive disorder and contextual risk: Contributions to the development of attachment security and behavior problems in toddlerhood. *Development and Psychopathology, 10,* 283–300.

Cicchetti, D., & Toth, S. L. (1998). The development of depression in children and adolescents. *American Psychologist, 53,* 221–241.

Cohn, J. F., & Campbell, S. B. (1992). Influence of maternal depression on infant affect regulation. In D. Cicchetti & S. Toth (Eds.), *Rochester symposium on developmental psychopathology: Vol. 4. A developmental approach to affective disorders* (pp. 103–130). Rochester, NY: University of Rochester Press.

Cole, P. M., Michel, M., & Teti, L. (1994). The development of emotion regulation and dysregulation: A clinical perspective. In N. Fox (Ed.), *The development of emotion regulation: Biological and behavioral considerations. Monographs of the Society for Research in Child Development, 2-3* (Serial No. 240), pp. 73–102.

Colin, V. (1996). *Human attachment.* New York: McGraw-Hill.

Conger, R., Patterson, G., & Ge, X. (1995). It takes two to replicate: A mediational model for the impact of parents' stress on adolescent adjustment. *Child Development, 66,* 80–97.

Cox, A. D., Puckering, C., Pound, A., & Mills, M. (1987). The impact of maternal depression in young people. *Journal of Child Psychology and Psychiatry, 28,* 917–928.

Coyne, J. C., & Downey, G. (1991). Social factors and psychopathology: Stress, social support, and coping processes. *Annual Review of Psychology, 55,* 347–352.

Coyne, J. C., Downey, G., & Boergers, J. (1992). Depression in families: A systems perspective. In D. Cicchetti & S. Toth (Eds.), *Rochester symposium on developmental psychopathology, Vol. 4: A developmental approach to the affective disorders* (pp. 211–249). Rochester, NY: University of Rochester Press.

Coyne, J., Schwoeri, L., & Downey, G. (1994). Depression, the marital relationship, and parenting: An interpersonal view. In G. P. Sholevar (Ed.), *The transmission of depression in families and children: Assessment and intervention* (pp. 31–57). Northvale, NJ: Jason Aronson.

Crockenberg, S. B., & Forgays, D. (1996). The role of emotion in children's understanding and emotional reactions to marital conflict. *Merrill-Palmer Quarterly, 42,* 22–47.

Cummings, E. M. (1995). Security, emotionality, and parental depression. *Developmental Psychology, 31,* 425–427.

Cummings, E. M., & Cicchetti, D. (1990). Toward a transactional model of relations between attachment and depression, (pp. 339–372). In M. T. Greenberg, D. Cicchetti, & E. M. Cummings (Eds.), *Attachment during the preschool years.* Chicago: University of Chicago Press.

Cummings, E. M., & Davies, P. T. (1992). Parental depression, family functioning, and child adjustment: Risk factors, processes, and pathways. In D. Cicchetti & S. Toth (Eds.), *Rochester symposium on developmental psychopathology, Vol. 4: A developmental approach to the affective disorders* (pp. 283–322). Rochester, NY: University of Rochester Press.

Cummings, E. M., & Davies, P. T. (1994a). Children and marital conflict: *The impact of family dispute and resolution.* New York: Guilford Press.

Cummings, E. M., & Davies, P. T. (1994b). Maternal depression and child development. *Journal of Child Psychology and Psychiatry, 35,* 73–112.

Cummings, E. M., & Davies, P. T. (1996). Emotional security as a regulatory process in normal development of psychopathology. *Development and Psychopathology, 8,* 123–139.

Cummings, E. M., & Davies, P. T. (1999). Depressed parents and family functioning: Interpersonal effects and children's functioning and development. In T. Joiner & J. C. Coyne (Eds.), *Recent advances in interpersonal approaches to depression* (pp. 299–327). Washington, DC: American Psychological Association.

Cummings, E. M., Davies, P. T., & Campbell, S. B. (in press). *Developmental psychopathology and family process: Theory, research, and clinical implications.* New York: Guilford Press.

Cummings, E. M., Goeke-Morey, M., & Dukewich, T. (1998, July). *Marital conflict, emotional security, and children's adjustment.* Paper presented at the XVth Biennial Meetings of the International Society for the Study of Behavioral Development, Berne, Switzerland.

Cummings, E. M., Zahn-Waxler, C., & Radke-Yarrow, M. (1981). Young children's responses to expressions of anger and affection by others in the family. *Child Development, 52,* 1274–1282.

Davies, P. T., & Cummings, E. M. (1994). Marital conflict and child adjustment: An emotional security hypothesis. *Psychological Bulletin, 116,* 387–411.

Davies, P. T., & Cummings, E. M. (1998). Exploring children's emotional security as a mediator of the link between marital relations and child adjustment. *Child Development, 69,* 124–139.

Davies, P. T., & Windle, M. (1997). Gender-specific pathways between maternal depressive symptoms, family discord, and adolescent adjustment. *Developmental Psychology, 33,* 657–668.

Downey, G., & Coyne, J. C. (1990). Children of depressed parents: An integrative review. *Psychological Bulletin, 108,* 50–76.

El-Sheikh, M., & Cummings, E. M. (1995). Children's responses to angry adult behavior as a function of experimentally manipulated exposure to resolved and unresolved conflict. *Social Development, 4,* 75–91.

Emery, R. E. (1992). Family conflict and its developmental implications: A conceptual analysis of deep meanings and systemic processes. In C.U. Shantz & W.W. Hartup (Eds.), *Conflict in child and adolescent development* (pp. 270–298). London: Cambridge University Press.

Emery, R. E., Fincham, F. D., & Cummings, E. M. (1992). Parenting in context: Systemic thinking about parental conflict and its influence on children. *Journal of Consulting and Clinical Psychology, 60,* 909–912.

Erel, O., & Burman, B. (1995). Interrelations of marital relations and parent-child relations: A meta-analytic review. *Psychological Bulletin, 188,* 108–132.

Feldman, S., & Downey, G. (1994). Rejection and sensitivity as a mediator of the impact of childhood exposure to family violence on adult attachment behavior. *Development and Psychopathology, 6,* 231–247.

Fendrich, M., Warner, V., & Weissman, M. M. (1990). Family risk factors. Parental depression and psychopathology in offspring. *Developmental Psychology, 26,* 40–50.

Fergusson, D. M., Horwood, L. J., & Lynskey, M. T. (1995). Maternal depressive symptoms and depressive symptoms in adolescents. *Journal of Child Psychology and Psychiatry, 36,* 1161–1178.

Fincham, F. D. (1994). Understanding the association between marital conflict and child adjustment: Overview. *Journal of Family Psychology, 8,* 123–127.

Geller, J., & Johnston, C. (1995). Depressed mood and child conduct problems: Relationships to mother's attributions for their own and their children's experiences. *Child and Family Behavior Therapy, 17,* 19–34.

Gold, P., Goodwin, F., & Chrousos, G. (1988). Clinical and biochemical manifestations of depression: Relations to neurobiology of stress. *New England Journal of Medicine, 319,* 348–353.

Goodwin, F., & Jamison, K. (1990). *Manic depressive illness.* New York: Oxford University Press.

Gotlib, I. H. (1982). Self-reinforcement and depression in interpersonal interaction: The role of performance level. *Journal of Abnormal Psychology, 93,* 19–30.

Gotlib, I. H., & Asarnow, R. F. (1979). Interpersonal and impersonal problem-solving skills in mildly and clinically depressed students. *Journal of Consulting and Clinical Psychology, 47,* 86–95.

Gotlib, I. H., & Robinson, L. A. (1982). Responses to depressed individuals: Discrepancies between self-report and observer-rated behavior. *Journal of Abnormal Psychology, 91,* 231–240.

Gottman, J. M., Katz, L. F., & Hooven, C. (1997). *Meta-emotion: How families communicate emotionally.* Mahwah, NJ: Erlbaum.

Greenberg, M. T., DeKlyen, M., Speltz, M., & Endriga, P. (1997). The role of attachment processes in externalizing psychopathology in young children. In L. Atkinson & K. J. Zucker (Eds.), *Attachment and psychopathology* (pp. 196–222). New York: Guilford Press.

Grych, J. H. (1998). Children's appraisals of interparental conflict: Situational and contextual influences. *Journal of Family Psychology, 12,* 437–453.

Grych, J. H., & Fincham, F. D. (1990). Marital conflict and child adjustment: A cognitive-contextual framework. *Psychological Bulletin, 108,* 267–290.

Harold, G. T., & Conger, R. D. (1997). Marital conflict and adolescent distress: The role of adolescent awareness. *Child Development, 68,* 333–350.

Harold, G. T., Fincham, F. D., Osborne, L. N., & Conger, R. D. (1997). Mom and dad are at it again: Adolescent perceptions of marital conflict and adolescent psychological distress. *Developmental Psychology, 33,* 333–350.

Harrington, R., Rutter, M., & Fombonne, E. (1996). Developmental pathways in depression: Multiple meanings, antecedents, and endpoints. *Developmental Psychopathology, 8,* 601–616.

Hetherington, E. M., Stanley-Hagen, M., & Anderson, E. R. (1989). Marital transitions: A child's perspective. *American Psychologist, 44,* 303–312.

Holmbeck, G. N. (1997). Toward terminological, conceptual, and statistical clarity in the study of mediators and moderators: Examples from the child-clinical and pediatric psychology literatures. *Journal of Consulting and Clinical Psychology, 65,* 599–610.

Hops, H., Biglan, A., Sherman, L., Arthur, J., Friedman, L., & Osteen, R. (1987). Home observations of family interactions of depressed women. *Journal of Consulting and Clinical Psychology, 55,* 341–346.

Jacobvitz, D. B., & Bush, N. F. (1996). Reconstructions of family relationships: Parent-child alliances, personal distress, and self-esteem. *Developmental Psychology, 32,* 732–743.

Laumakis, M., Margolin, G., & John, R. (1998). The emotional, cognitive, and coping responses of preadolescent children to different dimensions of marital conflict, (pp. 257–288). In G. Holden, B. Geffner, & E. Jouriles (Eds.), *Children and family violence.* Washington DC: American Psychological Association.

Lee, C. M., & Gotlib, I. H. (1991). Family disruption, parental availability, and child adjustment. *Advances in Behavioral Assessment of Children and Families, 5,* 171–199.

Margolin, G., Christensen, A., & John, R. (1996). The continuance and spillover of everyday tensions in distressed and nondistressed families. *Journal of Family Psychology, 10,* 304–321.

McElwain, N., & Volling, B. (1997). *The effects of depressed mood and marital conflict on parent-infant interaction: A family model.* Unpublished manuscript.

McGuffin, P., Katz, R., Watkins, S., & Rutherford, J. (1996). A hospital based twin registry study of the heritability of DSM-IV unipolar depression. *Archives of General Psychiatry, 53,* 129–136.

Miller, N. B., Cowan, P. A., Cowan, C. P., Hetherington, E. M., & Clingempeel, W. G. (1993). Externalizing in preschoolers and early adolescents: A cross study replication of a family model. *Developmental Psychology, 29,* 3–18.

Murray, L. (1992). The impact of postnatal depression on infant development. *Journal of Child Psychology and Psychiatry, 33,* 543–561.

Osborne, L A., & Fincham, F. D. (1996). Marital conflict, parent-child relationships, and child adjustment: Does gender matter? *Merrill-Palmer Quarterly, 42,* 48–75.

Radke-Yarrow, M., Cummings, E. M., Kuczynski, L., & Chapman, M. (1985). Patterns of attachment in two- and three-year-olds in normal families and families with parental depression. *Child Development, 56,* 884–893.

Rende, R. D., Plomin, R., Reiss, D., & Hetherington, E. M. (1993). Genetic and environmental influences on depressive symptomatology in adolescence: Individual differences and extreme scores. *Journal of Child Psychology and Psychiatry and Allied Disciplines, 34,* 1387–1398.

Rutter, M., & Quinton, D. (1984). Parental psychiatric disorder: Effects on children. *Psychological Medicine, 14,* 853–880.

Schwoeri, L., & Sholevar, G. P. (1994). The family transmission of depression. In G. P. Sholevar (Ed.), *The transmission of depression in families and children: Assessment and intervention* (pp. 123–144). Northvale, NJ: Jason Aronson.

Strack, S., & Coyne, J. C. (1983). Social confirmation of dysphoria: Shared and private reactions to depression. *Journal of Personality and Social Psychology, 44,* 798–806.

Teti, D., Gelfand, D. M., Messinger, D. S., & Isabella, R. (1995). Maternal depression and the quality of early attachment: An examination of infants, preschoolers, and their mothers. *Developmental Psychology, 31,* 364–376.

Thompson, R. A. (1994). Emotion regulation: A theme in search of definition. In N. Fox (Ed.), *The development of emotion regulation: Biological and behavioral considerations. Monographs of the Society for Research in Child Development, 59*(2–3, Serial No. 240), 25–52.

Thompson, R. A., & Caulkins, S. (1996). The double-edged sword: Emotional regulation for children at risk. *Development and Psychopathology, 8,* 163–182.

Weissman, M. M., Warner, V. Wickramaratne, P. Moreau, D. & Olfson, M. (1997). Offspring of depressed parents: 10 years later. *Archives of General Psychiatry, 54,* 932–940.

Wierson, M., & Forehand, R. (1992). Family stressors and adolescent functioning: A consideration of models for early and middle adolescents. *Behavior Therapy, 23,* 671–688.

Zahn-Waxler, C., Chapman, M., & Cummings, E. M. (1984). Cognitive and social development in infants and toddlers with a bipolar parent. *Child Psychiatry and Human Development, 15,* 75–85.

6
Self-Verification Theory: Expanding Current Conceptualizations of the Link Between Marital Distress and Depression

Jennifer Katz

The marital relationship may be more central to individual well-being than any other type of relationship among adults. Just as parents serve as primary attachment figures during childhood (see Cummings, DeArth-Pendley, Schudlich, and Smith, chapter 5), romantic partners serve as primary attachment figures during adulthood. For individuals who are either experiencing relationship problems, feeling depressed, or both, ongoing marital interactions often are problematic (see Whisman, chapter 1). Likewise, marital discord in the absence of depression may increase risk for later depression (Beach & O'Leary, 1993b). Depression in the absence of marital discord may increase risk for later marital discord as well (Beach & O'Leary, 1993a). In this book, Whisman (chapter 1) explores the relationship between depression and marital dissatisfaction within a meta-analytic framework, and Davila (chapter 4) discusses the reciprocal effects of depression and marital dysfunction within a stress-generation framework. Both Whisman and Davila highlight the potential value of explicating the mechanisms that account for these reciprocal influences.

Self-verification theory may provide one avenue for understanding some of the more complex ways in which individuals and their relationships exhibit mutual influences on each other. In this chapter, self-verification theory is introduced, and work applying this theory to understanding depression and marital quality is reviewed. Next, theoretical frameworks that have integrated self-verification theory into models of the association between depression and marital discord are discussed. In this context, an integrative model incorporating self-verification theory with the marital discord model of depression is described. This model illustrates how self-verification theory may contribute to an understanding of the link between marital discord and subsequent depression (Katz & Beach, 1997b). Strivings for self-verification among depressed individuals and effects on relationship quality also are discussed within the context of Joiner's integrative interpersonal theory of depression (Joiner, Alfano, & Metalsky, 1992, 1993; Joiner & Metalsky, 1995). The chapter concludes with a discussion of clinical implications of this work as well as directions for future research.

Self-Verification Theory

Self-verification theory, which is derived from theories concerned with self-concept and self-consistency, describes the individual's tendency to value social information about the self that is consistent with his or her self-views (Swann, 1983, 1987). Because stimuli that are predictable and familiar and reduce uncertainty may be perceived as especially trustworthy and accurate (Swann, Griffin, Predmore, & Gaines, 1987), information that confirms or verifies already-existing schemas is more likely to be remembered and evaluated as valid than information that runs counter to expectations and/or beliefs (cf. Swann & Read, 1981).

Individuals elicit (Joiner, 1994; Swann, Wenzlaff, Krull, & Pelham, 1992; Swann, Wenzlaff, & Tafarodi, 1992), remember (Swann & Read, 1981), and believe (Swann et al., 1987) self-verifying evaluations rather than nonverifying evaluations. These self-verification effects occur independently of the positivity or negativity of the feedback provided. That is, individuals appear to not only seek and value positive feedback concerning their positive self-conceptions, but also to seek and value negative feedback concerning their negative self-conceptions.

From the self-verification perspective, a primary motive of interpersonal behavior is to preserve the self-concept. It has been suggested that self-verification processes occur in an attempt to increase the individual's sense of predictability and control within social situations rather than for the sake of consistency itself (Swann, Stein-Seroussi, & Giesler, 1992). Specifically, self-verification strivings are thought to be motivated by intrapsychic, epistemic concerns about promoting existential security (e.g., "I really do know myself") and interpersonal, pragmatic concerns about promoting fluid interpersonal transactions (e.g., "My partner really does know me").

Self-Verification, Self-Enhancement, and the Cognitive–Affective Crossfire

Self-verification theory often is misunderstood as suggesting that individuals with negative self-views uniformly reject positive self-relevant feedback. Clearly, the self-verification motive does not exist in a vacuum. Individuals also seek and value positive, affectively pleasing feedback from others. Interest in positivity from others has been termed the *self-enhancement motive*. Research in the area of self-esteem is consistent with predictions made by both self-verification and self-enhancement theories. For instance, relative to individuals with low self-esteem, individuals with high self-esteem are more likely to engage in behaviors that elicit self-enhancing feedback about themselves (see Taylor & Brown, 1988, for a review). In contrast, individuals with low self-esteem seek self-enhancement only when there is little risk for humiliation or failure (Wood, Giordono-Beech, Taylor, Michela, & Gaus, 1994).

Both self-verification and self-enhancement motives appear to influence social behavior (Swann et al., 1987; Swann, Stein-Seroussi, et al., 1992), and data have suggested that needs for self-verification and self-enhancement operate independently of each other. For individuals with positive self-views, favorable feedback is both self-verifying and self-enhancing. Because favorable feedback simultaneously satisfies cognitive needs for self-verification and emotional needs for self-enhancement, these two motivations may be confounded with one another. For individuals with negative self-views, however, needs for self-verification and self-enhancement are at odds with one another. This conflict between motives for self-verification and self-enhancement among individuals with negative self-views has been termed the *cognitive–affective crossfire* (Joiner et al., 1993; Shrauger, 1975).

Individuals with negative self-appraisals appear to self-verify to confirm their self-concepts, despite the nonenhancing nature of such feedback (Swann, Stein-Seroussi, et al., 1992). This does not mean, however, that individuals with negative self-views lack the motivation to feel positively about themselves. In fact, dysphoric individuals with negative self-views appear to have conflicting needs for positive reassurance as well as negative self-verifying feedback (e.g., Joiner et al., 1993; Katz & Beach, 1997a; Swann, Wenzlaff, Krull, & Pelham, 1992). It may be postulated instead that individuals with negative self-views want to feel positively about themselves and want favorable feedback from others. They have difficulties, however, accepting such feedback as truthful and accurate.

Given that self-enhancing feedback meets affective needs for positivity and self-verifying feedback meets cognitive needs for consistency, it would be expected that self-verification and self-enhancement may have different and independent effects on relationship quality. Affective and cognitive needs should be congruent for individuals with positive self-views. In contrast, needs for cognitive consistency (met through self-verification) and positive affectivity (met through self-enhancement) among individuals with negative self-views are at odds with one another.

Self-Verification Theory and Relationship Quality

Do individuals really prefer partners who view them as they view themselves? Previous research in which self-verification theory has been applied to understanding marital quality generally has supported this theory. Swann, De La Ronde, and Hixon (1994) examined marital intimacy as a function of the interaction of spouses' self-views and the views of them held by their spouses. Findings were consistent with self-verification theory, as spouses with positive self-views were more intimate with their partners to the extent that their partners evaluated them positively. Likewise, spouses with negative self-views were more intimate with partners to the extent that their partners viewed them negatively (see also De La Ronde & Swann, 1998; Ritts & Stein, 1995; Schafer, Wickrama, & Keith, 1996; Swann, Hixon, & De La Ronde, 1992).

Using a different methodology, Katz, Beach, and Anderson (1996) also found evidence for the self-verification perspective. Spouses' self-views were assessed at the level of global self-esteem, and partner views of spouses were assessed using a measure of self-esteem support provision. Consistent with self-verification theory, greater congruence between spouses' self-esteem and perceived self-esteem support from partners was related to greater marital intimacy and satisfaction for spouses. Although positivity effects were apparent (i.e., greater self-esteem support was beneficial for relationship quality), it was concluded that self-verification effects contributed unique variance to dyadic adjustment as well.

Some more recent research has suggested that self-verification strivings may influence initial attraction to potential romantic partners. Katz and Beach (in press) conducted two experimental studies in which single participants responded to four scenarios in which potential partners provided them self-relevant feedback. Participants were most attracted to partners who provided feedback that was both self-enhancing and self-verifying and significantly less attracted to partners who provided either self-verification only or self-enhancement only. When feedback was explicitly labeled as incongruent with participants' self-views (Study 2), participants were significantly more attracted to self-verifying partners than to self-enhancing partners.

In contrast, Murray, Holmes, and Griffin (1996) found effects that may be viewed as consistent with individuals' preferences for positivity rather than self-verification. They studied positive illusions and dyadic adjustment among both married and dating couples. Individuals were more satisfied with their relationships to the extent that partners held overly positive or idealizing perceptions of them regarding specific interpersonal qualities (e.g., kind, lazy, childish). Murray et al. concluded that individuals are happier in relationships to the extent that their partners idealize them. Although self-verification hypotheses were tested in this study, evidence for the self-verification perspective was not obtained. Hypotheses about reconciling these discrepant findings are outlined in the last section of this chapter.

Why do self-verifying evaluations from partners enhance relationship quality in close dyads? And why does this occur even for individuals with negative self-views? Examination of the basic tenets of self-verification theory provides clues as to the effects of self-verifying feedback (or lack thereof) on relationship quality, although these hypotheses have not been empirically tested. Both positive and negative feedback that is inconsistent with an individual's self-views may lead to increased emotional distance between romantic partners. The recipient of positive nonverifying feedback may question whether his or her partner really knows him or her, may feel overvalued, and may fear inevitable rejection or humiliation given his or her partner's unrealistically high expectations that are certain to be disproved over time. For example, if a man who considered himself socially unskilled was married to someone who thought him socially adept, he may fear that his wife would expect him to be "the life of the party" at social functions. Conversely, if his wife held congruent negative views about his social skills, this concern would be minimized.

Negative nonverifying feedback may have even more damaging effects on relationship quality. For example, a woman who receives negative nonverifying feedback also may wonder about whether her partner really knows her. In addition, she may feel unappreciated or undervalued. This recipient of negative nonverifying feedback may experience rejection or humiliation given her partner's unreasonably poor evaluation. Although she may not have concerns about disappointing her partner in the future, as in the case of the overvalued spouse, the undervalued spouse may be concerned about having disappointed her partner in the past.

Self-Verification Theory and Depression

Thus far, the effects of self-verifying feedback and support from relationship partners have been discussed in terms of their effect on marital quality. Self-verification theory also provides an interpersonal perspective for examining self-discrepant feedback and its relation to negative mood. As discussed previously, nonverifying or discrepant feedback is thought to challenge the individual's sense of predictability and control over the environment (Swann, Stein-Seroussi, et al., 1992) causing cognitive discomfort and emotional distress.

Although nonverifying feedback from partners may influence relationship quality, individual well-being may be compromised as well because of concerns about personal failure or letting others down. This may occur in addition to or independent of direct effects on relationship quality. There are two types of nonverifying feedback, favorable and unfavorable, and both may be related to feelings of failure and disappointing others.

Favorable nonverifying feedback may lead to negative affect because of apprehension about failing in the future. Overly positive feedback may indicate that others hold unrealistically high expectations of the recipient, who feels unable to meet these expectations. In other words, when an individual is overvalued (i.e., receives positive but disconfirming self-relevant feedback), this may cause him or her to expect inevitable personal failure with regard to the standards held by others. Unfavorable nonverifying feedback may lead to negative affect because of the suggestion of already having failed in the eyes of the partner. Overly negative feedback may indicate that the partner holds excessively high standards that were not met. The undervalued spouse may feel that his or her partner is disappointed and that such disappointment is unwarranted.

Nonverifying feedback, both favorable and unfavorable, challenges the individual's sense of predictability and control over his or her social environment. Accordingly, nonverifying feedback may have effects similar to those described by the learned helplessness view of depression, which posits that depression may stem from an inability to act and control one's life (Seligman, 1974), and the hopelessness theory of depression (Abramson, Metalsky, & Alloy, 1989), which posits that depression may develop when an individual believes that he or she is unable to change an undesirable situation (e.g., being under- or overvalued).

Research applying self-verification theory to understanding depression is growing. Some research has suggested that negative self-verifying feedback from relationship partners may lead to depressive symptoms among individuals with negative self-views. Studies have been conducted with clinically depressed samples as well as with samples of individuals with subthreshold levels of depression.

Clinical Depression

To date, two studies have examined self-verification effects among individuals diagnosed with clinical depression. Giesler, Josephs, and Swann (1996) compared preferences for favorable versus unfavorable feedback among high self-esteem, low self-esteem, and depressed adults. Participants were identified as clinically depressed using both the structured clinical interview (*Diagnostic and Statistical Manual of Mental Disorders,* 3rd edition, revised; American Psychiatric Association, 1987) and a minimum score of 16 or higher on the Beck Depression Inventory (BDI; Beck, Ward, Mendelson, Mock, & Erbaugh, 1961). Each individual was provided with two bogus self-relevant summaries, one positive and one negative, that ostensibly summarized longer, more in-depth evaluative reports. Participants were asked to read the summaries and because of time constraints to choose the one in-depth evaluative report (favorable or unfavorable) they would be most interested in reading. Results indicated that 82% of the depressed group, 64% of the low self-esteem group, and 25% of the high self-esteem group selected the unfavorable evaluation. Results also suggested that depression exerted effects on preference ratings through influences of accuracy. That is, individuals in the depressed group perceived the unfavorable summaries as more accurate (i.e., self-verifying) than the favorable summaries, and this accounted for the effect of group membership on feedback preference.

Joiner, Katz, and Lew (1997) examined depressive symptoms, interest in negative, self-verifying feedback, and peer relationship functioning in a clinical sample of youth psychiatric inpatients. Approximately one half of their sample was diagnosed with major depression, depressive disorder not otherwise specified, or bipolar disorder. Consistent with Giesler et al. (1996), level of depression was associated with interest in negative feedback. Furthermore, interest in negative feedback was associated with rejection by peers within relatively long-standing peer relationships. Also of note, interest in negative feedback was more strongly associated with cognitive rather than emotional symptoms of depression and was associated with depression specifically rather than emotional distress more generally.

These findings provide support for the role of self-verification theory in understanding the negative social effects of clinically significant depression. Interest in negative self-verifying feedback by depressed individuals may help perpetuate their emotional distress and cause impaired social functioning. To the extent that such processes also occur within the marital context, self-verification strivings may influence both depression and relationship quality for some individuals.

Depressive Symptoms

To date, three reports focusing on self-verification theory and subclinical depression have been published. Swann, Wenzlaff, Krull, and Pelham (1992) proposed that depressed individuals are rejected because they gravitate toward relationship partners who view them unfavorably. In a series of four studies, they investigated whether individuals with negative self-views seek unfavorable appraisals from others. Preferences for unfavorable (i.e., self-verifying) feedback among individuals with negative self-views were of particular interest. Inclusion criteria for status as "depressed" varied somewhat across the studies, but generally were based on a BDI score of 9 or higher.

In Study 1, depressed individuals were inclined to prefer an unfavorable evaluator, whereas nondepressed individuals were inclined to prefer a favorable evaluator. In Study 2, depressed individuals preferred friends who viewed them less positively in a global sense than did nondepressed individuals. Although both depressed and nondepressed participants wanted to be seen in a positive manner by their current dating partners, depressed participants reported less liking for their current dating partners and a perception of being less valued by their current dating partners. In Study 3, which was a prospective study of college roommate pairs, negative feedback-seeking tendencies and the rejection of depressed participants by their roommates were investigated. Depressed participants were more inclined to seek unfavorable feedback than nondepressed or dysphoric (classified based on a BDI score of 5–14) participants. Furthermore, the more participants sought unfavorable feedback, the more likely their roommates were to derogate them later, intend to terminate the relationship, and plan to have a new roommate in the future.

Finally, in Study 4, cognitive versus affective precipitants of negative feedback seeking were examined among a sample of undergraduate women. Participants sought positive feedback about positive self-views but negative feedback about negative self-views, and these effects occurred independent of manipulations made to induce positive, negative, or neutral affect. Participants with negative self-views were significantly more likely to elicit unfavorable feedback than were participants with positive self-views, even though negative feedback was related to increases in both depressive and anxious symptoms.

These initial, provocative studies of self-verification and depression were criticized on a number of theoretical and methodological grounds (Alloy & Lipman, 1992; Hooley & Richters, 1992). First, the classification of chronic depression and dysphoria was inconsistent across studies and based solely on scores from the BDI, a nondiagnostic instrument administered over a period of 2–6 weeks. Next, the construct of negative feedback seeking, which was assessed through a hypothetical self-report measure, was criticized for being poorly operationalized and not reflective of actual feedback-seeking behaviors. In particular, because depressed individuals tend to withdraw from social interactions rather than seek feedback of a particular sort, it was suggested that the construct of negative feedback seeking needs to be better elucidated (Alloy & Lipman, 1992). Finally, the motivational underpinnings of the apparent self-verification effects were not substantiated by the research methods used. That is, it was not proven that negative feedback choices made by depressed individuals necessarily stem from motivation for self-verification. This point was substantiated by research from the depressive realism literature as well as from information processing models that suggested that negative content self-schemas bias attention to and selection of self-relevant information negatively (e.g., Markus & Wurf, 1987).

In partial reply to these criticisms, Swann, Wenzlaff, and Tafarodi (1992) conducted two additional studies of depression and self-verification strivings. In Study 1, dysphoric participants preferred to interact with an evaluator who appraised them unfavorably, whereas nondysphoric participants preferred to interact with an evaluator who appraised them favorably. Furthermore, all participants were more interested in interacting with their evaluator when they believed the evaluation was accurate. In Study 2, dysphoric participants responded to positive feedback by eliciting negative feedback, providing the first evidence for the motivational underpinnings of self-verification among dysphoric individuals.

This rebuttal article addressed some (but not all) of the major criticisms of the original article regarding negative feedback-seeking behaviors and the motivational underpinnings of self-verification strivings among individuals with depressive symptoms. In addition, the studies conducted by Giesler et al. (1996) and Joiner et al. (1997) successfully addressed concerns about the applicability of these findings to clinically significant depression. Because of the controversial nature of this work, efforts to replicate and extend self-verification findings to the context of depression are valuable. Additional support for the application of self-verification theory to understanding the development of depressive symptoms has been obtained outside of Swann's laboratory. Joiner (1995) hypothesized that individuals with negative self-views who seek self-verifying feedback from others are vulnerable to future increases in depression. He tested this hypothesis in a longitudinal study of same-sex roommate pairs. Consistent with his prediction, target individuals who were both interested in negative feedback from their roommates and who were evaluated negatively by their roommates were at increased risk for later depression, even after controlling for the targets' level of self-esteem. Thus, it was concluded that self-verification strivings among individuals with negative self-views may lead to the onset and maintenance of depressive symptoms, at least among individuals who are successful at soliciting negative self-verifying feedback from their relationship partners.

In summary, studies of both clinical and subclinical depression have provided some support for the application of self-verification theory to understanding depression. These findings suggest that (a) depression is related to interest in negative self-relevant feedback, (b) depressed individuals perceive negative feedback to be both accurate and self-verifying, (c) individuals who seek and receive negative self-relevant feedback experience increases in depressive symptoms over time, and (d) interest in negative feedback is related to interpersonal disruption across a variety of peer relationships.

Integrative Models of Self-Verification

Self-verification theory has been successfully applied to researchers' understanding of both depression and marital discord. Accordingly, several researchers have integrated self-verification theory into broader models of marital discord and depression, as reviewed below. First, an integrative model incorporating self-verification theory with the marital discord model of depression is described. This model provides one example of how self-verification theory adds to understanding the link between marital discord and subsequent depression (Katz & Beach, 1997b). Second, strivings for self-verification among depressed individuals are discussed within the context of an integrative interpersonal theory of depression (Joiner et al., 1992, 1993; Joiner & Metalsky, 1995).

Self-Verification, Relationship Quality, and Depression: A Multiple-Pathway Model

As reviewed previously, self-verifying feedback from partners contributes to relationship adjustment. Diverse measures of marital quality, such as satisfaction (Katz et al., 1996), commitment (Ritts & Stein, 1995; Swann, Hixon, et al., 1992), and intimacy (Katz et al., 1996; Swann et al., 1994) are positively related to receiving self-verifying evaluations from marital partners. Interestingly, self-verifying feedback also may contribute to depression for individuals with negative self-views (Joiner, 1995; Swann, Wenzlaff, Krull, et al., 1992).

Why is negative self-verifying feedback depressing? One likely mechanism involves the stability of self-views for individuals in self-verifying relationships. Individuals who receive self-verifying feedback appear to have more enduring and stable self-views, presumably because verification solidifies and strengthens those self-views. For example, Swann and Predmore (1985) found that individuals with self-verifying dating partners were significantly less likely to alter their self-appraisals when presented with non-verifying feedback about themselves. Likewise, Pelham and Swann (1994) found that partners were most likely to provide self-verifying feedback about highly certain self-appraisals (see also Swann & Guiliano, 1987).

Stability of self-esteem can be defined as the magnitude of fluctuations in an individual's level of self-esteem over time (Kernis, Grannemann, & Mathis, 1991). A growing body of evidence has indicated that stability of self-esteem may moderate the association between self-esteem level and depression (Butler, Hokanson, & Flynn, 1994; Kernis et al., 1991). That is, low self-esteem may be especially depressogenic among individuals with stable, rather than unstable, self-esteem.

Taken together, these findings suggest that self-verifying feedback leads to more stable self-conceptions (e.g., Swann & Predmore, 1985), which may increase risk for depression among individuals with low self-esteem. In contrast, stable self-conceptions may decrease risk for depression among individuals with high self-esteem (Butler, Hokanson, & Flynn, 1994; Kernis, Grannemann, & Mathis, 1991). Accordingly, self-verifying feedback may be expected to moderate the effect of self-esteem on depressive symptoms. Among self-verified individuals, low self-esteem may be robustly related to greater depression, and high self-esteem may be robustly related to lesser depression. In contrast, levels of self-esteem and depression should be less strongly related among non-verified individuals.

On the basis of these earlier works, Katz and Beach (1997b) suggested two distinct pathways through which self-verifying feedback from partners may influence depressive symptoms. In the first pathway, self-verifying feedback was expected to lead to increased relationship satisfaction, which was expected to lead to decreases in depression. In the second pathway, an indirect effect of self-verification on depressive symptoms was proposed. This effect was hypothesized to take the form of an interaction of self-verification and self-esteem level. In this pathway, self-verifying feedback was expected to intensify the effect of self-esteem level on depression. Accordingly, self-verifying feedback should have beneficial effects for depression among individuals with high self-esteem but detrimental effects among individuals with low self-esteem. Among non-verified individuals, self-esteem level should be less strongly related to depressive symptoms.

These hypotheses were investigated in two complementary studies of women's intimate relationships (Katz & Beach, 1997b). More specifically, pathways between self-verifying partner feedback and depression were examined within a community sample of married women (Study 1) and within a sample of undergraduate women involved in long-term dating relationships (Study 2). Support for the multiple-pathway model was obtained. The results of Study 1 suggested that self-verifying partner feedback was associated with enhanced relationship satisfaction, which, in turn, was associated with decreased depressive symptoms. At the same time, however, self-verifying feedback was associated with a stronger effect of self-esteem level on depressive symptoms. Level of self-esteem and depression were more strongly correlated for women with self-verifying marital partners than for women with nonverifying partners. Consequently, women with low self-esteem were at greater risk for depression when verified by their marital partners. The same pattern of findings was obtained in Study 2. Although the data were cross-sectional in nature, these results were not limited to a single type of intimate, romantic relationship, a single index of perceived partner verifying appraisals, or a single index of depressive symptoms.

It should be noted that many of the criticisms of the initial self-verification and depression studies may be applied to this work, and additional studies using more diverse methodologies are warranted. Regardless, however, the available evidence suggests an important extension of the original marital discord model of depression: There appears to be a trade-off between marital and individual well-being for individuals with negative self-views. Marital interactions that do not contribute to relationship discord still may be implicated in the development and maintenance of depression.

When a spouse holds negative self-views and his or her partner validates these self-views by providing negative self-verifying feedback, the spouse's negative self-conceptions may be stabilized and increase risk for depression. These partner behaviors may not be identified as problematic by the spouse, perhaps because they seem reasonable and justifiable. However, these partner behaviors still may have negative effects on the spouse's emotional well-being. In some cases, marital conflict can promote emotional health better than marital harmony. That is, when partner behaviors are more negative (or even less positive) than warranted based on a spouse's self-conceptions, rejection of this nonverifying feedback may lead to conflict but also help to preserve positive self-conceptions. Insofar as this conflict leads to general relationship discord, risk for depression may be heightened. If this conflict can be resolved successfully, risk for depression may be minimized and positive self-conceptions preserved.

Consider the case in which Deborah makes negative self-attributions that are verified by her partner Brian. Brian is upset because Deborah was late getting home from work. Deborah had anticipated Brian's reaction but was unable to avert the situation. If both Deborah and Brian attribute the problem as being internal to Deborah, her certainty that she is at fault for the problem is increased. Although there may be a relative absence of marital conflict in that both spouses agree that the problem is internal to Deborah, there may, nonetheless, be negative effects on Deborah's emotional well-being. For instance, Deborah may begin to develop other, more generalized negative self-conceptions (e.g., she is unable to meet the needs of her partner) and, consequently, may begin to feel dysphoric regarding her weaknesses and faults.

Alternatively, if Brian attributed the problem as being internal to Deborah but Deborah attributed the problem to an overly demanding supervisor (i.e., an external source), the probability of more severe marital conflict would be heightened. The spouses would disagree about the source of the problem, setting the stage for failure to validate or verify the other's perspective. However, this marital conflict may lead to depression only insofar as it affected marital discord more generally or only insofar as Deborah was persuaded by Brian's arguments to internalize the source of the problem.

As illustrated by these examples, the relationship between self-verifying partner feedback and well-being may be complex for individuals with negative self-views. Well-being in terms of relationship harmony may be at odds with well-being in terms of positive self-conception. The trade-off between relationship and individual well-being must be negotiated. Because both relationship harmony and a positive self-view influence depressive symptoms, this negotiation may be particularly difficult for people with negative self-views.

Integrative Interpersonal Theory of Depression

Self-verification theory also suggests avenues for partner behavior to influence relationship functioning when an individual is experiencing depression. These avenues of influence may hold whether or not that depression has been driven by marital problems. Joiner and colleagues (Joiner, et al., 1993; Joiner & Metalksky, 1995) have constructed an integrative theory of depression by merging Coyne's (1976) work with Swann's self-verification theory (1983). According to Coyne, depressed individuals seek positive, enhancing feedback about their worth from relationship partners through reassurance seeking. According to Swann, depressed individuals seek and value feedback about themselves that verifies or confirms their own self-views, even if that feedback is negative. Consistent with the crossfire model discussed previously (e.g., Shrauger, 1975), depressed individuals with negative self-views appear to have conflicting needs for positive reassurance from others as well as negative, self-verifying support.

Joiner et al. (1992) suggested that reassurance provided to depressed individuals may be emotionally satisfying but cognitively displeasing. Receiving positive nonverifying feedback thus triggers depressed individuals to seek negative verifying feedback from partners. In turn, this feedback is cognitively pleasing but emotionally unsatisfying. This prompts the depressed individual to seek more reassurance, creating a cycle of reassurance and negative feedback seeking. It was concluded that the confusing interpersonal demands of the depressed individual, whose needs for confirmation and enhancement are at odds with each other, may generate relationship stress. The partner may sense, rightfully so, that the depressed individual is never satisfied with the feedback that the partner provides. In addition to relationship stress, these interpersonal demands may contribute to rejection by the partner, relationship partner dissatisfaction, or both. In turn, partner rejection may exacerbate the depressed individual's depressive symptoms (Katz, Beach, & Joiner, 1998).

Empirical support for the integrative interpersonal theory of depression is growing. Findings have suggested that the three-way interaction of depression, interest in reassurance, and interest in negative feedback is associated with interpersonal disruption in close dyads. More specifically, reassurance-seeking and negative feedback-seeking behaviors among depressed undergraduates predicted rejection among same-sex roommates both cross-sectionally (Joiner et al., 1993) and longitudinally (Joiner & Metalksy, 1995) and partner relationship dissatisfaction (but not rejection per se) among heterosexual dating couples (Katz & Beach, 1997a).

Research substantiating this theory has provided additional evidence supporting the self-verification perspective as applied to understanding depression more generally. That is, these studies have demonstrated that mildly depressed individuals are interested in negative feedback from others. Importantly, interest in negative self-verifying feedback is consistent with the motivational view posited by Swann, Wenzlaff, Krull, et al. (1992). This theory also provides a more comprehensive account of the interpersonal context of depression, as it accounts for motivations for obtaining both positive self-enhancing and negative self-verifying feedback.

More recently, an entrainment model has been proposed (Joiner & Katz, 2000; see Joiner, chapter 7). Building on the integrative interpersonal theory, research efforts have focused on the relationship between reassurance seeking and negative feedback seeking within dyads. Preliminary data have suggested that the relationship between reassurance seeking and negative feedback seeking as indexed self-report measures is moderated by level of depression. Among dysphoric individuals, reassurance-seeking and negative feedback-seeking tendencies are significantly correlated. Among nondysphoric individuals, these two types of feedback seeking are not significantly correlated. Efforts are under way to examine feedback-seeking behaviors among depressed individuals and their dating partners' responses to both reassurance seeking and negative feedback seeking using observational methods.

Clinical Implications

Although no prevention or treatment work based on self-verification theory has been conducted at this time, many implications for clinical work may be drawn from both the initial theory and the models that incorporate self-verification theory. Of course, these speculations remain tentative until additional empirically based prevention or treatment work with couples has been conducted.

New components of marital therapy that target basic self-verification processes connecting marriage and depression may be useful. The assessment and conceptualization phases of therapy conducted with couples, depressed individuals, or both, may become more complex when self-verification considerations are taken into account. For instance, although assessment procedures for marital or couples therapy may typically involve gathering more couple-level, rather than individual, data, some degree of assessment of self-conceptions and partner conceptions of a spouse may be useful.

The basic research on self-verification theory has suggested that positive partner behaviors are attended to, believed, and remembered best when such behaviors are consistent with an individual's own self-views. Accordingly, enhancement of self-esteem and related interventions may be a useful adjunct to traditional couples therapy in some cases. It should be noted that this same principle may apply with regard to the therapist–client relationship in individual therapy. For example, challenging a client's negative self-views too quickly and without ample support for the therapist's claims may lead the client to feel misunderstood, limiting the effectiveness of the intervention.

Research applying self-verification theory to understanding depression has suggested that depressed clients attend to, believe, and remember negative self-verifying feedback from others. The theory and some research evidence have also suggested that depressed individuals are motivated to receive negative self-confirming feedback from others, at least on some level. Although somewhat controversial, clinical lore is replete with accounts of depressed individuals who have difficulty changing their lives in more positive directions. It should be helpful for therapists to acknowledge that change is difficult, even when such changes are positive, often because of challenges to predictability and control. An example of change relevant to the current topic is the acceptance of positive feedback from others as valid, which may lead to feeling overvalued. Accepting positive self-relevant feedback may be difficult because it feels insincere or transient. Discussion of these issues within therapy may be helpful in breaking a self-perpetuating cycle of attending to, believing, and internalizing negative feedback about the self.

Findings drawing on the multiple-pathway model have suggested that individual well-being and relationship quality are intertwined. The individuals who function the best both in terms of their individual emotional health and in their relationships are those who have positive self-conceptions and who have partners who verify those self-conceptions. Some spousal involvement in individual therapy for depression may be helpful in many cases, to interrupt seemingly benign interaction patterns that may stabilize the identified client's negative self-views. Negative self-verification effects suggest the need to uncover spousal transactions that may not be reported as aversive but may have important effects on recovery from depression. The challenge for marital therapy is to identify the problematic behavior while incorporating the spouse into the change process. Similarly, it is possible that spousal agreement with positive conclusions about a depressed individual's own self may intensify the effect of these self-beliefs on recovery. Accordingly, there may be an opportunity for marital therapy to use the spouse to reinforce beliefs that are changing in a positive direction.

Drawing on the integrative interpersonal theory of depression, attention to both positive and negative feedback seeking seems important. The negative reassurance-seeking effects obtained in supportive research have highlighted the need to identify requests from the depressed individual that are unanswerable and may serve to decrease empathy from that individual's spouse. At a minimum, such effects may provide one explanation for partner reluctance to become involved in marital therapy for depression even when the spouses agree that there are marital problems and they plan to stay in the relationship. Such considerations suggest the possibility of enhancing the effectiveness of marital therapy by finding ways to reduce partner avoidance and distancing.

Joiner's (Joiner et al., 1992, 1993) integrative theory further suggests that interventions to help depressed spouses tolerate positive self-relevant feedback may be beneficial. Self-esteem enhancement exercises that incorporate partner feedback may be one useful intervention aimed at achieving this goal. For instance, the depressed spouse could be encouraged to identify positive self-attributes that could be elaborated on by his or her partner. In this way, positive self-verifying feedback could be received and accepted.

Directions for Future Research

There are many avenues for future research in the area of self-verification, relationship quality, and depression. Certainly, the literature is not uniform in its support for self-verification theory. Furthermore, some of the research supportive of the self-verification perspective has been criticized on both theoretical and methodological grounds. Despite somewhat mixed results, however, it seems that self-verifying partner feedback does play a role in determining relationship quality—at least under certain conditions. Likewise, although the issue of specific motivational underpinnings involved in self-verification theory and depression remains controversial, evidence has accumulated to suggest that negative feedback from relationship partners does contribute to the development and/or maintenance of depressive symptoms.

Many speculations about the mechanisms of self-verification effects on depression and relationship quality have been outlined in this chapter. However, empirical research testing mechanisms underlying self-verification effects is sorely needed. In addition, recommended directions for future research include consideration of (a) individual-difference variables, (b) the larger relationship context, and (c) greater specification of the types of self-relevant feedback provided by relationship partners.

Individual-difference variables may moderate self-verification effects on relationship outcomes, but such variables have not been well studied. For instance, given that one benefit of self-verifying feedback is presumed to be increased predictability and control over the environment, it seems likely that self-verifying feedback would be particularly salient for individuals with heightened needs for predictability and control. In addition to differences specifically postulated as important by self-verification theory, many other individual-difference variables could influence the effect of self-verifying feedback from partners on depression and relationship quality. For example, attentiveness to self-relevant evaluations from others, perceived importance of self-relevant evaluations from others, accuracy in discerning self-relevant evaluations from others, and tendencies to experience evaluations from others as more or less positive all may heighten the salience of self-relevant evaluations offered by partners.

Dispositional empathy is one personality variable that may render partner evaluations more salient. A growing body of research has suggested that dispositional empathic tendencies can affect important social outcomes, including relationship quality in both heterosexual couples (Davis & Oathout, 1987, 1992) and same-sex friendship dyads (Davis & Kraus, 1990). In a recent study of self-verification effects on dyadic relationship quality, Katz and Joiner (1999) examined emotional empathy as a potential moderator of the association between self-verifying evaluations from roommates and targets' esteem for their roommates. As might be expected, individuals who endorsed the highest levels of emotional empathy appeared to be the most influenced by self-verifying evaluations provided by their roommates.

Clearly, consideration of additional individual-difference variables is warranted. Individual differences may be operationalized and studied in terms of both situational (e.g., current level of stress) and dispositional (e.g., extraversion) differences. Individuals with certain types of personality disorders, for instance, may be characterized by different types of preferences for feedback within close interpersonal relationships. The study of individual differences may help researchers better understand conditions under which self-verification effects are most consequential.

A second recommendation about future research on self-verification theory involves consideration of larger contextual factors. Additional research with ecologically valid, ongoing relationships is needed. Within such endeavors, the stage of the relationship may play an important role in determining whether self-verification effects emerge. Swann et al. (1994) have argued that individuals in dating relationships are primarily concerned with positive rather than self-verifying feedback. This conclusion was based on the notion that individuals pursuing dating relationships are more concerned with winning over potential partners than with issues that underlie self-verification effects (e.g., self-knowledge). The Swann et al. (1994) dating sample included couples who had been together for less than a month, suggesting that at least some of these couples were in the earliest stages of relationship formation. However, although positivity effects may be pronounced for individuals in newly formed romantic relationships, self-verification effects also may be relevant to understanding relationship quality (and perhaps depression) among dating couples in more long-standing relationships (Katz, Anderson, & Beach, 1997) or for those who are interested in becoming involved in a serious, long-standing relationship (Katz & Beach, in press).

Another contextual factor of interest may involve the level of safety or security perceived by the individual within a given relationship. It may be speculated that target individuals are interested in negative feedback from relationship partners only under certain safe conditions. For instance, when negative feedback is offered within a supportive relationship context, or when negative feedback is not excessively hurtful or damaging to their self-views, target individuals may be interested in negative partner feedback that confirms their self-views. Much of the evidence supportive of self-verification theory for spouses with negative self-views has been based on the relative absence of positive feedback rather than the presence of negative or critical feedback (Katz & Beach, 1997b; Katz et al., 1996, 1997).

The type of feedback being provided also may influence whether self-verification effects emerge. For instance, according to the self-verification perspective, abusive partner behavior may serve to verify individuals' negative self-views and thus increase relationship stability. However, abusive partner behavior differs in important ways from the types of partner feedback typically examined within a self-verification framework, rendering generalization to abuse potentially problematic. Katz, Arias, and Beach (2000) investigated the effects of both abusive and supportive feedback from partners on relationship outcomes. Predictions based on both self-verification and self-enhancement theories were tested. Only self-enhancement effects emerged with regard to psychological abuse, whereas both self-enhancement and self-verification effects emerged with regard to partner support. Both cross-sectional and longitudinal analyses were consistent with these predictions. Thus, application of this theory to understanding reactions to or tolerance for abuse seems unwarranted.

Broad review of the self-verification literature also is consistent with the notion that different types of feedback may be more or less amenable to self-verification effects on relationship quality. A distinction between performance or achievement versus socioemotional dimensions of the self-concept may be drawn. This distinction may have relevance for predicting when self-verification effects on relationship quality emerge. Swann, Hixon et al. (1992; Swann et al., 1994) studied self-views of competence in a variety of specific domains (e.g., athletic ability, artistic ability), and Katz et al. (1996, 1997) studied global self-esteem; both found evidence consistent with the self-verification theory. In contrast, Murray et al. (1996) studied socioemotional self-conceptions (e.g., kindness, dominance) and partner conceptions of self and did not find evidence consistent with self-verification theory. Perhaps self-enhancement effects predominate for socioemotional self-conceptions, as such evaluations are inherently ambiguous and subject to change given the relationship context. Performance- or achievement-related self-conceptions, however, may be somewhat more quantifiable and behaviorally driven, and therefore more subject to self-verification considerations. Studies of these different types of self-conceptions, partner conceptions, and relationship quality may be fruitful in substantiating this hypothesis.

Feedback about more diverse types of self-conceptions and the impact of feedback on more diverse measures of relationship adjustment also may be studied in future research. Potential areas for further growth involve self-attributions for negative relational events and body image concerns. Furthermore, sexual self-concepts and sexual interactions seem to be promising areas in which self-verification effects may be captured. For example, individuals' sexual self-schemas (e.g., Andersen & Cyranowski, 1994) may be verified directly through partner feedback or indirectly through the quality of a couple's sexual interactions. Self-verification of one's sexual self-views may influence sexual and relationship functioning and, in turn, emotional well-being. Problems with sexual functioning and marital functioning often co-occur, and sexual problems frequently characterize couples in which one or both members are depressed. Therefore, sexual interactions between marital partners also may be amenable to self-verification effects, with implications for sexual adjustment, general relationship adjustment, and depression.

Specific avenues for future research in the area of self-verification and depression remain as well. For instance, the major criticism of the Swann, Wenzlaff, Krull, and Pelham (1992) study that remains unresolved is the issue of motivational underpinnings of negative feedback seeking. Both the self-verification and the depressive realism literatures have suggested that depressed individuals are likely to experience negative social interactions with others and that these interactions may be related to the onset and maintenance of depressive symptoms. From the self-verification perspective, individuals are motivated to solicit unfavorable feedback from others in their social environment and prefer such feedback because it confirms their self-views. From the depressive realism perspective, depressed individuals lack the self-serving, falsely positive self-appraisals that may buffer against vulnerability to depression (Alloy & Clements, 1992) and are related to overall mental health. Despite the differences in these two perspectives, researchers in both areas have found preferences for seemingly accurate negative self-relevant feedback among depressed individuals. Clearly, additional work is needed to investigate the socially versus cognitively based motivational underpinnings of depressed individuals' preferences for negative feedback. It may be that certain types of motivations emerge for different individuals under different circumstances.

Despite powerful and reciprocal influences between depression and marriage, not all married individuals with negative self-views develop depression, and not all depressed individuals experience significant marital distress. Self-verification theory may help researchers better understand the complex ways in which partner behavior can influence both depression and relationship functioning. Research efforts that clarify issues about the applicability of self-verification theory to different individuals in different relationship contexts also may allow for increased clarity about the links between depression and marital distress.

References

Abramson, L. Y., Metalsky, G., & Alloy, L. B. (1989). Hopelessness depression: A theory-based subtype of depression. *Psychological Review, 96,* 358–372.

Alloy, L. B., & Clements, C. M. (1992). Illusion of control: Invulnerability to negative affect and depressive symptoms after laboratory and natural stressors. *Journal of Abnormal Psychology, 101,* 234–245.

Alloy, L. B., & Lipman, A. J. (1992). Depression and selection of positive and negative social feedback: Motivated preference or cognitive balance? *Journal of Abnormal Psychology, 101,* 310–313.

American Psychiatric Association. (1987). *Diagnostic and statistical manual of mental disorders* (3rd ed., rev.). Washington, DC: Author.

Andersen, B., & Cyranowski, J. C. (1994). Women's sexual self-schema. *Journal of Personality and Social Psychology, 67,* 1079–1100.

Beach, S. R. H., & O'Leary, K. D. (1993a). Dysphoria and marital discord: Are dysphoric individuals at risk for marital maladjustment? *Journal of Marital and Family Therapy, 19,* 355–368.

Beach, S. R. H., & O'Leary, K. D. (1993b). Marital discord and dysphoria: For whom does the marital relationship predict depressive symptoms? *Journal of Social and Personal Relationships, 10,* 405–420.

Beck, A. T., Ward, C. H., Mendelson, M., Mock, J., & Erbaugh, J. (1961). An inventory for measuring depression. *Archives of General Psychiatry, 4,* 561–571.

Butler, A. C., Hokanson, J. E., & Flynn, H. A. (1994). A comparison of self-esteem lability and low trait self-esteem as vulnerability factors for depression. *Journal of Personality and Social Psychology, 66,* 166–177.

Coyne, J. C. (1976). Toward an interactional description of depression. *Psychiatry, 39,* 28–40.

Davis, M. H., & Kraus, L. A. (1990, August). *Dispositional empathy in same-sex acquaintanceships.* Paper presented at the 98th Annual Convention of the American Psychological Association, Boston.

Davis, M. H., & Oathout, H. A. (1987). Maintenance of satisfaction in romantic relationships. Empathy and relational competence. *Journal of Personality and Social Psychology, 53,* 397–410.

Davis, M. H., & Oathout, H. A. (1992). The effect of dispositional empathy on romantic relationship behaviors: Heterosocial anxiety as a moderating influence. *Personality and Social Psychology Bulletin, 18,* 76–83.

De La Ronde, C., & Swann, W. B. (1998). Partner verification: Restoring shattered images of our intimates. *Journal of Personality and Social Psychology, 75,* 374–382.

Giesler, R. B., Josephs, R. A., & Swann, W. B., Jr. (1996). Self-verification in clinical depression: The desire for negative evaluation. *Journal of Abnormal Psychology, 105,* 358–368.

Hooley, J. M., & Richters, J. E. (1992). Allure of self-confirmation: A comment on Swann, Wenzlaff, Krull, and Pelham. *Journal of Abnormal Psychology, 101,* 307–309.

Joiner, T. E., Jr. (1994). The interplay of similarity and self-verification in relationship formation. *Social Behavior and Personality, 22,* 195–200.

Joiner, T. E., Jr. (1995). The price of soliciting and receiving negative feedback: Self-verification theory as a vulnerability to depression theory. *Journal of Abnormal Psychology, 104,* 364–372.

Joiner, T. E., Jr., Alfano, M. S., & Metalsky, G. I. (1992). When depression breeds contempt: Reassurance-seeking, self-esteem, and rejection of depressed college students by their roommates. *Journal of Abnormal Psychology, 101,* 165–173.

Joiner, T. E., Jr., Alfano, M. S., & Metalsky, G. I. (1993). Caught in the crossfire: Depression, self-consistency, self-enhancement, and the response of others. *Journal of Social and Clinical Psychology, 12,* 113–134.

Joiner, T. E., Jr., & Katz, J. (2000). [The entrainment hypothesis: What is the relationship between reassurance-seeking and negative feedback-seeking in dyads with a depressed partner?] Unpublished raw data.

Joiner, T. E., Jr., Katz, J., & Lew, A. J. (1997). Self-verification and depression among youth psychiatric outpatients. *Journal of Abnormal Psychology, 106,* 608–618.

Joiner, T. E., Jr., & Metalksy, G. I. (1995). A prospective test of an integrative interpersonal theory of depression: A naturalistic study of college roommates. *Journal of Personality and Social Psychology, 69,* 778–788.

Katz, J., Anderson, P., & Beach, S. R. H. (1997). Dating relationship quality: Effects of global self-verification and self-enhancement. *Journal of Personal and Social Relationships, 14,* 829–842.

Katz, J., Arias, I., & Beach, S. R. H. (2000). *Psychological abuse, self-esteem, and dating relationship outcomes: A critical examination of the self-verification perspective.* Manuscript submitted for publication.

Katz, J., & Beach, S. R. H. (1997a). Romance in the crossfire: When do women's depressive symptoms influence partner relationship satisfaction? *Journal of Social and Clinical Psychology, 16,* 243–258.

Katz, J., & Beach, S. R. H. (1997b). Self-verification and depressive symptoms in marriage and courtship: A multiple pathway model. *Journal of Marriage and the Family, 59,* 903–914.

Katz, J., & Beach, S. R. H. (in press). Looking for love? Self-verification and self-enhancement effects on initial romantic attraction. *Personality and Social Psychology Bulletin.*

Katz, J., Beach, S. R. H., & Anderson, P. (1996). Self-enhancement versus self-verification: Does spousal support always help? *Cognitive Therapy and Research, 20,* 345–360.

Katz, J., Beach, S. R. H., & Joiner, T. E., Jr. (1998). When does partner devaluation predict emotional distress? Prospective moderating effects of reassurance-seeking and self-esteem. *Personal Relationships, 5,* 409–421.

Katz, J., & Joiner, T. E., Jr. (1999). *Being known, intimate, and valued: Global self-verification and dyadic adjustment in couples and roommates.* Manuscript submitted for publication.

Kernis, M. H., Grannemann, B. D., & Mathis, L. C. (1991). Stability of self-esteem as a moderator of the relation between level of self-esteem and depression. *Journal of Personality and Social Psychology, 61,* 80–84.

Markus, H., & Wurf, E. (1987). The dynamic self-concept: A social-psychological perspective. *Annual Review of Psychology, 38,* 299–337.

Murray, S. L., Holmes, J. G., & Griffin, D. W. (1996). The benefits of positive illusions: Idealization and the construction of satisfaction in close relationships. *Journal of Personality and Social Psychology, 70,* 79–98.

Pelham, B. W., & Swann, W. B., Jr. (1994). The juncture of intrapersonal and interpersonal knowledge: Self-certainty and interpersonal congruence. *Personality and Social Psychology Bulletin, 20,* 349–357.

Ritts, V., & Stein, J. R. (1995). Verification and commitment in marital relationships: An exploration of self-verification theory in community college students. *Psychological Reports, 76,* 383–386.

Schafer, R. B., Wickrama, K. A. S., & Keith, P. M. (1996). Self-concept disconfirmation, psychological distress, and marital happiness. *Journal of Marriage and the Family, 58,* 167–177.

Seligman, M. E. P. (1974). Learned helplessness and depression. In R. J. Friedman & M. M. Katz (Eds.), *The psychology of depression: Contemporary theory and research.* New York: John Wiley & Sons.

Shrauger, J. S. (1975). Responses to evaluation as a function of initial self-perceptions. *Psychological Bulletin, 82,* 581–596.

Swann, W. B., Jr. (1983). Self-verification: Bringing social reality into harmony with the self. In J. Suls

& A. G. Greenwald (Eds.), *Social psychology perspectives* (Vol. 2, pp. 33–66). Hillsdale, NJ: Erlbaum.

Swann, W. B., Jr. (1987). Identity negotiation: Where the two roads meet. *Journal of Personality and Social Psychology, 53,* 1038–1051.

Swann, W. B., Jr., De La Ronde, C., & Hixon, J. G. (1994). Authenticity and positivity strivings in marriage and courtship. *Journal of Personality and Social Psychology, 66,* 857–869.

Swann, W. B., Jr., Griffin, J. J., Predmore, S. C., & Gaines, B. (1987). The cognitive-affective crossfire: When self-consistency confronts self-enhancement. *Journal of Personality and Social Psychology, 52,* 881–889.

Swann, W. B., Jr., & Guiliano, T. (1987). Confirmatory search strategies in social interaction: How, when, why, and with what consequences. *Journal of Social and Clinical Psychology, 5,* 511–524.

Swann, W. B., Jr., Hixon, J. G., & De La Ronde, C. (1992). Embracing the bitter "truth:" Negative self-concepts and marital commitment. *Psychological Science, 3,* 118–121.

Swann, W. B., Jr., & Predmore, S. C. (1985). Intimates as agents of social support: Sources of consolation or despair? *Journal of Personality and Social Psychology, 49,* 1609–1617.

Swann, W. B., Jr., & Read, S. J. (1981). Self-verification processes: How we sustain our self-conceptions. *Journal of Experimental Social Psychology, 17,* 351–372.

Swann, W. B., Jr., Stein-Seroussi, A., & Giesler, R. B. (1992). Why people self-verify. *Journal of Personality and Social Psychology, 62,* 392–401.

Swann, W. B., Jr., Wenzlaff, R. M., Krull, D. S., & Pelham, B. W. (1992). Allure of negative feedback: Self-verification strivings among depressed persons. *Journal of Abnormal Psychology, 101,* 293–306.

Swann, W. B., Jr., Wenzlaff, R. M., & Tafarodi, R. W. (1992). Depression and the search for negative self-evaluations: More evidence of the role of self-verification strivings. *Journal of Abnormal Psychology, 101,* 314–317.

Taylor, S. E., & Brown, J. D. (1988). Illusion and well-being: A social psychological perspective on mental health. *Psychological Bulletin, 103,* 193–210.

Wood, J. V., Giordono-Beech, M., Taylor, K. L., Michela, J. L., & Gaus, V. (1994). Strategies of social-comparison among people with low self-esteem: Self-protection and self-enhancement. *Journal of Personality and Social Psychology, 67,* 713–731.

7

Nodes of Consilience Between Interpersonal–Psychological Theories of Depression

Thomas E. Joiner, Jr.

E. O. Wilson's 1998 book, *Consilience: The Unity of Knowledge,* considered whether a set of fundamental laws and principles could be derived to explain all the universe, ranging from quarks to mind to galaxies to culture and so on. In this spirit, but less ambitiously and regarding a far smaller aspect, the goals of this chapter are to review, where possible, points of confluence between prominent interpersonal and psychological theories of depression; present empirical evidence regarding them; and suggest relevant areas for future empirical work.

Theories

1. *Coyne's (1976) interactional theory of depression:* To assuage emotional pain, dysphoric individuals engage in excessive and repeated reassurance seeking, which persists regardless of others' responses, often with deleterious consequences (e.g., interpersonal rejection, depression contagion) for all (see also Katz, chapter 6; cf. Coyne and Benazon, chapter 2).
2. *Swann's (1983) self-verification theory:* Individuals are fundamentally motivated to attain self-confirming feedback (even if negative) and, accordingly, will preferentially solicit, attend to, believe, and remember self-verifying feedback (see also Katz, chapter 6).
3. *Hopelessness theory of depression* (Abramson, Metalsky, & Alloy, 1989): A tendency to attribute negative events to stable and global causes, combined with the occurrence of negative events, produces hopelessness and, in turn, depression.
4. *Stress generation* (Hammen, 1991): Depressed individuals may engage in behaviors that produce stress, particularly interpersonal stress, that, in turn, may maintain or exacerbate depressive symptoms (see Davila, chapter 4).
5. *Social support theory* (Cohen & Wills, 1985): Social support, or the perception thereof, directly influences physical and mental well-being, including depression.
6. *Shyness research* (Kagan, Resnick, & Snidman, 1988): Shyness, a clearly enduring personality disposition, may, under certain conditions, serve as a vulnerability factor for depression and may further complicate the deleterious consequences of depressotypic interpersonal styles (cf. Karney, chapter 3; Davila, chapter 4).

Nodes of Consilience and Evidence

Reassurance and Negative Feedback Seeking

Depression has the effect of entraining excessive reassurance seeking and negative feedback seeking, which are otherwise independent processes. In general, reassurance seeking and negative feedback seeking should, at the least, be uncorrelated, even mutually exclusive (i.e., negatively correlated). If an individual desires negative feedback, how can he or she also desire reassurance, a form of positive feedback? Indeed, in unselected populations, these two variables have displayed a low, negative correlation (Joiner, Alfano, & Metalsky, 1993).

My colleagues and I have argued that depression changes all this (e.g., Joiner & Metalsky, 1995; Katz & Beach, 1997). The emotional pain of depression stimulates needs for interpersonal soothing (reassurance), whereas the negative self-concept of depression simultaneously stimulates the need for confirming negative feedback. According to this view, depressed individuals are motivated to obtain reassurance and negative feedback: reassurance to satisfy emotional needs and negative feedback to satisfy cognitive needs.

My colleagues and I have demonstrated in various ways that this combination leads to interpersonal difficulties (e.g., Joiner & Metalsky, 1995). We speculated that others become confused and frustrated by repeated requests for contradictory interpersonal feedback and, because of this, more likely to reject the depressed individual. However, it has not been demonstrated that these processes co-occur in individuals with depressive symptoms. In reanalyses of previous data sets (e.g., Joiner & Metalsky, 1995), a moderate, positive correlation emerged between negative feedback seeking and reassurance seeking among individuals with depressive symptoms. In contrast, as noted earlier, the correlation between these variables in unselected samples has been found to be negative. This finding is consistent with the view that depression has the effect of coupling the otherwise independent processes of excessive reassurance seeking and negative feedback seeking.

These correlational data, although consistent with the entrainment view, do not compellingly demonstrate that excessive reassurance seeking and negative feedback seeking co-occur among depressed individuals in a sequential, self-sustaining way, with one leading to the other, leading again to the first, and so on. More microanalytic research examining the following hypothesis among close relationship partners is currently under way: Given that one partner is depressed and that the depressed partner has received negative feedback from the other, the likelihood that the depressed partner will seek reassurance is greater than if he or she had received positive or neutral feedback. Similarly, given that the depressed partner has received reassurance from the other, the likelihood that the depressed partner will seek negative feedback is greater than if he or she had received negative or neutral feedback. Support for these hypotheses would make a compelling case for the entrainment perspective.

The possibility that excessive reassurance seeking and negative feedback seeking are entrained among depressed individuals is intriguing in itself, but it is also important from a general theoretical as well as clinical standpoint. From a theoretical standpoint, entrainment implies relative permanence. If entrainment is a relatively stable condition, and if entrainment leads to interpersonal difficulties (as it seems to; e.g., Joiner & Metalsky, 1995), then interpersonal difficulties may be relatively enduring (under conditions of depression-entrained reassurance seeking and negative feedback seeking). Entrainment can be seen as one explanation for the stress-generation effect among depressed individuals (i.e., depression leads to stress because it entrains aversive interpersonal behaviors) and can be considered as one source of social support depletion among depressed individuals. Of course, the generation of stress and the depletion of social support may serve to maintain or exacerbate depressive symptoms. Furthermore, enduring interpersonal difficulties may demoralize the depressed individual, even to the point of scarring cognitive style, so that, on symptom remission, vulnerability to relapse remains heightened (e.g., if attributional style is made more negative, ensuing difficulties may be attributed to stable and global causes, leading to hopelessness and thus possible relapse; Abramson et al., 1989). In this way, entrainment of excessive reassurance seeking and negative feedback seeking has implications not only for the particulars of depressive interpersonal processes, but also for theories involving stress generation, social support, and negative cognitive style.

If entrainment is demonstrated to be a feature of the interpersonal lives of depressed individuals, a clear target for treatment can be identified. According to the logic of the entrainment view, the uncoupling of excessive reassurance seeking and negative feedback seeking should reduce interpersonal strain, stress generation, and loss of social support. Straightforward psychoeducational and behavioral approaches to uncoupling excessive reassurance seeking and negative feedback seeking hold promise in the psychotherapy of depressed individuals.

Interpersonal Crucible of Particular Attributions

Social support buffers against depression by encouraging healthy attributions about negative events. Everyone (ranging from the hypercognitive to the staunchest cognitive critic) would likely agree that attributions do not occur in an interpersonal vacuum. Indeed, interpersonal feedback seeking (regardless of type) can be viewed as an effort to collect data in the service of forming attributions. For example, excessive reassurance seeking can be seen as an attempt to form self-relevant attributions ("Do you really love me?"), whereas negative feedback seeking can be seen as a means to interpersonally confirm negative attributions ("I'm no good at this, am I?").

It is well known that high social support serves as a buffer against the development of depressive symptoms (Cohen & Wills, 1985). Indeed, adequate interpersonal support often is viewed as a necessary condition for well-being and adaptive functioning. Low social support is associated with morbidity and mortality among medical patients as well as with a variety of other negative outcomes. For example, Collins, Dunkel-Schetter, Lobel, and Scrimshaw (1993) reported that pregnant women with low social support had more difficult labor, experienced more postpartum depression, and had babies with lower Apgar scores and lower birthweight than women with greater social support. But why and how is social support protective?

It has been suggested that social support encourages healthy attributions and that this relation accounts, in part if not in full, for the protective effect of social support on depressive symptoms. It has been predicted that good social support will cultivate positive attributions and that positive attributions, in turn, will lead to lowered depressive symptoms (Cohen & Wills, 1985).

I tested this prediction among a sample of undergraduates who completed questionnaires on social support, attributional style, and depressive symptoms at two questionnaire sessions held several weeks apart. Level of social support at the baseline session significantly predicted changes in depressive symptoms. Students with lower levels of support experienced increased depressive symptoms, whereas students with higher levels of support were buffered against the development of depressive symptoms. Baseline level of social support also predicted changes in cognitive style. Students with lower levels of support reported an increase in negative attributions about the causes of events, whereas students with higher levels of support did not. When changes in attributions were partialled from the relation between social support and changes in depressive symptoms, the latter relation was substantially diminished, suggesting that social support influenced depressive symptoms through its influence on attributions.

The hypothesis that depressotypic cognitions have an interpersonal source represents an obvious opportunity for the integration of interpersonal and cognitive theories of depression. Depression-related interpersonal processes, such as excessive reassurance seeking, negative feedback seeking, and the entrainment of the two, may erode positive cognitions by alienating socially supportive others. The absence of positive cognitions, in turn (as well as the presence of negative ones), may lead to the development of depressive symptoms. Despite reservations about integrating interpersonal and cognitive viewpoints, critics of cognitive theories of depression (e.g., Coyne, 1999) may find merit in this perspective, not only because an interpersonal variable is construed as a source variable, but also because this perspective allows interpersonal variables to affect depressive symptoms directly as well as indirectly through their influence on cognitions.

Partners'Attributions About One Another

Relationship partners' attributions about one another may explain the phenomenon of interpersonal contagion of depression. Depressive symptoms may be contagious (Coyne et al., 1987; Joiner, 1994). In a recent meta-analysis (Joiner & Katz, 1999), 12 studies on the contagion of depressive symptoms were found, and all reported significant results in favor of the view that depressive symptoms may be contagious.

Spouses' attributions about the nature of one another's behaviors may account, in part, for contagious depression among spouses. In a thorough review of the literature, Bradbury and Fincham (1990) concluded that negative attributions (e.g., blaming) by one spouse regarding his or her spouse's behavior are cross-sectionally (e.g., Baucom, Sayers, & Duhe, 1989) and prospectively (e.g., Fincham & Bradbury, 1987) associated with marital dissatisfaction. Furthermore, the causal status of attributions in producing marital distress has been well supported although not necessarily conclusive (cf. Hooley, 1987). Because they generate marital distress, marital attributions also may be predictive of depression. If so, the following scenario is implied: Given some behavior of one spouse (e.g., coming home late), the other spouse may make a negative attribution about his or her partner's behavior. This negative attribution (combined with other negative attributions about other spouse behaviors) may produce marital distress and, as a function thereof, produce depressive symptoms. Meanwhile, this very distress and depression may themselves affect the other spouse's attributions (e.g., ''My partner's always depressed, complaining, and unhappy''); these attributions, in turn, also may spark distress and depression. In this scenario, then, both spouses become distressed and depressed as a function of negative attributions regarding one another's behavior, including being distressed or depressed.

To my knowledge, this conceptualization has not been tested directly, but several studies are relevant nonetheless. As discussed above, the link between marital attributions and marital distress is well documented (see Bradbury & Fincham, 1990). Also, Fincham, Beach, and Bradbury (1989) reported that the attributions–marital distress relation remained when depression was controlled, which suggested that the relation is not an artifact of the attributions–depression connection. This is consistent with the sequence described above, which postulated that attributions lead to distress, which, in turn, leads to depression. Future research may benefit from examining whether a spouse's negative attributions about his or her partner's marital distress or depression serves as a vulnerability factor for his or her own depression.

From a slightly different perspective, emerging literature on the attributions parents make regarding their children's problems has provided further empirical support to the view that one individual's attributions about another may influence the emotional reactions of both (see Joiner & Wagner, 1996, for a review). For example, Grace, Kelly, and McCain (1993) reported that mothers' and adolescents' self-reported relationship conflict was related to the tendency of mothers and adolescents to attribute each other's negative behaviors to dispositional causes. Taken together with work on marital attributions, the research on parent–child dyads supports the idea that relationship-level attributions may be one viable explanation for contagious depression.

The work on marital and parent–child attributions has further demonstrated that attributional processes do not occur in an interpersonal vacuum. Attributional process per se, although typically viewed as an intrapsychic phenomenon even when applied to interpersonal events, may be generated interpersonally as well. For example, on experiencing a negative event, an individual may consult with a friend or a loved one and, as a product of that interaction, generate an attribution. In this case, it is not the attributional style of the individual who experienced the event that determines the eventual attribution. Nor is it the attributional style of the person consulted nor even the attribution of one individual about the behavior of the other, as in the marital and parent–child literatures. Rather it is the shared, collaborative attribution that produces the final attribution. If two or more individuals collaborate on an attribution for an event that affects them both, the attribution is likely to influence their emotional reactions in similar ways. And, if one collaborator is already depressed, his or her contribution to the process may influence the attribution negatively. Shared or collaborative attributions for negative events that affect two or more individuals also deserve consideration as a possible explanation for contagious depression.

Interpersonal Addendum to the Hopelessness Theory of Depression

Hopelessness acts as a depression and stress generator. The hopelessness theory postulates that hopelessness is one sufficient cause of depressive symptoms. In addition to generating depression, hopelessness also may generate interpersonal stress. That is, others may find the hopeless individual embittered and demobilized and reject the hopeless individual for this reason.

I conducted three studies that examined several issues related to stress generation in depression (Joiner, 2000; also see Davila, chapter 4). In the first two studies, the stress-generation effect reported by Hammen (1991) and Davila and colleagues (e.g., Davila, Bradbury, Cohan, & Tochluk, 1997) was replicated. That is, depressive symptoms at one point in time were predictive of increased stress at a later point in time.

Furthermore, the studies demonstrated that various interpersonal variables (e.g., avoidant coping style, excessive reassurance seeking) were not adequate explanations for the stress-generation effect. Depressive symptoms did not predict increased stress as a function of predicting increases in maladaptive interpersonal attitudes and behaviors. However, a cognitive variable—hopelessness—*was* a mediator of the stress generation effect. It appeared that individuals with depressive symptoms experienced increased stress because they became hopeless. Or, is it possible that they reported (but did not necessarily experience) increased stress because hopelessness generates the perception but not necessarily the occurrence of stress? A third study addressed this possibility and rejected it in favor of the view that hopelessness may be the key aspect of depression driving the generation of actual (not just perceived) stress.

Empirical support for this perspective would broaden the role of hopelessness in the hopelessness theory. Hopelessness currently is framed as the mediator between negative cognitive style and stress-induced depressive reactions. Hopelessness may perform this function by generating interpersonal stress. This interpersonal stress may, in turn, heighten depression and encourage depression persistence by producing stress that may further aggravate the negative cognitive style, leading to more hopelessness, more symptoms, more stress, and so on.

How specifically might hopelessness operate as a stress generator? There are several possibilities. (Note that these have not been empirically examined; they are intended as heuristics for future research.) First, depression chronicity may be involved in stress generation. There is little doubt that depression is chronic. The average length of major depressive episodes is approximately 8 months in adults (Shapiro & Keller, 1981) and 9 months in children (Kovacs, Obrosky, Gatsonis, & Richards, 1997). Incredibly, the mean length of dysthymic episodes may be as much as 30 years in adults (Shelton, Davidson, Yonkers, & Koran, 1997). In addition, Coryell and Winokur (1992) found that 70% of individuals who experienced one depressive episode subsequently experienced at least one more episode. As depression persists, people may become more and more hopeless, and significant others may become more and more burdened and disaffected. The notion that depression is contagious is consistent with this view (Coyne et al., 1987; Joiner, 1994). Sacco, Milana, and Dunn (1988) provided participants with transcripts of depressed individuals whose episodes were long lasting and transcripts of depressed individuals who experienced short episodes. Compared to short-episode transcripts, the transcripts of long-duration depressive individuals elicited more anger and more interpersonal rejection. In this analogue study, chronicity, as distinct from the mere presence of symptoms, accounted for the negative reactions of others. Interestingly, Hammen's (1991) study on stress generation in depression focused on women with chronic forms of depression. In summary, the hopelessness of chronic depression may burden others and thus account for interpersonal stress generation (e.g., interpersonal rejection, contagious depression).

A second possibility is that hopelessness, because of its embittering and stultifying interpersonal effects, may produce negative and persistent mental representations of depressed individuals in the minds of significant others. Sacco (1999) argued that, once developed, such representations take on an independent quality, in that they selectively guide attention and expectancies to confirm the representation (cf. Fiske, 1993) regardless of the actual behavior of the represented individual. The development of these mental representations may occur spontaneously and outside the awareness of the perceiver (Lewicki, Hill, & Czyzewska, 1992). Persistent representations may be particularly salient regarding negative versus positive behaviors. There is evidence that, compared with positive behaviors, negative behaviors are more likely to draw attention in the first place (Pratto & John, 1991) and when attributed to the individual (as opposed to the situation) are more likely to be remembered (Ybarra & Stephan, 1996). Furthermore, once encoded, representations of negative behaviors are more difficult to change than representations of positive behaviors (Rothbart & Park, 1986). Moreover, such representations may gain momentum with use, in that they disproportionately influence social cognition relative to actual subsequent behaviors of the represented individual (Sherman & Klein, 1994).

Hopelessness, then, may generate stress by instilling in others a schema that negatively biases subsequent perceptions of the hopeless individual and is difficult to alter. Others' negative views may, in turn, produce critical communications from others to the hopeless individual, and such communications have been shown to be strong predictors of depression and its recurrence (Hooley & Teasdale, 1989). As for others' perceptions, it appears that the hopeless and potentially depressed individual encounters an intractable problem: Continued hopelessness may serve only to maintain others' negative views and thus generate stress in the form of criticism; positive changes, because they do not match others' schemas, may be unnoticed or misattributed, leaving others' negative schemas unaffected. In addition, this does not address the problem of positive changes colliding with negative self-views, as emphasized by self-verification theory (see Katz, chapter 6).

Relatedly, it is important to consider that hopeless attitudes and their interpersonal expression may produce socially pragmatic rewards in that they reduce others' expectations for future performance and responsibilities. Weary and Williams (1990) reported that, compared with nondepressed participants, depressed individuals strategically failed at an experimental task when they expected that success would lead to others' future expectations of continued success (Baumgardner, 1990, obtained similar findings). Depressive cognitions (e.g., ''I'm just not up to it'') may thus encourage failure-inducing behavior (i.e., stress generation).

An integral element of socially pragmatic self-handicapping is the public disclosure of impairment or distress. Excessive or inappropriate self-disclosure has been found to characterize depressed individuals and to induce negative reactions from others (Jacobson & Anderson, 1982; Segrin & Abramson, 1994). In an effort to explain current performance deficits or reduce future performance demands, depressed individuals may self-disclose regarding distress and impairment, thereby generating interpersonal stress (e.g., negative reactions from others) and prolonging or reestablishing depression.

Taken together, these findings suggest an interpersonal elaboration to what is otherwise a cognitive model of depression; namely, the hopelessness theory of depression (Abramson et al., 1989). The hopelessness theory proposes that the tendency to attribute negative events to stable and global causes represents a diathesis that in the presence but not the absence of negative life stress increases vulnerability to depression. Furthermore, the theory specifies that those who possess a negative attributional style and who encounter negative life events are predicted to become hopeless and, as a function thereof, depressed. According to the hopelessness theory, hopelessness produces depression; according to the view presented in this chapter, hopelessness may generate stress. Thus, hopelessness may generate depression as a function of generating stress, or it may simultaneously generate depression and stress, with the latter maintaining the former.

Shyness

Shyness focuses the negative consequences of excessive reassurance seeking on just a few relationships. I theorized that shyness serves as a vulnerability factor for depressive symptoms in the absence but not in the presence of social support and that loneliness mediates the relation between shyness and increases in depressive symptoms (Joiner, 1997). A longitudinal study of 172 undergraduates supported this view. Participants who were shy and unsupported were likely to experience increases in depressive symptoms and decreases in positive affect over the course of the study, whereas other students were not. This effect was partially mediated by increases in loneliness and was specific to depressed symptoms and low positive affect; it did not apply to negative affect.

Like shy individuals, those who are excessive in reassurance seeking are vulnerable to later increases in depressive symptoms (e.g., Joiner & Schmidt, 1998), perhaps as a function of vulnerability to a host of negative interpersonal phenomena (e.g., rejection, depression contagion; Coyne et al., 1987). Consider, then, the plight of shy reassurance seekers. Because they are shy, they have fewer relationships than most (Jones, Briggs, & Smith, 1986). Because they excessively seek reassurance, the few relationships they have are particularly likely to break under the pressure of repeated reassurance seeking (Joiner, 1994; Joiner & Katz, 1999). In this way, shyness may function as a lens that focuses the effects of excessive reassurance seeking, making the latter's consequences even more profound (see also Karney, chapter 3, on neuroticism; Davila, chapter 4, on personality disorder).

Interconcatenating the Perspectives: An Integrative Statement

Based on the six theories discussed in this chapter, as well as their nodes of consilience, a broader picture of the interpersonal functioning of depressed individuals can be articulated. Depression and hopelessness may generate stress and erode social support as a result of the depressed individual's *excessive reassurance seeking, negative feedback seeking,* and *interpersonally inclusive negative attributions,* each of which may serve as depressogenic risk factors in itself. Generated stress and eroded social support may further encourage the development of depressive symptoms, and this may be a particularly acute problem for individuals who are both shy and excessive in reassurance seeking. Several of these processes induce and compound one another, making their scientific study challenging. This challenge is more likely to be met if researchers are equipped with inclusive theories, precise hypotheses, and powerful methodologies (cf. Coyne and Benazon, chapter 2; Karney, chapter 3).

Summary

Several strands of research on the clinical, social, and cognitive psychology of depression were touched on, each of which has illuminated important aspects of depression. These strands, enlightening in themselves, may be even more so when integrated. Examples of such integration were described with the hope that the examples themselves will be further pursued, and more important, the examples will stimulate still further integrative theoretical work. Notably, the crux of each of the five integrative examples can be clinically addressed by empirically supported psychotherapies, including interpersonal psychotherapy and cognitive behavioral psychotherapy.

References

Abramson, L. Y., Metalsky, G. I., & Alloy, L. B. (1989). Hopelessness depression: A theory-based subtype of depression. *Psychological Review, 96,* 358–372.

Baucom, D. H., Sayers, S., & Duhe, A. (1989). Attributional style and attributional patterns among married couples. *Journal of Personality and Social Psychology, 56,* 596–607.

Baumgardner, A. H. (1990). Claiming depressive symptoms as a self-handicap: A protective self-presentation strategy. *Basic and Applied Social Psychology, 12,* 97–113.

Bradbury, T. N., & Fincham, F. D. (1990). Attributions in marriage: Review and critique. *Psychological Bulletin, 107,* 3–33.

Cohen, S., & Wills, T. A. (1985). Stress, social support, and the buffering hypothesis. *Psychological Bulletin, 98,* 310–357.

Collins, N. L., Dunkel-Schetter, C., Lobel, M., & Scrimshaw, S. C. M. (1993). Social support in pregnancy: Psychosocial correlates of birth outcomes and postpartum depression. *Journal of Personality and Social Psychology, 65,* 1243–1258.

Coryell, W., & Winokur, G. (1992). Course and outcome. In E. Paykel (Ed.), *Handbook of affective disorders* (pp. 89–108). New York: Guilford Press.

Coyne, J. C. (1976). Toward an interactional description of depression. *Psychiatry, 39,* 28–40.

Coyne, J. C. (1999). Postscript. In T. Joiner & J. C. Coyne (Eds.), *The interactional nature of depression: Advances in interpersonal approaches* (pp. 363–392). Washington, DC: American Psychological Association.

Coyne, J. C., Kessler, R. C., Tal, M., Turnbull, J., Wortman, C. B., & Creden, J. F. (1987). Living with a depressed person. *Journal of Consulting and Clinical Psychology, 55,* 347–352.

Davila, J., Bradbury, T. N., Cohan, C. L., & Tochluk, S. (1997). Marital functioning and depressive symptoms: Evidence for a stress generation model. *Journal of Personality and Social Psychology, 73,* 849–861.

Fincham, F. D., Beach, S. R. H., & Bradbury, T. N. (1989). Marital distress, depression and attributions: Is the marital distress-attribution association an artifact of depression? *Journal of Consulting and Clinical Psychology, 53,* 510–517.

Fincham, F. D., & Bradbury, T. N. (1987). The impact of attributions in marriage: A longitudinal analysis. *Journal of Personality and Social Psychology, 53,* 510–517.

Fiske, S. T. (1993). Social cognition and social perception. In M. R. Rosenzsweig & L. W. Porter (Eds.), *Annual review of psychology (Vol. 44,* pp. 155–194). Palo Alto, CA: Annual Reviews.

Grace, N. C., Kelly, M. L., & McCain, A. P. (1993). Attribution processes in mother-adolescent conflict. *Journal of Abnormal Child Psychology, 21,* 199–211.

Hammen, C. (1991). Generation of stress in the course of unipolar depression. *Journal of Abnormal Psychology, 100,* 555–561.

Hooley, J. (1987). The nature and origins of expressed emotion. In K. Hahlweg & M. J. Goldstein (Eds.), *Understanding major mental disorder: The contribution of family interaction research* (pp. 176–194). New York: Family Process Press.

Hooley, J. M., & Teasdale, J. D. (1989). Predictors of relapse in unipolar depressives: Expressed emotion, marital distress, and perceived criticism. *Journal of Abnormal Psychology, 98,* 229–235.

Jacobson, N. S., & Anderson, E. (1982). Interpersonal skill deficits and depression in college students: A sequential analysis of the timing of self-disclosure. *Behavior Therapy, 13,* 271–282.

Joiner, T. E., Jr., (2000). *Three studies on stress generation.* Unpublished manuscript. Tallahassee, FL.

Joiner, T. E., Jr., (1994). Contagious depression: Existence, specificity to depressed symptoms, and the role of reassurance-seeking. *Journal of Personality and Social Psychology, 67,* 287–296.

Joiner, T. E., Jr., (1997). Shyness and low social support as interactive diatheses, and loneliness as mediator: Testing an interpersonal-personality view of depression. *Journal of Abnormal Psychology, 106,* 386–394.

Joiner, T. E., Jr., Alfano, M. S., & Metalsky, G. I. (1993). Caught in the crossfire: Depression, self-verification, self-enhancement, and the response of others. *Journal of Social and Clinical Psychology, 12,* 113–134.

Joiner, T. E., Jr., & Katz, J. (1999). Contagion of depressive symptoms and mood: Meta-analytic review and explanations from cognitive, behavioral, and interpersonal viewpoints. *Clinical Psychology: Science and Practice, 6,* 149–164.

Joiner, T. E., Jr., & Metalsky, G. I. (1995). A prospective test of an integrative interpersonal theory of depression: A naturalistic study of college roommates. *Journal of Personality and Social Psychology, 69,* 778–788.

Joiner, T. E., Jr., & Schmidt, N. B. (1998). Reassurance-seeking predicts depressive but not anxious reactions to acute stress. *Journal of Abnormal Psychology, 107,* 533–537.

Joiner, T. E., Jr., & Wagner, K. D. (1996). Parental attributions and outcome: A meta-analytic review. *Journal of Abnormal Child Psychology, 24,* 37–52.

Jones, W. H., Briggs, S. R., & Smith, T. G. (1986). Shyness: Conceptualization and measurement. *Journal of Personality and Social Psychology, 51,* 629–639.

Kagan, J., Resnick, J. S., & Snidman, N. (1988). Biological bases of childhood shyness. *Science, 240,* 167–171.

Katz, J., & Beach, S. R. H. (1997). Romance in the crossfire: When do women's depressive symptoms predict partner relationship satisfaction? *Journal of Social and Clinical Psychology, 16,* 243–258.

Kovacs, M., Obrosky, S., Gatsonis, C., & Richards, C. (1997). First-episode major depressive and dysthymic disorder in childhood: Clinical and sociodemographic factors in recovery. *Journal of the American Academy of Child and Adolescent Psychiatry, 36,* 777–784.

Lewicki, T., Hill, T., & Czyzewska, M. (1992). Nonconscious acquisition of information. *American Psychologist, 47,* 796–801.

Pratto, R., & John, O. P. (1991). Automatic vigilance: The attention-grabbing power of negative social information. *Journal of Personality and Social Psychology, 61,* 380–391.

Rothbart, M., & Park, B. (1986). On the confirmability and disconfirmability of trait concepts. *Journal of Personality and Social Psychology, 50,* 131–142.

Sacco, W. P. (1999). A social-cognitive model of interpersonal processes in depression. In T. Joiner & J. C. Coyne (Eds.), *The interactional nature of depression: Advances in interpersonal approaches* (pp. 329–362). Washington, DC: American Psychological Association.

Sacco, W. P., Milana, S., & Dunn, V. K. (1988). The effect of duration of depressive episode on the response of others. *Journal of Social and Clinical Psychology, 7,* 297–311.

Segrin, C., & Abramson, L. Y. (1994). Negative reactions to depressive behaviors: A communication theories analysis. *Journal of Abnormal Psychology, 103,* 655–668.

Shapiro, R. W., & Keller, M. B. (1981). Initial 6–month follow-up of patients with major depressive disorder. *Journal of Affective Disorders, 3,* 205–220.

Shelton, R. C., Davidson, J., Yonkers, K. A., & Koran, L. (1997). The undertreatment of dysthymia. *Journal of Clinical Psychiatry, 58,* 59–65.

Sherman, J. W., & Klein, S. B. (1994). Development and representation of personality impressions. *Journal of Personality and Social Psychology, 67,* 972–983.

Swann, W. B., Jr. (1983). Self-verification: Bringing social reality into harmony with the self. In J. Suls & A. G. Greenwald (Eds.), *Social psychological perspectives on the self* (Vol. 2, pp. 33–66), Hillsdale, NJ: Erlbaum.

Weary, G., & Williams, J. P. (1990). Depressive self-presentation: Beyond self-handicapping. *Journal of Personality and Social Psychology, 58,* 892–898.

Wilson, E. O. (1998). *Consilience: The unity of knowledge.* New York: Knopf.

Ybarra, O., & Stephan, W. G. (1996). Misanthropic person memory. *Journal of Personality and Social Psychology, 70,* 691–700.

PART III

EXPLORING CONTEXT, CORRELATES, AND CAUSES

8
Perceptions of Family Functioning of Suicidal and Nonsuicidal African American Women

Nadine J. Kaslow
Heather Twomey
Amy Brooks
Martie Thompson
Bettie Reynolds

This chapter explores African American women's perceptions of their families of origin and families of creation in relation to their vulnerability for suicidal behavior. This group of individuals is the focus of our attention for a number of reasons. First, suicidal behavior is often an extreme response to depression and thus merits attention in a book focusing on depression. Second, just as women tend to be more depressed than men, women also attempt suicide more often than do men. As such, a treatise on suicide attempts warrants attention paid to women. Third, there is a dearth of material on depression or suicidal behavior among people of color, and thus research with African American women who attempt suicide is an effort to begin to fill this gap. Finally, given the importance of the family unit within the African American community, a study of suicidal behavior in African American women must be conducted within a family context.

Before detailing the results of our empirical investigation of this relation, several relevant areas of research and literature are reviewed. First, the cultural characteristics specific to African American families in general and to African American women's roles in their families in particular are examined. Attention is paid to cultural and historical patterns as well as current demographic trends, with an emphasis on the topics of family strengths, marriage, intimate partner violence, and child maltreatment. Special consideration is given to the experiences and data relevant for low-income African American women. Next, the nature and prevalence of suicidal behavior in the United States and within the African American community are discussed. The focus is on suicidal behavior among women in general and among African American women specifically. Following is a review of the research investigating familial and interpersonal risk factors for suicidal behavior in general and for African Americans specifically. The final sections report the results from a systematic investigation of family-of-origin and family-of-creation characteristics that are risk factors for suicide attempts in low-income African American women. Those family risk factors that predict suicidal behavior in low-income African American women are identified. In addition, those variables that mediate and moderate the links between various aspects of family functioning and suicidal behavior are highlighted.

Background Literature

African American Families

Several cultural characteristics of African American families have been identified that are commonly viewed as derivatives of African worldviews. One fundamental aspect that tends to distinguish an Afrocentric perspective from a Eurocentric perspective is the high value placed on interdependence, unity, and collective responsibility (Greene, 1994). Consistent with this, there is an emphasis on family cohesiveness, kinship communities, and oneness rather than the rugged individualism valued in Western cultures. In other words, many, albeit not all, individuals within the African American community tend to consider the greater interest of the community before considering their own personal or individual needs.

One of the clearest manifestations of this worldview in African American families is the tendency to define family as an extended kinship network, as opposed to the typical Eurocentric cultural focus on the nuclear family (Greene, 1994). The evidence is clear that regardless of socioeconomic status (SES) African Americans are still more involved in extended kinship ties than are White Americans (Taylor, Chatters, Tucker, & Lewis, 1990). In kinship networks, individuals who have strong affectional ties with the family, although not biologically related, are considered and treated as family. They hold key roles and responsibilities in the family. There tends to be greater role flexibility than that commonly found in dominant cultural traditions. The rearing of children is commonly viewed as communal work that extends beyond the child's biological parents. As such, African American children typically are raised by many individuals, including key community members, older siblings, and "play" family members (nonbiological family members who serve as psychological and functional family members). Collins (1990) described the important role of "other mothers" in the African American community; that is, the other women (e.g., aunts, grandmothers) in the community who supervise and rear the children. The kinship networks of African Americans often include intergenerational family constellations as well. It is not uncommon, especially in lower income families, for grandmothers to raise their grandchildren or for children to reside in multigenerational homes (Boyd-Franklin, 1989). In addition, the extended kinship networks in the African American community serve as a vital source of support for single-parent families, particularly in low-income communities (Wilson et al., 1995). Furthermore, involvement with extended family is linked to greater personal self-esteem among African Americans, which, in turn, is related to lowered suicide risk (Walker, Taylor, McElroy, Phillip, & Wilson, 1995). Strong kinship bonds have been described as the most enduring legacy of African heritage (Boyd-Franklin, 1989).

Unfortunately, recent studies have suggested that supportive extended kin networks are less available for single mothers than previously presumed (Jayakody, Chatters, & Taylor, 1993). In a national sample, Jayakody et al. found that less than one fifth of never-married African American mothers received help with child care, and only one fourth received financial assistance. Clearly, the traditional sources of support are shrinking at the same time that single-female-headed households and households composed of unrelated individuals are becoming more prevalent, particularly within the low-income African American community.

African American families are embedded in a sociocultural and sociopolitical context of economic subordination and racism with historical roots in slavery that negatively affects educational opportunities, earning potential, and access to jobs. This burden is especially heavy for African American women, who occupy social and economic positions inferior to their White and male counterparts in that they have less access to positions of power and authority (Davis, 1981). The burden is greater still for those African American families who also contend with the oppression of poverty. Low-income African American families represent one of the most truly disadvantaged segments of American society. In fact, national statistics show that unemployment among African Americans is the highest in the country. Impoverished families often struggle not only with the frustrations of being unable to provide for the basic wants and needs of their members, but also with inadequate housing, unsafe living conditions, limited or nonexistent community resources, and seemingly constant unemployment. Tragically, the levels of acute and chronic stress and trauma are so high and so pervasive that they often erupt, releasing rage in the form of domestic violence, child abuse, and so-called ''Black on Black'' crime (Boyd-Franklin, 1989).

Family Strengths

A particular strength of the African American family that has been cited in the literature is the protective barrier the family serves against the racism and oppression of the dominant culture (Billingsley, 1992; Boyd-Franklin, 1989; Staples, 1994). By teaching children ways to recognize and cope with racism and oppression, the family helps the children develop the survival mechanisms necessary to master the special challenges posed by the racial barriers and disenfranchisement they face (Gibbs & Huang, 1989). Other noted strengths of the African American family include the extended kinship networks described earlier, strong religious and spiritual traditions, an ardent work ethic, a firm achievement motivation, flexible gender roles, a sense of optimism and determination, and resilient children (Boyd-Franklin, 1989; Gibbs & Hines, 1989; McAdoo, 1988; Staples & Johnson, 1993; Wilson & Tolson, 1990).

Marital Patterns

Existing data reveal differences in rates of marriage and single-parent households according to race, class, and age. Societywide changes in family organization (i.e., later marriage, more divorce, more singlehood, more births out of wedlock, more nonfamily living arrangements) have occurred over the past half century in the United States and have been shown to be more substantial for African Americans than other ethnic groups (Tucker & Mitchell-Kernan, 1995). As for single-headed households, recent census data, stratified by ethnicity and gender, revealed that these households are disproportionately African American and female headed (Bennett, 1995). For example, a 1992 survey revealed that 46% of African American families are headed by single women, compared with 24% of Latino and 17% of White families (McAdoo, 1988; U.S. Department of Commerce, 1992). According to this same report, this increase in the number of female-headed households has resulted in the reemergence of extended households involving cohabitation of these women with another family member or adult. However, a growing portion of these women (60% African American, 60% Latina, and 40% White) and children are living in poverty (Bennett, 1995).

Intimate Partner Violence

Intimate partner violence is an urgent social problem. The available national data reveal that annually a minimum of 1 in 6 couples experiences at least one violent act, 1 in 8 couples experiences serious injury, and 1 in 25 marriages is plagued with perpetual violence (Staples & Johnson, 1993). There is some evidence that intimate partner violence against women occurs at higher rates among African Americans than among European Americans (Hampton & Gelles, 1994; Stets & Straus, 1990; Straus & Gelles, 1986; Straus, Gelles, & Steinmetz, 1980). Specifically, national survey data (Staples & Johnson, 1993) collected from 1975 to 1985 revealed that severe violence toward African American female partners occurred at a rate of 113 per 1,000 versus 30 per 1,000 among European Americans (Stets & Straus, 1990; Straus & Gelles, 1986; Straus et al., 1980). Consistent with these findings, a more recent study revealed that African Americans were more likely to experience both minor and severe incidents of partner abuse in their primary relationships than their European American counterparts (1.2 and 2.4 times more likely, respectively; Hampton & Gelles, 1994). These between-group differences remained significant even after controlling for SES.

A number of explanations have been offered to account for the elevated rates of intimate partner violence within the African American community. The first set of explanations relates to the socialization of men within the United States and in the African American culture in particular. In the dominant U.S. culture, a man's masculinity is established by subordinating less powerful individuals. Men in the African American community, which is, as a whole, oppressed by the majority culture, have fewer opportunities for establishing power in the dominant culture because of limited access to jobs, political power, economic success, and so forth. It has been noted that two areas in which African American men can show their strength and prowess are sexual and intimate relationships (Boyd-Franklin, 1989; Greene, 1994). Therefore, the practice of subordinating women as a way of establishing male authority and masculinity may be particularly problematic within the African American community (Boyd-Franklin, 1989; Greene, 1994).

A second and related explanation for the higher rates of domestic violence among African Americans considers the socialization of women. Greene (1994) asserted that African American women's increased involvement in abusive relationships may, in part, reflect the internalization by African American women of the dominant cultural definition and value of masculine behavior as the power established through dominating others. Greene also stated that African American women may be at increased risk for internalizing this value because of the legitimacy of their partners' frustrations with racism and oppression. In these instances, African American women may either tolerate or believe that they deserve mistreatment from their partners. A common problem that African American women struggle with in such situations is a conflict of loyalty between their own needs and the needs of their families (Greene, 1994). In other words, they experience significant tension between their values of interdependence versus self-preservation. There often is a fear, with some basis in reality, that the criminal justice system will unfairly prosecute their African American male partner if charges are brought against him. Another issue specific to heterosexual African American women in abusive relationships has to do with the scarcity of African American men, which is largely due to high rates of incarceration and death secondary to illness or homicide among marriage-age eligible African American men. Because the paucity of African American men makes finding a mate difficult, many African American women endure their partner's maltreatment (e.g., physical violence, infidelity, emotional abuse) for fear they will lose him to the numerous other available female partners (Greene, 1994; Kanuha, 1994).

The third explanation offered to explain the elevated rates of intimate partner violence within the African American community pertains to economic factors. Specifically, African Americans are disproportionately represented in lower SES groups compared with other ethnic groups, and individuals from low-income groups are at elevated risk for domestic violence (Aldarondo & Sugarman, 1996; Belle, 1990; Hotaling & Sugarman, 1990;

Sorenson, Upchurch, & Shen, 1996; Staples & Johnson, 1993). Moreover, women living in poverty are more vulnerable to persistent violence because they have a particularly difficult time extricating themselves from an abusive relationship (Cardarelli, 1997). Consistent with this explanation, in an investigation of women residing in battered women's shelters, African American women were found to be more likely to have experienced severe abuse, live in poverty, have their children living with them, and not own a car than their European American counterparts (Sullivan & Rumptz, 1994).

A fourth dynamic believed to exacerbate the perniciousness of intimate partner violence within the African American community is the norm of silence. This demonstration of loyalty through silence is evidenced by the lack of condemnation by the church and other African American leadership organizations against wife battering and other domestic violence (Collins, 1990; Saunders, 1995). Collins (Collins, 1990) refers to a conspiracy of silence about African American men's physical and emotional abuse of African American women as part of a larger system that legitimizes and routinizes violence. An examination of popular media, including rap music, movies, television, and pornographic materials, reveals that the acceptance of violence against women is pervasive. The everyday occurrence of this violence, coupled with the implicit acceptance expressed through silence and lack of condemnation, leads many women to not perceive their partner's behavior as abusive or themselves as victims. Even when the violence is extreme, it can still be considered routine (Collins, 1990). Furthermore, there is a long-standing tradition, expectation, and stereotype that African American women are strong and can endure anything. The internalization of this stereotype also may prevent some African American women from acknowledging their need for help and support (Saunders, 1995).

Despite the above-cited statistics and corresponding explanations, contradictory explanations and findings also exist. It has been argued that official marital violence statistics overrepresent African Americans because of racial bias and the tendency for African Americans to be disproportionately represented in lower SES groups. Indeed, some have argued that there is no evidence to suggest that African Americans are inherently more violent than European Americans (Staples & Johnson, 1993). This explanation is consistent with the findings of other researchers who have found no differences in the prevalence of partner abuse when SES is statistically controlled (Coley & Beckett, 1988; Koss et al., 1994).

There are several explanations for these contradictory findings. Some social scientists indicate that African American women are less likely to report abuse because of their fear of losing their children, their desire to protect their partner from a perceived racist criminal justice system, and their concern that they will be viewed as a "traitor" in their community (Collins, 1990; Saunders, 1995). Conversely, others suggest a bias toward overreporting intimate partner violence as a consequence of limited financial means, which leaves African American women more dependent on the use of public services (e.g., emergency rooms, welfare services, community mental health clinics) and less able to protect their privacy (Asbury, 1987; Kanuha, 1994; Sullivan & Rumptz, 1994).

Child Maltreatment

There is a dearth of literature on the epidemiology and effects of childhood maltreatment among African Americans. The limited data available suggest African American families are overrepresented among substantiated cases of child maltreatment within the child-protection system and in foster care (Levine, Doueck, Freeman, & Compaan, 1996). This finding may be largely attributable to the differential income levels of the families served, as there is evidence that differences in the incidence and prevalence of child maltreatment in diverse populations may be due more to social class distinctions than to cultural or ethnic factors (Garbarino & Ebata, 1983). One of the most sophisticated studies pertinent to this topic was conducted by Wyatt (1990), who compared African American and White women's abusive sexual experiences throughout their lifetime. The results revealed few ethnic differences regarding the short- or long-term effects of abusive sexual experiences.

Suicidal Behavior

Epidemiology

A previous suicide attempt constitutes a significant risk factor for and predictor of suicide completion. Given that suicide is a leading cause of death for both men and women (among women and men ages 15–24 years, suicide is the fourth and third leading cause of death, respectively; among women and men ages 25–44, suicide is the fifth and fourth leading cause, respectively), it is a serious public health concern (National Center for Health Statistics, 1998). Women, despite having lower completion rates, make three times as many suicide attempts as do men (Canetto & Lester, 1995).

In the African American Community

Historically, it also has been purported that suicide completion rates are lower for African Americans than for European Americans (Chance, Kaslow, Summerville, & Wood, 1998). An examination of official suicide statistics, however, revealed that the highest rates of misclassification of cause of death are for women and African Americans (Phillips & Ruth, 1993). That is, on closer examination it was discovered that many deaths in which there was evidence of suicide were not, in fact, classified as suicides. This suggests that African American women may not be as protected from suicide as once thought.

The available research does suggest some risk and protective factors for suicidal behavior in the African American community. Protective factors include strong social support, Southern residence, older age, and church attendance and affiliation. On the other hand, risk factors include male gender, age between 25 and 34, psychiatric disorders (particularly depression and substance abuse), family dysfunction and violence, interpersonal discord and marital conflict, delinquency, homosexuality, and AIDS (Gibbs, 1997).

In our research, we found many variables to be risk factors for suicidal behavior among African American women. Specifically, compared with nonattempters, female suicide attempters were 7.4 times more likely to report global psychological distress, 8.5 times more likely to report hopelessness, 2.1 times more likely to report elevated levels of alcohol use, 4.9 times more likely to report drug use, 3.6 times more likely to have maladaptive coping skills, 2.4 times more likely to report poor interpersonal conflict-resolution skills, and 2.8 times more likely to report low levels of social support (Kaslow et al., 1998). Furthermore, for those African American women in our sample with a history of alcohol problems, the following variables were found to be risk factors for suicide attempts: global psychological distress, drug abuse, interpersonal loss, hopelessness, low social support, and poorly developed skills for dealing with interpersonal conflict (Kingree, Thompson, & Kaslow, 1999). Applying LISREL (linear structural relations) modeling to the data from the Epidemiologic Catchment Area study, Nisbet (1996) examined protective factors for suicidal African American women. Results from this analysis revealed that seeking and finding emotional and psychological support in friends and family members help to safeguard these women against suicidal behavior.

Families of Suicidal Individuals

Overview of Research

The bulk of research on the families of suicidal individuals has focused on youth. In a comprehensive and thoughtful review article of family risk factors for suicidal behavior in children and adolescents, Wagner (1997) provided empirical support for the claim that various aspects of family dysfunction are risk factors for attempted and completed suicide in youth. Specifically, prospective, presumed risk, and suicide risk studies have found poorer family system functioning, more conflicted parent–child relationships, higher rates of previous physical and sexual abuse, greater numbers of children residing with only one or neither parent, more losses due to mixed causes, and higher rates of family history of suicide attempts or psychiatric disorders in families of youth who attempt suicide compared with families of nonequated normal, equated normal, and, in some cases, clinical controls. Furthermore, the research evidence has shown that suicide attempts, as well as completions, often are preceded by family conflicts. There also have been consistent findings from correlational studies that indicate that suicide attempters are more likely than control groups to have poorer parent–child relationships, a history of abuse, and a family history of antisocial personality disorder. An important conclusion of Wagner's review was that the field has been hindered by a lack of attention to the temporal sequencing of putative risk factors and suicide symptoms. That is, the research designs and empirical findings typically used do not justify the majority of claims made regarding family risk factors for youth suicide. The summary provided above, however, reflects Wagner's careful attention to conclusions, albeit limited, that could reasonably be drawn from a significant number of the studies in this area.

There are a few studies that have examined the families of suicidal adults. Regarding family constellation, several factors have been explored, including marital satisfaction and number of children in the household. A large, 15-year prospective study of 989,949 women in Norway revealed a strong linear relation between an increase in number of children in marriage and a decrease in the relative risk for suicide (Hoyer & Lund, 1993). Several studies have revealed an increased risk for suicidal behavior in individuals never married, divorced, or widowed (Heikkinen, Isometsa, Marttunen, Aro, & Lonnqvist, 1995). The prevalence of marital conflict, poor intimate relationships, and interpersonal violence in the histories of suicidal women has been documented by several researchers (Kaslow et al., 1998; Maris, 1981; Stephens, 1985–1986). Not only has interpersonal discord been shown to be a risk factor and precipitant of suicidal behavior in women, but the opposite also has been shown to be true. That is, positive intimate relationships have been shown to decrease depression in women at increased risk for suicide (e.g., women with histories of sexual abuse; Feinauer, Callahan, & Hinton, 1996).

African American Families and Suicidal Behavior

There is a paucity of research on the families of suicidal African Americans. Only one study could be located that examined this issue among African American youth, despite the evidence that family functioning is related to adolescent suicide attempters in White samples. An examination of the perceived family functioning of a sample of 121 African American adolescent suicide attempters revealed that the bulk of the youth rated their families as moderately to significantly dysfunctional (Summerville, Kaslow, Abbate, & Cronan, 1994). Of those that rated their families as dysfunctional, the majority reported the most dysfunction on the cohesion dimension. More specifically, the families were perceived as disengaged; however, the nature of the disengaged presentation ranged across the adaptability spectrum. A unique family feature in a sample of primarily low-income suicidal African American adolescents was the tendency for the suicide attempter to manifest externalizing behavior problems (e.g., aggression, conduct problems, attention difficulties) rather than the internalizing behaviors (e.g., anxiety, depression, social isolation) often seen in nonminority samples of suicidal youth.

A few studies focusing on the families of suicidal African American adults were located. In a national study of the relation between marital status and suicide in African Americans and European Americans, a logistic regression analysis revealed that being divorced or widowed significantly raised the risk of death by suicide in African Americans but being single did not (Stack, 1996). Conversely, the impact of marital status on suicide was considerably stronger for European Americans than for African Americans, and being single did increase the risk of death by suicide for European Americans. The researchers contended that, in light of the well-documented data that African Americans have a greater degree of extended family support than European Americans, these data suggested a greater protective role for extended family ties within the African American community (Beck & Beck, 1989; Jayakody et al., 1993; Taylor et al., 1990; Wilson et al., 1995).

A few studies have specifically examined the link between partner abuse and suicidal behavior in African American women. Stark and Flitcraft (1996) found that African American women who attempted suicide were significantly more likely than their White counterparts to have a history of domestic violence. In their sample of women suicide attempters presenting to a hospital emergency room, only 22.2% of the White women who attempted suicide were identified as battered, whereas 48.8% of the African American women reported a history of partner abuse.

African American Women and Their Families: Programmatic Research on Suicidal Behaviors

Research Aims

Given the recent rise in rates of suicidal behavior within the African American community (Chance et al., 1998; Griffith & Bell, 1989), the fact that women are more likely to attempt suicide than are men (Canetto & Lester, 1995), and the extant data that indicates that family factors are associated with suicidal behavior in the majority population (Richman, 1986; Wagner, 1997), it is imperative that more research be conducted on suicidal behavior in African American women and their families. Thus, the overall purpose of our systematic line of research has been to examine and compare perceptions of family-of-creation and family-of-origin functioning between African American women who attempt suicide and those with no history of suicide attempts. The family-of-creation variables examined included family strengths, relationship satisfaction, family support, and physical and nonphysical partner abuse. The family-of-origin variables studied included various forms of childhood maltreatment, including physical, sexual, and emotional abuse and physical and emotional neglect. After the between-group differences were identified for these family-of-creation and family-of-origin variables, those family variables that predicted suicide attempt status were determined.

A second aim of our research endeavors was to examine those variables that mediate and moderate the link between suicidal behavior and various forms of family violence (physical partner abuse, nonphysical partner abuse, child maltreatment) and relationship discord. In these analyses, particular attention was paid to psychological symptoms, coping abilities, social support, and object relations development (a theoretical construct related to the quality of the early formative relationships in an individual's life).

Approach

The women we studied were recruited from Grady Health System, a large public health care system affiliated with Emory University, Atlanta, Georgia, that serves a primarily indigent, urban, and minority population. The sample consisted of two groups of African American women between the ages of 18 and 64: (a) women who presented to the hospital following a nonfatal suicide attempt ($n = 176$) and (b) women who presented to the hospital's medical walk-in clinics for nonemergency medical problems ($n = 185$). In addition, a subgroup of the overall sample, consisting of those women who reported a relationship within the past year, were analyzed separately: (a) women with a partner within the past year who presented to the hospital following a nonfatal suicide attempt ($n = 126$) and (b) women with a partner within the past year who presented to the hospital's medical walk-in clinics for nonemergency medical problems ($n = 112$). Detailed information about the sample and study procedures can be found elsewhere (Kaslow et al., 1998). Demographic information collected included both personal (age, education level, homeless status, and employment status) and family-related (marital status, number of children, mother and/or father living, birth order, and primary caretaker while growing up) information. Information collected on family of creation included self-report assessments of family strengths (Family Strengths; Olson, Larsen, & McCubbin, 1982), marital adjustment (Marital Adjustment Test; Locke & Wallace, 1959), and intimate partner abuse (Index of Spouse Abuse; Hudson & McIntosh, 1981). Information on family of origin included self-report assessments of childhood maltreatment, including sexual abuse, physical abuse, emotional abuse, emotional neglect, and physical neglect (Childhood Trauma Questionnaire; Bernstein, Ahluvalia, Pogge, & Handelsman, 1997; Bernstein et al., 1994). Data also were collected on psychological symptoms (Brief Symptom Inventory; Derogatis & Spencer, 1982), hopelessness (Hopelessness Scale; Beck, Weissman, Lester, & Trexler, 1974), alcohol problems (Brief Michigan Alcoholism Screening Test; Pokorny, Miller, & Kaplan, 1972), drug problems (Brief Drug Abuse Screening Test; Skinner, 1983), coping abilities (Preliminary Strategic Approach to Coping Scale; Hobfoll, Dunahoo, Ben-Porath, & Monnier, 1994), social support (Perceived Social Support; Cohen & Hoberman, 1983; Russell & Cutrona, 1984), and object relations (Bell Object Relations Inventory; Bell, Billington, & Becker, 1986, Object Relations Inventory [ORI]; Blatt, Chevron, Quinlan, Schaffer, & Wein, 1989).

Findings

Sample

The demographic variables of the African American women suicide attempters were comparable to the nonattempters with the exception of two personal demographic variables: Attempters had significantly fewer years of education and were less likely to be employed. The demographic variables of the African American women suicide attempters with partners were comparable to the nonattempters with partners with the exception of three personal demographic variables (attempters had significantly fewer years of education, were less likely to be employed, and were more likely to be homeless than were nonattempters) and one family-related demographic variable (attempters had significantly more children than did nonattempters). There were no other personal or family-related demographic variables that distinguished suicide attempters from nonattempters.

It is interesting to note that the only family demographic variable that differentiated between African American female suicide attempters and nonattempters was the number of children. However, unlike European American women, in which higher numbers of children serve to protect an individual from suicidal behavior (Hoyer & Lund, 1993), in this sample, more children was associated with attempting suicide. It may be that for low-income African American women, the presence of many children, without adequate financial resources to meet their basic needs, is more of a stressor than a protective factor.

Group Differences in Family-of-Creation Variables

Overall findings from the research, controlling for education, employment status, homeless status, and number of children in relevant analyses, revealed that suicide attempters reported fewer family strengths, poorer marital adjustment, and significantly higher scores on physical partner abuse and nonphysical partner abuse than did their nonattempter counterparts. Specifically, Kaslow and colleagues (1998) reported that African American women who attempted suicide were more likely to report being victims of intimate partner violence, both physical and nonphysical. In fact, female suicide attempters were 3.6 times more likely to report physical partner abuse and 3.9 times more likely to report nonphysical partner abuse than demographically matched nonattempters. These data suggest a clear link between problematic family relations in the current family constellation and an increased risk for suicidal behaviors.

Mediation of the Link Between Family-of-Creation Variables and Suicide Attempt Status

Several psychological symptoms were found to account for the link between partner abuse and suicidal behavior in women. Specifically, for African American women who experienced physical partner abuse within the past year, psychological distress, hopelessness, posttraumatic stress disorder (PTSD), and drug use mediated the link between intimate partner violence and suicidal behavior (Kaslow et al., 1998; Thompson et al., 1999). That is, the association between physical partner abuse and suicidal behavior is no longer significant when psychological distress, hopelessness, and PTSD are controlled for statistically. Furthermore, the association between nonphysical intimate partner violence was accounted for by psychological distress and hopelessness (Kaslow et al., 1998). That is, if psychological distress and hopelessness were controlled for statistically, nonphysical partner abuse was no longer associated with suicidal behavior in women. In addition, hopelessness mediated the link between relationship satisfaction and suicide attempt status.

Moderation of the Link Between Family-of-Creation Variables and Suicide Attempt Status

A variable moderating the link between partner abuse and suicidal behavior was also identified: social support (Kaslow et al., 1998). Women experiencing intimate partner violence (both physical and nonphysical) who had the belief that family members and friends would provide emotional support and assistance with practical matters were less likely to engage in suicidal behaviors than women experiencing intimate partner violence who did not have this belief.

Group Differences in Family-of-Origin Variables

Overall findings from this research, controlling for education, employment status, and homeless status, revealed that attempters reported significantly higher scores than did nonattempters on physical abuse, sexual abuse, emotional abuse, and emotional neglect during childhood. However, attempters and nonattempters did not report different levels of childhood physical neglect. Overall, women who attempted suicide in adulthood were much more likely to report a history of childhood maltreatment, including physical, emotional, and sexual abuse, as well as emotional neglect, than were adult women who never attempted suicide.

Mediation of the Link Between Family-of-Origin Variables and Suicide Attempt Status

Several variables were identified that accounted for the relation between the various types of childhood maltreatment and suicide attempt status in adult women. Overall, object relations deficits in several areas accounted for the association between childhood maltreatment and suicide attempts in women (Twomey, Kaslow, & Croft, 2000). Specifically, different dimensions of object relations differentially mediated the link between the various types of childhood maltreatment and suicide attempt status. The most robust mediator was the object relation dimension having to do with the ability to establish trustworthy and stable interpersonal relationships (alienation), which accounted for the association between all five types of childhood maltreatment and suicide attempt status. That is, for women with a history of any of the forms of childhood maltreatment who attempt suicide, it is not the child maltreatment per se but rather the difficulty establishing basic trust in relationships with others that makes them vulnerable to suicidal behavior. In addition, other aspects of object relations differentially mediate the links between specific forms of childhood maltreatment and later suicidal behavior. Specifically, childhood sexual abuse and childhood physical neglect were mediated by all aspects of object relations measured. That is, difficulties with the establishing trustworthy and stable interpersonal relationships (alienation), fears of rejection (insecure attachment), a deep mistrust of others (egocentricity), a sense of basic social ineptitude (social incompetence), and low levels of self–other differentiation–relatedness, all accounted for the link between childhood sexual abuse and childhood physical neglect and suicide attempts in women. As for the relations between the other types of childhood maltreatment and suicide attempt status, the link between suicide attempt status and physical abuse was also mediated by low levels of self-other differentiation–relatedness, and the link between suicide attempt status and emotional abuse also was mediated by the fear of rejection (insecure attachment).

Predicting Suicide Attempt Status

Further analyses were conducted to determine which family-of-creation and family-of-origin variables were significantly related to suicide attempt status while controlling for all other risk factors. Given that suicide is a phenomenon with a very low base rate, it is virtually impossible to predict whether a specific individual will attempt to or succeed at killing himself or herself. Although many risk factors associated with suicide attempts have been identified, specific case-by-case prediction of a suicide attempt is not possible. Given that the accurate identification of specific individuals who will attempt or complete suicide is highly unlikely, the goal is to enhance the ability to identify groups of individuals who are at increased risk for suicide. Thus, it is important to distinguish those variables associated with suicide attempts that enhance the predictive ability of applicable equations. Many risk factors are associated with each other and, therefore, do not improve the ability to identify individuals at increased risk for suicidal behavior. Thus, to identify those variables significantly related to suicide attempt status, multivariate logistic regression was used to control for other risk factors and confounding variables (e.g., education, employment status, homeless status, and number of children). All four family-of-creation (family strengths, marital adjustment, physical partner abuse, and nonphysical partner abuse) and four of the five childhood trauma (physical abuse, sexual abuse, emotional abuse, emotional neglect) variables that were significantly associated with suicide attempt status were included in this predictive model. Multivariate results revealed that only one family-of-creation (significant level of marital discord) and one family-of-origin variable (childhood sexual abuse) were uniquely associated with risk for suicide attempt among African American women. Women who reported a significant level of marital discord were 3 times as likely to have made a suicide attempt compared with women who did not experience significant levels of marital discord. In addition, women who reported experiencing childhood sexual abuse were 2 times as likely to have made a suicide attempt compared with women who had not experienced childhood sexual abuse.

Discussion and Conclusion

Results from this research revealed that African American women who attempt suicide have more negative perceptions of both their family of creation and their family of origin than do demographically matched women with no history of suicidal behavior. This overall finding is consistent with the literature, which has indicated that family dysfunction is a risk factor for suicidal behavior among adults (Aldridge, 1984; Keitner & Miller, 1990; Kosky, Eshkevari, Goldney, & Hassan, 1998; Richman, 1986) and suggests that, similar to their non–African American counterparts, family factors are associated with suicidal behavior in the African American community.

Compared with demographically similar nonattempters, African American women who attempt suicide report that their families of creation have fewer strengths and indicate that their intimate partnerships are less satisfying and more often characterized by both physical and nonphysical abuse. Given the emphasis within the African American community on the strengths of the family as protection against discrimination and oppression, and thus as a buffer against suicide, it is not surprising that those women who view their family as having more limited family resources in terms of family pride, positive values and beliefs, and a sense of mastery and competence (accord) are more likely to engage in self-harm. The findings that marital dissatisfaction and intimate partner violence are associated with increased risk for suicidal behavior among African American women is consistent with the literature on suicidal behavior in women more generally. Specifically, research has indicated that suicidal women experience their primary relationships as hostile and often characterized by psychological abuse, emotional neglect, and/or infidelity (Arcel, Mantonakis, Petersson, Jemos, & Kaliteraki, 1992; Bergman & Brismar, 1991; Stephens, 1985–1986; Wolk-Wasserman, 1986). In addition, several investigations have shown that women abused by their partner are more likely than nonabused women to have made suicide attempts (Abbott, Johnson, Koziol-McLain, & Lowenstein, 1995; Amaro, Fried, Cabral, & Zuckerman, 1990; Bergman & Brismar, 1991; Hampton & Gelles, 1994; Roberts, Lawrence, O'Toole, & Raphael, 1997) and women who attempt suicide have high rates of partner abuse (Kaslow et al., 1998).

Results from the mediational analyses suggested that the important factors that account for the association between intimate partner abuse and suicidal behavior in African American women and between relationship discord and suicidal behavior include various psychological problems, such as overall levels of distress, PTSD symptoms, feelings of hopelessness, and substance abuse. In other words, being involved in an abusive or discordant relationship increases a woman's risk for experiencing various psychological difficulties, which, in turn, increases her vulnerability to suicidal behavior. Thus, interventions with abused women and with women unhappy in their primary relationships should include strategies for ameliorating psychological symptoms and distress. Similarly, given that social support moderates the link between partner abuse and suicidal behavior, intervention efforts should target the bolstering of social support networks to reduce African American women's risk for suicidal behavior. Furthermore, community efforts that target the abuser rather than the abused are essential to ending the cycle of violence.

The results showing significant group differences in childhood maltreatment histories between African American women who attempted suicide and those who did not is consistent with the body of research that has clearly demonstrated that childhood trauma places individuals at risk for difficulties throughout the life span (Trickett & McBride-Chang, 1995) and for suicidal behavior in particular (Briere & Runtz, 1986, 1988a, 1988b, 1990; Briere & Zaidi, 1989; Romans, Martin, Anderson, Herbison, & Mullen, 1995; van der Kolk, Perry, & Herman, 1991; Young, 1992), the majority of this research has examined childhood physical and sexual abuse. In comparisons between various populations (psychiatric inpatients, psychiatric outpatients, college populations, community samples, and individuals of different nationalities) with reported histories of childhood physical and sexual abuse and control groups without abuse histories, higher rates of suicidal ideation and attempts have been found among both abuse groups (Briere & Runtz, 1986; Browne & Finkelhor, 1986; Gould et al., 1994; McCauley et al., 1997; Silverman, Reinherz, & Giaconia, 1996; van der Kolk & Fisler, 1994). As for emotional abuse, only one study that investigated the association between childhood emotional abuse and subsequent suicide attempts could be located (Gould et al., 1994). This study revealed that patients awaiting treatment in a university-based family medicine practice who reported a history of childhood emotional abuse were 3.7 times more likely to have made past suicide attempts than their nonabused peers. No empirical research investigating the link between physical and emotional neglect and suicidal behaviors could be located.

Results from the analyses examining various aspects of object relations as mediators between history of childhood maltreatment and suicide attempt status revealed that the inability to experience trust and emotional satisfaction in relationships fully accounted for the relation between the experience of all types of childhood maltreatment and the presence of a suicide attempt in adulthood. Considering the fact that childhood maltreatment in any form violates basic trust within the context of a dependent relationship, it is no wonder that, as a consequence, new objects and relationships are regarded with fear and apprehension (a lack of basic trust). Experiences of childhood maltreatment lead to an anticipation of interpersonal violence or rejection, not to the expectation of the types of loving, comforting, and caring interactions that build trust.

Data gleaned from this study also revealed that two family variables were predictive of suicide attempt status, marital adjustment (i.e., significant marital discord) and history of childhood sexual abuse, suggesting that these two variables are significant risk factors for suicide attempts among African American women. In fact, logistic regression revealed that women who reported a significant level of marital discord were 3 times as likely to have made a suicide attempt compared with women who did not experience significant levels of marital discord. In addition, women who reported experiencing childhood sexual abuse were 2 times as likely to have made a suicide attempt compared with women who had not experienced childhood sexual abuse.

It is interesting to speculate about this finding that relationship satisfaction was the only family-of-creation variable that was found to be predictive of suicidal behavior in this sample. This finding is consistent with the epidemiological and clinical literature revealing that an unhappy marriage constitutes a grave risk to a woman's mental health (Weissman, 1987). A review of the extant empirical research revealed that marital distress is strongly associated with both depressive symptoms and diagnostic depression (Whisman, chapter 1). For example, concordance rates between marital discord and depression as high as 50% have been reported (Beach & O'Leary, 1992). Marital distress and low spousal support also have been reported to predict depression onset (Brown & Harris, 1978), maintenance (Goering, Lancee, & Freeman, 1992), and relapse (Hooley & Teasdale, 1989). Given that depression is a major risk factor for suicidal behavior in women (Canetto & Lester, 1995), it is reasonable to hypothesize that the association found between depression and marital adjustment also may be found between suicidal behavior and relationship adjustment.

Still intriguing, however, is the fact that intimate partner abuse is not predictive of suicide attempt status whereas relationship dissatisfaction is (see O'Leary and Cano, chapter 9, for more information regarding the links between relationship discord and intimate partner violence). This suggests that the level of abuse in the relationship is distinct from how satisfying women find their intimate relationships. Although this appears contradictory, Collins's (1990) exploration of the conspiracy of silence in the African American community may shed some light. It may be that the African American women who experience intimate partner violence within a larger context in which violence against women is legitimized and routinized do not see themselves as victims. Therefore, the norms for evaluating happiness and satisfaction in an intimate relationship may not consider the presence or absence of abuse or violence because violence is expected, ignored, and condoned by the larger community. In this context, women learn to experience their partner's behavior as routine rather than alarming and unacceptable. If this is indeed the case, there are strong implications for broad community-focused interventions rather than exclusively individually focused ones.

Given that the deleterious effects of childhood maltreatment measured (in this and previous studies) are pervasive, far reaching, and clearly associated with suicidal behavior, it is striking that only childhood sexual abuse history was found to be a significant predictor of suicide attempt status in African American women. One possible explanation may involve the impact of history of sexual abuse on the subsequent relationships that women develop with their intimate partners. There is a growing body of empirical evidence that lends support for the long-standing clinical observations and theoretical formulations of the long-term consequences of childhood sexual abuse that are reflected in survivors' views of themselves and others. Several symptoms have been found to be associated with history of sexual abuse, including depression, feelings of helplessness, feelings of isolation, mistrust in interpersonal relationships, various sexual dysfunctions, and low self-esteem accompanied by a sense of oneself as damaged (Briere & Runtz, 1988a, 1988b; Browne & Finkelhor, 1986; Herman, 1981; Wyatt & Powell, 1988). More recently, researchers have pursued more theoretically based investigations to understand the lasting effects of childhood sexual abuse in adulthood. Specifically, Liem, O'Toole, and James (1996) explored the hypothesis that the experience of childhood sexual abuse that rendered these children markedly powerless, often as the result of betrayal or lack of protection by adults, results in a preoccupation with power and betrayal in subsequent relationships in an attempt to cope with intense feelings of betrayal and helplessness. The subsequent preoccupation with issues of betrayal and power interferes with psychological well-being. These researchers found that, compared with narratives of women without histories of childhood sexual abuse, the narratives of adult women with histories of childhood sexual abuse exhibited more frequent themes of personal powerlessness and betrayal by others (Liem, O'Toole, & James, 1992). Furthermore, a larger comparison of women with and without histories of childhood sexual abuse offered empirical support for a heightened need for power and a greater fear of power among survivors of childhood sexual abuse (Liem et al., 1996). These data are consistent with the conceptualization, from an interpersonal theoretical perspective (Benjamin, 1993; Strupp & Binder, 1984), that women may produce enactments with others consistent with their view of themselves as passive victims in a world of malevolent others which, in turn, reinforce feelings of depression, low self-esteem, and hopelessness. These feelings are significant risk factors for suicidal behavior both in non-African American (Canetto & Lester, 1995) and African American (Kaslow et al., 1998) women, and, therefore, it is not surprising that women with a history of sexual abuse are at particularly high risk for attempting suicide.

Findings from this study must be considered in light of study limitations. First, the measures were not developed specifically for use with African Americans, and the psychometric properties of the scales for low-income African American women deserve more study. This is particularly important given that the measures were designed for individuals who are functionally literate and thus able to complete the measures independently. Because of the low literacy levels of individuals who receive services at the hospital from which study participants were drawn, the measures were read to them. Second, all of the measures used were self-report in nature, and data were gathered from only one individual. Although this provides one family member's perceptions of her family, the lack of data from multiple informants or multiple methods of data collection limits the richness of the data and the generalizations that can be made. Third, the data gathered regarding family of origin were limited to one measure of child maltreatment and one index of family life and were retrospective in nature. Fourth, given that the suicide attempters completed the measures immediately following their suicide attempt, their reports of their family life may have been biased negatively as a result of their elevated distress levels. Fifth, given the cross-sectional nature of this study design, the conclusions that can be drawn regarding family factors predictive of suicidal behavior in African American women are limited.

Despite these limitations, this study offers one of the first investigations of the families of suicidal African American women. Therefore, the data gleaned can inform interventions with these women. There are a number of clinical implications of this research. First, the findings highlight the importance of focusing on concerns about family of creation and family of origin when working with suicidal African American women. This should entail asking questions about family functioning, current relationship satisfaction, partner abuse, and childhood history of maltreatment. The clinician should bear in mind the importance of assessing and addressing emotional abuse, in addition to physical and sexual abuse, when considering women's current and past family relationships. Interventions should focus on addressing the effect of parental depression and violence history on emotional well-being and interpersonal functioning and enhancing positive attachments and a sense of emotional security (Cummings, DeArth-Pendley, Schudlich, and Smith, chapter 5). Second, given that current relationship dissatisfaction is such a significant risk factor for suicidal behavior in African American women, couples therapy with these women and their partners could be particularly beneficial. However, it is important that clinicians be sensitive to the sociocultural and socioeconomic norms that govern interpersonal relating in the community of the individual targeted for intervention. Third, these findings also highlight the need for clinicians to be cognizant of the impact sociocultural and socioeconomic factors have on suicidal phenomena. For example, particular attention should be paid in interventions with suicidal, low-income African American mothers to assessing the amount of support and assistance they have with child care. Clearly, the more data amassed regarding the effect of the unique sociocultural, sociopolitical, and socioeconomic context on the risk of suicidal behaviors among low-income African American women, the more effective primary, secondary, and tertiary interventions will be. Especially considering the paucity of extant data, this investigation clearly constitutes a substantial contribution to the understanding of suicidal behavior in a historically disenfranchised and understudied group of individuals at recently increasing risk for suicide.

References

Abbott, J., Johnson, R., Koziol-McLain, J., & Lowenstein, S. R. (1995). Domestic violence against women: Incidence and prevalence in an emergency department population. *Journal of the American Medical Association, 273,* 1763–1767.

Aldarondo, E., & Sugarman, D. B. (1996). Risk marker analysis of the cessation and persistence of wife assault. *Journal of Consulting and Clinical Psychology, 64,* 1010–1019.

Aldridge, D. (1984). Family interaction and suicidal behaviour: A brief review. *Journal of Family Therapy, 6,* 309–322.

Amaro, H., Fried, L., Cabral, H., & Zuckerman, B. (1990). Violence during pregnancy and substance abuse. *American Journal of Public Health, 80,* 575–579.

Arcel, L. T., Mantonakis, J., Petersson, B., Jemos, J., & Kaliteraki, E. (1992). Suicide attempts among Greek and Danish women and the quality of their relationships with husbands and boyfriends. *Acta Psychiatrica Scandinavia, 85,* 189–195.

Asbury, J. (1987). African American women in violent relationships: An exploration of cultural differences. In R. L. Hampton (Ed.), *Violence in the Black family* (pp. 89–105). Lexington, MA: D.C. Heath.

Beach, S. R. H., & O'Leary, K. D. (1992). Treating depression in the context of marital discord: Outcome and predictors of response of marital therapy versus cognitive therapy. *Behavior Therapy, 23,* 507–528.

Beck, R. W., & Beck, S. (1989). The incidence of extended family households among middle aged Black and White women: Estimates from a five year panel study. *Journal of Family Issues, 10,* 147–168.

Beck, A. T., Weissman, A., Lester, D., & Trexler, L. (1974). The measurement of pessimism: The Hopelessness Scale. *Journal of Consulting and Clinical Psychology, 42,* 861–865.

Bell, M., Billington, R., & Becker, B. (1986). A scale for the assessment of object relations: Reliability, validity, and factorial invariance. *Journal of Clinical Psychology, 42,* 733–741.

Belle, D. (1990). Poverty and women's mental health. *American Psychologist, 45,* 385–389.

Benjamin, L. (1993). *Interpersonal diagnosis and treatment of personality disorders.* New York: Guilford Press.

Bennett, C. E. (1995). The Black population in the United States: March 1994 and 1993. *U.S. Bureau of the Census, Current Population Reports* (pp. 20–48). Washington DC: U.S. Government Printing Office.

Bergman, B., & Brismar, B. (1991). Suicide attempts by battered wives. *Acta Psychiatrica Scandinavia, 83,* 380–384.

Bernstein, D. P., Ahluvalia, T., Pogge, D., & Handelsman, L. (1997). Validity of the Childhood

Trauma Questionnaire in an adolescent psychiatric population. *Journal of the American Academy of Child and Adolescent Psychiatry, 36,* 340–348.

Bernstein, D. P., Fink, L., Handelsman, L., Foote, J., Lovejoy, M., Wenzelk, K., Sapareto, E., & Ruggiero, J. (1994). Initial reliability and validity of a new retrospective measure of child abuse and neglect. *American Journal of Psychiatry, 151,* 1132–1136.

Billingsley, A. (1992). *Climbing Jacob's ladder: The enduring legacy of African-American families.* New York: Simon & Schuster.

Blatt, S., Chevron, D., Quinlan, D., Schaffer, C., & Wein, S. (1989). *The assessment of qualitative and structural dimensions of object representations* (rev. ed.). Unpublished research manual, New Haven, CT: Yale University.

Boyd-Franklin, N. (1989). *Black families in therapy: A multisystems approach.* New York: Guilford Press.

Briere, J., & Runtz, M. (1986). Suicidal thoughts and behaviors in former sexual abuse victims. *Canadian Journal of Behavioral Science, 18,* 413–423.

Briere, J., & Runtz, M. (1988a). Multivariate correlates of childhood psychological and physical maltreatment among university women. *Child Abuse and Neglect, 12,* 331–341.

Briere, J., & Runtz, M. (1988b). Symptomatology associated with childhood sexual victimization in a nonclinical adult sample. *Child Abuse and Neglect, 12,* 51–59.

Briere, J., & Runtz, M. (1990). Differential adult symptomatology associated with three types of child abuse histories. *Child Abuse and Neglect, 14,* 57–64.

Briere, J., & Zaidi, L. Y. (1989). Sexual abuse histories and sequelae in female psychiatric emergency room patients. *American Journal of Psychiatry, 146,* 1602–1606.

Brown, G., & Harris, T. O. (1978). *Social origins of depression: A study of psychiatric disorder in women.* New York: Free Press.

Browne, A., & Finkelhor, D. (1986). Impact of child sexual abuse: A review of the research. *Psychological Bulletin, 99,* 66–77.

Canetto, S. S., & Lester, D. (1995). *Women and suicidal behavior.* New York: Springer.

Cardarelli, A. P. (1997). *Violence between intimate partners: Patterns, causes, and effects.* Needham Heights, MA: Allyn & Bacon.

Chance, S. E., Kaslow, N. J., Summerville, M. B., & Wood, K. (1998). Suicidal behavior in African American individuals: Current status and future directions. *Cultural Diversity and Mental Health, 4,* 19–37.

Cohen, S., & Hoberman, H. (1983). Positive events and social supports as buffers of life change stress. *Journal of Applied Social Psychology, 13,* 99–125.

Coley, S. M., & Beckett, J. O. (1988). Black battered women: A review of the empirical literature. *Journal of Counseling and Development, 66,* 266–270.

Collins, P. H. (1990). *Black feminist thought: Knowledge, consciousness, and the politics of empowerment.* New York: Routledge.

Davis, A. (1981). *Women, race, and class.* New York: Vintage Books.

Derogatis, L., & Spencer, P. (1982). *The Brief Symptom Inventory (BSI): Administration, scoring, and procedures manual.* Baltimore, MD: Johns Hopkins University.

Feinauer, L. L., Callahan, E. H., & Hinton, H. G. (1996). Positive intimate relationships decrease depression in sexually abused women. *American Journal of Family Therapy, 24,* 99–106.

Garbarino, J., & Ebata, A. (1983). The significance of ethnic and cultural differences in child maltreatment. *Journal of Marriage and the Family, 45,* 773–783.

Gibbs, J. (1997). African-American suicide: A cultural paradox. *Suicide and Life-Threatening Behavior, 27,* 68–79.

Gibbs, J. T., & Hines, A. M. (1989). Factors related to sex differences in suicidal behavior among black youth: Implications for intervention and research. *Journal of Adolescent Research, 4,* 152–172.

Gibbs, J. T., & Huang, L. N. (Eds.). (1989). *Children of color: Psychological interventions with minority youth.* San Francisco: Jossey-Bass.

Goering, P., Lancee, W., & Freeman, L. (1992). Marital support and recovery from depression. *British Journal of Psychiatry, 160,* 76–82.

Gould, D., Stevens, N., Ward, N., Carlin, A., Sowell, H., & Gustafson, B. (1994). Self-reported childhood abuse in an adult population in a primary care setting: Prevalence, correlates, and associated suicide attempts. *Archives of Family Medicine, 3,* 252–256.

Greene, B. (1994). Lesbian women of color: Triple jeopardy. In L. Comas-Diaz & B. Greene (Eds.), *Women of color: Integrating ethnic and gender identities in psychotherapy* (pp. 389–427). New York: Guilford Press.

Griffith, E., & Bell, C. (1989). Recent trends in suicide and homicide among Blacks. *Journal of the American Medical Association, 262,* 2265–2269.

Hampton, R. L., & Gelles, R. J. (1994). Violence toward Black women in a nationally representative sample of Black families. *Journal of Comparative Family Studies, 25,* 105–119.

Heikkinen, M. E., Isometsa, E. T., Marttunen, M. J., Aro, H. M., & Lonnqvist, J. K. (1995). Social factors in suicide. *British Journal of Psychiatry, 167,* 747–753.

Herman, J. L. (1981). *Father-daughter incest.* Cambridge, MA: Harvard University Press.

Hobfoll, S. E., Dunahoo, C. L., Ben-Porath, Y., & Monnier, J. (1994). Gender and coping: The dual axis model of coping. *American Journal of Community Psychology, 22,* 49–82.

Hooley, J. M., & Teasdale, J. D. (1989). Predictors of relapse in uniploar depressives: Expressed emotion, marital distress, and perceived criticism. *Journal of Abnormal Psychology, 98,* 229–233.

Hotaling, G. T., & Sugarman, D. B. (1990). A risk marker analysis of assaulted wives. *Journal of Family Violence, 5,* 1–13.

Hoyer, G., & Lund, E. (1993). Suicide among women related to number of children in marriage. *Archives of General Psychiatry, 50,* 134–137.

Hudson, W. W., & McIntosh, S. R. (1981). The assessment of spouse abuse: Two quantifiable dimensions. *Journal of Marriage and the Family, 43,* 873–888.

Jayakody, R., Chatters, L., & Taylor, R. (1993). Family support to single and married African American mothers: The provision of financial, emotional, and child care assistance. *Journal of Marriage and the Family, 55,* 261–276.

Kanuha, V. (1994). Women of color in battering relationships. In L. Comas-Diaz & B. Greene (Eds.), *Women of color: Integrating ethnic and gender identities in psychotherapy* (pp. 428–454). New York: Guilford Press.

Kaslow, N. J., Thompson, M. P., Meadows, L. A., Jacobs, D., Chance, S., Gibb, B., Bornstein, H., Hollins, L., Rashid, A., & Phillips, K. (1998). Factors that mediate and moderate the link between partner abuse and suicidal behavior in African American women. *Journal of Consulting and Clinical Psychology, 66,* 533–540.

Keitner, G. I., & Miller, I. W. (1990). Family functioning and major depression: An overview. *American Journal of Psychiatry, 147,* 1128–1137.

Kingree, J. B., Thompson, M. P., & Kaslow, N. J. (1999). Risk factors for suicide attempts among low-income women with a history of alcohol problems. *Addictive Behaviors, 24,* 583–587.

Kosky, R. J., Eshkevari, H. S., Goldney, R. D., & Hassan, R. (Eds.). (1998). *Suicide prevention: The global context.* New York: Plenum Press.

Koss, M. P., Goodman, L. A., Browne, A., Fitzgerald, L. F., Keita, G. P., & Russo, N. F. (1994). *No safe haven: Male violence against women at home, at work, and in the community.* Washington, DC: American Psychological Association.

Levine, M., Doueck, H. J., Freeman, J. B., & Compaan, C. (1996). African American families and child protection. *Child and Youth Services Review, 18,* 693–711.

Liem, J. H., O'Toole, J. G., & James, J. B. (1992). The need for power in women who were sexually abused as children. *Psychology of Women Quarterly, 16,* 467–480.

Liem, J. H., O'Toole, J. G., & James, J. B. (1996). Themes of power and betrayal in sexual abuse survivors' characterizations of interpersonal relationships. *Journal of Traumatic Stress, 9,* 745–761.

Locke, H. J., & Wallace, K. M. (1959). Short marital-adjustment and prediction tests: Their reliability and validity. *Marriage and Family Living, 21,* 251–255.

Maris, R. W. (1981). *Pathways to suicide, a survey of self-destructive behaviors.* Baltimore, MD: John Hopkins University Press.

McAdoo, H. P. (Ed.). (1988). *Black families* (2nd ed.). Newbury Park, CA: Sage.

McCauley, J., Kern, D., Koldner, K., Dill, L., Schroeder, A., DeChant, H., Ryden, J., Derogatis, L., & Bass, E. (1997). Clinical characteristics of women with a history of childhood abuse. *Journal of the American Medical Association, 277,* 1362–1368.

National Center for Health Statistics. (1998). *Monthly vital statistics report* (Vol. 46, No. 1, DHHS Publication No. PHS96–1120). Washington, DC: U.S. Department of Health and Human Services.

Nisbet, P. A. (1996). Protective factors for suicidal Black females. *The American Association of Suicidology, 26,* 325–341.

Olson, D. H., Larsen, A. S., & McCubbin, H. I. (1982). Family strengths. In D. H. Olson, H. I. McCubbin, H. Barnes, A. Larsen, M. Muxen, & M. Wilson (Eds.), *Family inventories* (pp. 56–70). St. Paul: University of Minnesota Family Social Science.

Phillips, D. P., & Ruth, T. E. (1993). Adequacy of official suicide statistics for scientific research and public policy. *Suicide and Life-Threatening Behavior, 23,* 307–319.

Pokorny, A., Miller, B., & Kaplan, H. (1972). The Brief MAST: A shortened version of the Michigan Alcohol Screening Test. *American Journal of Psychiatry, 129,* 342–345.

Richman, J. (1986). *Family therapy for suicidal people.* New York: Springer.

Roberts, G. L., Lawrence, J. M., O'Toole, B. I., & Raphael, B. (1997). Domestic violence in the emergency department: I: Two case-control studies of victims. *General Hospital Psychiatry, 19,* 5–11.

Romans, S. E., Martin, J. L., Anderson, J. C., Herbison, G. P., & Mullen, P. E. (1995). Sexual abuse in childhood and deliberate self-harm. *American Journal of Psychiatry, 152,* 1336–1342.

Russell, D., & Cutrona, C. (1984). *The provisions of social relationships and adaptation to stress.* Paper presented at the 92nd Annual Convention of the American Psychological Association, Toronto, Ontario, Canada.

Saunders, M. A. (1995). Long term physical complications of battering: An Afrocentric intervention of the ancestors. *Journal of Cultural Diversity, 2,* 75–82.

Silverman, A., Reinherz, H., & Giaconia, R. (1996). The long term sequelae of child and adolescent abuse: A longitudinal community study. *Child Abuse and Neglect, 20,* 709–723.

Skinner, H. (1983). The Drug Abuse Screening Test. *Addictive Behaviors, 7,* 363–371.

Sorenson, S. B., Upchurch, D. M., & Shen, H. (1996). Violence and injury in marital arguments: Risk patterns and gender differences. *American Journal of Public Health, 86,* 35–40.

Stack, S. (1996). The effect of marital integration on African American suicide. *Suicide and Life-Threatening Behavior, 26,* 405–414.

Staples, R. (1994). *Black family: Essays and studies.* (5th ed.). New York: Van Nostrand Reinhold.

Staples, R., & Johnson, L. B. (1993). *Black families at the crossroads: Challenges and prospects.* San Francisco: Jossey-Bass.

Stark, E., & Flitcraft, A. (1996). *Women at risk: Domestic violence and women's health.* Thousand Oaks, CA: Sage.

Stephens, J. B. (1985–1986). Suicidal women and their relationships with their parents. *Omega, 16,* 289–300.

Stets, J. E., & Straus, M. (1990). Gender differences in reporting marital violence and its medical and psychological consequences. In M. A. Straus & R. J. Gelles (Eds.), *Physical violence in American families: Risk factors and adaptations to violence in 8,145 families* (pp. 151–166). New Brunswick, NJ: Transaction.

Straus, M., & Gelles, R. (1986). Societal change and change in family violence from 1975 and 1985 as revealed by two national samples. *Journal of Marriage and the Family, 48,* 465–479.

Straus, M., Gelles, R., & Steinmetz, S. K. (1980). *Behind closed doors: Violence in the American family.* Garden City, NJ: Anchor Press.

Strupp, H. H., & Binder, J. L. (1984). *Psychotherapy in a new key: A guide to time-limited dynamic psychotherapy.* New York: Basic Books.

Sullivan, C. M., & Rumptz, M. H. (1994). Adjustment and needs of African-American women who utilized a domestic violence shelter. *Violence and Victims, 9,* 275–286.

Summerville, M. B., Kaslow, N. J., Abbate, M., & Cronan, S. (1994). Psychopathology, family functioning, and cognitive style in urban adolescents with suicide attempts. *Journal of Abnormal Child Psychology, 22,* 221–235.

Taylor, R. J., Chatters, L. M., Tucker, M. B., & Lewis, E. (1990). Developments in research on Black families: A decade in review. *Journal of Marriage and the Family, 52,* 993–1014.

Thompson, M. P., Kaslow, N. J., Kingree, J. B., Puett, R., Thompson, N. J., & Meadows, L. (1999). Partner abuse and posttraumatic stress disorder as risk factors for suicide attempts in a sample of low-income, inner-city women. *Journal of Traumatic Stress, 12,* 59–72.

Trickett, P. K., & McBride-Chang, C. (1995). The developmental impact of different forms of child abuse and neglect. *Developmental Review, 15,* 311–337.

Tucker, M. B., & Mitchell-Kernan, C. (Eds.). (1995). *The decline in marriage among African Americans: Causes, consequences, and policy implications.* New York: Russell Sage Foundation.

Twomey, H., Kaslow, N. J., & Croft, S. (2000). Childhood maltreatment, object relations, and suicidal behavior in women. *Psychoanalytic Psychology, 17,* 1–23.

U.S. Department of Commerce. (1992). Detailed occupation and other characteristics from the EEO file for the United States. Washington, DC: U.S. Government Printing Office.

van der Kolk, V., & Fisler, R. (1994). Childhood abuse and neglect and loss of self-regulation. *Bulletin of the Menninger Clinic, 58,* 145–168.

van der Kolk, V., Perry, C., & Herman, J. (1991). Childhood origins of self-destructive behavior. *American Journal of Psychiatry, 148,* 1665–1671.

Wagner, B. M. (1997). Family risk factors for child and adolescent suicidal behavior. *Psychological Bulletin, 121,* 246–298.

Walker, K., Taylor, E., McElroy, A., Phillip, D., & Wilson, M. (1995). Familial and ecological correlates of self-esteem in African American children. *New Directions for Child Development, 68,* 5–21.

Weissman, M. M. (1987). Advances in psychiatric epidemiology: Rates and risks for major depression. *American Journal of Public Health, 77,* 445–451.

Wilson, M., & Tolson, T. F. J. (1990). Family support in the Black community. *Journal of Clinical Child Psychology, 19,* 347–355.

Wilson, M. N., Greene-Bates, C., McKim, L., Simmons, R., Askew, T., Curry, J., & Hinton, I. (1995). African American family life. New *Directions for Child Development, 68,* 5–21.

Wolk-Wasserman, D. (1986). Suicidal communication of persons attempting suicide and responses of significant others. *Acta Psychiatrica Scandinavia, 73,* 481–499.

Wyatt, G. (1990). The aftermath of child sexual abuse of African American and White American women: The victim's experience. *Journal of Family Violence, 5,* 61–81.

Wyatt, G. E., & Powell, G. J. (Eds.). (1988). *Lasting effects of child sexual abuse.* Newbury Park, CA: Sage.

Young, L. (1992). Sexual abuse and the problem of embodiment. *Child Abuse and Neglect, 16,* 89–100.

9
Marital Discord and Partner Abuse: Correlates and Causes of Depression

K. Daniel O'Leary
Annmarie Cano

The lay and professional literatures have long linked marital problems and physical abuse to depression in one or both partners. However, almost everyone knows an individual in a supposed unhappy marriage who is not depressed. Although it may seem unlikely, this chapter provides documentation of individuals who are in relationships characterized by physical aggression but who are not depressed. In brief, there is no one-to-one correspondence between marital discord and depression or partner abuse and depression. This chapter first addresses the relationship of marital problems and depression. The second half of the chapter deals with the relationship of partner abuse and depression. In addressing these issues, we differentiate studies by assessment method (i.e., whether they measured depressive symptoms by questionnaire or clinical depression by standardized interview). We also address the strength of the relationships between marital discord and partner abuse to depressive symptoms and clinical depression.

Relationship Between Marital Discord and Partner Abuse

The relationship between marital discord and physical aggression by one or both partners is not as straightforward as might be expected, and it is not a central focus of this chapter. However, to provide some context for the interpretation of the relationship of marital discord and partner abuse and depression, it is important to have some understanding of the relationship between marital discord and partner abuse. The relationship depends on whether one is attempting to generalize from a clinical sample or a community sample.

In clinical samples of maritally discordant individuals seeking therapy for marital problems, between 50% and 65% of the relationships are characterized by some level of physical aggression. Work at our marital therapy clinic in suburban Long Island, New York, has suggested that about half of the couples who are physically aggressive engage in moderate levels of physical aggression. The other half of the physically aggressive couples engage in severe physical aggression (Ehrensaft & Vivian, 1996; O'Leary, Vivian, & Malone, 1992). Similar results were found by Holtzworth-Munroe et al. (1992). As might be expected, generally there is a significant association between the frequency and severity of physical aggression and the level of marital discord.

In community samples of young married couples, as many as 50% of the couples have relationships characterized by physical aggression, but the couples often do not perceive the physical aggression as problematic. In fact, the majority of men and women in such relationships do not report marital discord. For example, in our longitudinal research with young couples, we separated those women and men who were in stable physically aggressive relationships from those who were in stable nonaggressive relationships (O'Leary et al., 1989). The marital satisfaction of the two groups became increasingly discrepant across time. We used a cutoff of 90 on the Marital Adjustment Test (Locke & Wallace, 1959) as an optimal discriminator between distressed and nondistressed couples. With this cutoff, we found that 30% of the partners of stable aggressive men and 24% of the partners of stable aggressive women fell at or below the 90 cutoff at the 30-month assessment. Conversely, only 11% of the partners of stable nonaggressive men and 9% of the partners of stable nonaggressive women had scores below 90. Although it may not be surprising that partners of stable aggressive spouses were more likely to be discordant at the 30-month follow-up than partners of stable nonaggressive spouses, we anticipated that many more of the partners of stable aggressive spouses would report marital discord at 30 months.

The prevalence of self-reported physical aggression is between 21% and 43% of young married or cohabiting men and 36% and 51% of young married or cohabiting women (Leonard & Senchak, 1996; Magdol et al., 1997; Mihalic, Elliot, & Menard, 1994; O'Leary et al., 1989). However, marital discord usually is not present in the engagement year or the first year of the relationship, even when one (or both) of the partners is physically aggressive. If the physical aggression continues, however, marital satisfaction declines significantly (O'Leary et al., 1989; Quigley & Leonard, 1996). If the husband ceases to be physically aggressive, the drop in marital satisfaction will abate (Quigley & Leonard, 1996).

Depression and Marriage

Early theoretical accounts suggested that marriage was a risk factor for depression, especially for women (Bernard, 1972; Hafner, 1986). However, more recent large-scale studies have shown that married men and women actually have a lower risk for the incidence and recurrence of major depression compared to separated, divorced, or single individuals (e.g., Amenson & Lewinsohn, 1981; Anthony & Petronis, 1991; Aseltine & Kessler, 1993; Coryell, Endicott, & Keller, 1991). As for subclinical depression, studies have shown that married individuals also report lower rates of depressive symptoms than separated or divorced individuals, as measured by interviews and questionnaires (Amenson & Lewinsohn, 1981; Anthony & Petronis, 1991). These results have spurred researchers to consider the possibility that marriage may not be a predictor of depression in and of itself. Rather, as emphasized by Beach, Sandeen, and O'Leary (1990), poor marital quality, not marriage per se, appears to be the key risk factor for elevated depressive symptoms. This portion of the chapter reviews existing studies and is organized in terms of assessment method and sample used. That is, we note whether the researchers examined self-reported depressive symptoms assessed by questionnaires versus major depression assessed by structured or semistructured interviews and whether the sample was recruited from the community or a clinic setting.

Depressive Symptoms and Marital Discord

Researchers have conducted several studies examining marital discord as a potential predictor of depressive symptoms. A study of married couples in the community showed that men and women in discordant marriages were about 10 times more likely to report depressive symptoms than spouses in satisfactory marriages (O'Leary, Christian, & Mendell, 1994). The odds of experiencing depressive symptoms given marital discord remained significant even when the spouse's depressive symptoms and marital discord were held constant. In another study, Whiffen and Gotlib (1989) administered questionnaires to husbands and wives who were attending a prenatal medical clinic. They divided the respondents into four groups: (a) both partners reporting marital distress, (b) wives reporting marital distress, (c) husbands reporting marital distress, and (d) neither husbands nor wives reporting marital distress. They found that discordant wives reported significantly more depressive symptoms than nondiscordant wives. Likewise, discordant husbands reported significantly more depressive symptoms than nondiscordant husbands. Whiffen and Gotlib also found that husbands' marital discord predicted wives' depressive symptoms. That is, men's marital discord was associated with their own as well as their wives' depressive symptoms, whereas women's marital discord was associated only with their own depressive symptoms. The studies of Whiffen and Gotlib (1989) and O'Leary et al. (1994) have suggested that within-couple investigations are needed to increase understanding of the complexity of the depression–marital discord link, especially in terms of gender differences.

Longitudinal data also have shown a link between marital discord and later depressive symptoms as assessed by questionnaires. Christian-Herman, O'Leary, and Avery-Leaf (in press) used path analysis to determine the relationship between depressive symptoms and marital discord at two time points 2 months apart. They assessed women who reported that they had experienced a major negative event in their marriage, such as an affair, a threat of separation or divorce, or a physically abusive incident. To evaluate the role of the negative event on depressive symptoms, they restricted participation to women who had never been depressed. They assessed the women within 4 weeks of the negative marital event and 8 weeks after the event to evaluate the longitudinal effect of the negative marital event. The paths showed that marital discord was significantly associated with later depressive symptoms but that depressive symptoms were not associated with later marital discord. In fact, marital discord was as strong a predictor of later depressive symptoms as previous depressive symptoms.

In another longitudinal study, Fincham, Beach, Harold, and Osborne (1997) collected data from 116 community couples at 2 times 18 months apart. As expected, depressive symptoms and marital satisfaction were significantly related whether assessed cross-sectionally or longitudinally. Examining causal models, Fincham et al. found that depressive symptoms predicted marital discord in men whereas marital discord predicted depressive symptoms in women. This was one of the first studies to examine gender differences in a longitudinal manner to address the unidirectional and bidirectional association between depression and marital discord. It is hoped that researchers will continue to investigate such gender differences and examine the reasons for these differences. Fincham et al. interpreted these results by suggesting that men may respond to their own depression by denigrating their relationships or by withdrawing from the marital relationship more than women. Replication of these results would suggest that marital interventions for depressed men should be different from those for depressed women.

Studies involving clinical populations also have provided support for the association between depressive symptoms and marital discord. Christian, O'Leary, and Vivian (1994) examined the link between these two variables in a sample of married men and women seeking marital therapy (N = 139 couples). Mean Beck Depression Inventory (BDI) scores were 14.40 for wives and 9.64 for husbands. The researchers found that 39% of women and 24% of men scored above the cutoff of 14. In addition, 22% of women and 9% of men scored above the cutoff of 19, indicating moderate depressive symptoms (Beck, Steer, & Garbin, 1988). As reflected in their BDI scores, women reported significantly more depressive symptoms than men, but they also reported more marital discord than men. Despite these sex differences, depressive symptoms and marital discord were positively correlated for both men and women. These results again indicated that the association between depression and marital discord is not solely a female phenomenon.

Although research has shown a consistent, albeit moderate, relationship between elevated depressive symptoms and marital discord, some research has cast doubt on this association. To investigate the causal relationship between depressive symptoms and marital satisfaction, Burns, Sayers, and Moras (1994) conducted structural equation modeling with a sample of 115 patients undergoing cognitive–behavioral treatment for a mood disorder. Structural equation modeling was used to account for reciprocal associations between the two variables that Burns et al. suggested might have biased previous estimates. Participants' diagnoses included major depressive disorder, dysthymic disorder, adjustment disorder with depressed mood, and comorbid anxiety disorders. Participants completed questionnaires regarding depressive symptoms and relationship discord at a pretreatment screening and 12 weeks later. Patients either were married or had identified a significant other. Burns et al. found a weak causal asssociation between relationship discord and depressive symptoms assessed at the same time (i.e., at the 12-week follow-up). On the other hand, depressive symptoms did not cause relationship discord. The researchers concluded that the association between marital discord and depression had been overestimated in previous studies because these studies did not use methods such as structural equation modeling to account for the reciprocal relationships between depression and relationship discord. However, several sampling and methodological issues may qualify this conclusion.

First, the sample consisted of individuals seeking treatment for a mood disorder. It is possible that there was a stronger relationship between marital discord and depressive symptoms before the onset of the mood disorder. Second, not all participants were married. The absence of variance information in terms of marital discord brings into question whether the married and unmarried participants reported significantly different levels of marital discord. It is possible that Burns et al. may have found a stronger association between relationship discord and depressive symptoms if they had limited their study to married individuals. Third, because they assumed that any causal effect of pretreatment relationship discord on later depressive symptoms would be mediated by pretreatment depression scores or by follow-up discord they did not examine pretreatment discord as a predictor of follow-up depressive symptoms. Given the correlation between pretreatment relationship discord and follow-up depressive symptoms ($r = -.34$, p [.001), it would have been interesting to see this association examined. Although these problems exist, the Burns et al. (1994) study was important because it challenged researchers to reexamine the marital discord – depression links with different samples and techniques.

In addition, some researchers have found that depressive symptoms may lead to marital stress and discord. For example, Davila and colleagues (Davila, Bradbuy, Cohan, & Tochluk, 1997; Davila, Hammen, Burge, Paley, & Daley, 1995) conducted longitudinal studies that found that depressive symptoms generated relationship stress in married and dating women. In another longitudinal study of 264 young married women, Beach and O'Leary (1993) found that women with dysthymia were more likely to have marriages that became discordant than women without. Chronically dysphoric wives experienced a 23-point average decline in their marital satisfaction scores over the first 18 months of marriage. In contrast, nondysphoric wives showed a decline in marital satisfaction of only 4 points. In addition, Burns et al. (1994) found that participants who were diagnosed with dysthymia reported significantly greater marital discord compared with participants without dysthymia after treatment for depression. This effect was significant even when pretreatment marital discord was controlled for.

In summary, there are a number of studies that have shown a significant relationship between marital discord and elevated depressive symptomatology. Even studies conducted in the 1970s without standardized measures of either depression or marital discord showed a significant relationship between varied measures of the two constructs (for a review of these early correlational studies, see O'Leary et al., 1994). With the addition of standardized measures of depression and marital discord, the results remained basically the same. There was a significant, albeit moderate, correlation (r = .35) between marital discord and depressive symptoms. Moreover, the association between marital discord and depressive symptomatology usually was significant for both men and women. Furthermore, although there are only a few studies addressing the role of dysthymia and elevated depressive symptoms on marital discord, the results have indicated that dysthymia is associated both cross-sectionally and longitudinally with marital discord.

Severe Marital Problems and Major Depression

Although studies have shown that marital discord is associated with depressive symptoms, few studies have demonstrated a relationship between marital discord and diagnoses of major depression. Rather, researchers have examined the association between serious marital problems or negative marital events as precipitators of major depression. One of the oldest risk studies showed that the presence of marital problems increased the risk of being depressed approximately 25-fold (Weissman, 1987). This study did not use a standard measure of marital discord or marital satisfaction. Rather, it asked if the respondent "gets along with spouse" or "doesn't get along with spouse." Nonetheless, it was a seminal study in the field that pointed to the risk for clinical depression given some level of marital problems. The 6-month prevalence rate of major depression was 45.5% for those women who reported that they did not get along with their spouse. In contrast, only 2.9% of the women who reported that they got along with their spouse had major depression. The 6-month prevalence rate of major depression for men reporting that they did not get along with their spouse was 14.9%. Only 0.6% of men who reported that they got along with their spouse were depressed. Although the overall prevalence rates were quite different for men and women, the odds ratios were similar for men and women (men = 25.8; women = 28.1).

A study using the same methodology was conducted by Whisman and Bruce (1999), who investigated marital problems and the incidence of a major depressive episode (MDE) across a 1-year period. The sample (N = 904) was from the New Haven Epidemiological Catchment Area program. All respondents did not meet the criteria for MDE at baseline. As predicted, those individuals who reported marital problems at the initial assessment were more likely to develop clinical depression at 1-year follow-up than were those individuals who did not initially report such problems. More specifically, the incidence rates of MDE were 2.1% for nondistressed spouses and 5.3% for distressed spouses. The number of individuals in the overall sample who became depressed was too small (n = 26) to analyze their data by sex, so a direct comparison of odds ratios with the Weissman (1997) results was not possible. The overall sample did not exclude individuals who had previously been depressed, and it is possible that marital distress at baseline was a consequence of the history of major depression. However, even after controlling for history of major depression, maritally distressed spouses were still more likely to develop a MDE than nondistressed spouses.

Brown and his colleagues (Brown & Harris, 1978; Brown, Harris, & Hepworth, 1995) have investigated the impact of a variety of relationship problems on women. They found that objectively defined negative life events are powerful predictors of depression in women. Although Brown and his colleagues did not focus on events within marriage specifically, many of their participants experienced negative life events in close relationships, including marriage. For instance, in a study of humiliation events, Brown et al. (1995) found that 31% of a community sample of women in England who experienced a humiliation event became depressed according to the Present State Examination (Wing, Cooper, & Sartorious, 1974). Brown et al. defined a humiliation event as an event that devalues an individual's sense of self, attractiveness, or role (e.g., wife). Of the women who became depressed, the humiliation events they experienced were as follows: (a) 38% experienced a humiliation–putdown (e.g., discovery of partner's infidelity or affairs or verbal or physical attacks by anyone); (b) 35% experienced a humiliation–separation (e.g., separation or divorce initiated by the partner); (c) 34% experienced an entrapment event (e.g., paralyzed husband will not improve), and (d) 19% experienced a humiliation–other's delinquency (usually a child delinquency, such as a truant shoplifting daughter). Note that many of these humiliation events are relational in nature and suggest that humiliation events in marriage (HMEs) may be especially important in the etiology of depression.

Two studies specifically examined the effects of severe marital stressors on samples of married women (Cano & O'Leary, in press; Christian-Herman et al., in press). As noted earlier, Christian-Herman et al. recruited a sample of 50 married women who had recently experienced a severe marital stressor and who had no personal history of MDE. The rationale for this recruitment strategy was to minimize the potential for alternative explanations (e.g., biological) for the occurrence of MDE in the presence of marital stressors. Participants experienced marital stressors such as an extramarital affair by either partner, physical violence between spouses, or threats of divorce by either partner. Christian-Herman et al. found that 38% of these women experienced MDE according to the Diagnostic and Statistical Manual of Mental Disorders, third edition, revised (DSM-III-R; American Psychiatric Association, 1987) after experiencing the severe marital stressors. This incidence rate is substantially higher than rates found in epidemiological studies (1.8%; Eaton et al., 1989). Furthermore, path analyses indicated that marital discord predicted later depressive symptoms, but depressive symptoms did not predict later marital discord. This study provided preliminary evidence of the immediate and severe impact of highly negative marital events on depression in women.

Another study conducted with a sample of 50 married women also revealed the profound effect of severe marital stressors on depression in women (Cano & O'Leary, in press). This study differed from Christian-Herman et al.'s (in press) in several ways. First, participation was limited to women who experienced HMEs as defined by Brown et al. (1995) within 2 months of participating. HMEs experienced by the participants in the Cano and O'Leary study included the discovery of the husband's extramarital affair, the husband's threat of marital dissolution, or the wife's request for a separation or divorce because of her husband's extramarital affair or act of physical violence toward her. Second, a control group experiencing similar levels of marital discord but no severe marital stressors was also recruited to determine whether MDEs are precipitated simply by marital discord or by the occurrence of a HME. Third, women were excluded from the study if they had experienced other life stressors within 6 months of contact or had a MDE within 2 months of experiencing the marital stressor (HME group only). No one was excluded on the basis of lifetime history of depression.

Cano and O'Leary (in press) found that 72% of women who experienced a HME were diagnosed with a MDE according to the fourth edition of the DSM (DSM-IV; American Psychiatric Association, 1994) compared with 12% of the control group. In other words, it was the HMEs, not the marital discord, that precipitated depression. The high rate of MDEs in the HME group was not due to pre-HME depressive symptoms and marital discord, further demonstrating the strong association between HMEs and depression. The HME group also reported more nonspecific depressive and anxiety symptoms as measured by the Mood and Anxiety Symptom Questionnaire (Watson & Clark, 1991) than the control group. These MDE and symptom findings remained significant even when marital discord, lifetime history of depression, and family history of depression were partialled out. Furthermore, these researchers found that marital discord was associated with depressive symptoms in the control group but not in the HME group. This finding indicated that HMEs moderate the association between depressive symptoms and marital discord and suggested that researchers should assess for severe marital stressors when examining the depression–marital discord link. The Cano and O'Leary (in press) study was important for several reasons. First, similar to the Christian-Herman et al. (in press) study, it assessed both depression diagnoses and types of symptoms. Second, it investigated the relative importance of marital discord and negative events in marriage, whereas previous studies investigated only one or the other. Third, the statistical and methodological controls used strengthened its findings.

Other studies have examined the effect of marital stressors on both men and women, although these studies focused only on divorce or separation. Relationship dissolution increased the likelihood of a MDE by a factor of 12 in a large sample of female twins (Kendler, Kessler, Neale, Heath, & Eaves, 1995). In a large study of depressed individuals, their relatives, and their spouses (N = 1,319), participants who became divorced during a 6-year period were 3 times more likely to have a first onset of major depression than participants who remained married (Coryell et al., 1991). This result was stronger for women than for men. Specifically, 53% of the women who divorced became depressed, whereas 13% of the men who divorced became depressed. In a longitudinal community study, Aseltine and Kessler (1993) found that women but not men who became separated or divorced during a 3-year follow-up period experienced increased depressive symptoms. Additional analyses demonstrated that women without previous serious marital problems experienced an increase in depressive symptoms, whereas women with serious marital problems did not. In contrast, separated or divorced men who initially reported serious marital problems experienced a decrease in symptoms. Experiencing marital discord for a long time may lead to fewer depressive symptoms at the time of a separation or divorce, as the individual may desire to terminate the relationship. In contrast, becoming separated or divorced after a seemingly satisfactory marriage may result in more depressive symptoms because of the unexpected or unwanted dissolution of the relationship.

It appears that the bulk of the research on severe marital stressors has been conducted with women. Research is still needed to determine whether severe devaluing marital stressors have as negative an impact on men as on women. In addition, several other issues are important to research in this area. For instance, Aseltine and Kessler's (1993) work suggested that researchers need to account for the quality of marriage before marital dissolution when assessing the impact of negative marital events on depression. The work of Cano and O'Leary (in press) suggested that any study examining the depression–marital discord link should include an assessment of HMEs. In addition, assessing for a variety of symptoms that are specific and not specific to depression may help researchers better understand the sequelae of severe marital stressors.

Marital Therapy for Depression

On the basis of theory and research suggesting a possible causal relationship between depression and marital discord, several research teams suggested that improving the quality of the marriage may alleviate depression (Beach & O'Leary, 1992; Emanuels-Zuurveen & Emmelkamp, 1996; Jacobson, Dobson, Fruzzetti, Schmaling, & Salusky, 1991; O'Leary & Beach, 1990; Teichman, Bar-El, Shor, & Sirota, 1995). If this were the case, additional arguments could be made about the association between marital discord and depression. One of the first studies to investigate this hypothesis was conducted with 45 discordant couples in which the wife was diagnosed with major depression, dysthymia, or both according to a structured interview based on the DSM-III-R (American Psychiatric Association, 1987; Beach & O'Leary, 1992; O'Leary & Beach, 1990). Study participants were randomly assigned to behavioral marital therapy or standard individual cognitive therapy for depression. Not only was marital therapy just as beneficial as individual cognitive therapy in alleviating depressive symptoms, but marital therapy also was significantly better at improving marital discord than individual cognitive therapy.

Jacobson et al. (1991) conducted a similar study by randomly assigning 60 married couples in which the wife was diagnosed with major depression to behavioral marital therapy, individual cognitive therapy, or a combination treatment. However, couples were not selected for both marital discord and a diagnosis of a depressive disorder. Rather, Jacobson et al. selected depressed women, some of whom were discordant and some of whom were not. Behavioral marital therapy and cognitive therapy both decreased depressive symptoms in maritally discordant couples, whereas only behavioral marital therapy improved marital discord. However, for nondiscordant depressed wives, depressive symptoms improved more significantly with cognitive therapy than with behavioral marital therapy. Therefore, these results suggested that marital therapy for depression is effective when at least one spouse is depressed and discordant.

In a related vein, O'Leary, Riso, and Beach (1990) found that wives in the individual cognitive therapy group who attributed their depression to marital problems were more likely to be discordant after treatment than wives who did not attribute their depression to marital discord. Another study comparing marital therapy and individual therapy for depression showed that the most significant reductions in depression occurred following marital therapy (Teichman et al., 1995). Although the Teichman et al. study differed from the O'Leary and Beach (1990) and Jacobson et al. (1991) studies in that marital therapy was more effective than individual therapy in reducing depressive symptoms, all three studies showed that marital therapy was associated with decreases in depressive symptoms. Furthermore, in an analysis of the factors that may have led to changes in depressive symptoms, Beach and O'Leary (1992) found that marital therapy was effective in decreasing depressive symptoms by increasing marital adjustment. Taken together, these findings indicate that behavioral marital therapy is most effective in treating couples in which at least one partner is depressed and maritally discordant. Mismatches between couples and treatment modality may lead to insufficient treatment gains in terms of depression and marital discord.

Mediating Factors

Researchers also have focused on other factors that may contribute to the link between marital discord and depression. Attributions have probably been the most examined variable in terms of depression and marital discord. In a sample of couples seeking marital therapy, Christian et al. (1994) found that certain types of relationship attributions for marital problems were associated with marital discord but not with depressive symptoms for husbands and wives. Researchers also have found that causal and responsibility attributions were associated with marital discord and negative affect in community samples of husbands and wives (Horneffer & Fincham, 1995; Karney, Bradbury, Fincham, & Sullivan, 1994; Senchak & Leonard, 1993). For instance, Horneffer and Fincham (1995) found that negative relationship attributions (partner locus, stable, and global) about partner behaviors were associated with increased depressive symptoms and marital discord for both husbands and wives. However, a sex difference in this association has been demonstrated. For example, in a mixed sample of clinic and community couples, causal attributions for marital problems to themselves and marital discord were associated with depressive symptoms in women (Heim & Snyder, 1991). For men, only marital discord was associated with depressive symptoms. Although several studies have demonstrated that maladaptive attributions are positively associated with marital discord and depressive symptoms, questions remain. For instance, many of the studies reviewed in this chapter used different measures of attributions. Sample differences (i.e., clinic vs. community) also may have contributed to the mixed findings. Finally, some studies combined husband and wife data in analyses, making it difficult to detect sex differences.

Other factors that may play a role in the depression–marital discord relationship include social support and problem-solving ability. For instance, Aseltine and Kessler (1993) found that social interactions with friends alleviated depressive symptoms after a separation or divorce. In addition, conflicts with family worsened depression in women with previous marital problems. Whiffen and Gotlib (1989) found that nondiscordant wives reported more social support seeking than discordant wives and nondiscordant or discordant husbands. Other researchers have investigated the link between initial depressive symptoms and later marital stress. Davila et al. (1997) found that negative perceptions of future support and negative support behaviors mediated the association between depressive symptoms and marital stress for women but not for men. It appears that social support is an important factor in the link between depressive symptoms and marital satisfaction. Problem-solving ability may be another important factor to investigate in terms of depressive symptoms and marital discord, at least for men. Problem-solving appraisal was associated with depressive symptoms and marital discord for men and women in a clinic sample (Christian et al., 1994). Couples who appraise themselves as poor problem solvers may find that marital problems and discord are difficult to approach and therefore become depressed.

Summary

In the 1970s, researchers suggested that being married was associated with higher rates of depression. However, as the research concerning the link between depression and marriage developed, it appeared that the quality of the marriage was more important than marital status in precipitating depression. That is, being maritally discordant was associated with increased depression (Beach et al., 1990). Most studies have shown a moderate relationship between self-reported depressive symptoms and marital discord; however, some studies have shown that dysthymia may predict marital discord (Beach & O'Leary, 1993; Burns et al., 1994) and that depressive symptoms may lead to discord in men (Fincham et al., 1997). On the other hand, several longitudinal studies on marriage have found a greater impact of discord and divorce on women's depressive symptoms. Most of the studies using self-report measures of depressive symptoms were conducted with women in community samples. Perhaps additional research with clinic populations and with men will shed light on possible measurement, sample, and gender differences.

In addition, researchers have investigated the role of severe marital problems in precipitating MDEs as assessed with structured interviews. Early studies showed that self-reported marital problems were associated with increased risk of major depression for both men and women (e.g., Weissman, 1987), and a longitudinal study confirmed the negative impact of marital problems on depression for both men and women (Whisman & Bruce, 1999). Cross-sectional and longitudinal studies have shown a robust association between negative marital events such as separation, divorce, and extramarital affairs and major depression in community samples of community women (Aseltine & Kessler, 1993; Cano & O'Leary, in press; Christian-Herman et al., in press). In addition, the use of various measures of symptoms and assessments of pre-event functioning and the examination of the context in which these marital stressors occur have improved researchers' understanding of this relationship.

Marital therapy outcomes studies have suggested that improving the quality of the marriage alleviates depressive symptoms (Beach & O'Leary, 1992; Jacobson et al., 1991; O'Leary & Beach, 1990). However, the treatment literature has focused on marital treatment of depression in wives. More research needs to be conducted before the same can be concluded for husbands. Additional research has begun exploring other factors that may contribute to depression in marriage, including severe marital problems, attachment, attributions, and social support. Examining these factors will improve researchers' understanding of the association between depression and marital discord.

Partner Abuse and Depression

It may not be surprising to find that many physically abused women report "feeling blue" or that many of these women can be diagnosed with a depressive disorder. Newspaper accounts of women's suicide attempts following an abusive incident reinforce such impressions. On the other hand, some abused women simply get angry, become dissatisfied with the marriage, and want to leave the relationship. A woman's psychological (e.g., fear) and practical (e.g., financial resources) abilities and resources to leave an abusive relationship can be expected to play a role in the extent to which she might feel trapped in the relationship and, in turn, feel depressed.

Predictions about the sequelae of partner abuse are less clear for a man in a relationship in which he perceives himself as abused. Far fewer men perceive themselves as physically abused and seek help for the problem. On average, men are physically injured less often than women in both clinical and community populations (Cantos, Neidig, & O'Leary, 1994; Cascardi, Langhinrichsen, & Vivian, 1992; Straus & Gelles, 1990). Given these facts, one might expect that men who are abused by their female partners would be depressed, especially because they likely perceive themselves as being in a very unusual situation.

The scenarios depicted above represent what is often believed to be the norm in partner abuse situations. In fact, these scenarios may represent the extremes of partner abuse for which clinical, supportive, and/or legal services are sought. However, the epidemiological facts from community surveys and nonclinical samples present a different picture. In these nonclinical samples, the majority of women and men in physically aggressive relationships both engaged in acts of physical aggression (Magdol et al., 1997; O'Leary et al., 1989; Schafer, Caetano, & Clark, 1998; Straus & Gelles, 1990). In such cases, the predictions about depressive symptoms and clinical depression are less clear than in more extreme cases.

Given that marital discord may be present in relationships characterized by physical aggression, it also is possible that marital discord itself may be an important predictor of depressive symptoms and/or clinical depression. The first half of this chapter presented evidence indicating that marital discord is a predictor of depressive symptoms and/or clinical depression. However, it appears that negative marital events involving loss and humiliation (e.g., infidelity, separation, and divorce) seem to be critical in precipitating clinical depression (Aseltine & Kessler, 1993; Brown et al., 1995; Cano & O'Leary, in press; Christian-Herman et al., in press). Future research will be necessary to determine the relative importance of partner physical aggression and loss and HMEs in predicting clinical depression.

Another factor that has become important to assess is the role of psychological abuse and its relative importance to physical abuse. Although the body of evidence addressing this issue is quite new, there are data that show that psychological abuse is more detrimental to women's mental health than physical abuse (see O'Leary & Maiuro, 1999, Mini-Series on Psychological Abuse, Violence and Victims). Such information comes directly from women in relationships characterized by both physical and psychological abuse (Follingstad, Rutledge, Berg, Hause, & Polek, 1990; Vivian & Langhinrichsen-Rohling, 1994). Given the perceived impact of psychological and physical aggression it may be that physical aggression is less important than psychological aggression in predicting depressive symptoms. These and related issues are addressed later in this chapter. The material on partner abuse and depression is divided into two sections, one dealing with community sample results and another dealing with clinical sample results. The organization of this part of the chapter differs from that of the previous part because there has been more research on physical abuse conducted with clinical samples. Nonetheless, as in the first part of this chapter, the sections are related to the use of depressive symptoms and clinical depression as the dependent measures.

Community Sample Results

The largest community sample study to address the association of physical aggression and depressive symptoms is that of Stets and Straus (1990). In this study, a nationally representative sample of 2,947 women was surveyed by telephone. The research had numerous goals, but one aim was to assess the possible impact of partner aggression on depressive symptoms. Overall, approximately 12% of women reported that their partner had engaged in some act of physical aggression against them in the past year. The investigators divided the physically abused women into two groups: (a) those who reported minor physical aggression and (b) those who reported severe physical aggression. Minor acts of physical aggression included behaviors such as pushing, slapping, and shoving, whereas severe acts of physical aggression included behaviors such as beating, threatening with a knife or gun, and/or using a knife or gun. Seven percent of women reported that their partner had engaged in minor acts of physical aggression against them, and 5% reported that their partner had engaged in severe acts of physical aggression against them.

Stets and Straus's (1990) main research objective was not to examine the association of depression and partner abuse. Consequently, the measure of depressive symptoms consisted simply of six questions about the presence or absence of depressive symptoms (e.g., sadness, hopelessness, worthlessness, wondering about whether things were worthwhile, suicidal thoughts, suicidal behavior). The investigators summed the symptom scores and then looked at the percentage of women whose depressive symptom scores were above the 75th percentile. Thirty-three percent of women who reported that their partner had engaged in minor physical aggression against them, and 58% of women who reported that their partner had engaged in severe aggression against them had depressive symptom scores above the 75th percentile. In contrast, only 21% of women who reported no physical aggression against them had depressive symptom scores above the 75th percentile. These results underscore the need to separate individuals experiencing moderate and severe violence into different groups. As is illustrated repeatedly, mild-to-moderate and severe acts of physical aggression have different consequences on a wide variety of measures.

In another community sample population, where the focus of the research was on the epidemiology of depression, Weissman and Klerman (1992) found that the rate of depression in physically abused women was 10.2%. This rate of depression is higher than that in the general population but lower than the rates reported earlier in this chapter when discussing the results for maritally discordant women from the New Haven Catchment Area study (Weissman, 1987). However, the earlier results refer to a 6-month prevalence rate of MDE for women who didn't get along with their spouse and does not refer to physical aggression specifically. In the National Comorbidity Study, Kessler et al. (1994) found that 21.3% of the abused women were depressed, again a rate higher than in the general population.

In a large random sample of men in the military ($N = 11,870$), Pan, Neidig, & O'Leary (1994) examined a number of predictors, including depressive symptoms, for their relative value in predicting physical aggression against a female partner. Physical aggression was assessed with a modified version of the Conflict Tactics Scale (CTS; Straus, 1979), and depressive symptoms were assessed with a 15-item measure similar to the BDI. Both physical aggression and depressive symptoms were assessed using self-reports. Nonordered multinomial logistic models were used to estimate the odds of mild and severe husband-to-wife physical aggression. The demographic variables age and salary were controlled before the role of depressive symptoms was estimated. In calculating the odds ratios, a comparison was first made between mild aggression and no aggression. A comparison was then made between severe aggression and no aggression. For every 20% increase in depressive symptoms, the odds of being mildly physically aggressive increased by 30%. For every 20% increase in depressive symptoms, the odds of being severely physically aggressive increased by 74%. Although these odds ratios clearly indicate that men's depressive symptoms are associated with their use of physical aggression against a female partner in a large military sample, it is unclear whether the depression was driving the physical aggression or vice versa. It would seem plausible that if a man was physically aggressive toward his wife he might later feel badly about having acted in a physically aggressive manner and, in turn, have elevated symptoms of depression such as difficulty sleeping and feeling hopeless.

Clinical Samples

Documentation of the elevated risk of depressive symptoms and/or MDE has been provided in a number of studies of physically abused women. A summary of 14 such studies appears in Cascardi, O'Leary, and Schlee (1999) and will not be reviewed in detail here. Taken together, these studies indicated that women using battered women's shelters or other domestic violence services appear to have some of the highest rates of depression. For example, in a battered women's shelter Gleason (1993) found a 1-month (past month) Diagnostic Interview Schedule (Robins, Helzer, Crouhan, & Ratcliff, 1981) prevalence rate for major depression of 69%. However, it is interesting to compare the depressive symptom elevations of the samples reviewed by Cascardi et al. (1999) and those of samples of women who are maritally discordant but not physically abused. With the exception of women in battered women's shelters, it appears that depressive symptoms are not significantly higher in physically abused samples than in maritally discordant samples. As expected, the mean depression scores are higher for severely abused women than for women who have experienced mild to moderate physical aggression. However, as will be documented in this chapter, the variance between groups is such that the mean differences generally are not significant.

To assess the relationship between physical aggression against a female partner and depressive symptoms, Cascardi and O'Leary (1992) gathered information from 33 battered women seeking counseling at a county center for victims of partner abuse. Seventy-five percent of the women at the center reported being beaten by their partner. Thirty-four percent had broken bones and/or required stitches, and 31% required surgery and/or suffered a concussion. Fifty-two percent of the women had BDI scores greater than 20, and approximately 70% had BDI scores greater than 14. Moreover, there was a strong and significant association between frequency and/or severity of physical aggression against the women and depressive symptoms. More specifically, the correlation of the frequency of physical aggression and depressive symptoms was .54; the correlation of the severity of physical aggression and depressive symptoms was also .54. In an attempt to better understand the mechanisms leading to elevated depressive symptoms, we looked at the extent to which self-blame was correlated with depressive symptoms. As predicted, self-blame was significantly correlated with depressive symptoms and low self-esteem. However, it should be noted that only 18% of these women blamed themselves for the physical aggression inflicted on them by their partner. However, if self-blame was evident, depressive symptoms were elevated.

In another study focusing on clinical samples, Vivian and Malone (1997) assessed the level of depressive symptoms in 327 discordant women seeking marital therapy with their husbands. The sample was broken down into three groups: (a) discordant women with nonaggressive husbands (n = 132), (b) discordant women with moderately aggressive husbands (n = 112), and (c) discordant women with severely aggressive husbands (n = 83). Depressive symptoms were assessed with the BDI, and comparisons were made across the three groups. Physical aggression was assessed with a modification of the CTS. Women in the severely aggressive group reported that their husbands had engaged in a mean number of 4.5 acts of aggression in the past year, whereas women in the moderately aggressive group reported that their husbands had engaged in 2.8 acts of physical aggression against them. As expected, the mean level of depressive symptoms was highest in the women who reported severe aggression by their husbands (M = 16.9). Women who reported that their husbands were moderately physically aggressive toward them had the second highest levels of depressive symptoms (M = 14.6). Women who reported that they were in a discordant marriage but whose husbands were not physically aggressive had the lowest depression scores (M = 12). The women in the severely aggressive group were significantly more depressed than the women in the discordant nonaggressive group, but there were no other group differences. The most noteworthy result from this study was that all three clinical groups experienced elevated depressive symptoms.

Although a control group was not included in the Vivian and Malone (1997) study, related work by Cascardi et al. (1992) reported results of a control group of community couples selected for the absence of marital discord and physical aggression. From that comparison as well as from data collected from normative samples (Beach & O'Leary, 1993) it is known that the mean BDI scores reported by community women usually are between 4 and 6, indicating mild, if any, depressive symptoms. Thus, it is clear that women in discordant relationships have elevated depressive symptoms and that the presence of physical aggression increases the likelihood that those depressive symptoms will be even higher. On the other hand, the differences within the clinical groups are smaller than the differences between the clinical groups and the community group. It is also clear from these results that many women who experience physical aggression and who seek treatment for marital problems are not clinically depressed. Their mean BDI scores did not meet the cutoff of 19 often used in depression treatment studies and were not within the moderate range (19–28) recommended by Beck (Beck et al., 1988). These results suggest that future research should address the multiple factors that might predict highly elevated depression scores and clinical depression. Being hopeless about the relationship, blaming oneself, having few financial resources, and perceiving few alternatives to the relationship seem to be worthwhile factors to address in future research on predicting clinical depression.

In related research, Boyle and Vivian (1996) focused on depressive symptoms of men in discordant nonviolent relationships and men in discordant violent relationships. They presented data on men in the groups just mentioned in the Vivian and Malone (1997) study, although the groups were not identical in terms of the numbers per group. The clinical sample was broken down into three groups: (a) discordant nonaggressive husbands (n = 94), (b) discordant aggressive husbands (n = 69), and (c) discordant severely aggressive husbands (n = 100). There was also a community control group (n = 49). Depressive symptoms were assessed with the BDI, and comparisons were made across the three groups. Physical aggression was assessed with a modification of the CTS. Mean BDI scores across the three clinical groups were as follows: (a) discordant nonaggressive husbands = 8.3; (b) discordant moderately aggressive husbands = 10.2; and (c) discordant severely aggressive husbands = 12.0. The community control group had a mean BDI score of 3.1. The three clinical groups had higher levels of depressive symptoms than the community control group, and the severely aggressive men had higher BDI scores than the men in the other two clinical groups.

We also were interested in the prevalence of major depressive disorder (MDD) and posttraumatic stress disorder (PTSD; Cascardi et al., 1999) in another clinical sample of women ($N = 92$). These women were in physically aggressive marriages and were seeking treatment directed at reducing their partner's psychological and physical aggression. The Structured Clinical Interview (SCID; First, Spitzer, Gibbon, & Williams, 1995) for the DSM-III-R was used to determine the prevalence of MDD and PTSD. Physical aggression was assessed with a modification of the CTS. To be selected as an abused woman for this study, a woman had to report that her husband had engaged in at least two acts of physical aggression against her in the previous year. Seventy-six percent of the women had experienced severe physical aggression.

Thirty-two percent of the abused women met SCID criteria for MDD, and 30% of the abused women met SCID criteria for PTSD. Seventeen percent of the women were comorbid for both MDD and PTSD. The symptom severity correlation (BDI score with number of PTSD symptoms) was significant but small ($r = .25$). The mean BDI score was 15.45 for the entire sample, placing them in the mild to moderate range of depressive symptoms according to Beck et al. (1988). Depressive symptoms were predicted by marital discord and intensity of husband's physical aggression. PTSD symptoms were predicted by husband's dominance and isolation tactics and intensity of husband's physical aggression. Any clinician treating such women should consider the presence of these problems when developing an intervention. Although it is beyond the scope of this chapter to consider treatment issues in depth, it is noteworthy that PTSD symptoms were not predictive of treatment outcome for these and other women in a treatment outcomes study (Schlee, Heyman, & O'Leary, 1998). The larger treatment outcome study assessed the value of gender-specific and couples treatments when both treatments had as their primary goal reducing psychological and physical aggression (O'Leary, Heyman, & Neidig, 1999). Moreover, the level of depressive symptoms dropped significantly from pre- to posttreatment, and it remained at a relatively steady level from posttreatment to follow-up.

In a somewhat parallel study, Feldbau-Kohn, Heyman, and O'Leary (1999) assessed the presence of clinical depression and depressive symptoms in men seeking treatment for the reduction of psychological and physical aggression. The question addressed in this research was whether physically aggressive men would have elevated rates of clinical depression and whether the physical aggression was associated with level of depressive symptoms. In addition, the reseachers were interested in whether depressive symptoms would predict physical aggression after anger had been controlled. Following psychodynamic theory that suggests that depression is anger turned inward (Freud, 1917/1957), it was predicted that depressive symptoms would be associated with anger. However, it also was predicted that acts of physical aggression toward a female partner would be predicted by depressive symptoms. As expected, depressive symptoms were associated with acts of physical aggression toward a partner, but the absolute level of the correlation was small (r = .21). Moreover, when levels of anger were controlled, the association of depressive symptoms and physical aggression became nonsignificant. In short, although depressive symptoms and physical aggression toward a female partner were related, anger, not depressive symptoms, accounted for the variance in the prediction of physical aggression. Finally, only 11% of the men in this treatment-seeking sample met the criteria for clinical depression. Although this rate is higher than the overall prevalence rate of 4%–5% for men in epidemiological studies, the rate is such that depression per se would not need to be seen as a major treatment target.

Suicide of Female Victims of Partner Abuse

There have been clinical descriptions of suicide attempts of women who have been battered for decades. Stark and Flitcraft (1995) found that 1 battered woman in 6 (17%) attempted suicide. Another study found that a significant percentage of battered women who attempted suicide had made multiple attempts after the first abusive injury (Bergman & Brismar, 1991). In this Swedish study, few women who made suicide attempts actually presented with a physical injury. Thus, prolonged psychological abuse may be a key predictor of women's suicide attempts.

In one of the largest studies of suicide attempts, Kaslow et al. (1998) compared partner abuse in African American women in suicide attempters (n = 148) and nonattempters (n = 137). A suicide attempt was defined as a self-injurious act that required medical attention. After it was determined that a woman had made a suicide attempt, a research team member went to the hospital and recruited the patient for the study once she was medically stable enough to participate. The attempters were primarily unmarried and unemployed and had relatively limited education (M [12 grades). Control participants were recruited at medical walk-in clinics. The Index of Spouse Abuse, which conceptualizes partner abuse as both physical and nonphysical partner abuse, was used. As predicted, physical and nonphysical abuse were more common in suicide attempters than nonattempters. Moreover, both physical and nonpartner abuse were reported almost twice as often for the suicide attempters than for the nonattempters. Among other factors, the researchers also assessed hopelessness, alcohol problems, drug problems, and social support. These factors mediated the link between partner abuse and suicide attempts.

Association of Reductions in Physical Aggression and Reductions in Depressive Symptoms

One method of developing an understanding of the causal relationship between physical aggression against a female partner and the depressive symptoms of the female partner is to examine naturally occurring changes in these two variables across time. This strategy was used by Quigley and Leonard (1996) in a longitudinal study with newly married partners. Depression scores decreased for those women whose husbands ceased being physically aggressive. In contrast, women whose husbands continued to be physically aggressive experienced increases in depression. At Time 1, there was no difference between the depression scores of the women in either group, but by Year 3, the women whose husbands ceased to be physically aggressive were significantly less depressed than those whose husbands did not cease their aggression. Such results strongly imply that the physical aggression led to the changes in the depressive symptoms.

In one of the few longitudinal studies of battered women, R. Campbell, Sullivan, and Davidson (1995) assessed 129 battered women 6 months after their exit from a shelter for wife abuse. When the women left the shelter, 26% of the women had scores in the severe range of the CES-D depression scale, and 20% of the women had scores in the moderate range of depression. Depression scores were lower 10 weeks following shelter exit, but they did not change further at 6 months. Feelings of powerlessness and level of abuse were predictive of depressive symptoms at 6 months.

In a different longitudinal study, J. Campbell and Soeken (1999) analyzed 98 women's responses to battering over a 3.5-year period. A battered woman was defined as a woman who had experienced at least one act of severe violence or two acts of minor violence or had been forced into sex by her intimate partner during the previous year. Although Campbell and Soeken examined a number of variables and changes therein over time, in keeping with the central theme of this chapter, only the results for depressive symptoms are reported here. The sample was primarily African American (80%). Overall, the largest group of women in the sample was single, and about half were unemployed. However, the sample covered the full range of occupational categories, with 11% having jobs in "professional occupations." The women were assessed three times over the 3-year period. The analyses were broken down as follows: women abused only at Time 1 (Y, N, N; n = 28), women abused at Times 1 and 2 (Y, Y, N; n = 22), and women abused at all three times (Y, Y, Y; n = 39). The women abused at Times 1 and 3 but not at Time 2 were not included in the analyses. Overall, trend analyses indicated that there was a decrease in BDI scores from Time 1 to Time 2 and an increase at Time 3. Graphic presentation of BDI scores by group revealed the following: Means for Group 1 (Y, N, N) decreased slightly from Time 1 to Time 2, then rose again slightly. A similar trend was seen for Group 2 (Y, Y, N). The group of women reporting physical abuse at all three times showed an increase in mean BDI scores from approximately 16 to 24.

It may be a surprise to some that the overall mean BDI score at Time 1 in the Campbell and Soeken (1999) study was only 16. This mean score is very similar to those means in maritally discordant groups discussed in the first section of this chapter (e.g., Christian et al., 1994). In keeping with the results of the R. Campbell et al. (1995) study, it is possible that single women feel less powerless or trapped than married women. It also is possible that psychological abuse exacts a negative toll across time that renders the maritally discordant, nonphysically abused women as depressed as women who have been seriously battered.

Treatment research also offers some supporting documentation for the view that reductions in physical aggression can lead to reductions in depressive symptoms. That is, when husbands in physically aggressive relationships reduce their physical aggression, the women's depressive symptoms decrease significantly (O'Leary et al., 1999). More specifically, as previously mentioned, in treatments designed to reduce psychological and physical aggression, women's depressive symptoms decreased significantly in programs that led to reductions in their husband's physical aggression. Because the treatment also led to significant increases in marital satisfaction, it is possible that the decreases in physical aggression led to increases in marital satisfaction, which in turn led to decreases in depressive symptoms. At any rate, if a treatment can lead to decreases in physical aggression, it is possible that there will be concomitant decreases in depressive symptoms.

Summary

In community and representative samples, there was a significant association between physical aggression against a female partner and her depressive symptoms. Furthermore, in women in shelters or receiving services for battered women, the prevalence of MDEs was elevated. In turn, depressive symptoms were associated with frequency and severity of physical aggression against the female partner in women who are repeatedly abused. In several studies, there was an association between men's depressive symptoms and use of physical aggression against a female partner. However, in one study, when anger was controlled, the association between depressive symptoms and physical aggression became nonsignificant. Thus, anger, not depressive symptoms, seems to be the key factor predicting aggression.

According to the information presented in this chapter, it is clear that marital discord and negative marital events are critical factors in predicting depressive symptoms and clinical depression. Physically abused women often do not have significantly higher rates of depressive symptoms than maritally discordant nonphysically abused women. These results have a number of implications. First, it is possible that psychological abuse may be a more important predictor of depressive symptoms than physical abuse. Given that women find psychological abuse more aversive than physical abuse, this conclusion seems quite reasonable. Second, the impact of affairs or loss and anticipated loss of a partner may be just as or more predictive of depressive symptoms and clinical depression than physical aggression.

References

Amenson, C. S., & Lewinsohn, P. M. (1981). An investigation into the observed sex difference in prevalence of unipolar depression. *Journal of Abnormal Psychology, 90,* 1–13.

American Psychiatric Association. (1987). *Diagnostic and statistical manual of mental disorders* (3rd ed., rev.). Washington, DC: Author.

American Psychiatric Association. (1994). *Diagnostic and statistical manual of mental disorders* (4th ed.). Washington, DC: Author.

Anthony, J. C., & Petronis, K. R. (1991). Suspected risk factors for depression among adults 18–44 years old. *Epidemiology, 2,* 123–132.

Aseltine, R. H., & Kessler, R. C. (1993). Marital disruption and depression in a community sample. *Journal of Health and Social Behavior, 34,* 237–251.

Beach, S. R. H., & O'Leary, K. D. (1992). Treating depression in the context of marital discord: Outcome and predictors of response of marital therapy versus cognitive therapy. *Behavior Therapy, 23,* 507–528.

Beach, S. R. H., & O'Leary, K. D. (1993). Marital discord and dysphoria: For whom does the marital relationship predict depressive symptomatology? *Journal of Social and Personal Relationships, 10,* 405–420.

Beach, S. R. H., Sandeen, E. E., & O'Leary, K. D. (1990). *Depression in marriage.* New York: Guilford Press.

Beck, A. T., Steer, R. A., & Garbin, M. G. (1988). Psychometric properties of the Beck Depression Inventory: Twenty-five years of evaluation. *Clinical Psychology Review, 8,* 77–100.

Bergman, B., & Brismar, B. (1991). Suicide attempts by battered wives. *Acta Psychiatrica Scandinavica, 83,* 380–384.

Bernard, J. (1972). *The future of marriage.* New York: World.

Boyle, D., & Vivian, D. (1996). Generalized versus spouse-specific anger/hostility and men's violence against intimates. *Violence and Victims, 11,* 293–218.

Brown, G. W., & Harris, T. O. (1978). *Social origins of depression: A study of psychiatric disorder in women.* London: Tavistock.

Brown, G. W., Harris, T. O., & Hepworth, C. (1995). Loss, humiliation and entrapment among women developing depression: A patient and non-patient comparison. *Psychological Medicine, 25,* 7–21.

Burns, D. D., Sayers, S. L., & Moras, K. (1994). Intimate relationships and depression: Is there a causal connection? *Journal of Consulting and Clinical Psychology, 62,* 1033–1043.

Campbell, J. C., & Soeken, K. L. (1999). Women's responses to battering over time: An analysis of change. *Journal of Interpersonal Violence, 14,* 21–40.

Campbell, R., Sullivan, C. M., & Davidson, W. S. (1995). Women who use domestic violence shelters: Changes in depression over time. *Psychology of Women Quarterly, 19,* 237–255.

Cano, A., & O'Leary, K. D. (in press). Humiliating marital events precipitate major depressive episodes and symptoms of nonspecific depression and anxiety. *Journal of Consulting and Clinical Psychology.*

Cantos, A. L., Neidig, P. H., & O'Leary, K. D. (1994). Injuries of women and men in a treatment program for domestic violence. *Journal of Family Violence, 9,* 113–124.

Cascardi, M., Langhinrichsen, J., & Vivian, D. (1992). Marital aggression, impact, injury, and health correlates for domestic violence. *Archives of Internal Medicine, 152,* 1178–1184.

Cascardi, M., & O'Leary, K. D. (1992). Depressive symptomatology, self-esteem, and self-blame in battered women. *Journal of Family Violence, 7,* 249–259.

Cascardi, M., O'Leary, K. D., & Schlee, K. A. (1999). Co-occurrence and correlates of post traumatic stress disorder and major depression in physically abused women. *Journal of Family Violence, 14,* 227–249.

Christian, J. L., O'Leary, K. D., & Vivian, D. (1994). Depressive symptomatology in maritally discordant women and men: The role of individual and relationship variables. *Journal of Family Psychology, 8,* 32–42.

Christian-Herman, J. L., O'Leary, K. D., & Avery-Leaf, S. (in press). The impact of negative events in marriage on depression. *Journal of Social and Clinical Psychology.*

Coryell, W., Endicott, J., & Keller, M. (1991). Major depression in a nonclinical sample: Demographic and clinical risk factors for first onset. *Archives of General Psychiatry, 49,* 117–125.

Davila, J., Bradbury, T. N., Cohan, C. L., & Tochluk, S. (1997). Marital functioning and depressive symptoms: Evidence for a stress generation model. *Journal of Personality and Social Psychology, 73,* 849–861.

Davila, J., Hammen, C., Burge, D., Paley, B., & Daley, S. E. (1995). Poor interpersonal-problem solving as a mechanism of stress generation in depression among adolescent women. *Journal of Abnormal Psychology, 104,* 592–600.

Eaton, W. W., Kramer, M., Anthony, J. C., Dryman, A., Shapiro, S., & Locke, B. Z. (1989). The incidence of specific DIC/DSM-II mental disorder: Data from MINH epidemiology catchment area program. *Acta Psychiatric Scandinavia, 79,* 163–178.

Ehrensaft, M., & Vivian, D. (1996). Spouses' reasons for not reporting existing physical aggression as a marital problem. *Journal of Family Psychology, 10,* 443–453.

Emanuels-Zuurveen, L., & Emmelkamp, P. M. G. (1996). Individual behavioral-cognitive therapy v. marital therapy for depression in maritally distressed couples. *British Journal of Psychiatry, 169,* 181–188.

Feldbau-Kohn, S. R., Heyman, R. E., & O'Leary, K. D. (1999). Major depressive disorder and depressive symptomatology as predictors of husband to wife physical aggression. *Violence and Victims, 13,* 1–4.

Fincham, F. D., Beach, S. R. H., Harold, G. T., & Osborne, L. N. (1997). Marital satisfaction and depression: Different causal relationships for men and women? *Psychological Science, 8,* 351–357.

First, M., Spitzer, L., Gibbon, M., & Williams, J. (1995). Structural clinical interview for axis I DSM-IV disorders (SCID). Washington, DC: American Psychiatric Association.

Follingstad, D. R., Rutledge, L. L., Berg, B. J., Hause, E., & Polek, D. (1990). The role of emotional abuse in physically abusive relationships. *Journal of Family Violence, 5,* 107–120.

Freud, S. (1957). Mourning and melancholia. In J. Strachey (Ed. and Trans.), *Complete psychological works* (Vol. 14, pp. 152–170). London: Hogarth Press. (Original published 1917)

Gleason, W. J. (1993). Mental disorders in battered women: An empirical study. *Violence and Victims, 8,* 53–68.

Hafner, R. J. (1986). *Marriage and mental illness: A sex-roles perspective.* New York: Guilford Press.

Heim, S. C., & Snyder, D. K. (1991). Predicting depression from marital distress and attributional processes. *Journal of Marital and Family Therapy, 17,* 67–72.

Horneffer, K J., & Fincham, F. D. (1995). Construct of attributional style in depression and marital distress. *Journal of Family Psychology, 9,* 186–195.

Holtzworth-Munroe, A., Waltz, J., Jacobson, N. S., Monaco, V., Fehrenbach, P. A., & Gottman, J. M. (1992). Recruiting non-violent men as control subjects for research on marital violence: How easily can it be done? *Violence and Victims, 7,* 79–88.

Jacobson, N. S., Dobson, K., Fruzzetti, A. E., Schmaling, D. B., & Salusky, S. (1991). Marital therapy as a treatment for depression. *Journal of Consulting and Clinical Psychology, 59,* 547–557.

Karney, B. R., Bradbury, T. N., Fincham, F. D., & Sullivan, K. T. (1994). The role of negative affectivity in the association between attributions and marital satisfaction. *Journal of Personality and Social Psychology, 66,* 413–424.

Kaslow, N. J., Thompson, M. P., Meadows, L. A., Jacobs, D., Chance, S., Gibb, B., Bornstein, H., Hollins, L., Rashid, A., & Phillips, K. (1998). Factors that mediate and moderate the link between partner abuse and suicidal behavior in African American women. *Journal of Consulting and Clinical Psychology, 66,* 533–540.

Kendler, K. S., Kessler, R. C., Neale, M. C., Heath, A. C., & Eaves, L. J. (1995). Stressful life events, genetic liability, and onset of an episode of major depression in women. *American Journal of Psychiatry, 152,* 833–842.

Kessler, R., McGonagle, K., Nelson, C., Hughes, M., Swartz, M., & Blazer, D. (1994). Sex and depression in the National Comorbidity Survey: II. Cohort effects. *Journal of Infectious Disease, 30,* 15–26.

Leonard, K. E., & Senchak, M. (1996). Prospective prediction of husband marital aggression within newlywed couples. *Journal of Abnormal Psychology, 105,* 396–380.

Locke, H. J., & Wallace, K. M. (1959). Short marital adjustment and prediction tests: Their reliability and validity. *Marriage and Family Living, 21,* 251–255.

Magdol, L., Moffitt, T. E., Caspi, A., Newman, D. L., Fagan, J., & Silva, P. A. (1997). Gender differences in partner violence in a birth cohort of 21–year-olds: Bridging the gap between clinical and epidemiological approaches. *Journal of Consulting and Clinical Psychology, 65,* 68–78.

Mihalic, S. W., Elliot, D. S., & Menard, S. (1994). Continuities in marital violence. *Journal of Family Violence, 9,* 195–226.

O'Leary, K. D., & Beach, S. R. H. (1990). Marital therapy: A viable treatment for depression and marital discord. *American Journal of Psychiatry, 147,* 183–186.

O'Leary, K. D., & Maiuro, R. D. (1999). Psychological abuse in domestically violent relationships. *Violence and Victims, 14,* 3–117.

O'Leary, K. D., Barling, J., Arias, I., Rosenbaum, A., Malone, J., & Tyree, A. (1989). Prevalence and stability of physical aggression between spouses: A longitudinal analysis. *Journal of Consulting and Clinical Psychology, 57,* 263–268.

O'Leary, K. D., Christian, J. L., & Mendell, N. R. (1994). A closer look at the link between marital discord and depressive symptomatology. *Journal of Social and Clinical Psychology, 13,* 33–41.

O'Leary, K. D., Heyman, R. E., & Neidig, P. H. (1999). Treatment of wife abuse: A comparison of gender specific and conjoint approaches. *Behavior Therapy, 30,* 475–505.

O'Leary, K. D., Riso, L. P., & Beach, S. R. H. (1990). Attributions about the marital discord/depression link and therapy outcome. *Behavior Therapy, 21,* 413–422.

O'Leary, K. D., Vivian, D., & Malone, J. (1992). Assessment of physical aggression in marriage: The need for a multimodal method. *Behavioral Assessment, 14,* 5–14.

Pan, H., Neidig, P. H., & O'Leary, K. D. (1994). Predicting mild and severe husband to wife aggression. *Journal of Consulting and Clinical Psychology, 62,* 975–981.

Quigley, B. M., & Leonard, K. E. (1996). Desistance of husband aggression in the early years of marriage. *Violence and Victims, 11,* 355–370.

Robins, L., Helzer, J., Crouhan, J., & Ratcliff, K. (1981). The NIMH diagnostic interview schedule. *Archives of General Psychiatry, 38,* 381–389.

Schafer, J., Caetano, R., & Clark, C. (1998). Rates of domestic violence among U. S. couples. *American Journal of Public Health, 88,* 1702–1704.

Schlee, K. A., Heyman, R. E., & O'Leary, K. D. (1998). Group treatment for spouse abuse: Are women with PSTD appropriate participants? *Journal of Family Violence, 13,* 1–20.

Senchak, M., & Leonard, K. E. (1993). The role of spouses' depression and anger in the attribution-marital satisfaction relation. *Cognitive Research and Therapy, 17,* 397–409.

Stark, E., & Flitcraft, A. (1995). Killing the beast within: Woman battering and female suicidality. *International Journal of Health Services, 25,* 43–64.

Stets, J. E., & Straus, M. A. (1990). Gender differences in reporting marital violence and its medical and psychological consequences. In M. M. Straus & R. J. Gelles(Eds.), *Physical violence in American families: Risk factors and adaptations to violence in 8,145 families* (pp. 151–165). New Brunswick, NJ: Transaction.

Straus, M.A. (1979). Measuring intrafamily conflict and violence: The Conflict Tactics (CT) Scales. *Journal of Marriage and the Family, 41,* 75–88.

Straus, M. M., & Gelles, R. J. (1990). *Physical violence in American families: Risk factors and adaptations to violence in 8,145 families.* New Brunswick, NJ: Transaction.

Teichman, Y., Bar-El, Z., Shor, H., & Sirota, P. (1995). A comparison of two modalities of cognitive therapy (individual and marital) in treating depression. *Psychiatry: Interpersonal and Biological Processes, 58,* 136–148.

Vivian, D., & Langhinrichsen-Rohling, J. (1994). Are bi-directionally violent couples mutually victimized? A gender sensitive comparison. *Violence and Victims, 9,* 107–124.

Vivian, D., & Malone, J. (1997). Relationship factors and depressive symptomatology associated with mild and severe husband to wife physical aggression. *Violence and Victims, 12,* 3–18.

Watson, D., & Clark, L. A. (1991) *Mood and anxiety symptom questionnaire.* Iowa City: Department of Psychology, University of Iowa.

Whiffen, V. E., & Gotlib, I. H. (1989). Stress and coping in maritally distressed and nondistressed couples. *Journal of Social and Personal Relationships, 6,* 327–344.

Whisman, M. A., & Bruce , M. L. (1999). Marital distress and incidence of major depressive episode in a community sample. *Journal of Abnormal Psychology, 108,* 674–678.

Weissman, M. M. (1987). Advances in psychiatric epidemiology: Rates and risks for major depression. *American Journal of Public Health, 77,* 445–451.

Weissman, M. M., & Klerman, G. (1992). Depression: Current understanding and changing trends. *Annual Review of Public Health, 13,* 319–339.

Wing, J. K., Cooper, J. E., & Sartorious, N. (1974). The measurement and classification of psychiatric symptoms: An instruction manual for the present state examination and CATEGO program. England: Cambridge University Press.

PART IV

APPLICATION: MARRIAGE AS A POINT OF INTERVENTION IN THE TREATMENT OF DEPRESSION

10

Couples Therapy for Depression: Using Healthy Relationships to Treat Depression

James V. Cordova
Christina B. Gee

The concordance rates between depression and marital distress have been reported to be as high as 50% (Beach, Jouriles, & O'Leary, 1985). Evidence has suggested that relationship distress frequently precedes the development of depressive symptoms (Beach & O'Leary, 1993; Markman, Duncan, Storaasli, & Howes, 1987; Schaefer & Burnett, 1987) and increases an individual's vulnerability to depression (e.g., Beach, Whisman, & O'Leary, 1994). Although not all depressive episodes are preceded by relationship distress, depression invariably has a negative effect on the quality of a couple's intimate relationship (Billings, Cronkite, & Moos, 1983; Birtchnell, 1988; Horwitz & White, 1991; Schuster, Kessler, & Aseltine, 1990; Weiss & Aved, 1978; Weissman, 1987). Given the reliable association between depression and marital distress, treating an individual's depression within the context of his or her marital relationship often may be a logical choice (Beach, Sandeen, & O'Leary, 1990). The individual is embedded within his or her marital relationship, and the depression inevitably both affects and is affected by the couple's ongoing day-to-day interactions (see Coyne and Benazon, chapter 2; Davila, chapter 4; and Katz, chapter 6). That partnership, therefore, can either be a source of strength and an asset to the individual's recovery or a source of further suffering and a hindrance to the health of both partners (see Whisman, chapter 1, for more detail).

Although several state-of-the-art treatments for unipolar depression have demonstrated some degree of effectiveness, there is certainly room for improvement. The National Institute of Mental Health Collaborative Depression Study reported recovery rates of 57% for imipramine plus clinical management, 55% for interpersonal psychotherapy (IPT), and 51% for cognitive–behavior therapy (Elkin et al., 1989). Similarly, in a component analysis of cognitive therapy (CT) for depression, Jacobson et al. (1996) reported a 58.3% recovery rate for a complete CT package and 50% and 56.4% recovery rates for the behavioral activation and automatic thoughts components, respectively. In addition, such treatments appear to result in long-term recovery for only about one half of treated individuals (e.g., Gortner, Gollan, Dobson, & Jacobson, 1998).

One possible reason that many individuals do not recover or relapse over time is that current treatments focus on treating the individual and do not attempt to directly affect his or her ongoing relationships. These treatments do not place a strong emphasis on factors such as having a supportive and responsive home environment. Indeed, some evidence has suggested that simply being married, in and of itself, increases the effectiveness of treatments for depression (Elkin et al., 1989; Jarrett, Eaves, Grannemann, & Rush, 1991; Thase & Simons, 1992). Furthermore, there also is evidence that the supportiveness of a spouse decreases the incidence of depression following stressful life events (Brown & Harris, 1978) and that marital distress increases the incidence rate of depression even above the rate for single individuals (Ross, 1995). Therefore, it appears reasonable to hypothesize that treating depression in couples therapy, regardless of the presence or absence of co-occurring relationship distress, may result in faster recovery rates and lower relapse rates by fostering and maintaining a supportive marital relationship that responds effectively to the symptoms of depression.

Given such a likely benefit, couples treatments for depression have been explored several times. To date, however, systematized couples treatments for depression have focused exclusively on treating the depression by focusing on the marital distress (see Baucom, Shoham, Mueser, Daiuto, & Stickle, 1998). In this chapter, we explore the possibility of designing a couples therapy that addresses depression directly and that may therefore be equally applicable to couples who are not maritally distressed as well as to couples reporting significant marital distress. Specifically, we provide a detailed description of a treatment adapting couples therapy techniques for promoting acceptance, intimacy, and collaboration to the goals of a behavioral treatment for depression. We discuss methods for uniting the couple with a common perspective toward the depression and fostering a sense of ''we-ness'' and collaboration against the depression. We also discuss fostering partners' ability to respond flexibly to situations that might exacerbate the depression as well as their ability to effectively handle day-to-day challenges. In addition, we discuss building tolerance, preparing for relapse, and participating in active self-care. Finally, we discuss the importance of continual active engagement as partners both within the relationship and outside of the relationship. First, however, we present a brief review of the existing literature regarding marital therapy as a treatment for depression.

Previous Studies

Behavioral Marital Therapy

Behavioral marital therapy (BMT) as a treatment for depression has been the subject of several studies. Beach and O'Leary conducted one of the few well-controlled studies (Beach & O'Leary, 1992; O'Leary & Beach, 1990). In their study, maritally distressed couples in which the wife met the *Diagnostic and Statistical Manual of Mental Disorders (DSM-III;* American Psychiatric Association, 1980) criteria for major depression or dysthymia were randomly assigned to BMT, Beck's (Beck, Rush, Shaw, & Emery, 1979) CT, or a wait-list control condition. The BMT procedures used are described in Beach, Sandeen, and O'Leary (1990) and consisted of the instigation of positive behavior, communication training, problem-solving training, and relapse prevention procedures (see also Jacobson & Margolin, 1979). The following results were found: (a) BMT and CT were equally effective at reducing depressive symptoms in comparison to the wait-list condition, and (b) BMT significantly outperformed CT in the alleviation of wives' marital distress. Interestingly, Beach and O'Leary (1992) found that for husbands, BMT and CT resulted in equal improvement in marital satisfaction. Beach and O'Leary noted, however, that the positive effects of CT on husbands' marital satisfaction may hold only for the mildly discordant subset as a result of attrition of the more discordant husbands in the CT sample.

At 1-year follow-up, Beach and O'Leary (1992) found that BMT wives continued to report significantly greater marital satisfaction than CT wives. Moreover, the effect of BMT on depression appeared to be mediated by marital satisfaction. That is, wives' depressive symptoms improved because their marital satisfaction improved. Furthermore, the evidence suggested a differential response to CT based on pretreatment levels of marital discord and cognitive distortion. Specifically, higher levels of pretreatment marital discord (and fewer cognitive distortions) were significantly more predictive of remaining depressive symptoms for CT wives than for BMT wives. CT, however, did perform as well as BMT when wives reported lower levels of marital discord (and greater cognitive distortions).

Taken together, these two studies suggest that, for distressed couples, improving marital functioning is as effective as modifying individuals' cognitive distortions in the treatment of depression. In fact, the studies suggest that BMT may be more effective than CT at alleviating the symptoms of depression when relationship distress is high. Thus, if the goal is to treat depression, it appears that the clinician can target either the relationship between the individual and his or her partner or the individual's cognitions. However, if the goal is to treat marital distress, it appears that the clinician must target the relationship directly. One implication of these results is that marital therapy may be a more broadly applicable treatment for distressed couples, as it is capable of treating both relationship distress and individual depression.

To address the efficacy of BMT for depression when the couple is not maritally distressed, Jacobson and colleagues (Jacobson, Dobson, Fruzzetti, Schmaling, & Salusky, 1991) studied both distressed and nondistressed couples with a depressed wife. Couples were randomly assigned to BMT, CT, or a treatment in which individual CT sessions were interspersed with conjoint BMT sessions. Results of this study once again demonstrated a significant reduction in depressive symptoms in all three conditions. Furthermore, this study demonstrated that this symptom reduction occurred regardless of whether couples were distressed or not. As with the Beach and O'Leary (1992) study, only BMT resulted in significant gains in marital satisfaction. However, whereas Beach and O'Leary demonstrated that BMT and CT were equally effective as treatments for depression in a maritally distressed sample, the Jacobson et al. (1991) study demonstrated that the two treatments were not equivalent in a maritally nondistressed sample. Specifically, CT significantly outperformed BMT as a treatment for depression with nondistressed couples, whereas the two treatments were equivalently effective with distressed couples. It should be noted, however, that nondistressed couples' depressive symptoms did significantly improve (effect size = 1.67); they simply demonstrated less improvement than the couples in the CT group (effect size = 3.98).

Six- and 12-month follow-up of these couples revealed no differential relapse rates between the three conditions (Jacobson, Fruzzetti, Dobson, Whisman, & Hops, 1993). In fact, relapse rates were low in all conditions at 12 months (10%–15%). At 6-month follow-up, wives of nondistressed couples treated with BMT were more depressed than those treated with CT or with the combined treatment. However, at 12-month follow-up, there were no significant differences in wives' depression scores among the treatment conditions.

In summary, these studies suggest that treatments directed at improving the quality of the marital relationship effectively reduce the symptoms of depression and increase reported levels of marital satisfaction. Furthermore, treating the relationship appears to be as effective as treating an individual's dysfunctional thoughts for alleviating depressive symptoms and more effective for increasing marital satisfaction over the long run. However, the major caveat appears to be that, when a couple is not maritally distressed, individual CT is initially more effective for depression than marital therapy. In contrast, it appears that depressed individuals who also are maritally distressed are best served by marital therapy.

Cognitive Marital Therapy

Teichman, Bar-El, Shor, Sirota, and Elizur (1995) investigated the efficacy of cognitive marital therapy (CMT) as a treatment for depression. The primary aim of CMT "is to increase the insight of the spouses regarding their respective part in maintaining the depression and then to motivate the search for alternative reciprocal patterns'' (p. 138). Three categories of depression-maintaining patterns were described: (a) overprotection (e.g., the depressed spouse's depression is maintained by the caretaking of his or her spouse); (b) hostility or ambivalence (e.g., the nondepressed partner both positively reinforces depressive behavior by caretaking and punishes the depressed partner by communicating irritation and contempt); and (c) complementary dysfunctional needs (e.g., self-enhancement, mutual dependency, irrational role assignments). This structured therapy is limited to 15 sessions and focuses on the cognitive, affective, behavioral, and interactive components of these depression-maintaining patterns (see Teichman & Teichman, 1990, for more detail).

Couples in which one spouse met *DSM-III-R* (American Psychiatric Association, 1987) criteria for major depression or dysthymia were randomly assigned to CMT, CT, or a wait-list control condition. Participants were not assessed for marital distress. Results indicated that the CMT group's depressive symptoms decreased significantly from pre- to post-therapy, whereas the CT group did not change significantly. Posttherapy, the CMT group reported significantly lower depression scores than the other groups, and CMT resulted in the fewest unrecovered patients compared with the CT and wait-list groups (33%, 87%, and 93%, respectively). Finally, the spouses of the depressed patients in the CMT group also reported significantly lower posttreatment depression scores than did the spouses of CT patients. In short, CMT outperformed CT as a treatment for depressive symptoms from pre- to posttherapy for both depressed patients and their spouses.

However, at 6-month follow-up, the CMT and CT groups both showed significant decreases in depressive symptoms, with no significant differences between the groups. In addition, both CMT and CT demonstrated equivalent rates of unrecovered patients (41.6% and 54.5%, respectively). Results were similarly equivalent for patients' spouses.

In a follow-up report, Teichman (1997) compared the three groups to a pharmacotherapy group (PT) treated primarily with amitriptyline. Results of the posttreatment comparisons demonstrated that the CMT group reported a marginally significant lower mean depression score than the other groups, with no significant differences emerging among the other groups. At 6-month follow-up, the CMT and CT groups reported significantly lower depression scores than the PT group, although the CMT and CT groups did not differ from each other. The results of these studies supported the results of the previous studies in demonstrating that marital therapy and CT appear to be equally effective treatments for depression in the long run (i.e., 6–12 months). Additionally, this study also suggested that a marital therapy designed to address marital interactions that maintain depression may result in faster symptom reduction for both depressed patients and their spouses than individual therapy. Addition of the PT group allowed these investigators to demonstrate that, although PT resulted in significant reductions in reported depressive symptoms, it performed poorly compared to CMT in the short run and poorly compared to both CMT and CT in the long run.

Unfortunately, because this study did not include a measure of marital satisfaction, it did not address questions regarding (a) the efficacy of CMT as a treatment for marital distress, (b) the potential mediating role of marital satisfaction in the relationship between CMT and depressive symptoms, or (c) the potential differential effects of CMT on maritally distressed versus nondistressed couples. It is highly likely that a substantial number of study couples were also maritally distressed, and a comparison of these two groups would have added substantially to the previous research.

Conjoint Marital Interpersonal Psychotherapy

Foley, Rounsaville, Weissman, Sholomaskas, and Chevron (1989) conducted a pilot study investigating the efficacy of conjoint marital interpersonal psychotherapy (IPT–CM) as a treatment for depression. The premise of IPT–CM is that depression develops within interpersonal contexts and that a treatment directed at interpersonal marital issues can be an effective treatment for depression. IPT–CM is described as focusing on five marital areas: communication, intimacy, boundary management, leadership, and attainment of socially appropriate goals. Specific problems in these areas are targeted for improvement, primarily by focusing on dysfunctional communication between spouses. Details of the IPT approach can be found in Klerman, Weissman, Rounsaville, and Chevron (1984).

Eighteen couples who attributed the presence of depression to discord within their marriage were randomly assigned to 16 weeks of either IPT–CM or individual IPT. Patients in both groups reported significant improvement in depressive symptoms and social adjustment from pre- to posttreatment; however, no significant differences were found between the two treatments. On the other hand, assessments of marital functioning revealed that IPT–CM patients were significantly better adjusted following treatment than IPT patients. In addition, patients' spouses also improved significantly in marital functioning from pre- to posttreatment regardless of treatment condition.

Consistent with the above studies, conjoint and individual treatments for depression appeared to be equally effective at reducing depressive symptoms. Differences between the two treatments emerged when level of marital adjustment was measured, with the individual treatment having had little effect on marital quality compared to the marital treatment.

Enhancing Marital Intimacy Therapy

Waring, Chamberlaine, Carver, Stalker, and Schaefer (1995) conducted a pilot study comparing enhancing marital intimacy therapy (EMIT) to a wait-list control group. EMIT is described as a therapy designed to "facilitate self-disclosure of personal constructs" (p. 4) as a means of building intimacy in the relationship. Waring et al. described the techniques of EMIT as involving self-disclosure of (a) each partner's explanation for the depression, (b) each partner's observations and experiences of their parents' marriages, (c) each partner's perspective on the early history of the relationship, and (d) each partner's relating of the current relationship to past relationships.

Participants were 17 couples with a depressed wife randomly assigned to either EMIT or a 10-week wait-list. Although both the Beck Depression Inventory (Beck, Ward, Mendelson, Mock, & Erbaugh, 1961) and the Hamilton Depression Inventory (HDI; Hamilton, 1960) were used, depressed wives in the EMIT group showed improvement over the wait-list group only on the HDI. Following the treatment of some wait-list couples, analyses were conducted again on the somewhat larger sample ($n = 23$). This reanalysis revealed significant reductions on both measures of depressive symptoms. Thus, although it reflected the results of a pilot study with a small sample, this report demonstrated the robust nature of the effect of marital therapy on depression.

Replication From Outside the United States

These results also have been supported by research conducted in The Netherlands. Emanuels-Zuurveen and Emmelkamp (1996) compared the efficacy of a cognitive–behavioral individual treatment to a communication skills-based marital therapy in the treatment of unipolar depression. Marital therapy procedures were based on those described by Beach et al. (1990) and on the communication-skills training techniques described by Emmelkamp and colleagues (Emmelkamp, Van Linden van der Heuvel, & Ruphan, 1988). This therapy consisted of 5 initial sessions devoted to examining any problems stemming from the depression that might have hindered marital therapy, such as complicated grief or low activity level, followed by 10 sessions focusing on communications-skills training, including active listening, assertiveness, and problem-solving training.

Thirty-six participants reporting depressive symptoms and significant marital distress were randomly assigned to one of the two treatment conditions. As with the above studies, the individual cognitive–behavioral treatment and the marital treatment were equally effective treatments for depression. Again, as with the above studies, marital treatment resulted in significantly greater improvements in marital satisfaction than individual treatment. The authors noted, however, that the marital treatment condition experienced more dropouts than the individual treatment condition and that many of the couples were disappointed that depression was not addressed specifically in the marital treatment.

Summary

Results are remarkably consistent across a variety of marital therapies. Marital therapy as a treatment for depression is significantly better than no treatment at all. Furthermore, marital therapy is as good or better than standard CT when applied in cases in which the depressed individual is also significantly maritally distressed. However, marital therapy has not been shown to be as effective a treatment for depression as CT when partners are not also maritally distressed. This, of course, makes perfect sense when one considers that these marital treatments were not intended to be direct treatments for depression, but instead were intended to have an effect on depression by alleviating marital distress. Without the presence of marital distress, traditional marital therapies may be limited in their effectiveness. However, a couples therapy designed to address depression as well as increase marital support and cohesion may be effective regardless of the presence or absence of marital distress.

Therefore, the remainder of this chapter describes a couples therapy designed for the treatment of depression regardless of the presence or absence of self-reported marital distress. The therapy described integrates the acceptance- and change-promoting approach of integrative behavioral couples therapy (IBCT; Christensen & Jacobson, 1991, 2000; Christensen, Jacobson, & Babcock, 1995; Cordova & Jacobson, 1993; Jacobson & Christensen, 1996) with a behavioral approach to the treatment of depression (Cordova & Jacobson, 1997).

Acceptance in Couples Therapy

IBCT rose from the desire to help those couples not benefiting from traditional BMT. Studies have suggested that the one third of couples least likely to benefit from BMT (Jacobson, Schmaling, & Holtzworth-Munroe, 1987) have tended to be severely distressed, older, emotionally disengaged (Baucom & Hoffman, 1986; Hahlweg, Schindler, Revenstorf, & Brengelmann, 1984), and polarized on basic issues (Jacobson, Follette, & Pagel, 1986). BMT was designed to teach couples new relationship skills and requires that partners work together to learn those skills. Partners who are too distressed and polarized simply cannot work together well enough to learn what BMT has to teach. IBCT was designed to repair the collaborative capacity of these couples by fostering intimacy and closeness through acceptance.

Acceptance can be understood as a graceful coming to terms with those things about a relationship that are unlikely to change while at the same time working efficiently toward changing those things that can be changed (Cordova & Jacobson, 1993; Cordova & Kohlenberg, 1994). Acceptance techniques function to increase closeness and intimacy within a relationship despite the presence of specific irreconcilable differences. In therapeutic terms, couples are encouraged to "give up the struggle" to change the unchangeable and, therefore, to free up the time and energy previously lost to destructive change efforts for more healthy relationship behavior. It should be noted, however, that the type of acceptance proposed does not promote hopeless resignation or subjugation to unhealthy power differences. Therapy is not intended to promote depressive withdrawal from relationship engagement but instead to promote the ability to differentiate between what can be changed with hard work and what cannot. In essence, IBCT is intended to produce an active and effective couple by emphasizing both emotional acceptance and relationship change skills.

For example, when skill deficits are contributing to a couple's distress, fostering acceptance can promote the collaboration necessary to learn those skills. Alternatively, distressed couples may not have skill deficits, but may simply be too embattled to use the skills they do have effectively. In such cases, fostering acceptance can move the couple past destructive and unwinnable conflicts and allow them to use their skills more effectively. An approach designed to foster both emotional closeness and relationship skillfulness provides the appropriate blend of compassion and action necessary for effectively addressing unipolar depression regardless of the presence or absence of relationship distress (Cordova & Jacobson, 1997). If the couple is concurrently distressed, then the already empirically supported indirect approach to the treatment of depression is an immediate option. If, on the other hand, the couple is happily married, then that happy marriage can become the context in which the partners learn about and address the depression as a team.

We are emphasizing an acceptance-based approach to the treatment of depression for several reasons. First, it has been theorized that such an approach may simply be more generally effective than an exclusively change-oriented approach (Christensen & Jacobson, 1991, 2000; Christensen et al., 1995; Cordova & Jacobson, 1993; Jacobson & Christensen, 1996), and preliminary evidence has been presented to support this supposition (Cordova, Jacobson, & Christensen, 1998; Jacobson, Christensen, Prince, Cordova, & Eldridge, in press). In short, we believe this is a uniquely powerful form of couples therapy. Second, because depression may be a recurring condition (cf. Shea et al., 1992), the use of acceptance-based techniques for coping with recurrences seems appropriate. Coming to terms with depression as a potentially chronically recurring condition may aid couples in becoming effective agents of primary and secondary prevention as well as facilitators of tertiary intervention. Third, many of the ways in which depressed individuals and their partners respond to depression do more harm than good, and it is the unique goal of acceptance interventions to decrease the frequency and destructiveness of a couple's dysfunctional change attempts.

Couples Therapy for Depression

Couples therapy for depression (CTD) uses the techniques of IBCT to achieve the goals of a behavioral therapy for depression (i.e., increased effective action). CTD is intended to be effective regardless of the depression's etiology and is intended to address both depression and marital distress simultaneously. It also is intended to be an effective treatment for depression in the absence of significant marital distress. Working with nondistressed couples presents the challenge of fully integrating the nondepressed spouse and the relationship itself into a treatment for what is most commonly considered an individual problem. However, it also presents the advantage of a couple with an easily established collaborative set. In other words, although both partners may be affected by the depression, they are not also struggling directly with each other and are therefore in a better position to take advantage of the strengths inherent within their partnership. On the other hand, working with couples who are also significantly maritally distressed provides multiple targets for intervention. The relationship distress itself can be targeted as a means of both improving relationship satisfaction and alleviating depressive symptoms. Alternatively, the depression can be targeted as a means of not only treating the depression, but also as an issue through which the couple can reestablish intimacy, collaboration, and trust in their relationship. In other words, establishing a partnership in relation to the depression can serve as a vehicle for establishing relationship satisfaction. In summary, couples therapy can serve as a treatment context for depression, for relationship distress, or for both simultaneously, with the main difference being the range of possible intervention targets.

Given that several sources of information already exist describing acceptance in the treatment of marital distress (Christensen & Jacobson, 1991, 2000; Christensen et al., 1995; Cordova & Jacobson, 1993; Jacobson & Christensen, 1996), this chapter addresses treatment in the absence of significant marital distress. The absence of significant marital distress allows the therapist to target the depression directly. The following sections describe how a partnership that deals effectively with unipolar depression can be established.

The following are the basic therapeutic goals of CTD: (a) uniting the couple with a common perspective toward the depression, (b) increasing the partners' behavioral flexibility, (c) increasing the effective handling of aversive situations, and (d) promoting active exploration of the relationship and the environment. These treatment goals address the symptoms of depression by strengthening the couple's relationship and their capacity to work together to solve problems and pursue both common and individual goals. The following sections describe the pursuit of each goal in the treatment of depression.

Uniting the Couple With a Common Perspective

Uniting the couple with a common perspective from which to address the depression is initially the key goal of CTD. The idea of uniting a couple in relation to problems that may be difficult or impossible to solve is an adaptation of IBCT's unified detachment (e.g., Christensen et al., 1995; Jacobson & Christensen, 1996). Fostering a united perspective is the first goal of CTD because the remainder of therapy depends on the partners having adopted a position from which they are addressing the depression as a team. The goal is to actively involve both partners in treatment and to develop the relationship as a dependable source of social support. A unified perspective allows partners to regard the depression more accurately as a joint problem and not the sole responsibility or fault of either partner individually. Developing a somewhat detached perspective also allows partners to stay close to each other despite the depression rather than allowing the depression to drive them apart. The key to developing a unified detachment is to depict depression as an entity or process that is in a sense separable from the individual partners. In essence, depression is framed not as something residing inside the individual, but as a third party present within the relationship with its own agenda and effects.

Developing a Sense of "We-ness"

In the pursuit of a unified detachment, we talk of the couple developing a sense of "we-ness" similar to that described by Gottman (1994), in which the couple feels united in the struggle with depression rather than divided by it. As noted, this sense of we-ness is essential to CTD in that it is the context from which depression can be addressed by the couple as partners. We-ness undermines blame and criticism by allowing the couple to blame the depression rather than each other. We-ness provides a sense of being able to work together effectively and facilitates both partners taking an active role in addressing their common enemy. Once this sense is developed, the depressed partner no longer has to cope with the depression alone, but is joined by his or her partner, thus tapping into a powerful source of support. In addition, the nondepressed partner is included in treatment as a genuinely essential component, thus avoiding any sense of being excluded from a fundamentally important part of his or her partner's life and fostering a sense of effectiveness and agency to counteract feelings of helplessness in the face of the other's depression.

The first step to developing a sense of we-ness is to provide the couple with a thorough and objective education about depression. The rationale is to begin to objectify depression as a thing, to educate the partners about their common enemy, and to clarify any misinformation about depression that the partners might have brought with them into therapy. The therapist should explain how depression is conceptualized in the DSM, discuss the possible causes debated in the literature, and outline what is known about the effects of depression on intimate relationships. Partners are encouraged to take personal responsibility for learning as much as they can about the condition they are dealing with. The goal is to promote a sense of agency through which the couple begins to face their problem as fully integrated partners.

We-ness also can be promoted through an adaptation of the empty-chair method. The empty-chair method simply involves talking about the depression as though it were seated in an empty chair in the therapy room. The idea is to use a physical prop to facilitate the partners' conceptualization of the depression as a third party in their relationship, with its own causes, its own effects, its own agenda, and its own existence apart from either partner. Essentially, depression is formulated as an unwelcome guest in the couple's relationship. Furthermore, it is discussed as something for which neither partner is to blame, but something for which both partners ultimately are responsible. In other words, once the depression is placed in the chair, it is acknowledged that neither partner is to blame for it but that both partners are responsible for actively addressing it, monitoring it, coping with it, and working to prevent its recurrence.

Promoting Self-Observation

Unified detachment also can be promoted through assisting couples in objective, non-judgmental self-observation. Self-observation is an important component of treatment because depressed individuals frequently use destructive strategies (e.g., substance abuse, excessive distraction, and suicide) to escape from their own feelings of despair. However, escape from one's own thoughts and feelings is practically impossible, and attempts to do so are ultimately fruitless and self-destructive. Self-observation facilitates acceptance of distressing thoughts and feelings because the act of observing oneself is incompatible with the avoidance, withdrawal, and aggression that often interfere with more appropriate responses (Cordova, 1998). The goal of CTD is to foster acceptance of private experiences exactly because those experiences cannot be effectively addressed in any other way. Self-observation provides the perspective from which the depressed individual can simply attend to the ebb and flow of his or her thoughts and feelings without attempting to control them. In addition, the shared outlook that the partners construct allows them to observe their own private experiences, get to know them, become comfortable with them, and begin to accept them without the disheartening work of trying to deny, denigrate or destroy them. In particular, the depressed individual is provided a perspective from which he or she can watch the thoughts and feelings associated with the depression without "buying into" them, without struggling with them, and without evaluating them as necessarily good, bad, foolish, or shameful. The depressed individual is allowed the perspective from which to simply watch these thoughts and feelings come and go of their own accord. The short-term goal of promoting a repertoire of active self-observation is to undermine the depression about the depression and establish a sense of nurturance and acceptance toward the depressed individual's own experience. The long-term goal is to free up the time and energy wasted on ineffective attempts to destroy undeniable feelings for the pursuit of other more attainable goals.

Self-observation is also beneficial to the nondepressed partner. The nondepressed partner may seem to experience two competing inclinations in response to the other's depressive behavior. One inclination is to respond solicitously (e.g., offering help and comfort), whereas the other is to be irritated and frustrated (which precipitates verbal aggression and withdrawal; e.g., Biglan, 1991; Coyne, 1976; Lovejoy & Busch, 1993). The nondepressed partner may initially act on his or her first inclination and engage in a great deal of caretaking behavior intended to alleviate the depressed partner's suffering. However, that behavior often carries undertones of irritation, providing the depressed individual with a mixed message of both loving support and critical anger. Over time, the nondepressed partner often becomes more openly angry as solicitous responses become increasingly fruitless. Furthermore, the nondistressed partner may find himself or herself actively avoiding his or her partner or physically withdrawing when depressive symptoms are present. As with the depressed partner, self-observation from a shared perspective allows the nondepressed partner to begin the process of coming to terms with his or her own undeniable private experiences. Because it appears that these mixed emotions are unavoidable, fostering their acceptance allows both partners to recognize that these feelings are normal, nonmalicious, and inescapable and that they need not be denied or eliminated to respond well as partners. Although self-observation is sometimes difficult to learn, it is made easier when it initially requires that the individual simply describe out loud the thoughts and feelings he or she is observing.

In addition, self-observation can help the couple recognize the interaction patterns that may be common within relationships with a depressed partner. For example, there is evidence that depressed individuals engage in excessive reassurance and negative feedback seeking (see Joiner, chapter 7), which may, in turn, lead their partners to respond with solicitousness, then irritation, and eventually withdrawal. By observing the interaction pattern, the couple can learn to tolerate these occasional aversive interactions without completely withdrawing from interacting altogether. The couple can see that they sometimes get stuck in this pattern and that they are able to move through it without damaging their relationship, so long as they do not wholly withdraw from each other to avoid this type of interaction.

Increasing Partners' Behavioral Flexibility

A second goal of CTD is to increase both partners' behavioral flexibility. Behavioral flexibility is an important objective of treatment because rigidity and passivity predispose individuals to depression by limiting their ability to actively adapt to changing environments (Cordova & Jacobson, 1997). In other words, the absence or suppression of responses that enable adaptation to changing contingencies results in a shrinking repertoire of effective behavior and a subsequent increase in contact with aversive relational stimuli (i.e., arguments and unresolved problems). As an individual's ability to behave effectively diminishes, he or she becomes increasingly vulnerable to depression. The depressed individual is gradually left with little he or she can do to effect positive change, resulting in depressed mood, irritability, loss of motivation, anhedonia, and the host of other symptoms commonly associated with clinical depression.

For example, the transition to parenthood is a predictably stressful time for couples and has been associated with deterioration in marital satisfaction (Belsky, 1990). Such a transition requires a great deal of adaptive coping from both partners. Partners who attempt to carry on exactly as they did before parenthood are likely to find that a great deal of that behavior is no longer functional and that much of the behavior necessary for parenting is missing. Intimacy between partners may begin to deteriorate as the demands of parenthood increase. Failure to adapt increases vulnerability to depression by decreasing positive interactions within and outside of the relationship and increasing negative interactions. CTD aims to foster the emergence of flexible repertoires capable of adapting to changing circumstances, rebuilding depleted resources, and preparing for future transitions.

Another type of rigidity that couples are susceptible to involves becoming stuck in emotionally negative ways of thinking about and responding to specific problems in the relationship. Specific topics or issues in the relationship can set the stage for repetitive patterns characterized by negative assumptions about each other and heated, angry exchanges. These patterns, because they are practically guaranteed to be exceptionally aversive and ultimately ineffective, are classically depressogenic because they require an enormous amount of time and energy with absolutely no positive payoff. In such cases, promoting greater mutual empathic understanding of each partner's role in the pattern fosters partners' behavioral flexibility. Promoting empathy increases flexibility by changing the emotional context within which the problematic interaction has characteristically occurred. It is often the case that affecting the emotional climate surrounding a particular issue can have a dramatic effect on the interaction itself. Sometimes an emotional shift from blaming accusation to empathic understanding eradicates the problematic interaction pattern altogether. Other times it aids in easing the partners in and out of the pattern, therefore limiting the amount of damage that pattern does to the relationship.

These rigid patterns are also likely to develop in relation to the depression itself. Therefore, partners are encouraged to talk about their experiences of the depression and the feelings involved in the struggle to overcome it. The nondepressed partner is encouraged to share the softer, more vulnerable feelings (e.g., fear, desperation, hurt, or loneliness) that may be motivating the harder expressions of anger, criticism, and withdrawal in response to the depression. This effort is necessary because it is important for the depressed spouse to experience genuine empathy for the struggles of the nondepressed spouse in relation to the depression. In addition, reestablishing empathy from the nondepressed spouse to the depressed spouse is necessary because of the previously mentioned evidence that the behavior of depressed individuals tends to erode empathy over time and elicit feelings of irritation and withdrawal (e.g., Biglan, 1991; Coyne, 1976; Lovejoy & Busch, 1993).

Reestablishing empathy provides other benefits as well. First, couple cohesion increases when each partner feels equally supported by the other. Second, the elicitation of empathy from the depressed spouse toward the nondepressed spouse, if done in a way that does not feed into already established feelings of guilt, provides the depressed partner with a focus outside of the self. Because the salience of positive environmental stimuli is diminished by a preoccupation with private thoughts and feelings, drawing the depressed individual out of himself or herself and back into the relationship is theorized to begin the process of reestablishing environmental control over positively reinforced behavior. Third, reestablishing empathy not only increases understanding about the effects of depression on the partners, but also creates the emotional closeness necessary to collaborate in its treatment and monitoring. Finally, and perhaps most important, building intimacy in the relationship and the competence with which the partners facilitate and engage in intimate interactions is exactly the type of effective interpersonal behavior that is theorized to alleviate depression.

Increasing the Effective Handling of Aversive Situations

Increasing the effective handling of aversive situations is another goal of CTD. A great deal of depressogenic behavior consists of passive or passive–aggressive responses to problems that are genuinely solvable. Similarly, depressogenic behavior often consists of struggles to avoid or destroy problems that cannot be changed. In such cases, learning to distinguish those things that can be changed from those that cannot helps partners manage their efforts more effectively and avoid unproductive struggles. In general, problems that are amenable to active problem-solving strategies are overt, operantly shaped, or otherwise changeable through direct action. Problems that are not amenable to problem-solving strategies tend to be private (e.g., thoughts, feelings), unconditionally respondent, or simply unavailable for manipulation. For solvable problems, therapy promotes collaborative problem solving and active social support. On the other hand, for unsolvable problems (e.g., partner or relationship characteristic that cannot be changed constructively), acceptance is promoted as the most effective type of response (Cordova & Jacobson, 1997). Struggling to change the unchangeable is depressogenic, and freeing up the time and energy devoted to that struggle should be a central aspect of effective therapy.

Relinquishing the struggle to change the unchangeable is often best accomplished through strategies that foster tolerance. Tolerance-promoting techniques include providing understandable reasons for the depression and the behaviors associated with it, highlighting the positive features of the relationship despite the depression, and preparing in advance for relapse.

Providing understandable reasons for the depression and the behaviors associated with it was discussed earlier as a means of uniting couples with a shared perspective. Understandable reasons also promote tolerance by emphasizing that neither partner is to blame for the depression. For example, if a couple considers the depression to be caused by an environmental insufficiency, rather than personal inadequacy, then they are much less likely to feel shame and self-loathing and more likely to actively address those environmental deficiencies. In addition, if partners come to understand that learning to genuinely tolerate occasional feelings of depression is the surest means of getting on with an active and meaningful life, then they are less likely to become completely distracted by misguided attempts to control day-to-day variations in mood.

Highlighting the positive features of the relationship places the depression within its proper context as simply one aspect of a much larger life together. Tolerance develops as a result of recognizing that the symptoms of depression coexist with many other enjoyable and meaningful experiences. CTD involves redirecting partners toward those meaningful activities that remain available to them in living a quality life. The message conveyed is that an individual can value himself or herself, his or her life, his or her partner, and his or her relationship as vital components of a life that also sometimes includes the symptoms of depression. It is assumed that a depressed mood cannot simply be willed away and that vulnerability to depression may be a chronic condition. Depressive moods may come and go as a function of the transactions between an individual and his or her environment, and a meaningful life can be pursued despite moment-to-moment variations in mood.

Tolerance is also built by preparing couples for depressive relapse. Such preparation accomplishes two things. First, it prepares partners emotionally for the possibility that depression may recur. Preparing a couple for relapse decreases the probability that they will be emotionally devastated by future episodes. Second, discussing the possibility of relapse allows partners to prepare effective responses to reemergent symptoms and depressogenic life events (e.g., a death in the family or relocation). Again, the assumption is that a vulnerability to depression may be chronic and that additional depressive episodes may occur. Given this, it seems prudent to prepare depressed individuals and their spouses for possible recurrences. This discussion with the couple evolves naturally from previous discussions of the depression as an unwelcome guest for which neither partner is to blame. Such unwelcome guests, much like the flu or misfortune, at times cannot be avoided, but can still be dealt with successfully. CTD discusses the concept of living with and despite the occasional period of depressive mood, rather than living in fear of it or in response to it.

Preparation for relapse involves working with the couple to identify foreseeable events that might set the stage for subsequent depressive episodes. Identifying such events in advance allows the couple to be prepared by allowing them the opportunity to discuss active coping strategies and means of broadening their available repertoires as an inoculation against depression. Preparation for relapse also involves preparing the couple to recognize and respond to early signs of relapse. Recognition of the early signs of relapse requires becoming familiar with depressive symptoms as they might manifest themselves in overt behavior (or the lack of it), in mood, and in thinking processes. It also requires understanding the partners' vulnerabilities and the types of environmental changes that might interact with those vulnerabilities. For example, if one partner recognizes that he is often strongly affected by criticism at work, then he and his partner are better able to recognize when that might be affecting his mood. Recognizing such events allows the couple to tap directly into their skills for dealing with such events, such as discussing what can be done to address the criticisms or the critic, recognizing that the mood will pass, or focusing on other areas of life that are sources of effective activity.

Communication and Problem-Solving Training

Another means of promoting the effective handling of aversive circumstances is through training in effective communication and problem-solving skills. The implementation of communication and problem-solving training is described only briefly, as detailed descriptions of these techniques can be found in numerous other sources (e.g., Cordova & Jacobson, 1993).

Communication training consists primarily of teaching couples simple, concrete steps to ease communication and decrease the probability of misunderstandings. These steps include (a) keeping the message short, (b) focusing on the speaker's perspective, (c) avoiding blame and criticism, and (d) paraphrasing the speaker's message. Although treatment does not require couples to adhere to a particular style of communication, for those couples experiencing severe communication difficulties, communication training provides a useful structure within which other therapy goals can be pursued. A tool such as communication training may be necessary only with those couples whose communication skills are inadequate for dealing effectively with the presence of depression in their relationship. However, for those couples, communication training may be an essential step toward tapping into their capacity to support each other and work together collaboratively in the treatment of the depression. In addition, improving their communication skills may, in and of itself, contribute to improvement as it adds to their repertoire of effective interpersonal behaviors.

Problem-solving training teaches couples concrete strategies for dealing with negotiable problems in their relationship. Problem-solving techniques are taught as a means of effectively approaching problems that can be changed through problem identification and concrete solutions. Problem solving begins with problem definition, proceeds through brainstorming solutions to sorting solutions into the feasible and unfeasible, and finally moves to deriving a change agreement. As with communication training, problem-solving training is hypothesized to aid in the treatment of depression by providing partners with more effective relationship skills. This cooperative problem-solving strategy usually is implemented in the context of relationship problems, and it has been found to be remarkably effective. Additionally, within CTD, this cooperative problem-solving strategy is promoted as a means for a couple to jointly address problems they can face together. Cooperative problem solving is also useful even when one partner must ultimately implement the solution independently. In such cases, problem solving works as a social support tool in that both partners can work together to develop a response plan for one of them.

Beyond focusing on how partners can function as a team in the context of depression, individual self-care skills are also promoted. CTD helps each partner identify areas in which his or her individual efforts are required and guides the development of appropriate self-care skills. Thus, although partners work together, neither can afford to delegate ultimate responsibility for his or her own well-being. No relationship can fulfill every individual need and desire completely, and each partner must be willing and able to supplement his or her relationship with outside sources (e.g., outside friendships, activities).

Promoting Active Exploration and Reactivation

A broad, flexible, and active repertoire is believed to be the key to preventing depression as well as a key to recovery (Cordova & Jacobson, 1997). Therefore, the final component of CTD is promoting an active exploration of and engagement in both the interpersonal and external environment. Exploration of the interpersonal environment is aided by the increased emotional closeness and relationship skills promoted during therapy. Active exploration of the external environment is promoted in therapy through exploration of activities that both members of the couple can participate in together as well as activities that each can participate in individually. Partners are encouraged to seek out opportunities to increase the number and variety of activities available to them as a means of building and maintaining large, effective repertoires.

In individual treatments for depression, behavioral activation often takes the form of coaching an individual to brainstorm a list of possible activities and to try each systematically. The downside of this individual approach is that the individual is sent out alone to try to implement those suggestions without any guarantee of social or other environmental support. By including the spouse as an integral aspect of this endeavor, the depressed individual is not alone in his or her efforts but is instead part of a loving team working toward a mutual goal. In individual approaches, even if the depressed partner wants the spouse's assistance, the spouse must first be convinced of the importance of participating. This often is easier to accomplish in couples therapy where the mutual benefits can be made obvious by the therapist.

The therapist describes the rationale behind actively increasing both joint and individual activity. The rationale is that developing a repertoire of active exploration fosters increased closeness and satisfaction in the relationship and decreases both partners' vulnerability to depression. As in individual therapy, the couple is asked to brainstorm and create a list of possible joint activities, including ideas that might seem silly or unreasonable. The brainstorming process is intended to be enjoyable in and of itself, and couples should be encouraged to take a lighthearted and playful approach to the task. The couple is then directed to talk about the items and choose one they will do together before the next session. Explicit plans are made, including selecting a day and a time and preparing for foreseeable difficulties. Choosing one or more joint activities for the week remains at least a brief part of subsequent sessions. These activities can be new ones or can include activities that become a regular part of the couple's routine (e.g., breakfast out once a week).

Enjoyable or meaningful individual activities are also chosen in the same fashion. Both partners work together to think of things each can do to be active and effective over the course of the next week. Daily schedules like those used in CT are useful in this endeavor, especially for individuals whose activity levels are limited. Again, once a list has been compiled for each partner, a handful of activities can be chosen by each, those activities can be scheduled, and potential obstacles can be prepared for.

The couple also should be engaged in a discussion emphasizing the necessity of being actively exploratory on an ongoing basis. The rationale to be shared with the couple is that continually exploring within and outside of the relationship for new activities and new responses will add to the richness of their lives and will nurture a growing and flexible repertoire more resilient to the vicissitudes of life. Thus, couples should come to understand that actively pursuing novel experiences is essential, and that continually adding to their abilities and experiences is something to be valued and pursued.

Conclusion

To date, marital therapies for depression have treated the symptoms of depression indirectly by directly treating the causes of marital distress. The empirical literature has consistently demonstrated that this indirect approach to the treatment of depression is as effective as individual treatments for depression, with the added benefit of being significantly more effective at improving partners' marital satisfaction. However, it appears that such indirect treatments are of lesser value to depressed individuals whose relationships are not distressed. It has been our contention that a couples treatment designed to treat depression directly rather than indirectly can be a benefit to depressed individuals regardless of the presence or absence of concurrent relationship distress. Furthermore, we have speculated that such a treatment could potentially be more powerful than individual treatments, both in terms of speeding the process of symptom reduction and in terms of decreasing the likelihood of depressive relapse.

CTD is a couples treatment specifically applicable to depression. Based on behavioral theories of depression and relationship distress, and incorporating techniques for fostering acceptance and facilitating change, CTD is intended to be flexible enough to help most couples effectively cope with unipolar depression and relationship distress. This treatment, however, has yet to be tested empirically. Thus, although our hopes for its usefulness are high and the bases for its success as a treatment appear sound, its efficacy remains to be demonstrated.

References

American Psychiatric Association. (1980). *Diagnostic and statistical manual of mental disorders* (3rd ed.). Washington, DC: Author.

American Psychiatric Association. (1987). *Diagnostic and statistical manual of mental disorders* (3rd ed., rev.). Washington, DC: Author.

Baucom, D. H., & Hoffman, J. A. (1986). The effectiveness of marital therapy: Current status and applications to the clinical setting. In N. S. Jacobson & A. S. Gurman (Eds.), *Clinical handbook of marital therapy* (pp. 597–620). New York: Guilford Press.

Baucom, D. H., Shoham, V., Mueser, K. T., Daiuto, A. D., & Stickle, T. R. (1998). Empirically supported couple and family interventions for marital distress and adult mental health problems. *Journal of Consulting and Clinical Psychology, 66,* 53–88.

Beach, S. R., Jouriles, E. N., & O'Leary, K. D. (1985). Extramarital sex: Impact on depression and commitment in couples seeking marital therapy. *Journal of Sex and Marital Therapy, 11,* 99–108.

Beach, S. R., & O'Leary, K. D. (1992). Treating depression in the context of marital discord: Outcome and predictors of response for marital therapy vs. cognitive therapy. *Behavior Therapy, 23,* 507–528.

Beach, S. R., & O'Leary, K. D. (1993). Marital discord and dysphoria: For whom does the marital relationship predict depressive symptoms? *Journal of Social and Personal Relationships, 10,* 405–420.

Beach, S. R. H., Sandeen, E. E., & O'Leary, K. D. (1990). *Depression in marriage: A model for etiology and treatment.* New York: Guilford Press.

Beach, S. R. H., Whisman, M. A., & O'Leary, K. D. (1994). Marital therapy for depression: Theoretical foundation, current status, and future directions. *Behavior Therapy, 25,* 345–371.

Beck, A. T., Rush, A. J., Shaw, B. F., & Emery, G. (1979). *Cognitive therapy for depression.* New York: Guilford Press.

Beck, A. T., Ward, C., Mendelson, M., Mock, J., & Erbaugh, J. (1961). An inventory for measuring depression. *Archives of General Psychiatry, 4,* 53–63.

Belsky, J. (1990). Children and marriage. In F. Fincham & T. Bradbury (Eds.), *The psychology of marriage* (pp. 87–117). New York: Guilford Press.

Biglan, A. (1991). Distressed behavior and its context. *The Behavior Analyst, 14,* 157–169.

Billings, A. G., Cronkite, R. C., & Moos, R. H. (1983). Social environmental factors in bipolar depression: Comparisons of depressed patients and controls. *Journal of Abnormal Psychology, 92,* 119–133.

Birtchnell, J. (1988). Depression and family relationships: A study of young, married women on a London housing estate. *British Journal of Psychiatry, 153,* 758–769.

Brown, G. W., & Harris, T. O. (1978). *Social origins of depression: A study of psychiatric disorders in women.* New York: Free Press.

Christensen, A., & Jacobson, N. S. (1991). *Integrative behavioral couple therapy.* Unpublished treatment manual.

Christensen, A., & Jacobson, N. S. (2000). *Reconcilable differences.* New York: Guilford Press.

Christensen, A., Jacobson, N. S., & Babcock, J. C. (1995). Integrative behavioral couple therapy. In N. S. Jacobson & A. S. Gurman (Eds.), *Clinical handbook of couple therapy* (pp. 31–64). New York: Guilford Press.

Cordova, J. V. (1998). Acceptance theory: Understanding the process of change. In E. V. Gifford (Chair), *Finding the clinical core: Theory in practice.* Symposium conducted at the meeting of the Association for Advancement of Behavior Therapy. Proceedings of the 32nd annual convention of the Association for Advancement of Behavior Therapy, Washington, DC.

Cordova, J. V., & Jacobson, N. S. (1993). Couples distress. In D. H. Barlow (Ed.), *Clinical handbook of psychological disorders: A step-by-step treatment manual* (2nd ed.; pp. 481–512). New York: Guilford Press.

Cordova, J. V., & Jacobson, N. S. (1997). Acceptance in couple therapy and its implications for the treatment of depression. In R. J. Sternberg & M. Hojjat (Eds.), *Satisfaction in close relationships* (pp. 307–334). New York: Guilford Press.

Cordova, J. V., Jacobson, N. S., & Christensen, A. (1998). Acceptance vs. change in behavioral couples therapy: Impact on client communication processes in the therapy session. *Journal of Marital and Family Therapy, 24,* 437–455.

Cordova, J. V., & Kohlenberg, R. J. (1994). Acceptance and the therapeutic relationship. In S. C. Hayes, N. S. Jacobson, V. M. Follette, & M. J. Dougher (Eds.), *Acceptance and change: Content and context in psychotherapy* (pp. 125–142). Reno, NV: Context Press.

Coyne, J. C. (1976). Depression and the response of others. *Journal of Abnormal Psychology, 85,* 186–193.

Elkin, I., Shea, T., Watkins, J. T., Imber, S. D., Sotsky, S. M., Collins, J. F., Glass, D. R., Pilkonis, P. A., Leber, W. R., Fiester, S. J., Docherty, J., & Parloff, M. B. (1989). National Institute of Mental Health Treatment of Depression Collaborative Research Program. Archives of General Psychiatry, 46, 971–982.

Emanuels-Zuurveen, L., & Emmelkamp, P. M. G. (1996). Individual behavioral-cognitive therapy v. marital therapy for depression in maritally distressed couples. *British Journal of Psychiatry, 169,* 181–188.

Emmelkamp, P. M. G., Van Linden van der Heuvel, C. G., & Ruphan, M. (1988). Cognitive and behavioral interventions: A comparative evaluation with clinically distressed couples. Journal of Family Psychology, 1, 365–377.

Foley, S. H., Rounsaville, B. J., Weissman, M. M., Sholomaskas, D., & Chevron, E. (1989). Individual versus conjoint interpersonal therapy for depressed patients with marital disputes. *International Journal of Family Psychiatry, 10,* 29–42.

Gortner, E. T., Gollan, J. K., Dobson, K., & Jacobson, N. S. (1998). Cognitive-behavioral treatment for depression: Relapse prevention. *Journal of Consulting and Clinical Psychology, 66,* 377–384.

Gottman, J. M. (1994). *What predicts divorce: The relationship between marital processes and marital outcomes.* Hillsdale, NJ: Erlbaum.

Hahlweg, K., Schindler, L., Revenstorf, D., & Brengelmann, J. C. (1984). The Munich marital therapy study. In K. Hahlweg & N. S. Jacobson (Eds.), *Marital interaction: Analysis and modification* (pp. 3–26). New York: Guilford Press.

Hamilton, M. (1960). A rating scale for depression. *Journal of Neurology, Neurosurgery and Psychiatry, 23,* 56–62.

Horwitz, A. V., & White, H. R. (1991). Becoming married, depression, and alcohol problems among young adults. *Journal of Health and Social Behavior, 32,* 221–237.

Jacobson, N. S., & Christensen, A. (1996). *Integrative couple therapy: Promoting acceptance and change.* New York: Norton.

Jacobson, N. S., Christensen, A., Prince, S. E., Cordova, J. V., & Eldridge, K. (in press). Integrative behavioral couple therapy: An acceptance-based, promising new treatment for marital discord. *Journal of Consulting and Clinical Psychology.*

Jacobson, N. S., Dobson, K., Fruzzetti, A. E., Schmaling, K. B., & Salusky, S. (1991). Marital therapy and a treatment for depression. *Journal of Consulting and Clinical Psychology, 59,* 547–557.

Jacobson, N. S., Dobson. K. S., Truax, P. A., Addis, M. E., Koerner, K., Gollan, J. K., Gortner, E., & Prince, S. E. (1996). A component analysis of cognitive-behavioral treatment for depression. *Journal of Consulting and Clinical Psychology, 64,* 295–304.

Jacobson, N. S., Follette, W. C., & Pagel, M. (1986). Predicting who will benefit from behavioral marital therapy. *Journal of Consulting and Clinical Psychology, 54,* 518–522.

Jacobson, N. S., Fruzzetti, A. E., Dobson, K., Whisman, M., & Hops, H. (1993). Couple therapy as a treatment for depression: II. The effects of relationship quality and therapy on depressive relapse. *Journal of Consulting and Clinical Psychology, 61,* 516–519.

Jacobson, N S., & Margolin, G. (1979). *Marital therapy: Strategies based on social learning and behavior exchange principles.* New York: Brunner/Mazel.

Jacobson, N. S., Schmaling, K. B., & Holtzworth-Munroe, A. (1987). Component analysis of behavioral marital therapy: Two-year follow-up and prediction of relapse. *Journal of Marital and Family Therapy, 13,* 187–195.

Jarrett, R. B., Eaves, G. G., Grannemann, B. D., & Rush, A. J. (1991). Clinical, cognitive, and demographic predictors of response to cognitive therapy for depression: A preliminary report. *Psychiatry Research, 37,* 245–260.

Klerman, G. L., Weissman, M. M., Rounsaville, B. J., & Chevron, E. S. (1984). *Interpersonal psychotherapy of depression.* New York: Basic Books.

Lovejoy, M. C., & Busch, L. M. (1993). Emotional and behavioral responses to aversive interpersonal behaviors. *Journal of Abnormal Psychology, 102,* 494–497.

Markman, H. J., Duncan, S. W., Storaasli, R. D., & Howes, P. W. (1987). The prediction of marital distress: A longitudinal investigation. In K. Hahlweg & M. Goldstein (Eds.), *Understanding major mental disorder: The contribution of family interaction research* (pp. 266–289). New York: Family Process Press.

O'Leary, K. D., & Beach, S. R. (1990). Marital therapy: A viable treatment for depression and marital discord. *American Journal of Psychiatry, 147,* 183–186.

Ross, C. E. (1995). Reconceptualizing marital status as a continuum of social attachment. *Journal of Marriage and the Family, 57,* 129–140.

Schaefer, E. S., & Burnett, C. K. (1987). Stability and predictability of quality of women's marital relationships and demoralization. *Journal of Personality and Social Psychology, 53,* 1129–1136.

Schuster, T. L., Kessler, R. C., & Aseltine, R. H. (1990). Supportive interactions, negative interactions and depressed mood. *American Journal of Community Psychology, 18,* 423–438.

Shea, M. G., Elkin, I., Imber, S. D., Sotsky, S. M., Watkins, J. T., Collins, J. F., Pilkonis, P. A., Beckham, E., Glass, D. R., Dolan, R. T., & Parloff, M. B. (1992). Course of depressive symptoms over follow-up: Finding from the National Institute of Mental Health Treatment of Depression Collaborative Research Program. *Archives of General Psychiatry, 49,* 782–787.

Teichman, Y. (1997). Depression in a marital context. In S. Dreman (Ed.), *The family on the threshold of the 21st century: Trends and implications* (pp. 49–70). Mahwah, NJ: Erlbaum.

Teichman, Y., Bar-El, Z., Shor, H., Sirota, P., & Elizur, A. (1995). A comparison of two modalities of cognitive therapy (individual and marital) in treating depression. *Psychiatry, 58,* 136–148.

Teichman, Y., & Teichman, M. (1990). Interpersonal view of depression: Review and integration. *Journal of Family Psychology, 3,* 349–367.

Thase, M. E., & Simons, A. D. (1992). Cognitive behavior therapy and relapse of nonbipolar depression: Parallels with pharmacotherapy. *Psychopharmacology Bulletin, 28,* 117–122.

Waring, E. M., Chamberlaine, C. H., Carver, C. M., Stalker, C. A., & Schaefer, B. (1995). A pilot study of marital therapy as a treatment for depression. *American Journal of Family Therapy, 23,* 3–10.

Weiss, R. L., & Aved, B. M. (1978). Marital satisfaction and depression as predictors of physical health status. *Journal of Consulting and Clinical Psychology, 46,* 1379–1384.

Weissman, M. M. (1987). Advances in psychiatric epidemiology: Rates and risks for major depression. *American Journal of Public Health, 77,* 445–451.

11

Marital Therapy for Co-Occurring Marital Discord and Depression

Steven R. H. Beach

The rapid pace of development in the underpinnings of marital therapy for co-occurring marital discord and depression is well documented throughout this book. However, change suggests both progress and the possible need to reevaluate currently used forms of intervention. Has anything useful been learned? If so, how should researchers and clinicians modify, eliminate, or expand the various aspects of marital therapy for depression? At a minimum, thinking about intervention in the context of recent theoretical developments is likely to prompt developments in clinical techniques (see Beach & Fincham, 2000). Asking these questions is also an open acknowledgment that we are not yet where we need to be in our efforts to help couples who are struggling with co-occurring marital discord and depression.

Can we help improve the relationships of those with depression? Can we help relieve or prevent episodes of depression by helping clients develop stronger relationships? Can we reduce the misery level of depressed individuals who may be facing difficult interpersonal situations? Can we reverse the cycle of felt isolation, rejection, and hopelessness that is all too common for depressed individuals in discordant relationships and replace it with an expanding circle of health? Admittedly, these goals are lofty. Perhaps, as is suggested by Coyne and Benazon (chapter 2), the most enthusiastic among us may sometimes promise more than we know or more than we can deliver. Exaggerated claims, however, are not in the best interests of the field or of those who are suffering and in need of treatment. We will do far better for the field and for our clients to acknowledge what we know and admit what we do not know. This underscores the important contribution of careful attention to efficacy research (see O'Leary and Cano, chapter 9; Cordova and Gee, chapter 10). Focusing interventions on efficacious treatments provides useful benchmarks against which to measure success and a useful check on "false advertising."

Happily, recent research has led to considerable consensus regarding many basic issues, and this must be seen as encouraging at a theoretical level. There is consensus regarding the robust relationship between depression and marital discord (see Whisman, chapter 1; O'Leary and Cano, chapter 9; Cordova and Gee, chapter 10). There is growing consensus that the nature of this relationship is bidirectional (see Karney, chapter 3; Davila, chapter 4; Katz, chapter 6). And, there is consensus that marital discord may interact with personal vulnerabilities (Coyne and Benazon, chapter 2; Davila, chapter 4; Katz, chapter 6; Joiner, chapter 7), both in producing increased depressive symptoms and in generating increased interpersonal difficulties. Likewise, there is growing recognition of the likely familial precursors of depression and marital discord (Cummings, DeArth-Pendley, Schudlich, and Smith, chapter 5; Kaslow, Twomey, Brooks, Thompson, and Reynolds, chapter 8). These developments place marital interventions for depression on a firmer conceptual foundation than ever before. As a result, we have moved beyond the simplistic suggestion that marital discord alone is a sufficient explanation for depression and the potentially problematic view that marital partners cause depression (cf. Coyne and Benazon, chapter 2). Instead, the field appears to be gradually moving toward a consensus model that identifies personal vulnerabilities, interpersonal events, and causal loops as pivotal in understanding the emergence of co-occurring marital discord and depression.

The ongoing changes in the underpinnings of the field of marital processes and depression indicate that the field of marriage and depression is expanding and developing in a healthy manner (cf. Beach, Fincham, & Katz, 1998). From the clinical intervention standpoint, we can view these developments as auguring well for the future of the field and heralding positive developments regarding clinical applications. On the other hand, basic knowledge about close relationships and depression promises to outstrip current clinical wisdom. This suggests that neither behavioral marital therapy (BMT) for depression (see Beach, Sandeen, & O'Leary, 1990, for details) nor currently available empirically supported alternative approaches to marital therapy (see Baucom, Shoham, Mueser, Daiuto, & Stickle, 1998, for a list) are likely to capture the full range of possible techniques that may be useful in the treatment of co-occurring marital discord and depression. It seems likely that additional points of intervention remain to be identified and that, as clinicians and researchers continue to probe the interplay of interpersonal processes and depressive symptoms, new clinical interventions are likely to be forthcoming (see Joiner & Coyne, 1999, for a broader discussion of interpersonal processes in depression).

Meanwhile, a large population of depressed individuals need help with marital and family relationships (Whisman, chapter 1), and successful interventions for relationship problems may have a beneficial effect on recovery from depression (O'Leary and Cano, chapter 9; Cordova and Gee, chapter 10). The importance of these considerations notwithstanding, however, what may be more significant is that marital therapy has potentially important implications for easing suffering and misery. Helping depressed individuals improve their interpersonal relationships may be useful in reducing their symptoms even if it does not relieve the depressive episode. That is, clinicians should think about the use of marital therapy with some depressed clients, even if its only effect is to reduce the acute suffering associated with marital disputes. Marital disputes are not trivial events for individuals who are already experiencing depression, and having a better way to handle marital problems is likely to reduce symptoms substantially. To the extent that marital disputes are painful, and particularly so for depressed individuals, marital therapy may often be called for as a component of treatment for depression, whether or not it is intended to treat the depression. In addition, evidence has suggested that a substantial number of depressed individuals receiving marital therapy also will experience remission of their depressive symptoms (O'Leary and Cano, chapter 9; Cordova and Gee, chapter 10).

The focus of this chapter is BMT, an empirically supported treatment for marital difficulties that has been shown to be safe and effective for use with depressed individuals (Beach et al, 1998; Craighead, Craighead, & Ilardi, 1998).

Why Behavioral Marital Therapy?

BMT is an efficacious and specific treatment for marital discord (Baucom et al., 1998). It has been successfully applied cross-culturally (Hahlweg & Markman, 1988) and has been developed into a widely disseminated prevention program with readily available self-help books and videotapes (Markman, Stanley, & Blumberg, 1994). Recently, BMT has been reformulated for use within the context of managed care (Rathus & Sanderson, 1999). The Rathus and Sanderson treatment manual includes suggestions for dealing with third-party payers and session limitations. Accordingly, as a starting point for helping depressed individuals with relationship difficulties, BMT has the advantages of widespread availability, proven efficacy, and readily available advice regarding application within likely clinical constraints. These considerations suggest that BMT may be a good practical choice when selecting a framework to guide marital therapy for depression (see also Beach et al., 1990). However, marital therapy does not appear to be widely used in the treatment of depression. It may be presumed, then, that BMT for depression is also not widely used. Why is this?

Four Things Are Needed

To offer marital therapy as a component of a multifaceted intervention for depression, therapists need four things that have not been widely available. First, therapists need an understanding of depression that gives them the confidence necessary to use marital therapy when it is warranted and that helps them identify those clients who are most likely to benefit. Marital therapy for depression is unlikely to be used in the treatment of depression if it is difficult to discriminate between likely responders and nonresponders. Because it is widely understood that marital therapy will not be the treatment of choice for all depressed individuals who are married or in committed relationships, being able to make this determination is critical for good practice (but see Cordova and Gee, chapter 10, for an alternative). Second, therapists need a readily available justification for using marital therapy for depression when it is appropriate. Because most therapists do not work in isolation, their choice of therapeutic modality needs to be easily justified to colleagues and to those who may have decision-making authority in managed care organizations, third-party payers, or clinic settings. Marital therapy is unlikely to be used if doing so will elicit negative reactions from colleagues, supervisors, or administrators. Third, therapists need a description of at least one form of marital therapy for depression. Although familiarity with many forms of marital therapy may be useful, a solid grounding in at least one approach is critical for the successful application of marital therapy as a treatment for depression. Accordingly, a detailed description of techniques and an opportunity for supervised practice with their implementation seems important in preparing therapists to implement marital therapy for depression. Fourth, therapists need permission to be a part of creating the next generation of marital therapy for depression (Beach et al., 1998), including the creative generation of new techniques. Generating new techniques, particularly when these new techniques are grounded in basic research on marital or interpersonal processes in depression and do not contradict the larger aims of the overall program of intervention, is an excellent way for a practitioner to maintain his or her enthusiasm for working with a complex population. This chapter briefly addresses each of these needs and references more detailed discussions when appropriate.

Confidence in the Use of Marital Therapy for Depression

Is marital therapy for depression indicated when there is significant co-occurring marital distress that is a focus of current concern for the depressed individual? For nonpsychotic, nonbipolar outpatients, the answer appears to be a qualified yes (Beach et al., 1998; O'Leary and Cano, chapter 9). Marital therapy has proven to be a potent intervention for depression. Four outcomes studies found marital therapy superior to wait-list or equally as effective as cognitive therapy (CT) for the treatment of depression. These studies are described by O'Leary and Cano (chapter 9) and Cordova and Gee (chapter 10). Jointly, these outcomes studies provide good justification for the application of marital therapy to the treatment of depression. The reason the yes is qualified is that practical considerations, such as one spouse's unwillingness to attend conjoint therapy sessions, may preclude marital therapy in an unknown percentage of cases that might otherwise seem suitable (see Coyne and Benazon, chapter 2, for more discussion). However, data have indicated that BMT is as safe and effective when applied to depressed individuals as when applied to a broader population of maritally discordant couples. Accordingly, therapists should feel free to use BMT with depressed clients when marital therapy seems indicated.

Identifying Individuals Most Likely to Benefit From Marital Therapy for Depression

Salience of Marital Problems

One approach to the identification of depressed individuals likely to benefit from marital therapy is to examine the relative salience of marital problems in the individual's life. When marital problems are significant and of considerable concern to the depressed individual, it is likely to be useful to consider the potential merits of marital therapy.

In one variation of this approach, Beach and O'Leary (1992) contrasted pretherapy marital environment and pretherapy cognitive style as two potential predictors of treatment outcome. Depressed wives receiving individual CT did worse if they reported relatively more marital problems but relatively fewer cognitive errors (on the Cognitive Error Questionnaire; Lefebvre, 1980). In contrast, depressed wives receiving marital therapy did as well regardless of the salience of their pretreatment marital problems. These results suggest that within the overall population of discordant couples with a depressed partner, marital therapy is likely to be an increasingly good therapeutic strategy as the salience of marital problems increases. A caveat is that spouses who state a firm decision to leave the relationship are unlikely to be good candidates for marital therapy, and marital therapy would not be indicated even if marital problems were highly salient to the depressed spouse.

Perceived Etiology

A second possible approach for the identification of depressed individuals likely to benefit from the use of marital therapy for depression is to examine the individual's understanding of his or her difficulties and the way that he or she sees marital problems fitting in with them. In particular, it may be useful to identify the extent to which marital problems are seen as having preceded and contributed to the onset of the depressive episode.

Following this logic, O'Leary, Riso, and Beach (1990) attempted to predict differential responses to treatment from patient reports of order of problem onset (depression first or marital problems first). Women entering the treatment protocol were asked which problem came first, marital discord or depression. Depressed women who reported that marital problems preceded their depression had poor marital outcomes when assigned to CT, but more positive marital outcomes when assigned to marital therapy. These results suggest that if resources for providing marital therapy are limited, marital therapy should be provided first to those who report that their marital problems preceded their current depressive episode. Such individuals will commonly also state that they are depressed about the state of their marriage.

In another investigation of the predictive power of client perceptions, Addis and Jacobson (1996) examined the relationship between clients' reasons for depression and their responses to treatment. They found that clients who viewed relationship factors as strongly related to their depression responded less well to CT. These clients completed less CT homework, viewed CT as less helpful, and showed less improvement in their level of depressive symptoms. This work is in keeping with the assumption that therapy is less effective when there is a mismatch between client expectations and treatment model (Whisman, 1993). In addition, these results suggest once again that marital therapy for depression may be the treatment of choice when the client believes that marital problems are related to his or her depression.

Not Severity of Depression

It is natural to think that certain other symptoms or diagnostic factors might result in better or worse outcomes when marital therapy is attempted as a treatment for depression. For example, the results of the Treatment of Depression Collaborative Research Program (Elkin et al., 1989) suggested that CT might be a relatively ineffective treatment for severely depressed outpatients (but see Hollon et al., 1992, for a failure to replicate). Likewise, O'Leary, Sandeen, and Beach (1987) reported that, for practical reasons, it was difficult to conduct marital therapy when the depressed spouse was experiencing significant and persistent suicidal ideation. However, it does not appear that marital therapy for depression is contraindicated by higher levels of depressive symptoms (excluding acute suicidal ideation).

With a score of 30 on the Beck Depression Inventory (Beck, Steer, & Garbin, 1988) as the cutoff for severe depression (cf. Hollon et al., 1992), the recovery rate in the Beach and O'Leary (1992) sample did not differ as a function of severity for either CT or marital therapy (Beach, 1996). Although the issue of severity as a criterion for assignment to marital therapy may best be considered undetermined at present, there is no evidence to contraindicate marital therapy for moderately to severely depressed individuals or for those with dysthymia.

Decision Rules

Are there decision rules that may be used to help decide when BMT for co-occurring marital discord and depression is most likely to be useful as a primary intervention and when it is not? Again, the answer appears to be yes. BMT for depression (i.e., the approach outlined by Beach et al., 1990) is most useful when marital problems are salient to the depressed individual or the depressed individual believes that the marital problems caused the current depressive episode. Symptoms within the mild to moderate range or dysthymia may influence the ease of treatment (see Foley, Rounsaville, Weissman, Sholomaskas, & Chevron, 1989). However, these factors do not appear to diminish the outcomes of marital therapy for depression more than they diminish the outcomes of individual CT for depression (Beach, 1996). This suggests that severe symptoms or dysthymia do not automatically contraindicate the use of marital therapy for depression, nor do such symptoms preclude changes in the marital relationship.

In brief, BMT is a safe and effective intervention with proven efficacy in relieving marital discord. It can be used with depressed individuals and has been shown to relieve marital discord in this population. It is possible to identify individuals who believe their marital problems are related to their depression simply by inquiring about these issues, and such individuals appear to be good candidates for marital therapy for depression. For such individuals seen in an outpatient setting, marital therapy appears to enhance marital functioning and relieve depressive symptoms.

Justification for Using BMT in the Treatment of Depression

Once a couple has been identified as a good candidate for marital therapy for depression, the therapist must be ready to justify the decision to use one of the various approaches to marital therapy. This chapter details procedures from the BMT tradition. However, the available data can be used to justify the use of other forms of marital therapy as well.

Because most of the outcomes research on marital therapy for depression used some version of BMT, this form of marital therapy may be the easiest to justify to colleagues and third-party payers. The key to justifying other forms of marital therapy lies in identifying the mechanism of change. If the beneficial effects of marital therapy are attributable to enhanced marital satisfaction, then any approach to marital therapy that is able to produce enhanced marital satisfaction should be considered of potential benefit in the treatment of co-occurring marital discord and depression. If so, it is likely that a number of approaches to marital therapy could have beneficial effects.

Does enhancing marital satisfaction decrease depression? It appears that much of the effect of marital therapy on depression is mediated by enhanced marital satisfaction. Two studies, in particular, indicated that the effect of BMT on depression is mediated by changes in marital satisfaction. Beach and O'Leary (1992) found that posttherapy marital satisfaction fully accounted for the effect of marital therapy on depression. Likewise, Jacobson, Dobson, Fruzzetti, Schmaling, and Salusky (1991) found that marital adjustment and depression changed together for depressed individuals who received marital therapy, but not for those who received CT. Therefore, it appears that BMT for depression may reduce the level of depressive symptoms primarily by enhancing the marital environment, whereas CT appears to work through a different mechanism of change (i.e., cognitive change, see Whisman, 1993). Accordingly, although the issue is not settled, it seems likely that all efficacious approaches to marital therapy may have something to offer in the treatment of co-occurring marital discord and depression.

Baucom et al. (1998) reviewed the outcomes literature on marital therapy and indicated that BMT can be considered efficacious and better than several alternatives in the treatment of marital discord. This lends considerable support to the use of BMT for depression as outlined by Beach et al. (1990; see also Craighead et al., 1998). The Beach et al. version of BMT has the additional advantage of having been tailored to fit common circumstances of depressed individuals. At the same time, Baucom et al. (1998) found emotion-focused therapy (EFT) to be efficacious in the treatment of marital discord. Given the grounding of EFT in attachment theory, and the links between disrupted attachment and depression (see Anderson, Beach, & Kaslow, 1999; Cummings et al., chapter 5; Kaslow et al., chapter 8), EFT also should be considered a potentially viable form of treatment for discordant couples with a depressed partner. Finally, cognitive, insight-oriented, and strategic marital therapies have been found to be possibly efficacious in the treatment of marital discord as well. Accordingly, these therapies may provide useful interventions in the treatment of marital discord. They also may prove to be useful sources of additional interventions suggested by emerging lines of basic research (e.g., self-verification, stress generation, and emotional insecurity; see Davila, chapter 4; Cummings et al., chapter 5; Katz, chapter 6; Joiner, chapter 7).

BMT for Depression

BMT for depression (Beach et al., 1990) begins with a focus on increasing positive interactions. This focus was designed to directly enhance support provision within the marital dyad. In view of recent conceptual developments, this stage may also be thought of as attempting to enhance felt security in the relationship (e.g., Cummings et al., chapter 5) and helping the partners shift from defensive, prevention-oriented, avoidance goals and toward constructive, promotion-oriented, approach goals (Fincham & Beach, 1999). As a result, this initial stage of BMT for depression relies heavily on the BMT techniques for instigating positive behavioral exchanges through the use of caring items, positive communication, joint pleasant activities, and positive tracking. However, interventions aimed at providing a different and less blaming understanding of the partner's behavior (e.g., interventions from EFT, insight-oriented marital therapy, cognitive marital therapy, and integrative couples therapy) also might be useful at this stage. Interventions designed to provide the depressed spouse with a limited sick role might be useful early in therapy as well (see Coyne and Benazon, chapter 2).

Once some progress has been made in building positive, supportive interactions, the focus of BMT for depression shifts to restructuring the couple's approach to problem-oriented communication. This is to further reverse tendencies toward blame, coercion, and vicious cycles of interaction. At the same time, interventions at this stage are designed to introduce and foster collaboration within the dyad and protect the couple from falling back into well-established depressogenic patterns. This stage of BMT for depression uses many of the BMT techniques for communication and problem-solving training. However, recent conceptual developments have suggested the need to address as well expectations of negative partner behavior (Davila, chapter 4), long-standing tendencies to avoid potentially negative interpersonal situations (Joiner, chapter 7), and unintended confirmation by the spouse of dysfunctional beliefs the depressed individual may have about himself or herself (Katz, chapter 6).

The final stage of BMT for depression focuses on identifying potential obstacles to maintenance of gains. Because both depression and marital discord tend to recur (Coyne and Benazon, chapter 2), a focus on relapse prevention and strategies for coping with future relapse is an essential part of any marital approach to the treatment of co-occurring marital discord and depression. However, this stage of marital therapy for co-occurring marital discord and depression has received relatively little empirical attention.

Within each of the three stages of BMT for depression, therapists may be seen as attempting to intervene in one of two broad domains. However, because understanding of the targets or mediating goals of therapy is changing, the list of suggested techniques is likely to grow and evolve as well. Accordingly, the following suggestions may be viewed as proven techniques, but they should not be considered a final or exhaustive list of potentially useful techniques.

Increase Felt Security and Support in the Relationship

Promote Cohesion-Building Activities

The cohesiveness of a marriage can be thought of as the extent of positive interaction between the partners and may be indexed by such activities as simple displays of affection to one another or positive time in interaction with each other. This definition of cohesiveness is similar to Berscheid's (1983) definition of closeness in that it emphasizes the number of causal effects between the partners rather than their felt intensity. However, cohesive behaviors represent a subset of the causal sequences considered by Bersheid. Cohesiveness refers only to the positive activities that serve to bind the partners together. These positive causal connections are hypothesized to constitute a great reservoir of stability, familiarity, and positive experience. In addition, cohesive activities provide reassurance that occasional arguments or strained interactions with one's spouse or other family members are not as serious as they might otherwise seem.

Because cohesive activities are both reassuring and encouraging, they may have the effect of increasing felt security while decreasing defensiveness. As a result, increasing cohesive behaviors may serve as one strategy to activate approach goals and deactivate the defensive goals that often come to dominate the marital interactions of discordant couples (see Fincham & Beach, 1999), and may especially dominate the interaction of couples in which one partner is depressed. Interventions aimed at increasing couple cohesion by the prescription of activities such as caring gestures may therefore be particularly helpful in alleviating depression and may also improve collaboration between spouses. It is important that the behaviors prescribed by the therapist already be doable for the couple. That is, no new learning should be required. In addition, the activities suggested by the therapist should be small actions that can be repeated often. The goal of prescribing these small activities is to increase the frequency of positive, enjoyable experiences shared by the couple.

The therapist's main task is to present the assignment in a manner that facilitates a changed view of the partner and helps both spouses identify, prompt, recognize, and reward small, positive changes. It is useful, therefore, to emphasize that the goal of this assignment is to identify things that can convey the feelings of caring each spouse has for the other. Many spouses need considerable help in discovering what will convey caring to their partner. It often is helpful to have each spouse compile a list of small gestures or behaviors he or she can do to show his or her true caring for his or her partner. The therapist must ensure that these lists are conceptualized as menus rather than as demands and that listed items would indeed be perceived as showing caring. Moreover, spouses should be educated about the importance of engaging in these behaviors frequently, and of recognizing and responding positively when their partner displays them. Because many individuals come to therapy focused exclusively on the negative aspects of their spouse's behavior, helping discordant couples and couples with a depressed partner increase their positive activities typically requires considerable direction from the therapist. A number of suggestions for working with couples have been developed. More detailed suggestions regarding the enhancement of positive couple interactions may be found in Beach et al. (1990), Markman et al. (1994), and Rathus and Sanderson (1999).

Encourage Acceptance of Emotional Expression

A second target of intervention highlighted in BMT for depression is the opportunity to express one's feelings and to feel understood and accepted by one's partner. Feeling understood by one's partner is a key element of perceived support and one that should have a powerful effect on depressive symptoms (Beach, 1996). Importantly, it is disclosure of feelings to one's partner and the perception that one's partner will be accepting of that disclosure of one's feelings that is most uniformly protective against depression (Cutrona, 1996). Activities related to expression of feelings and the belief that the spouse will be accepting and appropriately responsive also may be understood as helping the depressed spouse view his or her partner as a more secure target of attachment. For many depressed individuals, however, there is a strong perception that their partner will not listen to their concerns or that if he or she does listen, his or her reaction will not be appropriately responsive. Moreover, in the context of marital discord and depression, this perception may be a relatively accurate reflection of the partner's likely reaction. This is why it may be advantageous to work with the couple conjointly and direct interventions toward enhancing listening skills in the dyad. Such interventions often can function to improve both reported marital satisfaction and mood.

Husbands of depressed wives often show a minimal response to their wives' complaints. Thus, empathic listening can be introduced as one way for spouses to better understand each other. Empathic listening skills training may begin with a brief didactic overview of the listening skills of summarizing, reflecting, validating, and question asking. The therapist typically models the skills for the couple, and then the spouses practice the skills with feedback from the therapist. Because good empathic listening may decrease unnecessary misunderstandings, these skills may decrease the perceived need to solve problems or make changes in the relationship, leading both partners to feel more secure and to perceive the other as more committed to the relationship.

Markman et al. (1994) provided an extended discussion of these issues (see also their videotaped PREP materials, which may be used as an adjunct to marital therapy for depression). Another resource to guide communication training is the self-help manual developed by Fincham, Fernandes, and Humphreys (1993). This manual has many useful forms and suggestions for initiating communication training. One particularly useful form suggested by Fincham et al. is the therapy contract, which provides a structured way of initiating communication training while ensuring that both partners are ready to move forward with this approach. In addition, the provision by the therapist of a good formulation of the couple's problems may be useful in fostering greater acceptance of the depressed spouse's emotional disclosures (see Cordova and Gee, chapter 10; Jacobson & Christensen, 1996).

Actual and perceived coping assistance offered by a depressed individual's spouse buffers stress and can protect against depression, particularly when it matches the needs of the depressed individual (Cutrona, 1996). Joint problem solving and improved communication between spouses often will allow the nondepressed spouse to offer concrete assistance in a way that seems responsive and appropriate to the depressed spouse. This may help decrease depressive symptoms by providing the depressed individual with an enhanced sense of environmental mastery (cf. Joiner, chapter 7), or it may work by increasing felt security in the relationship (cf. Cummings et al., chapter 5). Aid that is perceived as responsive may also increase the perceived commitment of the partner and further decrease defensiveness within the relationship (see also Stanley, 1998).

Enhancing a couple's joint problem-solving skills typically begins by conveying a basic problem-solving attitude. It is important that the therapist convey that problems are a normal part of married life, that marital problems have solutions (or partial solutions) worth searching for, and that win–win solutions are always preferable to outcomes in which one spouse "loses." In addition to mobilizing hope, this type of introduction to problem solving also may help deactivate defensiveness and encourage teamwork. As has been suggested by work on positive life events in remission from depression (e.g., Brown, Adler, & Bifulco, 1988), a believable promise of positive change can prompt substantial change in mood and may be critical for improvement in depressive episodes that have lasted for more than 6 months. Importantly, couples should not be encouraged to engage in a problem-solving discussion until they both feel that they understand the other's perspective and that their perspective has been understood (see Markman et al., 1994, for more discussion of this point).

The problem definition stage is especially important for discordant couples. Because of depressed individuals' tendencies to perceive and talk about negative events in global, general terms, it is particularly important that couples be helped to make their concerns as concrete and specific as possible. This increases the chances that brainstorming will result in the couple generating useful potential solutions to their problems. Likewise, it is important that depressed couples not discount possible solutions out of hand. In some cases, the best solution will involve something the couple has not done because they simply assumed it could not work. Indeed, it is useful for the therapist to ask about solutions that the couple has already considered but rejected. In some cases the rejected solutions will turn out to be excellent foundations for a workable solution. Finally, after the couple learns to select and implement solutions, it is important that the therapist be involved in teaching them how to effectively evaluate the outcomes of their solutions (see Fincham et al., 1993; Markman et al., 1994; or Rathus & Sanderson, 1999, for more detailed suggestions).

Increase Self-Esteem Support

Self-esteem support is generally considered to include behaviors such as expression appreciation, complimenting, and noticing positive traits in the spouse or other family members. Interestingly, in a study conducted by Vanfossen (1986), affirmation was the variable that was most strongly and consistently related to feelings of well-being for wives. This type of support may be particularly important to wives because they tend to be more self-critical than husbands (Carver & Ganellen, 1983). Moreover, it is more common for wives to feel unappreciated by their husbands and for discordant wives to actually receive less in the way of nonverbal positive behaviors from their husbands (Noller, 1987). Likewise, an individual's perception that his or her spouse is overly critical or negative can promote relapse of depression (see Whisman, chapter 1). In contrast, when partners are appreciative, complimentary, and affirming, threats to self-esteem or minor criticisms even from one's partner are more easily tolerated. This may be important in facilitating effective problem solving. As difficult problems are approached and resolved, it is useful for both partners to understand that disagreements need not imply that their partner no longer values them.

It is important to focus on each spouse's ability to notice positive attributes and behaviors in the other and to comment on them openly. This form of positive communication typically is presented as expressing what is normally taken for granted. The therapist's task is to help spouses verbalize sincere positive feelings about their partner, in the form of thanks, acknowledgments, or compliments. Couching the assignment as expressing sincere positive feelings and reactions helps to keep the positive verbalizations believable and avoids the potentially negative effects of overly positive or overly vague positive comments (see Katz, chapter 6). The therapist may need to prompt spouses to compliment each other and explain the importance of noticing and commenting on things they like.

The therapist can explain that being able to express positive feelings and appreciation is important both for helping to keep the marriage healthy and for providing each partner with a more accurate view of himself or herself and the relationship. This intervention is especially powerful when it follows the instigation of cohesive behaviors, as described earlier. In this case, the therapist can talk about ways to "let your partner know that you are noticing the positive changes that are occurring in your relationship." Or, the therapist may say "It is hard to keep doing positive things if you are not sure it makes any difference to anyone" or "Noticing the positive things your partner does helps your partner know he/she is on the right track and helps you allow those positive things to have an impact on your mood." A natural extension of this assignment is "Let your partner know other positive things you notice about him/her." Accordingly, noticing positive things can lead to complimenting the spouse in other ways.

Enhance Spousal Dependability and Perceived Partner Commitment

Another aspect of social support is spousal dependability. It has been hypothesized (Beach, Fincham, Katz, & Bradbury, 1996) that the most important aspect of social support may not be supportive behavior that actually occurs, but rather the perception that supportive others would be available if they were needed. In particular, this may take the form of believing that one's partner is committed to the relationship and will not leave just because things are difficult in the relationship (see also Stanley, 1998). Such a perception may directly increase an individual's perceived control over his or her environment, thereby reducing reactivity to stressful situations. It also may make giving up a self-defensive stance toward one's partner and adopting a more cooperative pattern of interaction seem more reasonable.

Establishing an increased sense of spousal dependability sometimes occurs as an outgrowth of other positive changes in the relationship over the course of marital therapy for depression. When it does not occur spontaneously, however, it is important to address this issue directly (see also Markman et al., 1994; Stanley, Trathen, McCain, & Bryan 1998).

Enhancing the depressed individual's perception that his or her partner is dependable and committed to the relationship may require helping the spouse express his or her commitment in clear, direct ways. However, it also may require attention to dysfunctional attributions of blame for negative, old behaviors that prevent one spouse from giving the other credit for the positive, new behaviors that have been resulted from therapy. In line with attributional accounts of marital dysfunction (Fincham, Beach, & Nelson, 1987), it has been found that it is possible to decrease blame by helping partners develop a less blaming view of each other's motivations. In particular, if partner behavior can be seen as being merely self-defensive and automatic, or if the partner can be seen as experiencing little choice in what he or she did, old hurts can be more readily forgiven (cf. Cordova and Gee, chapter 10; Jacobson & Christensen, 1996; Notarius, Lashley, & Sullivan, 1997). Often, in the aftermath of positive and constructive marital change, spouses are willing to review and change previous constructions about their partner's behavior and accept more benign interpretations.

Several interventions have been proposed to help increase the perception of spousal dependability and commitment. Some of these techniques were described by Markman et al. (1994) in their discussion of commitment. For example, they proposed that encouraging couples to discuss feelings of hurt or to directly raise and discuss the issue of commitment may be a useful approach to increasing commitment. Likewise, Jacobson and Christensen (1996) raised the possibility that having the therapist provide a couple with a new understanding of their problems may have the potential to increase perceived availability and commitment (see also Cordova and Gee, chapter 10).

Increase Intimacy and Confiding

A final aspect of social support that is emphasized in BMT for depression is increased spousal intimacy. In this context, intimacy refers to a relationship state in which spouses' innermost feelings, thoughts, and dispositions can be revealed and explored (cf. Waring, 1988; see Prager, 1995, for a more comprehensive discussion). Interventions designed to increase intimacy have been related to decreased depression (see Cordova and Gee, chapter 10). Taking a risk by sharing thoughts, feelings, and beliefs can be a powerful mood elevator and can engender or rekindle strong feelings of attraction and love. Conversely, sharing one's feelings but receiving criticism or rejection may lead to intense dysphoria or anger. When there is marital discord, the loss of trust engendered by the ongoing discord may serve to inhibit self-disclosure. Moreover, when a spouse does self-disclose or share reactions, the probability of a rejecting response from his or her partner is likely to be higher in a discordant marriage than in a nondiscordant one. Given depressed individuals' tendency to avoid negative outcomes and their anticipation of negative partner behavior (see Davila, chapter 4), one might anticipate a general pattern of withdrawal from marital conflict, which could, in turn, lead to further marital deterioration (Gottman & Krokoff, 1989; McGonagle, Kessler, & Gotlib, 1993). Therefore, given the context of avoidance of significant marital issues, it could be expected that intimacy would be particularly vulnerable to deterioration.

For many couples, intimate self-disclosures will begin to occur more frequently as a natural outgrowth of the marital interventions outlined above aimed at improving listening and speaking skills and engendering a calmer, more cohesive marital atmosphere. However, on occasion, despite gains in other areas, couples lack the usual settings for relaxed, positive self-disclosure and other intimate exchanges. In these cases the therapist may need to help the couple begin to develop new routines that create comfortable, natural relaxed time together. More specifically, the therapist may focus on helping the couple structure their time to allow for shared mealtimes, a common bedtime, shared time over tea or coffee, or other regular times together. When such settings are lacking, the therapist might consider encouraging the couple to develop new daily routines that produce such shared time. Additional suggestions for increasing intimacy have been proposed by Prager (1995) and by Markman et al. (1994). It should be noted that engendering such shared routines also may be a necessary precursor for work on enhancing sexuality in the marital relationship, another venue for intimacy that is problematic for many discordant, depressed spouses.

Decrease Defensiveness, Coercive Cycles, and Stress in the Marriage

Depressed individuals report feeling vulnerable to marriage-related stress; stress related to the marital and parenting relationships have been found to represent prominent concerns for depressed individuals (Bothwell & Weissman, 1977); and stress within the family has been found to be related to level of depressive symptoms (Beach, Martin, Blum, & Roman, 1993). Accordingly, when high-intensity stressors such as marital violence (see Kaslow et al., chapter 8; O'Leary and Cano, chapter 9) can be identified and are occurring within the marriage, they need to be given priority in treatment. When not addressed, such stressors block an individual's recovery.

There are several patterns of marital behavior that are chronic, negative, and threatening and that commonly occur in discordant couples and couples with a depressed spouse. Marital patterns involving the following should be addressed: (a) verbal and physical aggression (see O'Leary and Cano, chapter 9); (b) threats of separation or divorce; and (c) explicitly denigrating references, severe criticism, and blame (see also Davila, chapter 4; Katz, chapter 5). It is important to note that because negative exchanges of this sort typically are reciprocated, these incidents may exacerbate feelings of depression regardless of who initiates the exchange. There often are other idiosyncratic areas that function as major stressors for a particular couple. These patterns may be perceived as intensely stressful by a given couple or individual and cannot be ignored simply because they do not fit into one of previously mentioned categories.

Eliminate Overt Hostility and Verbal and Physical Aggression

The results of a number of studies have demonstrated that discordant, depressed couples show considerable hostility and tension in their interactions (see Whisman, chapter 1). There are couples in which long periods of perceived isolation and relative silence are punctuated by outbursts of accusation and recrimination. Even more destructive is a pattern that involves rapidly escalating arguments culminating in violence. Interaction patterns of this type leave even nondepressed spouses exhausted and drained. For depressed spouses, they provide a level of stress well above what is conducive to reduction of depressive symptoms. For recovered individuals, this pattern may lead to relapse of depression. Yet, depressed individuals are likely to find themselves locked in coercive patterns of stressful interaction with both their spouses and their children (Biglan et al., 1985; Hops et al., 1987; Davila, chapter 4). Thus, a pattern of high-intensity arguments associated with verbal or physical abuse, whether between spouses or involving children, should be an early target of treatment. Recent work by O'Leary and colleagues suggested that both individual and couple formats that focus on violence might be useful in reducing this troubling pattern (see O'Leary and Cano, chapter 9).

Address Threats of Separation or Divorce

Another stressor associated with marital discord is the fear of separation. Discordant couples often are plagued by a sense of uncertainty about the future of their relationship. A frequent concern of couples entering therapy is that if the problems they are experiencing are not quickly resolved, separation may be imminent. Accordingly, concerns about divorce often represent a significant element linking marital discord to stress. This uncertainty about the future of the relationship often can be conceptualized as a low level of perceived spousal dependability, to be dealt with in due course during marital therapy or to be addressed by a careful formulation of the couple's problems. However, when spouses use the threat of divorce as a potent way of underscoring a point during disagreements, particularly when this is done in front of their children, it is a stressor deserving early attention in therapy.

For the depressed spouse, the idea of divorce can create ambivalence. On one hand, the notion of divorce can represent escape and surcease of conflict; whereas, on the other hand, the idea of separation or divorce can be extremely threatening given the elevated dependency needs characteristic of many depressed individuals. For the nondepressed spouse, the threat of divorce may be a realistic representation of his or her level of frustration with his or her depressed partner. The threat of divorce also helps create needed distance from the spouse and thus may be reinforced in the short run. Thus, explicit statements about divorce or actions that strongly imply thoughts of divorce can become established aspects of a couple's ongoing interaction in the context of discord and depression. Such events are not uncommon and can be disruptive to therapy if not addressed promptly. Accordingly, if this pattern is observed, it should be an early direct target of intervention.

Reduce Explicitly Denigrating Spousal References, Severe Criticism, and Blame

As discussed above, it is clear that feedback from one's spouse plays an important role in self-evaluation. Thus, chronic denigrating or devaluing statements by one spouse about the other take a considerable toll on the spouse's self-esteem over time. In addition, recent work has underscored the potential for devaluing statements or behavior to intensify the effect of a depressed individual's low self-esteem (Katz, chapter 6). In the context of depression and marital discord, the devaluation of one partner by the other can escalate from being nonverbal and implicit to being stated directly in harsh and uncompromising terms. A spouse may refer to the depressed spouse in vulgar terms or may explicitly call him or her lazy, worthless, and bad. At low levels, this type of behavior can be viewed as representing a lack of self-esteem support or affirmation. As such, it may recede as positive interactions are encouraged throughout therapy. However, when a shift occurs from low-level stress to the high-level stress of explicit denunciation, devaluation represents a major stressor, a threat to remission of depressive symptoms, and a likely source of relapse. As such, it must be managed explicitly and very early in therapy (see Beach et al., 1990, for more detailed suggestions).

Summary

Severe marital stressors may require attention before attempts to facilitate a positive focus or establish new communication and problem-solving patterns can be made. Alternatively, couples may be on good behavior early in therapy and so may not report certain problems until later in therapy. In either case, the therapist faces the task of helping the couple eliminate an entrenched pattern and replace it with something new. Marital therapy techniques emerging from the strategic, object relations, and behavioral traditions have been reported to help in such cases. Interestingly, these approaches share the view that neither partner is to be blamed for the marital problems, although partners are encouraged to view themselves as responsible for changing (see O'Leary and Cano, chapter 9). Accordingly, as therapists work with especially challenging cases, it may be useful to keep this principle in mind.

In summary, identifying major stressors in the marriage or family early in therapy and either reducing them or decreasing their perceived impact is critical if a positive focus is to emerge in the early phase of therapy. Accordingly, careful assessment of the more common major stressors outlined above as well as of couple-specific stressors should have high priority in the initial sessions of therapy.

Search for New Targets of Intervention in Marital Therapy for Depression

One implication of the research reviewed in the other chapters of this book is that marital therapy for depression should be expanded to include new targets of intervention and should be open to new ways of dealing with common impasses or patterns that may lock couples in cycles of depression and discord. Especially important will be new techniques that better target reciprocal processes connecting marriage and depression, such as negative verification, reassurance seeking and feedback seeking, and stress generation. These processes can act as building blocks for potentially vicious cycles that may cause longer or more serious episodes of depression. Because these processes may not be addressed adequately in current versions of marital therapy for depression (or in current individual therapy approaches), they represent an opportunity for collaboration between clinicians and researchers in the search for ways to further enhance the effectiveness of marital approaches to the treatment of depression.

Negative Verification

Negative verification refers to marital interactions that may not be reported as negative but nonetheless may inhibit the recovery process. In particular, spousal agreement with negative self-beliefs may intensify the effect of those self-beliefs. However, negative verification may be relatively invisible to both partners because it does not cause distress and may not be associated with conflict. Therefore, to identify negative self-verification processes, the therapist may need to assess for areas in which the depressed spouse makes global negative evaluations of himself or herself and views his or her partner as agreeing with those negative evaluations. All such cases of perceived spousal negative verification are likely to merit attention. In cases in which a perception is incorrect (i.e., the partner does not agree with the negative self-evaluation), intervention may take the form of a special case of cognitive therapy (e.g., helping the depressed spouse examine his or her distorted beliefs within a supportive framework). In cases in which the partner does agree, however, it is important that the therapist develop interventions to help the nondepressed spouse's evaluation change in conjunction with the depressed spouse's self-evaluation. In addition, there may be opportunities to identify areas in which the depressed spouse has positive self-beliefs but views his or her partner as overlooking or not agreeing with them. In such instances, there may be the opportunity for the therapist to use the spouse to reinforce beliefs that are changing positively and therefore increase their impact.

Reassurance Seeking and Feedback Seeking

Reassurance seeking and *feedback seeking* refer to requests from the depressed spouse that may be unanswerable. Depressed individuals may ask repeatedly for reassurance from their partners that the partners are not tired of them. Repeated instances of this request can become tiring and then the reassurance seeking becomes a source of the feared outcome (see Joiner & Coyne, 1999). Such requests may serve to decrease empathy from the nondepressed spouse. For example, some depressed individuals are preoccupied with concerns that their spouse may leave them, and anxiety about the spouse leaving may intensify the depressogenic effects of marital distress. The therapeutic challenge associated with reassurance seeking and feedback seeking is to provide the nondepressed spouse with some way to handle such a request and to short-circuit his or her likely negative reaction. In many cases, providing an explanation of the negative reaction may prove useful (e.g., Kobak, Ruckdeschel, & Hazan, 1994; Notarius et al., 1997). In this approach, the nondepressed spouse is encouraged to understand his or her negative reaction to the request for reassurance or feedback as an automatic response to a partner behavior that is perceived as threatening the relationship or the self. This provides a nonblaming way to understand the tendency to be rejecting of the depressed spouse and can set the stage for a more functional alternative response to reassurance seeking or feedback seeking from the depressed spouse.

After identifying that he or she has negative reactions to reassurance seeking or feedback seeking, the nondepressed spouse may be provided with new responses that provide support at a general level but do not encourage either reassurance seeking or feedback seeking. In particular, the partner may be encouraged to provide both statements of affection and compliments spontaneously, but not to provide either reassurance or feedback in response to reassurance seeking or feedback seeking. Such an intervention might decrease the depressed spouse's preoccupation while simultaneously decreasing the nondepressed partner's desire to withdraw. To be effective, however, an intervention of this sort must involve both partners and be presented as a collaborative effort to reduce depressive symptoms.

Stress Generation

Depressed individuals may also benefit from new interventions designed to reduce their contribution to ongoing marital difficulties (e.g., stress generation). Interventions designed to remedy depression-specific obstacles to problem solving and support provision in marriage are likely to be particularly important in the next generation of marital interventions for depression. Although effective marital treatments for depression already include both problem-solving and communication-training components, interventions addressing stress generation focus particular attention on the depressed individual's negative expectations for problem-solving interactions and tendency to criticize. Because many distressed couples reciprocate negative behaviors, negative expectations and criticism may prompt either a destructive pattern of partner behavior or lead to spousal verification of a negative self-view. Accordingly, new interventions to reduce negative behavior from the depressed spouse to his or her partner seem warranted.

Emanuels-Zuurveen and Emmelkamp (1996) raised the possibility that existing communication-focused interventions may have some effect in reducing partner-directed criticism. Likewise, because problem-solving training is well designed to interrupt coercive cycles associated with depression (Beach, Whisman, & O'Leary, 1994), it may be that techniques already used in BMT interrupt the stress-generating patterns associated with depression or related personal characteristics.

Emotional Security Enhancement

Although enhancing emotional security has been an implicit goal of BMT for depression, this construct has assumed increasing prominence in recent research. Particularly when depression is examined from an attachment perspective, reestablishing a felt sense of emotional security assumes a central role in marital therapy for depression. Accordingly, it may be useful to consider techniques with the potential to more rapidly and powerfully address concerns related to emotional security. For example, it may be useful to consider marital therapy techniques proposed by attachment theorists (e.g., Greenberg & Johnson, 1988; Kobak et al., 1994) or techniques proposed in the context of integrative couples therapy (Jacobson & Christensen, 1996). Alternatively, it may be that the use of religious metaphor (Stanley, 1998) or a direct focus on the enhancement of intimacy (Prager, 1995) may prove useful in stabilizing or enhancing emotional security for some couples. Whatever the approach, efforts to more reliably influence emotional security seem likely to remain an important focus of efforts to enhance marital therapy for depression.

Concurrent Antidepressant Medication

Sometimes a marital therapist will be the first professional to see a depressed individual or possibly the first mental health professional to recognize that he or she is depressed. In such cases, the issue of referral for antidepressant treatment arises. Antidepressants are widely used, and the newer generations of antidepressant medications are relatively well tolerated. Although some depressed individuals show a strong initial bias against medication, this often can be overcome with encouragement from the therapist. However, some depressed individuals will get better without antidepressant medication, and for some, marital therapy alone will be sufficient. How is a marital therapists to decide when to refer a depressed client for medication and when to take a wait-and-see approach?

Reviews of the literature (e.g., Thase et al., 1997) have suggested that medication may be particularly strongly indicated when the depressed individual has a history of severe or recurrent depression. More recently, Whisman and Ubelacker (1999) suggested that antidepressant medication might be a useful adjunct to marital therapy for depression when the depressed spouse has marked difficulty with emotional regulation. In particular, antidepressants may help some depressed spouses reduce feelings of anger and resentment, enabling them to engage more fully in marital therapy. O'Leary, Sandeen, and Beach (1987) suggested that individual or pharmacological approaches were preferable to marital therapy for actively suicidal patients. Accordingly, although considerable additional research is needed before there is clear guidance on the best ways to combine antidepressant medication and marital therapy, some guidelines may be inferred from the available literature. First, if the depressed spouse has recurrent or severe depressive episodes, the marital therapist should encourage a trial of antidepressant medication. Second, if the depressed spouse has marked difficulty in emotional regulation, the potential usefulness of antidepressant medication should be discussed. Finally, because it is always useful to underscore that many options are available to depressed clients, it is likely to be useful for the therapist to mention the possibility of referral for medication or for individual therapy to all depressed clients (see Beach et al., 1990). In addition, if clients being seen for marital therapy do not show improvement in mood within the first 4 to 6 weeks of therapy, the therapist should probably raise again the possibility of referral for a trial of antidepressant medication.

Conclusion

Marital therapy appears to have a role in the treatment of depressed individuals who are in discordant marital relationships. However, the appropriate use of marital therapy in the treatment of co-occurring marital discord and depression has been hampered by four key factors. There has been a lack of confidence, a lack of good sources of information about marital therapy approaches, difficulty justifying the use of marital therapy to decision makers, and a lack of openness to innovation. These four problems have led to hesitancy by therapists to use marital therapy techniques. This chapter addressed each of these potential obstacles.

The efficacy of BMT in the treatment of co-occurring marital discord and depression notwithstanding, the development of new and more powerful marital interventions for depression should remain a top priority for clinical scientists studying marital and family processes in depression. Meanwhile, the available efficacy literature has indicated that BMT may be considered a safe and effective intervention for marital discord. For couples with salient marital problems that appear to be related to ongoing depression or depressive symptoms, marital therapy for depression (Beach et al., 1990) appears to be an excellent foundation for beginning a course of marital therapy. Because direct tests of this approach also have suggested that it is effective in treating depression, it has additional credibility as a first approach to marital therapy when one of the partners is depressed. On the other hand, because process research has suggested that much of the benefit of BMT for depression derives from its ability to enhance marital satisfaction, it appears that any marital therapy capable of enhancing marital satisfaction for depressed individuals also may be useful in the treatment of depression. Likewise, recent empirical work identifying new potential targets of intervention suggested the value of remaining open to new techniques. In addition, marital therapy has yet to be adequately tested in combination with pharmacological approaches to treatment. It can be hoped, therefore, that even as marital therapy for depression becomes more widely available and used, the modality will continue to evolve along with the scientific evolution of the field.

References

Addis, M. E., & Jacobson, N. S. (1996). Reasons for depression and the process and outcome of cognitive-behavioral psychotherapies. *Journal of Consulting and Clinical Psychology, 64,* 1417–1424.

Anderson, P., Beach, S. R. H., & Kaslow, N. J. (1999). Marital discord and depression: Exploring the potential of attachment theory to guide clinical intervention. In T. Joiner & J. C. Coyne (Eds.), *The interactional nature of depression: Advances in interpersonal approaches.* (pp. 271–298). Washington, DC: American Psychological Association.

Baucom, D. H., Shoham, V., Mueser, K. T., Daiuto, A. D., & Stickle, T. R. (1998). Empirically supported couple and family interventions for marital distress and adult mental health problems. *Journal of Consulting and Clinical Psychology, 66,* 53–88.

Beach, S. R. H. (1996). Marital therapy in the treatment of depression. In C. Mundt, M. J. Goldstein, K. Hahlweg, & P. Fiedler (Eds.), *Interpersonal factors in the origin and course of affective disorders* (pp. 341–361). Gaskell: London.

Beach, S. R. H., & Fincham, F. D. (2000). Marital therapy and social psychology: Will we choose partnership or cyptomnesia? In G. Fletcher & M. Clark (Eds.), *Blackwell handbook of social psychology: Vol. 2, Interpersonal processes.* Oxford, UK: Blackwell.

Beach, S. R. H., Fincham, F. D., & Katz, J. (1998). Marital therapy in the treatment of depression: Toward a third generation of therapy and research. *Clinical Psychology Review, 18,* 635–661.

Beach, S. R. H., Fincham, F. D., Katz. J., & Bradbury, T. N. (1996). Social support in marriage: A cognitive perspective. In G. R. Pierce, B. R. Sarason, & I. G. Sarason (Eds.), *The handbook of social support and the family* (pp. 43–65). New York: Plenum.

Beach, S. R. H., Martin, J. K., Blum, T. C., & Roman, P. M. (1993). Effects of marital and co-worker relationships on negative affect: Testing the central role of marriage. *American Journal of Family Therapy, 21,* 312–322.

Beach, S. R. H., & O'Leary, K. D. (1992). Treating depression in the context of marital discord: Outcome and predictors of response for marital therapy vs. cognitive therapy. *Behavior Therapy, 23,* 507–528.

Beach, S. R. H., Sandeen, E. E., & O'Leary, K. D. (1990). *Depression in marriage: A model for etiology and treatment.* New York: Guilford Press.

Beach, S. R. H., Whisman, M., & O'Leary, K. D. (1994). Marital therapy for depression: Theoretical foundation, current status, and future directions. *Behavior Therapy, 25,* 345–372.

Beck, A. T., Steer, R. A., & Garbin, M. G. (1988). Psychometric properties of the Beck Depression Inventory: Twenty-five years of evaluation. *Clinical Psychology Review, 8,* 77–100.

Berscheid, E. (1983). Emotion. In H. H. Kelley, E. Berscheid, A. Christensen, J. H. Harvey, T. L. Huston, G. Levinger, E. McClintock, L. A. Peplau, & D. R. Peterson (Eds.), *Close relationships.* New York: Freeman Press.

Biglan, A., Hops, H., Sherman, L., Friedman, L. S., Arthur, J., & Osteen, V. (1985). Problem-solving interactions of depressed women and their spouses. *Behavior Therapy, 16,* 431–451.

Bothwell, S., & Weissman, M. M. (1977). Social impairments four years after an acute depressive episode. *American Journal of Orthopsychiatry, 47,* 231–237.

Brown, G. W., Adler, Z., & Bifulco, A. (1988). Life events. Difficulties and recovery from chronic depression. *British Journal of Psychiatry, 152,* 487–498.

Carver, C. S., & Ganellen, R. J. (1983). Depression and components of self-punitiveness: High standards, self-criticism, and over-generalization. *Journal of Abnormal Psychology, 92,* 330–337.

Craighead, W. E., Craighead, L. W., & Ilardi, S. S. (1998). Psychosocial treatments of major depressive disorder. In P. E. Nathan & J. M. Gorman (Eds.), *A guide to treatments that work* (pp. 226–239). Oxford, UK: Oxford University Press.

Cutrona, C. E. (1996). *Social support in couples.* New York: Sage.

Elkin, I., Shea, T., Watkins, J. T., Imber, S. D., Sotsky, S. M., Collins, J. F., Glass, D. R., Pilkonis, P. A., Leber, W. R., Docherty, J. P., Fiester, S. J., & Parloff, M. B. (1989). National Institute of Mental

Health Treatment of Depression Collaborative Research Program. *Archives of General Psychiatry, 46,* 971–982.

Emanuels-Zuurveen, L., & Emmelkamp, P. M. G. (1996). Individual behavioral-cognitive therapy v. marital therapy for depression in maritally distressed couples. *British Journal of Psychiatry, 169,* 181–188.

Fincham, F. D. & Beach, S. R. H. (1999). Conflict in marriage. *Annual Review of Psychology, 50,* 47–77.

Fincham, F. D., Beach, S. R. H., & Nelson, G. (1987). Attribution processes in distressed and nondistressed couples: 3. Causal and responsibility attributions for spouse behavior. *Cognitive Therapy and Research, 11,* 71–86.

Fincham, F. D., Fernandes, L. O. L., & Humphreys, K. (1993). *Communicating in relationships.* Champaign, IL: Academic Press.

Foley, S. H., Rounsaville, B. J., Weissman, M. M., Sholomaskas, D., & Chevron, E. (1989). Individual versus conjoint interpersonal therapy for depressed patients with marital disputes. *International Journal of Family Psychiatry, 10,* 29–42.

Gottman, J. M., & Krokoff, L. J. (1989). Marital interaction and satisfaction: A longitudinal view. *Journal of Consulting and Clinical Psychology, 57,* 47–52.

Greenberg, L. S., & Johnson, S. M. (1988). *Emotionally focused therapy for couples.* New York: Guilford Press.

Hahlweg, K., & Markman, H. J. (1988). Effectiveness of behavioral marital therapy: Empirical status of behavioral techniques in preventing and alleviating marital distress. *Journal of Consulting and Clinical Psychology, 56,* 440–447.

Hollon, S. D., Derubeis, R. J., Evans, M. D., Weimer, M. J., Garvey, M. J., Grove, W. M., & Tuason, V. B. (1992). Cognitive therapy and pharmacotherapy for depression: Singly and in combination. *Archives of General Psychiatry, 49,* 774–781.

Hops, H., Biglan, A., Sherman, L., Arthur, J., Friedman, L., & Osteen, V. (1987). Home observation of family interactions of depressed women. *Journal of Consulting and Clinical Psychology, 55,* 341–346.

Jacobson, N. S., & Christensen, A. (1996). *Integrative couple therapy: Promoting acceptance and change.* New York: Norton.

Jacobson, N. S., Dobson, K., Fruzzetti, A. E., Schmaling, K. B., & Salusky, S. (1991). Marital therapy as a treatment for depression. *Journal of Consulting and Clinical Psychology, 59,* 547–557.

Joiner, T., & Coyne, J. C. (1999). *The interactional nature of depression: Advances in interpersonal approaches.* Washington, DC: American Psychological Association.

Kobak, R. R., Ruckdeschel, K., & Hazan, C. (1994). From symptom to signal: An attachment view of emotion in marital therapy. In S. M. Johnson & L. S. Greenberg (Eds.), *The heart of the matter: Perspectives on emotion in marital therapy* (pp. 46–71). New York: Brunner/Mazel.

Lefebvre, M. F. (1980). Conitive distortion in depressed psychiatric and low back pain patients (Docteral dissertation, University of Vermont, 1980). *Dissertation Abstracts International, 41,* 693B. University of Vermont microfilms No. 60–17, 652.

Markman, H., Stanley, S., & Blumberg, S. L. (1994). *Fighting for your marriage.* San Francisco: Jossey-Bass.

McGonagle, K. A., Kessler, R. C., & Gotlib, I. H. (1993). The effects of marital disagreement style, frequency, and outcome on marital disruption. *Journal of Social and Personal Relationships, 10,* 385–404.

Noller, P. (1987). Nonverbal communication in marriage. In D. Perlman & S. Duck (Eds.), *Intimate relationships: Development, dynamics, and deterioration* (pp. 149–175). Beverly Hills, CA: Sage.

Notarius, C. I., Lashley, S .L., & Sullivan, D. J. (1997). Angry at your partner? Think again. In R. J. Sternberg & M. Hojjat (Eds.), *Satisfaction in close relationships* (pp. 219–248). New York: Guilford Press.

O'Leary, K. D., Riso, L. P., & Beach, S. R. H. (1990). Attributions about the marital discord/depression link and therapy outcome. *Behavior Therapy, 21,* 413–422.

O'Leary, K. D., Sandeen, E. E., & Beach, S. R. H. (1987, November). *Treatment of suicidal, maritally discordant clients by marital therapy or cognitive therapy.* Paper presented at the 21st annual meeting of the Association for Advancement of Behavior Therapy, Boston.

Prager, K. J. (1995). *The psychology of intimacy.* New York: Guilford Press.

Rathus, J. H., & Sanderson, W. C. (1999). *Marital distress: Cognitive and behavioral interventions for couples.* Northvale, NJ: Jason Aronson.

Stanley, S. (1998). *The heart of commitment.* Nashville, TN: Thomas Nelson.

Stanley, S., Trathen, D., McCain, S., & Bryan, M. (1998). *A lasting promise.* San Francisco: Jossey-Bass.

Thase, M. E., Greenhouse, J. B., Frank, E., Reynolds, C. F. R., Pilkonis, P. A., Hurley, K., Grochocinski, V., & Kupfer, D. J. (1997). Treatment of depression with psychotherapy or psychotherapy-pharmacotherapy combinations. *Archives of General Psychiatry, 54,* 989–991.

Vanfossen, B. E. (1986). Sex differences in depression: The role of spouse support. In S. E. Hobfoll (Ed.), *Stress, social support, and women* (pp. 69–84). New York: Hemisphere.

Waring, E. M. (1988). *Enhancing marital intimacy through facilitating cognitive self-disclosure.* New York: Brunner/Mazel.

Whisman, M. A. (1993). Mediators and moderators of change in cognitive therapy of depression. *Psychological Bulletin, 114,* 248–265.

Whisman, M. A., & Ubelacker, L. A. (1999). Integrating couple therapy with individual therapies and antidepressant medications in the treatment of depression. *Clinical Psychology: Science and Practice, 6,* 415–429.

Commentary:
Understanding and Alleviating Depression in Couples and Families: Can We Get There From Here?

Thomas N. Bradbury

The chapters in this book are essential reading for scientists and practitioners concerned with depression, marital and family dysfunction, and their complex interplay. In these chapters, leading scholars provide thoughtful analyses of these existing literatures, outline their views on the directions in which we need to head to advance our understanding of family processes and depression, and specify the steps they believe we need to take to achieve this understanding. As with any good book and, indeed, any great puzzle, this one holds great appeal while also serving as a source of consternation and frustration and creating the unrealistic wish for simple solutions.

The appeal of this book, and the broader field it represents, comes from the fact that intraindividual and interpersonal distress are commonplace and detrimental—even lethal—and thus are in need of scientific and therapeutic attention. This book succeeds in highlighting this fact and adds more specifically to the literature through reviews of established empirical associations (in terms of both reliable interventions and replicable findings in basic research); presentation of a wide range of emerging ideas and hypotheses; and suggestions for new theoretical, methodological, and intervention-related developments. By itself, the central message of this book—that depression develops in significant interpersonal contexts and that, over time, each can transform the other in complex and important ways—provides a valuable correction to the views that (a) affective disorder is intrinsically biological in nature and thus is optimally studied and treated from this perspective (characteristic of biological psychiatry) and (b) marriage begins with two psychologically healthy individuals and unfolds primarily as a function of their communication rather than their psychological make-up and the individual problems and symptoms they encounter (characteristic of earlier social learning conceptions of marriage).

On the other hand, the frustration that comes from reading this book arises from the limited scope of established associations in this domain, the realization that much work remains in determining which of the proposed ideas are viable and which are not (and for which purposes they are and are not viable), the sense that there could be more agreement about the important questions that now confront the field, and the hurdles that stand between us and the implementation of effective procedures that might prevent or alleviate depressive symptoms and interpersonal distress in couples and families. This frustration is no fault of the contributors; in fact, it is primarily because the chapters are clear in outlining what we do and do not know that we can grapple with broader questions about how progress in this field can be sparked. The purpose of this commentary is to ask a series of five questions that, as far as I can discern, underlie some of the frustration I experience when I read about depression in couples and families. As important as it is to acknowledge the impressive accomplishments recorded to date in this area (e.g., Beach, chapter 11), addressing the factors that may be hindering progress seems far more profitable and informative at this stage. And, doing so seems particularly important in view of the observation made by Coyne and Benazon (chapter 2) that ''there has been relatively little in the way of new empirical work in the last decade examining the role of marriage and marital functioning in major depression. Most recent writings consist of integrative reviews and consolidations of existing data, and there is a relative paucity of new data being published.'' The questions addressed below are raised with the intent of guiding theoretical efforts and, in particular, shaping the kinds of data that are collected in future studies.

Are We Conducting Basic Research That Is an End in Itself or That Is a Means to an Applied End?

On rare occasions, research on depression in marriages or families is undertaken solely to understand some basic psychological mechanism. More common, however, is research that has as its immediate or eventual goal the application of findings so that depression, interpersonal distress, or both are in some way alleviated. The chapters in this book illustrate these two basic goals well, with some focusing more on basic phenomena in this domain (e.g., Katz, chapter 6; Joiner, chapter 7) and typically emphasizing correlational or quasi-experimental designs, and with others focusing more on the development and testing of interventions in clinical outcomes trials (e.g., Cordova and Gee, chapter 10; Beach, chapter 11) and typically emphasizing experimental designs. In the next section I outline some concerns with the strategy that seems to underlie most outcome studies in this area, but here I argue that the generation of viable treatment strategies is absolutely fundamental to all research on depression in marital and family relationships. Hypothetically speaking, if a highly effective intervention or set of interventions were developed for the alleviation of depression in marriage, for example, we could reasonably expect that basic research on depression and marriage would slow considerably. Researchers naturally would turn to questions about the factors that mediate change, what might be learned from unsuccessful cases, or how to disseminate the intervention on a large scale. On the other hand, if we were to account for a high proportion of variability in the complex interplay between depression and interpersonal functioning, crucial research on the translation of these basic findings to the treatment context would remain to be conducted. From this, I think it is fair to conclude that effective intervention is the raison d'etre for the study of depression in interpersonal contexts.

Of course, many would argue that the development of effective psychological interventions depends heavily on rigorous basic research. This link between basic research and intervention is widely acknowledged as the hallmark of contemporary models of training in clinical psychology, and it is implicit in the basic research chapters in this book. But is it reasonable to assume that basic research on depression and family relationships can directly shape intervention? To what degree can we expect that basic research will fulfill this promise? Because we can never really know whether profoundly important results might emerge from any given line of basic research, it would be unwise to recommend against it. However, careful analysis of the link between basic research and intervention might lead us to be less sanguine about the applied value of the kinds of basic research that are now conducted, and it might suggest some basic research strategies that could prove more fruitful.

I believe there is a gulf between basic psychological research on depression in family relationships and interventions directed at alleviating affective and interpersonal disorders. This gulf exists because our basic research examines couples or families as groups while our interventions must be tailored and delivered to individual couples and families who may not abide by some established empirical association. For example, if it is shown that a particular kind of interaction sequence discriminates between depressed, distressed marriages and nondepressed, distressed marriages, it does not follow that this sequence is particularly characteristic of or salient for the distressed couple with a depressed spouse who is seeking therapy. An interaction sequence that does not differentiate between distressed marriages with and without a depressed spouse may be exceedingly important for the couple with a depressed spouse who is seeking help. Even if basic research studies reliably confirm a longitudinal association between, say, depression and marital functioning, there is a good chance that working to reduce the depression in the hopes of enhancing marital functioning may not provide much relief for many couples. At present it seems that basic research in this area can provide only rough estimates of what might and might not be targeted in interventions, and a change in approach might be needed to ensure that basic research on depression in marriages and families can accomplish more than this. It seems that progress toward effective interventions occurs not so much because basic research suggests new treatments or modifications to existing ones but because experimental outcome studies, probably combined with healthy doses of clinical insight, lead to better outcome studies and, in turn, to refined interventions. Indeed, outcome studies may have more of an effect on basic research than the reverse, as putatively active therapeutic ingredients (e.g., attributions, acceptance) may spawn lines of study. This is not a problem, of course, but it does seem important to acknowledge that the payoff of basic research may not be as great as seems to be assumed.

This gulf is in part the result of the difficulty in translating group-level findings to individual couples and in part the result of the sheer difficulty of conducting research that captures simultaneously the ebb and flow of interpersonal relationships and individual psychological functioning, particularly when the picture is complicated by factors such as interpersonal aggression (see O'Leary and Cano, chapter 9). This problem is compounded by the fact that individuals differ widely in the point at which they present for intervention, with some presenting, for example, when depressive symptoms overwhelm a fragile marital relationship and others presenting when marital problems become too much for a depressed individual or an individual with a history of depression to manage. Thus, at different times, the same couple or family might function in ways that are very much in line with basic empirical findings or in ways that are directly opposed to them. The limited impact of basic research on intervention is compounded further when data are not collected from all members of the family system of interest (e.g., only wives), are collected from individuals without regard for their significant interpersonal relationships, are collected using sampling methods that do not include individuals who might seek assistance for difficulties with depressive symptoms or with relationships, are collected in cross-sectional studies, or are collected using two-wave longitudinal designs.

The important question is whether this gulf between basic research and interventions is necessary or whether basic research can be retooled in some way to make it more germane to the shaping and refining of interventions for depression and interpersonal dysfunction. Before concluding that the former is true, it would seem profitable to develop basic research programs not on the basis of what naturally causes depression and marital dysfunction to occur, as seems to be the case with most basic research, but on the basis of what factors in the marital and therapeutic environments might be manipulated and capitalized on to bring about reductions in these problems. This shift would recognize that the factors that give rise to a disorder may not be coterminous with the factors that would alleviate it—that is, the solution to a problem may take a different form from the cause of the problem. It would also seem profitable to conduct fine-grained idiographic studies of individual symptom patterns over time, as is often done in psychiatric research, integrated with reports of marital functioning, for individuals with differing relationship backgrounds and histories of affective disorder (cf. Karney, chapter 3). This would reveal the heterogeneity in how these important variables unfold with time, and it would give us the opportunity to begin to identify meaningful subgroups of couples and families.

Are We Studying Individuals With Symptoms or Individuals With Diagnoses?

In one way or another the authors of these chapters are seeking to understand, and in some cases alter, variability in depression. For some, this means variability in depressive symptoms; for others, this means variability in whether or not someone has a diagnosis of depression. For some, this means analysis of between-group variability; for others, it means analysis of within-individual variability, whether in symptoms or diagnoses. It would be misguided to assert that any one approach is better in some absolute sense, as all of these approaches are probably needed to understand how interpersonal functioning and depression interrelate. However, it does seem safe to say that there are a lot of different conceptions of depression represented in these chapters and not much recognition of how these differing conceptions make different assumptions and may require different explanatory models.

At a simple level, the symptom-based and diagnosis-based conceptions each have strengths and weaknesses. A diagnostic, *DSM*-based view of depression promotes the use of interview data, is usually associated with studying clinical or community populations, and is adopted in studies that typically capture poorer levels of personal and interpersonal functioning. On the other hand, the categorical approach often assumes more homogeneity within a particular diagnosis than is warranted; often does not include the fluctuation of symptoms within the subsyndromal range (and into the diagnosable range); reveals little about the interpersonal meaning associated with particular symptoms; and, as more disturbed populations are studied, raises questions about other syndromes that may be comorbid with the depression. Adopting the categorical view seems most valuable in treatment outcome studies, where it is necessary to demonstrate that a particular intervention, such as marital therapy, actually can bring about significant marital and individual change.

Symptom-based approaches to depression are valuable in that they typically remain close to specific symptom data; yield continuous data and hence do not require assumptions about when an individual is or is not a member of a particular diagnostic category; and permit researchers the opportunity to study between-subjects and within-subject variability in emotional, cognitive, and vegetative signs. However, it is well known that the symptom-based view is limited because it relies on self-reports, is often associated with the study of undergraduate or otherwise psychologically healthy or resourceful populations, and implies a correspondence between dysphoria and depression that simply may not exist. Thus, although this approach would seem to hold many advantages for understanding the full range of symptoms associated with depression and its link with marital and family factors, this ideal is not being achieved in many studies.

The point is not simply to enumerate the strengths and weaknesses of a categorical versus continuous approach to depression or to advocate for one view over the other, but instead to observe that one's stance on this issue has numerous and far-reaching implications for the kinds of research conducted. It subsequently becomes difficult to integrate this research and to even see findings generated by the two approaches as reflecting some common set of underlying phenomena. Similar kinds of difficulties might be expected as researchers explore depression and interpersonal functioning in relation to personality disorders (see Davila, chapter 4), which themselves can be conceived either categorically or dimensionally. Perhaps the most important recommendation in this regard comes from Cummings, DeArth-Pendley, Schudlich, and Smith (chapter 5), who argue for more sophisticated and fine-grained analyses of depression and family environments. At the very least, this implies that we should devote more time to interviewing our clients or study participants, alone and in important relationships, about their relationships and about their individual symptoms, so that we can appreciate their unique experiences before trying to establish nomothetic systems for explaining and changing these experiences.

Are We Committed to Efficacy or Effectiveness?

In the parlance of psychotherapy outcomes researchers, a treatment is efficacious if it yields the desired outcomes under rigorous, controlled conditions, and it is effective if it yields the desired outcomes under externally valid conditions in the field. The chapters in this book that deal most explicitly with intervention—chapter 9 by O'Leary and Cano, chapter 10 by Cordova and Gee, and chapter 11 by Beach (cf. Coyne and Benazon, chapter 2)—are concerned primarily with the efficacy of interventions. Their reviews of research highlight evidence that improving the quality of a marriage can result in the alleviation of depressive symptoms, that a marital intervention typically is better than standard cognitive therapy for depression with co-occurring marital distress, and that improvements in marital quality may mediate the association between treatment and change in depression. This is important information because it indicates that a practitioner working with a distressed couple in which one spouse is depressed can use marital therapy for depression (see Beach, chapter 11) or something like it with the expectation that both sets of problems will likely diminish. Although I would argue that these data do not prove that marital functioning is therefore a cause of depression in the natural environment, certainly it is a major contributor in some situations, whereas in others it is not—they do at least indicate that therapeutic modification of marital patterns can lead to improvements in depressive symptoms. I would also argue, the importance of efficacy studies in general and these efficacy studies in particular notwithstanding, that it is the widespread dissemination of an intervention (or integrated sets of interventions) with a reasonable chance of alleviating the problem in question that must drive the field. Thus, in the same way that basic research is conducted in the service of applied research and thus would be secondary to it, it would seem that efficacy research is secondary to, and ultimately conducted in the service of, effectiveness research.

The efficacy data reported to date can be viewed as providing a foundation on which to build better interventions and intervention strategies. But how strong a foundation is this? How far does current efficacy research get us in being able to help the large numbers of couples and families in which at least one member is depressed? A number of issues about these couples and families arise in thinking about filling this gap. First, little is known about the process by which individuals and couples initiate and pursue a search for help. The symptoms of depression (e.g., pessimism, lack of energy) do not seem to lend themselves to high levels of help seeking, except perhaps when they are relatively severe and debilitating. Unfortunately, many unhappy couples turn first to a divorce attorney rather than to a mental health professional. In any case, we know relatively little about the eventual target population for our interventions and the settings in which these individuals appear for help, and this would seem to necessarily constrain the relevance of the efficacy data.

Second, assuming that individuals are seeking help for marital or individual difficulties (or if they are seeking help for some other problem, and marital or individual difficulties are subsequently detected), there remains the question of whether the professionals with whom these individuals come into contact are aware of the relevant research and clinical literatures, either in their general form (e.g., depression and marital dysfunction often co-occur) or their specific form (e.g., depression sometimes can be alleviated with specialized forms of marital therapy). The efforts in this book to disseminate knowledge to practitioners are laudable and timely (e.g., Beach, chapter 11). However, information is needed to determine the degree to which relevant groups of practitioners who routinely come into contact with key target populations are aware of this knowledge. At least as important is the need to determine the willingness and capability of these practitioners to implement specific clinical procedures that are known to be efficacious. The viability of efficacy research is dependent on established procedures being adopted by relevant practitioners. In the absence of strong, FDA like guidelines for the administration of psychotherapeutic interventions, it is possible that efficacious treatments, and even effective treatments, may be developed that simply are not used on a large scale.

Third, even if the desirable situation arises in which an individual, couple, or family seeks help for marital problems or depression, which is detected by a practitioner aware of and trained in an efficacious mode of treatment for these problems, the couple or family may nonetheless choose to not receive this treatment. As Coyne and Benazon (chapter 2) note, many depressed clients referred to marital therapy reject this suggestion, ''whereas others accept it, only to fail to enlist their partner or fail to come for subsequent sessions as a couple.'' Efficacy studies by design collect data from individuals with a demonstrated commitment to a particular approach to alleviating their problems, but these individuals might be a select subgroup of the population that encounters these problems.

Fourth, even if the couple or family does avail themselves of the efficacious treatment that is offered, the possibility remains that the couple or family will not benefit from it—due, perhaps, to patient characteristics, practitioner training and experience, or their interaction—or that any benefits that do accrue are short-lived. The chapter by Kaslow, Twomey, Brooks, Thompson, and Reynolds (chapter 8) is a valuable reminder that the socioeconomic context of affective disorder, which is not well understood in current efficacy studies, may affect the onset, course, and treatment of the disorder. Moreover, the follow-up intervals in outcome studies conducted to date have tended to be relatively short, and given that depression is marked by recurrence, treatments may be operating primarily to manage a particular episode rather than to help shape a marital environment that decreases the likelihood of subsequent symptoms or reduces their duration if serious symptoms do develop. Successful management of a particular episode is no small task, of course, but efficacy studies tend to have a short-term focus on what is a long-term, chronic condition that places ongoing stress on an individual's marriage and family relationships.

In short, I believe that I am not alone in maintaining that we should be committed to effectiveness data or, more to the point, to getting effective interventions to the individuals who need them at the time they are most likely to benefit from them. Efficacy data are one part of the puzzle, but I believe they are a smaller part than is typically acknowledged. Furthermore, the distinct possibility remains that the treatments carefully designated as being efficacious may take a different form when effectiveness is established. The burden of filling the gap between efficacious and effective treatments should not fall solely on the shoulders of researchers committed to identifying efficacious treatments. Efforts to build a bridge from efficacious treatments to effective treatments typically have begun on the side where the laboratory is, yet it may prove most expeditious to build from both sides while coordinating efforts along the way.

Are We Primarily Pursuing Treatment or Prevention?

When intervention is addressed in this book, emphasis typically is on clinical treatment of individuals experiencing depression, marital dysfunction, or both. The debilitating effects of these problems necessitate such an approach, yet several arguments can be made in favor of more fully embracing a preventive orientation. First, compared to clinical treatment, larger numbers of couples can be reached with preventive interventions. This would be especially important if it is the case that many couples would not avail themselves of relationship-focused treatments for depression, although there is no complementary assurance that prevention programs would reach the individuals who could benefit most from them. Second, such an approach would extend the logic of using marital therapy for the treatment of depression. That is, if the marital relationship is, in some sense, used as leverage for alleviating depression in therapy, then greater leverage should result from relationship-focused prevention programs because these relationships are stronger and more amenable to change. The power of relationships to help individuals struggle more successfully with adverse circumstances in the past is well reflected in Kaslow et al.'s research, chapter 8, which indicates that the association between childhood maltreatment and suicide attempt status is mediated fully by individuals' ability to experience trust and satisfaction in their relationships. Coyne and Benazon make a similar point about the protective advantage of positive marital relationships in chapter 2. Important practical questions about how to promote these kinds of experience remain, but the mental health benefits of strong interpersonal connections do appear to be profound—perhaps as profound as the high costs associated with conflicted interpersonal connections. Similarly, Cordova and Gee (chapter 10) note that ''the use of acceptance-based techniques for coping with recurrences seems appropriate. Coming to terms with depression as a potentially chronically recurring condition may aid couples in becoming effective agents of primary and secondary prevention as well as facilitators of tertiary intervention.'' Finally, there is an inherent logic in prevention that cannot be overlooked: Addressing a problem early is beneficial because individuals and their loved ones do not have to suffer as much and because it is likely to be harder and more costly to address the problem when it is more chronic and entrenched.

It is useful to consider what it is we might seek to prevent and how this might be accomplished. For example, a prevention program designed to strengthen marriage might be implemented, with the assumption that this would have many benefits, including a decrease in the likelihood of depression. This approach, particularly to the extent that it focused on helping couples and families understand and manage stressful events and moods in their relationships, might be most effective with subsyndromal symptoms of depression. Because it is unclear whether an intervention that does not focus explicitly on depression could modify the recurrence and course of diagnosable depression, it would seem plausible to develop an intervention that provides couples or families with an understanding of depression and the skills needed to handle it successfully. This approach might be most effective with couples and families in which one member has a history of major depression and would therefore be considered a form secondary prevention. Least plausible, perhaps, would be a program focused specifically on depression administered with at-risk populations (i.e., individuals with a history of depression) with the expectation that this would yield collateral benefits for marital functioning. Davila (chapter 4) and others review evidence to indicate that a history of affective disorder appears to predict early age at marriage, which has been shown to predict more marital adversity. Thus it appears that efforts to intervene strictly around depression in at-risk married populations will be unsuccessful unless the marriage itself is also part of the intervention.

Of course, the notion of prevention is not new to the marital domain, where a growing tradition of research and intervention shows that working early with couples (particularly on conflict management skills) may result in slower rates of marital deterioration relative to untreated control couples and in reduced rates of marital disruption. However, little attention has been given to the possible consequences of these interventions for individual symptoms, including symptoms of depression. On one hand, this is surprising in view of the links between depression and marital functioning and the more specific links between depression and negative behavior in marital interaction. On the other hand, programs designed to prevent marital dysfunction focus strongly on marital outcomes, and outcome studies that evaluate these programs typically involve couples who are not at high risk for marital dysfunction. Nevertheless, examination of individual (and child) functioning following participation in primary or secondary marital prevention and preparation programs appears to be a valuable means of collecting further experimental data on the link between depression and marital functioning, of establishing a broader impact for these programs, and of opening up new avenues for strengthening marriages and families. As marital prevention programs continue to improve, it can be expected that there will be growing interest in administering them to couples and families with greater risk for marital difficulties and higher levels of depression. In the same way that the basic literatures on marital interaction and marital therapy expanded to include depression and other problems such as violence, it is likely that the prevention literature will begin to recognize and attend to these higher risk populations.

In undertaking research that will promote the well-being of marriages and families and that will enhance management of depression (i.e., decrease the likelihood of recurrences or shorten their severity and duration), I believe it is important to recognize that basic research in support of prevention efforts can be quite different from basic research in support of therapeutic interventions. In the former there is a great need to identify factors that place couples and families at risk for particular outcomes. These can then be used as selection criteria for identifying target populations and to identify processes that transform this risk into adverse outcomes (e.g., stress generation processes described by Davila, chapter 4; self-verification processes described by Katz, chapter 6; reassurance-seeking and negative feedback-seeking processes described by Joiner, chapter 7). Strong emphasis is therefore placed on the onset and course of the outcomes of interest (e.g., depressive symptoms, marital complaints), and longitudinal research with a focus on the development of these outcomes is essential. Research that begins with individuals who have already been beset with marital or individual problems are less informative when prevention is the ultimate goal, because understanding the cause of the problem—which is what one hopes to alter in any resulting preventive intervention program—then becomes difficult. As I argued earlier, basic research conducted to inform therapeutic interventions is fraught with difficulties, particularly because of the great heterogeneity in case presentations. Couples and families seeking therapy after marital problems or depression already exist place different demands on the clinician because he or she must address not only how a particular set of symptoms originated but also the consequences these symptoms have had for the individual, the marriage, and the family. Whereas a prevention program might have the advantage of working with, for example, a newly married individual who has a history of depression in the hopes of managing that depression and preventing marital discord, the clinician is confronted with, in essence, this same couple several years later for whom the depression has contributed to marital discord and vice versa. Basic developmental research therefore seems more pertinent to the preventionist than to the clinician.

In summary, the research presented in this book suggests that it may be timely to take advantage of the opportunity to view marriages and families as possessing both actual and potential resources that, if tapped and educed through preventive interventions, could strengthen them while also enhancing individual functioning. This opportunity has not been recognized much within the marital prevention literature, and it is only beginning to be exploited by researchers interested in depression in marital and family contexts. The research needed to determine the nature of these interventions may well differ from that directed toward couples and families already struggling with depression and interpersonal tension. Thus, although there is a tendency toward thinking about primary, secondary, and tertiary interventions along a common dimension, the research needed to achieve effective primary or secondary prevention may differ qualitatively from that needed to achieve effective tertiary treatment.

Are We Imposing Our Views or Exposing the Phenomena?

In any area of research there is a continuing struggle to determine whether the variables being studied are those most likely to predict and explain the phenomena of interest and whether the factors we seek to modify with interventions are those most likely to bring about lasting change. Determining whether we are working with the most important variables can be a long and difficult process because a great deal of effort must be expended in ensuring that our measures of selected constructs are valid, because several studies often are required before we can conclude that we are on the wrong track, and because we often give our hypotheses the benefit of the doubt in empirical tests. Nevertheless, constant monitoring of our work in relation to the problem under consideration is essential, and even with constant monitoring, there is a risk that our attempts to understand and alter some problem say as much about the concepts, methods, and designs that we use as about the phenomena themselves.

In the literature on the marital and familial context of depression, the most obvious disparity between the phenomena of interest and our approach to them is, I believe, the failure to capture fully the developmental nature of individual and interpersonal functioning. This literature seems to be marked by relatively few data spread, not always evenly, across a wide range of important and interesting questions, and few of these data come from strong longitudinal studies over significant spans of time. Whereas it is clear from clinical work that symptoms of depression fluctuate and that the quality of marital and parent–child relationship changes with time, a good deal of research on these topics neglects these fundamental features. There are times when a more static approach is acceptable in research, such as when measures are being developed and refined, when we are simply trying to describe what a population looks like (e.g., in terms of comorbid conditions at any one point in time), when we are trying to establish epidemiological estimates on the extent of some problem in the population, when we are trying to identify a mediator for some demonstrated longitudinal effect (i.e., to examine whether a putative mediator is in fact associated with independent variables that predict some important outcome), or when a third-variable artifact for some established cross-sectional association is being ruled out. Generally, however, studies that attend to the development and course of relationships, and the individual symptoms that develop within them, will prove to be more informative, and in many cases far more informative, than those taking isolated snapshots of these variables.

It could be argued that establishing associations in cross-sectional studies is a desirable and necessary step to take before undertaking more time-consuming longitudinal studies. In one sense, cross-sectional research is indeed valuable, because it helps establish how specific measures and procedures might perform in a particular population. In another sense, however, cross-sectional studies can be counterproductive. The observational literature on marital interaction in relation to marital quality provides a useful example. Clear evidence has accumulated in cross-sectional studies to demonstrate that maritally dissatisfied spouses, compared with their maritally satisfied counterparts, are more negative and more recipro- cally negative when discussing important marital difficulties. Behavioral marital therapy (see chapter 11) developed, in part, on the basis of these and other cross-sectional findings, with the goal of teaching maritally distressed couples to perform more like maritally satisfied ones. This approach to treatment was an improvement over existing models (particularly because of its focus on establishing empirically rather than assuming treatment effects), yet behavioral marital therapy appears to help only about one half of the couples receiving it, and many of those couples slip back into poor marital functioning with time. As a result, rather different treatment models are being developed and tested.

Of course, it is easy to be wise in hindsight, and it must be noted that this cross-sectional research has been unusually important in refining how we quantify and study marital interaction. We can still learn from this progression of research, however, particularly because we might imagine a very different history to this field had there been some recognition that the interaction patterns that differentiated happy and unhappy couples may not have been the main cause of marital dysfunction. Longitudinal research might have made salient the possibility that these behavioral differences were a consequence of marital distress; that, as research is beginning to show, the association between observed behavior is sometimes weak and somewhat elusive; or that some other variable, such as the severity of the problems that couples were discussing, was contributing to the observed effects. Longitudinal research at that point might have provided more information about how marital distress develops naturally in initially satisfied couples and the factors associated with that development. Different treatment models, possibly even models that approximate those now being tested, might have been explored earlier.

The more general point is that we cannot know whether the effects obtained in most nonexperimental cross-sectional studies provide a valid reflection of these associations over time until we actually examine them over time. This said, it is important to temper the call for developmental research by noting that (a) development is not always well captured in longitudinal studies, and (b) longitudinal research is not a sure and straightforward solution to important questions now confronting the field, in part because conducting nonexperimental longitudinal research can mislead us into inferring causation where it is not justified. And, as I argued earlier, basic research, even good longitudinal research, can sometimes provide only a rough approximation of where to focus interventions. However, with appropriate caution and rigor, studies of key variables over time would no doubt illuminate processes that are now only the source of informed speculation.

One important strength of this book is the frequent referencing of recent longitudinal studies of depressive symptoms and interpersonal functioning. This suggests that there is growing recognition of the value of these studies and that they will appear at an increased rate in the years to come. A more important strength is that these chapters present some of the methodological tools needed to make longitudinal studies more effective (Karney, chapter 3) and some of the inherently developmental ideas that can be tested in these studies. These ideas include, for example, the sensitizing effects of stress (Whisman, chapter 1), the developmental histories that individuals bring into marriage (Davila, chapter 4), the entrainment of excessive reassurance seeking and negative feedback seeking (Katz, chapter 6; Joiner, chapter 7), and the strong emphasis placed on depression as a chronic, recurring condition (Coyne and Benazon, chapter 2; O'Leary and Cano, chapter 9). This shifting of focus toward developmental, temporal aspects of depression in important interpersonal contexts is perhaps the most exciting aspect of the chapters in this book, and it seems most likely to shape future progress in this field.

Conclusion

Considered separately, depression and troubled interpersonal relationships in couples and families involve considerable suffering and comprise many complex phenomena. Efforts to address these problems as they relate to one another are therefore faced with a tremendous challenge. The chapters in this book outline this challenge well and present valuable reviews of the field along with a panoply of promising ideas for advancing it. The intent of this commentary has been to identify some of the sources of tension in research on depression in marriages and families. The five themes that were identified are common predicaments in the behavioral sciences—basic versus applied research, categorical versus continuous variables, efficacy versus effectiveness of interventions, prevention versus treatment, and cross-sectional versus longitudinal studies—yet, when considered in relation to social functioning and depression, they take on unique and interesting features. Addressing these themes will, I believe, contribute to our ability to understand and alleviate the individual difficulties and interpersonal strife that render marriages and families more turbulent and less effective.

Author Index

Numbers in italics refer to listings in reference section.

Subject Index

ABOUT THE EDITOR

Steven R. H. Beach received his PhD from the State University of New York at Stony Brook in 1985. He joined the faculty of the Psychology Department at the University of Georgia in 1987 after working as a practicing clinician in outpatient, hospital, and private practice settings. He was elected Fellow of the American Psychological Association in 1994. He currently serves as professor of psychology and is the associate director of the Institute for Behavioral Research at the University of Georgia. Dr. Beach has published more than 80 articles on marital processes, close relationships, and depression in numerous scholarly journals. He currently serves as associate editor of *Personal Relationships* and has served as an editorial board member for the *Journal of Personality and Social Psychology,* the *Journal of Psychopathology and Behavioral Assessment, Psychological Assessment,* and the *Journal of Personal and Social Relationships.*